Abstracts
of
Wills Recorded in
Orange County, North Carolina
1752-1850

and

(202 Marriages Not Shown in the Orange County Marriage Bonds)

Compiled By:
Ruth Herndon Shields

2 volumes in 1

Southern Historical Press, Inc.
Greenville, S.C.
2001

This volume was reproduced from
the 1957 & 1966 editions located in the
publisher's private library,
Greenville, South Carolina

Please Direct all Correspondence & Orders to:

Southern Historical Press, Inc.
P.O. Box 1267
375 West Broad Street
Greenville, S.C. 29602-1267

Originally published: Chapel Hill, N.C.
Vol. #1- 1957 & Vol. #2 -1966
Reprinted: Southern Historical Press, Inc.
Greenville, S.C., 2001
ISBN # 0-89308-769-6
Printed in the United States of America

ABSTRACTS OF WILLS

RECORDED 1752 THROUGH 1800
in

ORANGE COUNTY, NORTH CAROLINA

WILL BOOKS A B and C

PLUS 20 PAGES IN BOOK D

and

202 EARLY MARRIAGES NOT SHOWN

in the

ORANGE COUNTY MARRIAGE BONDS

Compiled by

Ruth Herndon Shields, Chairman
Genealogical Records Committee
Davie Poplar Chapter, NSDAR
Chapel Hill, North Carolina

A FEW FACTS ABOUT ORANGE COUNTY

Orange County was formed in 1752 largely from Granville, partly from Bladen and Johnston.

From Orange were taken:

All of Chatham in 1771.
Part of Guilford in 1771.
All of Wake in 1771

The bill for the formation of Chatham, Guilford and Wake was passed at the 1770-1771 Assembly.

All of Caswell in 1777.
All of Person, which was formed from Caswell in 1791.
All of Alamance in 1849.
Part of Durham in 1881.

Randolph and Rockingham Counties were formed partly from that part of Guilford which was taken from Orange.

- - - - -

Please read the note following A-184, and one following A225.

- - - - -

FOREWORD

This book was begun in 1955 as a project of the Genealogical Records Committee of Davie Poplar Chapter, NSDAR, of which I was a member. Memory Alldredge Lester was then Chairman of the Committee, and Edna Allen Lane was Regent of the Chapter. The work was continued in 1956.

Knowing how valuable such a record would be to the many thousands of descendants of Orange County residents now scattered over the United States, I undertook to complete and publish this volume. In this I have been greatly helped by our former Regent, Mrs. Lane.

In the INDEX TO WILLS in the Courthouse at Hillsboro, only the testator, and the legatees are indexed. Many other persons are mentioned in the wills, deeds, and powers-of-attorney recorded in the Will Books. Many children are mentioned who had already received their part of estates, and thus were not legatees. Executors, neighbors, and others are mentioned, and each will has two or more witnesses who sre not indexed in Hillsboro. All such persons are indexed in this book.

This book has been a labor of love, and it is the sincere wish of the Committee that it will prove of value to future genealogists.

Ruth Herndon Shields, Chairman

Memory Alldredge Lester (Mrs. Robert M.), Chapter Regent
Edna Allan Lane (Mrs. B.B.), Past Regent

THESE ORIGINAL PAPERS ARE PRESERVED IN THE ARCHIVES IN RALEIGH, BUT ARE NOT RECORDED IN HILLSBORO.

Will of THOMAS BOWLS of Orange Co., N.C. Recorded 1789

wife: Elizabeth Bowls

sons Thomas Bowls & William Bowls receive "land on N. Fork of Little River, 220 acres, bought from John Embry.

son: John Bowls granddau: Sarah Clark

daus: Elizabeth Murdak, Sarah Bowls

Executors: sons Thomas and William Bowls
Witnesses: Jane x Davis, James Latta, Jr.

- - -

"September 24th 1782. The subscriber having business to travel to the Westward & over the Mountains & thru the uncertainty of life & and the precarious Traveling at this critical time doth assign all his Right Title & Claim to her the deed of his land to Eliz'a Lemon the Relict of Henry Lemon deceas'd in Security for a certain sum of money that he the subscriber owes her. In witness whereunto he hath set his hand the day & year above written.

(Signature very bad)

Signed in presence of
Philip Jackson
Elizabeth Williams

James ? Gideaon ? "
(Indexed in Archives as I. Gideon.)

- - -

Will of WILLIAM HANNAH of Orange Co., N.C. Date of probate not known.

wife; Sarah Hannah Date of will: 12 October 1785

son: David Wiley Hannah, under age.

daus: Mary and Sarah

Executors: wife Sarah, and son David Wiley Hannah.
Witnesses: Robert Gray, Jane Mordak.

Note on back of will " Sarah Hannah qualified"(as Executrix).

- - - - -

Will of William Hooper. Dated 24 April 1788 Date of probate not known.

wife: Anne

daughter Elizabeth, under age

sons: Thomas, William , both under age.

- continued -

Pages 1,2,3 and 4 indexed on page 5

Original wills in Archives, but not recorded in Hillsboro.

Will of WILLIAM HOOPER continued -

This will is 12 pages long, devises a number of slaves, and several parcels of land, eight lots in Hillsboro, some property in Charlotte, N.C., etc.

Executors: wife Anne, and sons William and Thomas,
James Hogg, and Jesse Benton.

Friends to advise executors: Samuel Johnston, Archibald Maclaine, Alfred Moore, James Iredell, and John Huske.

Witnesses: McDonald Hogg, Walter Alves, Helen Hogg.

This is a paper attempting to free a slave, not a will, though it is endorsed on the back "\Martha Nial's will". The spelling is confusing, in the body of the instrument it is spelled Nail, the signature is MARTHA x NIAL, the paper is indexed in the Archives as NEIL !

"I, Martha Nail, widow of Robert Nail late of Orange County, N.C." .... frees her slave Lucy and her issue"if the law allows it"..... her son-in;law is to attempt to handle the matter if the instrument itself is not sufficient. Lucy is to be no part of her estate in any future will she (Martha) makes.

son-in-law: Daniel Cloud.

signed: Martha x Nial

Witnesses: Jonathan Lindly
Thomas Lindly

Dated 29 (month not clear) 1797, date of probate not shown.

- - -

Will of WILLIAM PHILLIPS of Orange County, N.C. Dated 9 May 1794

wife: Elizabeth

son Joel
son David "tract where he now lives" (100 acres)
son William "tract where he now lives " bounded by Trousdell.. on Haw River.

daus: Susannah and Pheby and Elizabeth

"My four daughters by my first wife" Mary, Lucy, Hannah, Sarah.

Executors: wife Elizabeth, sons David and Joel
Witnesses: William Rainey, Mary Simmons.

Note on back of will: "Widow and Joel Phillips qualified".

- - -

Pages 1,2,3 and 4 indexed on 5

Original will in Archives, but not recorded in Hillsborough.

Will of SUSANA RAY of Orange County, N.C. Dated 11 Oct 1794, date of probate not on will

daughter: Mary Ray

Mother is to raise Mary Ray and "school her". If Mary dies, estate is to go to testator's brothers and sisters (names not stated). Mother is to have use of estate to care for Mary.

Executors: "Two brothers-in-law William Ray and Joseph Buckner ? (or Brecken ?)"
Witnesses: Jno. Baker, Agnes (x) Few ? Margaret Baker.
Note on back of will "Executors qualified".

- - -

Will of WILLIAM RAY of Orange County, N.C. Dated 11 March 1794, date of probate not on will

wife: Martha

sons: Robert, John, William, James

daus: Christian, Elizabeth, Isabell

(Testator has sold land to John Homes, son of Robert Homes.)

Executors: wife, and Benjamin Rainey.
Witnesses: William Rainey, Mary (x) Rainey, James Stockedd.

- -

Probate of the two wills below in the Court Minutes for Orange County, N.C., but the wills are not in GRIMES or in the will books in Hillsborough.

Court of July 1754. "On motion of Richard Parker the last will and testament of SAMUEL HARLAN and the codicil annexed thereto was proved in open court by the oath of James Vassey (?) and affirmation of Valentine Hollingsworth, Quaker. Elizabeth Harlan widow of the deceased and Aaron Harland, Executors thereof, qualified as such ..."

Court of July 1754. The will of JOSEPH HARDIN deceased was proved by the oath of Benjamin Martin. Elizabeth Harlan, widow, appeared and qualified as Executrix.

Pages 1, 2, 3 and 4 are indexed on page 5

Five abstracts of Orange County wills from "GRIMES".

J. Bryan Grimes' wonderful book NORTH CAROLINA ABSTRACTS of WILLS 1690-1760 lists just seven wills for Orange County. Of these seven only two are now on record in the will books in Hillsborough, and the originals have been lost. They are the wills of MICHAEL ELLETT (Grimes says ELIOT), and JOSEPH WADE.

Grimes, page 124 Will of JAMES FORASTER. Dated 5 Sept 1755, proved Dec 1755
sons: William and James, land on Eno River
sons: Benjamin and Thomas, "my plantation"
son-in-law: John Manning, land on Eno River
Executrix: wife Ann. Witnesses: Pat McCulloch, Hugh Wood.
The Clerk of Court was James Watson.
No mention of the probate of this will is in the Court Minutes.

Grimes, page 358 Will of JOHN STANFIELD. Dated 4 Aug 1755, proved Sept 1755
wife: Hannah
sons: John (land on Haw River), Thomas (land known as the Meeting House Tract), Samuel ("plantation whereon I now live"). Thomas and Samuel also get land near the Rich Hills.
Executors: John Jones, Joseph Maddox.
Witnesses: Thos. Lindley, Hugh Laughlin, Thos. Lowe.
(probate of this will not in Court Minutes but items about the estate in Minutes for June 1759 and March 1760)

\- - -

Grimes, page 395 Will of HENRY WEBB. Dated 10 Jan 1756, proved March 1759
sons: Wentworth and John.

Executrix: wife Elizabeth Webb. Witnesses: George Laws,
Witnesses: George Laws, Elias Downs.
(Probate of this will in Minutes for March 1759.)

\- - -

Grimes, page 171 Will of JAMES HOPKINS. Dated 8 Feb 1759, of St Mathews Parish proved March Court 1759.
"Children" mentioned but not named. (Probate is in Minutes)

Executors: William Hopkins, William Phillips, John Hopkins.
Witnesses: Allicksander Ferguson, John Dobbins, David Smith.

\- - -

Grimes, page 246 Will of ROBERT MELTON. Dated 24 April 1759, proved Nov 1759
sons: James, Nathaniel
Nathan, Isesum, Ancel
Executor: son Nathan Melton.
Witnesses: James Sellers, Mary Stratton. Clerk: James Watson.
(Probate of this will is in Court Minutes for June 1759, by "oath of Richard Parker one of the witnesses" (he was an attorney). Mary Stratton and James Sellers were summoned to appear at next court as witnesses.)

\- - -

Pages 1, 2, 3 & 4 indexed on 5

Index to pages 1,2 and 3

- - -

Index to page 4 - "GRIMES"

- - - - - - - - - - - - - - - - -

Note by R.H.S. A woman's name indexed thus - Mary (..) Smith - means that she is married, and that I do not know her maiden name.

- - - - - - - - - - - - - - - - -

The will of SARAH COTTON of Northampton County is among the Orange County, N.C. wills in the State Archives. It appears to be a copy, and was probably used in a suit concerning an estate settlement. Since it is not an Orange County will I did not abstract it. R.H.S.

ABSTRACTS OF ORANGE COUNTY, N.C. WILL BOOKS A, B and C.

A-1 Will of MICHAEL ELLETT. Dated 5 Oct 1756, proved 10 Dec 1756.

Sole heir: Wm Phillips, no relationship stated.
"A saddle & 4 shillings to be demanded of Joseph Bugg...
7 shillings, etc to be demanded of David Phillips ...
1 pound 10 shillings to be demanded of James Lindsey ...
3 shillings 4 pence to be demanded of Samuel Mains."

Executor: Wm. Phillips.
Witnesses: Wm. Offill, James Hopkins, Wm. Hopkins.

- - -

A-2 Will of CHARLES FOSHEE. see A-62 for same will.
Dated 23 Nov 1757, proved Dec 1757.
wife: Susanna
sons: William and Charles Foshee, get land.
After wife's death - everything else to be divided among "my children".
Executors: Joseph Foshee, and wife Susannah.
Witnesses: Wm (x) Marsh, Elmore or Elmon (x) George.

- - -

A-3 Will of JONATHAN FINCHER. Dated 20 March 1757, proved May 1757.
wife: name not stated, ten shillings.
sons: "eldest son" name not stated,but called Joshua in Codicil.
Jonathan, Richard, Joseph, Benjamin (he is to be bound to Joseph Mattox).
daughters: Mary,Hannah

No Executors named.
Witnesses: Benj. Cate, Charles Jonas, (Margaret (x) Whitehead.

- - -

A-5 Will of DUNCAN BOHANNON Dated 1760

wife: Susannah. sons: John, Benjamin, Richard

daus: Frankey Boyd, Mary Bohannon
granddaughter: Betty Bohannon

son Benjamin "one survey of land at the mouth of Second creek of New Hope joining land formerly John Rhodes" ..."

Executors: sons Benjamin and Richard, and John Brantley.
Witnesses: Hannah Brantley, Jos. Fuller, Jos. Brantley.

A-7 Will of JOSHUA HADLEY. Dated 20 Sept 1760, proved Nov 1760.

wife: Patience
sons: Joseph, Joshua, Thomas, Simon
Benjamin gets "land on James River in Virginia"
daus: Ruth Marshel, Mary Piggott, Sarah Ford,
Hannah, Deborah, Katherine ? or Hatherner ?

- continued -

Book A, page 7 Will of Joshua Hadley continued-

Executors: wife Patience, son Joshua
Witnesses: Simon Di....., Wm. Holmes, Francis Dorset.

- - -

A-9 Will of AARON VAN HOOK. Dated 10 May 1760, proved Aug 1760.

wife: Katherine

sons: Lawrence, David.

Executors: wife, and sons Lawrence and David.
Witnesses: Lidia Van Hook, Bridget Van Hook, Thos. Morgan.

- - -

A-11 Will of MARY ANN CURRIE. Dated 20 Sept 1759, proved Nov 1759.

sons: John, James. daus: Margaret, Mary.

Executors: sons John and James
Witnesses: Edward Nash

- - -

A-12 Will of HENRY MAYNOR. Dated 3 March 1760, proved March 1760.

"loving wife", name not stated.

daus: Rachel, Mary, Elizabeth, Susanna, Betty

Executors: friends Anthony Champness, and John Marshal.
Witnesses: Charles Davis, John Pike, William Marshall.

- - -

A-13 Will of JAMES ALSTON. Dated 28 Feb 1760, proved 2 May 1760.

wife: Christian sons: John, James

daus; Mary, Charity, Sarah brother: Joseph John Alston

"... that Warham Glenn make my son John a deed for land where Warham Glenn and Ann Downs lived .."
he mentions "John Woods line" ..." Josiah Sumner to pay "

"son John land on Neuse River and 2 lots in Newbern ... land in Chowan Co. on Bird's Creek where my father lived ... son James land in Halifax and Granville counties"

Executors: sons John and James
Witnesses: Warham Glenn, James Alston,James Boyd, Thos. Hines

- - -

A-17 Will of MARY SHEPHEARD, Widow. Dated 5 May 1761,
proved Aug 1761

son: Jacob Slater
daughters: Mary Whitehead, Mary Dennis
granddaughter: Mary Dennis

"to Isaac Dennis .. to children of John Dennis & John Slater"

Executors: John Dennis, John Slater.
Witnesses: Isaac Jackson, Samuel Maury, Samuel Jackson.

- - -

A-16 Will of RICHARD BRACEWELL, BRASWELL or BRANWELL.
Dated Aug 1761, proved Aug 1761

wife: Joyce
daus: Mary, Tabitha
sons: Valentine Jacob, Richard William

He devises land on S side of Haw River bought of H. Mackneel.

Executors: wife,"loving friend Hector Mackneel, brother Henry."
Witnesses: Thomas Tucker, Henry Bracewell, John Records.

- - -

A-19 Will of THOMAS BERRY. Dated 10 April 1761, proved May 1761

wife:Elizabeth son-in-law: James Morrow

sons: James, Thomas, Benjamin
daus: Elizabeth, Margaret Morrow, Nancy
grandchildren: William & Jane Berry children of Wm Berry dec'd.

No executor named. Witnesses: Paul Harmon, Wm. McMath.

- - -

A-23 Will of JOHN BOOKER. Dated 18 Aug 1761, proved Nov 1761.

wife: Patience dau: Patience son: James

No executor named.
Witnesses: Wm. Brevard, Susannah Brown, Mary Richards.

- - -

A-25 Will of ADAM MASON. Dated 4 Aug 1763, proved Nov 1763.

sons: Anthony, Francis, Tobias, Jacob
daughters: Elizabeth, Anne Phillipina
Executors: sons Tobias and Jacob.
Witnesses: Francis Nash, Ralph McNair, Phillip Jackson.

- - -

A-27 Will of JOHN BONNEY. Dated 10 April 1761, proved May 1761.

"loving wife", name not stated.

sons: Richard, Simon, Daniel, John, William.

Executors: wife,"with help of my son John".
Witness: William Clark

- - -

A-27 Will of JAMES COLLINS. Dated 4 Dec 1762, proved May 1763.

wife: Elizabeth (writing not clear)

sons: James (oldest), John

No executor named. Witness: Elizabeth ..(?)

- - -

A-27 Will of JOHN COLLINS. Dated 4 Nov 1762, proved Nov 1762.

brother: "all mother left me to go to my brother William Collins"

sister: Catherine

Executor: brother-in-law Enos Ellmore
Witnesses: Lawrence Thompson, Thos. Thompson, Enos Ellmore.

- - -

A-29 Will of TIMOTHY TERRELL. Dated 1 Feb 1763, proved Feb 1763.

wife mentioned, name not stated.

sons: Solomon, Micajah, Nimrod (under age), Simon (minor), Daniel, Richard, Aron, Moses (under age).

daus: Jemima, Ruth, Millie, Mary, Betty, Cuzziah,

Executors: wife, and John Pills (?).

Witnesses: Abraham Teague, Jos McLester, Moses Teague.

- - -

A-31 Will of WILLIAM BROWN. Dated 18 Feb 1764, proved May 1764.

heirs, relationship not stated:
Margaret Ray, Wm. Brown McClintock,
Janette and David Alsoms

No Executor named.
Witnesses: Geo. Johnston, John Kornegay, Thos. Holygam (?).

- - -

A-32 Will of WILLIAM FORBIS. Dated 28 Nov 1763,
proved Feb 1764

wife: Margaret

sons: William, Hugh, George.
After 3 years George is to be bound to a trade.

"other 6 young children...."

Executors: Andrew Finley, William Willis.
Witnesses: John Willis, James Mathews, Martha Willis, Thomas Willis, Hugh Willis.
"Approved: Margaret Forbis, John Forbis, Thomas Morgan, Rachel Forbis, Arthur Forbis.

- - -

A-34 Will of JOEL BROOKS. Dated 26 Aug 1764, proved Sept 1764

wife: Mary son: John

Executor: brother James
Witnesses: Wm. Brown, Charles Stout, Joseph Kyes.
This will was very hard to read, but the Court Minutes give the names of the witnesses in the probate of the will. This BROOKS family is given in the BROOKS genealogy by Mrs. Ida Brooks Kellam.

- - -

A-36 Will of WILLIAM (x) LOUNG (LONG) Dated 6 April 1764,
proved May 1764

wife: Catrin

sons: "oldest son George", & "youngest son" name not stated.

Executors: Charles Johnson, David Craig.
Witnesses: Mary Mitchell, John Craig.
The handwriting of the Clerk is extremely hard to read, it looks beautiful, but the elaborate capital letters are much like one another. OLDS has this name as SAWNEY, and I read it as YOUNG, but the Court Minutes prove that LONG is correct.

- - -

A-37 Will of DANIEL NORRIS. Dated 27 May 1760, proved
Aug 1765

wife: Mathews son-in-law: Thomas Beale

No relationship stated to: Evan Jones, Elizabeth Hart.

Executors: wife Mathews, and son-in-law Thomas Beale.
Witnesses: John Thompaon, Peter Bornal, Mary Jones.

- - -

Book A, page 39 Will of HUGH LAUGHLIN. Dated 24 Feb 1765,
Proved 26 Feb 1765.

wife: Mary brother: William Laughlin

daus: Elizabeth, Mary, Rebecca, Charrity, Joannah, Susanna.

Testator owns a Mill. No witnesses. No Executors.

Proved 26 Feb 1765 by the oath of John Laughlin.

- - -

A-45 Will of JOHN (x) THOMAS. Dated 24 April 1765, proved May 1766.

wife: Elizabeth daughter Mary

sons: eldest son John, James

he says "my three children" No Executor named.

Witnesses: Henry Ledbetter, John (x) Hamlett, Ann (x) Hamlett

- - -

A-42 Will of JAMES ROONEY (or RONEY), of St. Matthew's Parish, Orange Co., N.C. Dated 2 Aug 1765, proved 2nd Tuesday, Nov 1765.

sons: Benjamin, Thomas

daus: Elizabeth, Ann. He says "my four children".

Sole Executor: John Sample
Witnesses: James McCarley, Mary Sample, John Bul....

- - -

A-44 Will of ANDREW CALDWELL. Dated 26 March 1765, proved 2nd Tuesday, May 1766.

wife: Jannet

sons: Samuel, William.
daus: Mary, Elizabeth. "my four children"

Executors: wife Jannet, and James Freeland.
Witnesses: Alex'r Mebane, Jno. Sample, A..... Sanford.

- - -

A-45 Will of CHARLES (x) SINKLER. Dated 5 June 1766 Proved 2nd Tues. Aug 1766.

wife: Ann dau: Catherine
son: Charles

"All my children, being seven in number".

Executors: wife and "well beloved friend John Buchanon of Augusta Co., Va." to settle affairs in Augusta Co., Va., and wife and "my trusty friend Amoss Evans to settle affairs in this province."
(His land in Augusta Co., Va. was on South Fork of Hototin River, called Indian River.) -continued-

A-45. Witnesses: Joseph McLester, Amoss Evans, James Harvey.

- - -

A-48 Will of THOMAS MELER or MILES, or MILLS. Dated 14 March 1766 Proved 2nd Tues. May'66.

wife: Hannah

sons: Aquilla, Moses, Abraham, John, Thomas, Peter, Jacob.

daus: Hannah Slade, Pottiet , No Executor named.

Witnesses: Lewis Bartow, Isaac (x) Robuck,Joseph Peterson.

- - -

A-49 Will of HUGH (x) SINON. Dated 1 June 1766, proved Nov 1766.

He seems to be a bachelor, no relationships to heirs given.

Thomas Lindsey, Jr. 525 acres on Pine Hill Creek.
William Welsh, 125 acres, same location.
"Thomas Lindsey, Sr. and his wife Ruth should have my slave Sarah".
William Lindsey, son of James Lindsey, Daniel McCavoy, Owen Dowd (?), Samuel Stuart.

"If my brothers or brothers-in-law come in from Ireland" they are to receive some property.

Executors: "my friends Samuel Stuart, William Lindsey".
Witnesses: Michael (X) Wufner (?), Thomas Lindsey, Sr.

- - -

A-52 Will of William Asten. Dated 16 Nov 1766, proved Feb 1767.

wife: Mary

sons-in-law: Peter Downey, Archibald McLeroy

grandsons: William Asten Downey, Thomas Stinky (?) McLeroy, William McBride

Executors: wife, and Archibald McLeroy and George Finley.
Witnesses: David Fulton, Andrew Dark, Henry Cowden.

- - -

A-53 Will of WILLIAM COX. Dated 20 Jan 1767, proved 2nd Tues Feb 1767.

sons: Harmon Cox, land on east side of Deep River
William Cox, land on west side of Deep River
John Cox, land lying on the Mill Creek adjoining Wm. McFarson's
Solomon Cox, land "on Little Brush Creek where Benjamin William's formerly lived"
Thomas Cox gets the mill. He says "my five sons".

-continued-

A-53 Will of WILLIAM COX continued

daus: "Rebecca Dixon in Pennsylvania, 4 shillings"
"Mary Lindley wife to James Lindley"
"Martha Terrell wife to William Terrell"
"Marjory Nicholas wife to Isaac Nicholas"
"Catherine Hunt wife to Elizor Hunt"

Executors: "My trusty and well beloved son and cousin, William Cox and Isaac Cox."
Witnesses: John Cox, William Moffitt (?), John Allen.

\- - -

A-56 Will of JOHN (x) FIELDS. Dated 16 Nov 1766, proved Feb 1767

wife: name not stated

son John one-half of estate
son Roger other half of estate

Abeneasar Starnes and Ann Starnes his wife and Roger Murphy "should have the care of the child" - the oldest to live with the Starnes - the younger to live with Roger Murphy,Sr. If Murphy Sr should die, he is to live with Roger Murphy,Jr.

Witnesses: William Ward, James Morgan, Roger Murphy, Jr, Rachel (x) Fields.

\- - -

A-57 Will of ISAAC HOLDING. Dated 13 Jan 1767, proved Feb 1767

wife: Sarah father: Thomas Holding

"well beloved brother John Douglass..."
"loving brother Thomas Holding ..."
"beloved brother John Kelly ..."

sons: Thomas Holding, Isaac Holding

If sons die without issue land goes to Margaret Douglas, daughter of John Douglas, Ann Holderness daughter of John Holderness, Fanny Wood daughter of John Wood, John Holderness son of Thomas Holderness, Sr, and Thomas Kelly son of John Kelly.

Executors: John Douglas and Sarah Holding.
Witnesses: John McVinchey, Benjamin Fincher, Richard Fincher.

\- - -

A-59 Will of JOSEPH AKIN. Dated 4 Jan 1766, proved Feb 1767

sons: Thomas, Joseph Akin.

daus: Mary Akin, Suillah ?, Sarah, "my three daughters"

"Joseph Ostin - 370 acres of land lying on the head of Sandy River in Hallyfax CO. in Va. which he bought of me."

- continued -

A-59 Will of JOSEPH AKIN continued -

"George Jefferson - 600 acres on Lick Fork of Moore's Creek in Orange County, N.C. which he bought of me."

Executor: "Thomas Asgah living in Hallyfax County in Va."
Witnesses: Alex (x) Montgomery, John (x) Luis, Sam Barton.

\- - -

A-62 Will of CHARLES FOSHEE. Dated 23 Nov 1757, proved, 2nd time, Feb 1759.

wife: Susannah

"... my two sons" William Foshee and Charles Foshee get land

After wife's death everything else is to be sold and "divided among all my children."

Executors: Susannah Foshee, Joseph Foshee.
Witnesses: William (x) Marsh, Elmon or Elmore George.

Note by R.H.S. Evidently there were two copies of this will. Neither copy was ever signed. Susabbah proved the will in Dec 1757, and qualified as Executrix. Joseph Foshe proved the will again in Feb 1759, and renounced his right as Executor. He began a suit against Susannah, accusing her of wasting the estate, but dropped it. Susannah died in 1761, and Joseph Foshee was appointed Administrator of her estate and of Charles'. She seems to have been Charles' second wife, as Joseph Foshee was appointed Guardian to the orphan daughter of Charles and Christian Foshee. There are several items about these two estates in the Orange County Court Minutes. I have abstracted and published these Court Minutes for the years 1752 through 1766--see page 5.

\- - -

A-60 Will of ALEXANDER STUART or STEWART Dated 18 Aug 1764, proved Feb 1767

wife: Elizabeth

eldest son: Robert, under age
youngest son: John, under age

daughter: Abigal Stuart

Executors: William Piggott, Jeremiah Piggott.
Witnesses: John Pike, Samuel Pike.

\- - -

A-63 Will of SAMUEL (x) LEHMAN. Dated 18 Oct 1766, proved May 1767

wife: Priscilla

son: Gorabebel? Lehman

Executrix: wife Priscilla.
Witnesses: Wm (x) Barker, Lewis (x) Barker, Chris. Woodward.

\- - -

A-64 Will of ADAM ROGER. Dated --, proved May 1767

Wife, her name not stated, is pregnant...."child that my wife is with now ..."

daughter: Mary

"brother John's children, William and John .."

"Guardian over this my estate brother Hugh Roger and Robert Rea."

Executors: brother Hugh Roger and I_r_abel or I_s_abel Roger.
Witnesses: John Patton, Elinore Rogērs.
(Proved by John Patton and Eleanor Rogers.)

- - -

A- 66 Will of THOMAS CATE. Dated 5 Nov 1765, proved May 1767

wife: Elizabeth

son: Richard "plantation whereon I now live"

daughter Sarah "daughters" mentioned

granddaughter Ann " daughter of my son Thomas .."

Executors: sons Thomas and Joseph.
Witnesses: William Smith, Eliza beth (x) Cate.

- - -

A-67 Will of JOSEPH WADE. Dated 3 Jan 1757, proved Aug 1767

wife: Sarah

sons: John, James

daus: Mary Strawther, Susannah Hart, Elizabeth Talley, Lucy Powell, Sarah Fountain

grandson: Joseph Strawther

Executors: "son Joseph Wade and my son-in-law Joseph Powel".
Witnesses: William Bradford (GRIMES says this is Burford), Samuel Burton.

- - -

A-68 Will of DAVID HALLIBURTON. Dated 3 Jan 1767, proved Aug 1767.

Wife, name not stated, is pregnant.

Sons: Thomas, David, John, William, all under 21 years.

"son Charles which is now a cripple" to be educated.

Executors: wife, and George Moore.
Witnesses: John (x) Adams, Thomas (x) Beach (?), Susannah Adams.

- - -

A-70 Will of WALTER(x) THEDFORD. Dated 13 August 1767, proved Nov 1767.

wife: Rebecca

sons: Josias (eldest), William (land on Stony Creek).

dau: Deborah

son-in-law: William Williams.

Executors: wife Rebecca, and eldest son Josias.
Witnesses: Abigal Bracken, John Baker.

- - -

A-72 Will of WILLIAM BASKETT. Dated 17 July 1767, proved Nov 1767.

Wife: Ruth Baskett

"my three daughters Mary, Elizabeth and Ruth, as they marry or arrive to the age of twenty years"

sons: Thomas, William.

Executors: "trusty and beloved friends William White and John Baskett".
Witnesses: Jane (x) Dael (?), Dianah (x) Collingsworth.

- - -

A- 74 Will of SOLOMON DEBOW. Dated 1 Sept 1767, proved Nov 1767.

wife: Hannah

Sons: John, tract of land lying on Winn's Creek.
Frederick, land on Cain Creek and land on Hyco Creek.
Benjamin (now under 21)

-continued-

A-74 Will of SOLOMON DEBOW continued-

daus: Hannah, Jane (unmarried)
"daughters Ann, Mary, Sarah and Elizabeth to have reasonable schooling" etc.

Executors: wife Hannah, and son John Debow.
Witnesses: John Pearson, Rachel (x) Gold, L.?. V.Hook.

- - -

A-76 Will of Michael Holt. Dated 31 June 1765, proved Nov 1767.

wife: Elizabeth son: Peter

"my children" name and number not stated.

Executors: "my dear son Michael Holt, Junior, and Nicholas Holt, Junior."
Witnesses: John Butler, William Carlisle.

- - -

A-77 Will of WILLIAM (x) SERJANT, SENIOR.

Dated 11 Feb 1768, proved April 1768.

wife: Sarah son-in-law: Joseph Gold

sons: Joseph, Thomas, James, Stephen

dau: Elizabeth "100 acres which I purchased of Thos. Bailey".

Executors: Sons Stephen Bryant and Joseph Gold".
Witnesses: John Lea, Sarah Serjant.

- - -

A-79 Will of FREDERICK (x) NALL. Dated 7 March 1768, proved April 1768.

Wife: Martelenor Nall

Executrix: wife
Witnesses: John Watson, John Campbell, Peter Wolf, .. ?.. Bavin.

- - -

A-80 Will of CHARLES (x) MURROW. Dated 16 Dec 1767, proved April 1768.

cousin: Robert Barnhill, one half of estate.

"well beloved brother Adam Murrow" other half of estate if he comes to America.

Executor: cousin Robert Barnhill.
Witnesses: James Humphill, Thomas Humphill, John Hood (?).

- - -

A-81 Will of ALEXANDER MONTGOMERY. Dated 27 July 1767
proved April 1768.

wife; name not stated

son: Alexander Montgomery

son-in-law: Robert Barnett in Amhurst Co., Va. "my plantation that lyeth in Rockfish settlement".

son: William Montgomery 5 shillings.

"rest of my children namely John, Elizabeth, and my daughters Ann and Mary ... one shilling sterling"

Sole Executrix: "well beloved wife".
Witnesses: William Robinson, Charles Crawford, Wm. Maxwell.

- - -

A-83 Will of JAMES (x) HAYGOOD. Dated 20 Feb 1768,
proved 29 July 1768.

Wife: name not given

sons: George, Benjamin, James, William.

dau: Rebecca.

Executors: wife, and William Partin.
Witnesses: Philip Gee, George (x) Haygood, William (x) Partin.

- - -

A-84 Will of JOHN (x) McCALLISTER. Dated 11 July 1768
proved July 1768.

wife: Rosannah

sons: James, Joseph

unmarried daus: Sarah, Mary, Martha, Margaret McCallister.
married daus: Margaret Patent? I .?.., Elizabeth.

Executors: brother James McCallister,
son-in-law Andrew Patent ? or Poteat ?
Witnesses: Henry Petillo, Cairns Tinnin, Margaret (x) Tinnin.

- - -

A-86 Will of PETER (x) POOR. Dated 31 May 1768, proved
Oct. 1768.

wife: Elizabeth

son: Peter Poor (under age)

daus: Mary Ann, Ann Phillipinia, Eva Catarina, Elizabeth, "my four daughters", (all under age).

Guardians: John Oliver, George Fogleman.
Executrix: wife.
Witnesses: Josias Mogar, Joseph Bogs, Anthony ...?...

- - -

A-89 Will of ISAAC (x) GREASON. Dated 10 Sept 1768, proved Oct 1768.

wife: Margaret

sons: Nicholas, Jacob "land on west of Beaver Creek", John.

daus: Margaret Loew, Unitie Lionburger.

Sole Executor: son Nicholas Greason.
Witnesses: George Fogleman, John Oliver.

- - -

A-92 Will of JOHN McCOY, of St. Mathew's Parish, Orange Co.

Dated 4 April 1767, proved October 1768.

Wife, name not stated.

"oldest son Francis", daughter Elizabeth, "younger children".

Guardian: "well beloved friend, Robert Rea".
Executor: W. McCoy.
Witnesses: John Armstrong, Matthew J. Cobey (?).

- - -

A-93 Will of WILLIAM BORING. Proved 11 October 1768.

On his death bed William Boring orally left to Charles and Joseph Boring, brothers, a slave, etc.

John Currie and James Culbertson swore to the above before William Lee, Justice of the Peace, on June 20 1768.

- - -

A-94 Will of JOHN McCOMB. Dated --, proved April 1769.

wife: Rachel wife's sons: John, William

"my son Jesse"

daus: Mary, Jane, Darcas, Harrow (?),
Sarah, Margaret, Elizabeth

Executors: John McComb, Rachel McComb, Mary McComb,
Jane McComb, Jesse McComb, Darcas McComb.
Overseer of Executors: James Allison.
Witnesses: John Smith, Elizabeth Smith.

- - -

A-95 Will of OWEN THOMAS. Dated 17 March 1769, proved April 1769.

wife: Mary

"six small children: Hester, Joana, Lewis, Jonathan, John, Elizabeth". -continued-

A-95 Will of OWEN THOMAS continued-

brother James Thomas "as long as he lives with them" (the children).

sons: William, James, George, Michal.

daus: Mary Hard (or Hart), Ann Wilks.

Executors: John Gray, Thomas Cate son of Robert.
Witnesses: John Baskett, Frederick Williams.

- - -

A-97 Will of JOHN RECORD. Dated 26 Dec 1768 / , proved April 1769.

wife: Comfort dau: Mary Record

sons: David, John, Sion

Executors: wife Comfort, and Joseph Brantley Idison.
Witnesses: James Brantley, Wm. Brantley.

- - -

A-99 Will of THOMAS PETTEY. Dated 26 Aug 1766, proved July 1769.

wife: Mary dau: Martha Pettey

sons: Thomas, land on George Herndon's line
Reubin, John. All the sons seem to be under age.

Friend Robert Marsh to care for children if wife dies before children come of age.

"youngest children, Thomas and Martha".

Executors: Robert Marsh, James Younger.
Witnesses: James Stewart, Robert Carlile.

- - -

A-101 Will of WILLIAM WALKER. Dated 24 March 1769, proved July 1769.

"beloved wife"

sons: James, John, William, Abraham, Alexander.

Testator mentions money received in Pennsylvania.

Executors: John Robertson, John Corry.
Witnesses: John Corry, Jr., Shasana (x) Corry.

- - -

A-102 Will of SAMUEL REED. Dated 4 Sept 1765, proved July 1769.

wife: Mary

"Samuel Stewart now living with me".. to him at the age of 21...

Elizabeth Jones ... to be of age at 18 -continued-

A-102 Will of SAMUEL REED continued-

Executors: wife Mary, and Thomas Lindley, Sr.
Witnesses: Wm. Lindley, John Maroon.

- - -

A-105 Will of JOHN GEER. Dated 12 Aug 1769, proved Jan 1770.

beloved wife, name not stated

sons: David, Frederick, William, John.

daus: Mimma, Tabitha, Mary Burnett, Siny (?), Sarah.

son-in-law: James Roper.

Witnesses: Jacob Garrard, Jr, Michael Dent.

- - -

A-106 Will of ROBERT DONALDSON. Dated 20 March 1770, proved April 1770.

wife: Hannah

sons: Thomas (married), Robert

daus: Margaret, wife of William Ray
"Undutiful daughter Mary 2 shillings"
"Hannah, Elizabeth, Jean, Ritteren (?), Sarah and Robert, I allow equal shares."

Executors: wife Hannah, & Wm. Ray. Overseer: Thomas Donaldson.
Witnesses: Honor Nicks, Elizabeth Thomas, Thomas Douglass.

- - -

A-107 Will of SAMUEL YARBOROUGH. Dated 5 Nov 1769, proved April 1770.

wife: Sarah

sons: William, "land in Amelia Co., Va. whereon his grandfather lived lying between Cold and Nottoway ... likewise land on Tarr River adjoining Robert Bumpas..."

Samuel, John, both are under 21 years of age.

daus: Elizabeth Yarborough, Sarah Yarborough, Lewcey Yarborough, all under 18 years of age.

Executors: wife Sarah, Wm. Yarborough, John Bumpass.
Witnesses: Abraham Womack, Jr., Isaac Johnston, James Evans.

- - -

A-109 Will of ROBERT MOTHEREL. Dated 8 Jan 1769, proved April 1770.

wife: name not stated

sons: John, Samuel, Joseph, Robert "100 acres each when they come of age".

-continued-

A-109 Will of ROBERT MOTHEREL contiued-

Executors: wife, and David Mitchell
Witnesses: James Culbertson, Jr., John Carson, David Porter.

- - -

A-111 Will of WILLIAM PEGGOTT. Dated 9 Feb, proved April 1770.

wife: Sarah

sons: eldest son John, youngest son William "all land bought of Richard Henderson on middle fork of Rocky River .. adjoining Thos Ransom's line" ...

"second son Samuel"; "third son Jeremiah".

"six daughters, Abigail, Marjory, Sarah, Marah, Elizabeth, Rachel."

Executors: Jeremiah and Benjamin Peggott.
Witnesses: Henry Underwood, Thos. Molborough, Simeon Adamson.

This will is signed William Piggotte.

- - -

A-112 Will of JAMES TALBERT. Dated 5 Oct 1769, proved April 1770.

wife: Mary

"My father and mother to live where they are now without being disturbed."

sons: oldest son John to be bound to his uncle Joseph to learn tailor's trade at age of fifteen.

sons Benjamin and Loran (?) to be bound to him when fifteen till they are twenty-one years of age.

daughter mentioned but name not stated," 3 sons and 1 dau."

Executors: "loving brothers Abraham Miles and George Sea".
Witnesses: Thomas McNeil, George See. (Possibly Lee)

- - -

A-114 Will of JOSEPH DIXSON. Dated 5 Dec 1769, proved April 1770.

wife: Mary

sons: Nathan, Stephen
dau: Anne Bailey wife of Caleb
sons: Solomon land on Terrell's Creek on waters of Haw River adjoining John Lambral's land.
Jesse land bought of John May.
Eli land bought of Howil Brown, adjoining Geo. Dixson.
Samuel and Joseph to enter into full possession of their land when they reach 21 years of age.

-continued-

A-114 Will of JOSEPH DIXSON continued-

Executrix: wife Mary.
Witnesses: William Moffitt, Joab Brooks, Jr., Solomon Cox.

- - -

A-116 Will of JAMES McGOWN. Dated Nov 1769, proved April 1770.

Wife: name not stated

sons: James, William

daus: Mary, Susannah, Ettar.

Executor: George Tate. Witness: Robert Mebane.

- - -

A- 117 Will of ALEXANDER LARKIN. Dated 19 August 1772 proved - no date given.

Wife: Mary

sons: Thomas, William.

daus: Mary and her husband Mordecai Moor
Margaret, Sarah,
Elizabeth Boring.

Executors: wife, and son Thomas.
Witnesses: John Tinnin, Jane Tinnin, William Anderson.

- - -

A-119 Will of JOHN MILES. Dated 6 May 1769, no probate date

Wife: Mary

sons: Charles, Thomas, John, youngest son William.

Executors: Charles Smith, Christopher Smith.
Witness: Charley Smith.

- - -

A-121 Will of ROBERT SMITH, of St. Mathew's Parish.

Dated 20 June 1772, no probate date.

Wife: Mary sons: John, Andrew, Robert

daus: Elizabeth, Mary, Isabel.

Executors: Joseph McCaffrity, and son William.
Witnesses: John Walker, Robert Chassen (?).

- - -

A-122 Will of JOSEPH ALLEN. Dated --

Wife: Sarah daus: Elizabeth, Sarah

-continued-

A-122 Will of JOSEPH ALLEN continued-

sons:John, William, Daniel, George, Joshua.

"other children, Solomon, Samuel, Elisha, Joseph".

Executors: sons William and Daniel, and friend Wm. Clark.
Witnesses: Daniel Allen, William Allen, Joshua Allen,
George Allen, William Clark.

- - -

A-124 Will of EDMUND HARDIN. Dated 20 August 1769,
no probate date.

Wife: Mary

"Estate to be divided between wife and 3 children and unborn child".

Executors: wife Mary, and Thomas Cate.
Witnesses: John Baskett, Jonathan Hardin, Moses Rice.

- - -

A-125 Will of HOSEA TAPLEY. Hatdded 21 March 1770.

Affidavit: "This day came Victory Rankin and made oath that she was at Hosea Tapley's Jr. before he died and he said land to go to sons John Pryor Tapley and Hosea Tapley. One part to go to another son if his wife have one".

Witness: John Pryor. Affidavit made 22 March 1770.

- - -

A-125 Will of JOSEPH GEORGE. Dated 14 Feb 1770, proved --

Wife: Ellenor

sons: Ambrose, Daniel Pegg, William, Isaac, James, Jesse.

daus: Mary Hinsford, Cathrine Riddle, Peggy George.

Executors: sons Ambrose and James, and wife Ellenor.
Witnesses: James Younger, John Page, Jr.

- - -

A-127 Will of JOHN PENDEXTER. Dated 23 Oct 1772, proved --

Wife: Elizabeth

sons: William, John, Lionel (?), Chapman, Thomas, Francis.

Executors: James McCann, John Hart
Witnesses: Abraham Whittiker, Nelly Ruby*, Elizabeth Tate.

- - - * Witness is Nelly Reily, not Ruby.
All three witnesses signed with a "mark", x.

A-128 Will of GEORGE BOWER. Dated 15 July 1770, proved --

Wife: Margaret

"sons as they come of age", name and number not stated
"daughters as they come of age", name and number not stated

Executrix: wife Margaret
Witnesses: Edward Turner, James Browning, Hugh Finley.

- - -

A-129 Will of WILLIAM BLACKWOOD. Dated 8 Oct. 1772, proved -

Wife: Elizabeth sons: James, John, William

daus: Martha, Mary, Jennet, Elizabeth, Ann.

Executors: son William, daughter Margaret.
Witnesses: Alex. Mebane, William Tate, Mary Sample.

- - -

A-131 Will of NATHANIEL WALTON. Dated 31 July 1771, proved -

Wife: Mary "Peter, only son now living"

daus: Mary, Jemima, Keziah.

Executors: wife Mary, and son Peter.
William Durbin, John Reeves, Lancelot Johnston.

Codicil dated 4 August 1771.

- - -

A-135 Will of JOHN BASKETT. Dated 26 Feb. 1771, proved --

Wife: Ann brother: James

sons:William, Thomas (under age).

Executors: friends Thomas Cate and James Baskett.
Witnesses: John Cate, Elizabeth Cate.

- - -

A-137. Will of JOHN MORDAUGH. Dated 8 July 1771, proved --

Wife: Elizabeth

sons: James "plantation bought of Enos Elliman"
David, John

daus: Catrin, Agness, Janet, Elizabeth.

Executors: wife Elizabeth, and son James Sr.
Witnesses: Wm. Rutherford, John Mordaugh.

- - -

A-140 Will of ANDREW HARRISON. Dated 16 May 1773,
proved May 1774.

Wife: Jane

sons: Ninian, youngest son Andrew.
"William and Thomas 1 shilling, already having received their part"

daus: Milley Moore, Elizabeth Harrison, Anne Ware, Molly, Jane.

Executors: Wm. Harrison, Thomas Harrison, John Ware, Wm. Moore.
Witnesses: Robert Payne, Charles Burton.

– – –

A-143 Will of PRISCILLA (x) BURTON. Dated 22 May 17--,
proved May 1774.

son: Robert Burton

granddaughters Sarah Burton, daughter of Robert, Judah Coleman.

dau: Priscilla Burton, daughter of Robert Burton.

Executor: son Robert Burton.
Witnesses: Abram Perkins, Thomas Dudley, Charles Burton.

– – –

A-144 Will of GEORGE TATE. Dated Feb 1774, proved May 1774.

sons: George Tate, James Tate wife

daus: Kitturah (oldest), Akness, Mary, Elizabeth, Litia, Janet, Margaret, "my seven daughters". All seem to be minors.

Sole Executrix: wife.
Witnesses: William Tate, Hugh Willson, James Smith.

– – –

A-146 Will of NATHANIEL HARRIS of the Parish of St Mathews.

Dated June 1773, proved May 1774.

Wife: Ellender

sons: Nathaniel, Archer, Edward, Charles Harris

daus: Unity Callahan, Lenora Burks

granddaughter: Mary Harris.

Executor: Edward Harris.
Witnesses: Wortham Glenn, Ann Glenn, Mildred Woods.

Note: OLDS' ABSTRACTS OF N. C. WILLS lists the above will as NATHANIEL HARRISON, but HARRIS is correct.

– – –

A-147 Will of ALEXANDER ROBBINSON or ROBERTSON 23 April 1774, will proved May 1774

sisters: Esthy Robeson
Ellenor Ceasey wife of John Ceasey
nephews: James Ceasey, David Ceasey
brother-in-law: John Ceasey

Executors: Hugh McAden, William Powell.
Witnesses: Hugh McAden, Wm Powell, William Maxwell.

\- - -

A-148 Will of SAMUEL UNDERWOOD. Dated March 1773, proved May 1774.

wife: Anna

sons: Henry, Alex, Samuel, Benjamin, James

daus: Mary Cloud eldest, Anne
"Jane, Ruth, Sarah, Elizabeth, four youngest"

Executors: wife Anna, son Alexander.
Witnesses: John Marshall, William Ward, Jacob Marshall.

\- - -

A-150 Will of HENRY SEARS. Dated 8 Nov 1768, proved May 1774.

wife: Rose sons: John, Edward, Harry, Barbey*

daughters: Sally, Nancy and Sears (Henry Sears' wife w Rosannah Barbee)

Executors: wife Rose, and John Barbee, Jr.
Witnesses: Mark Morgan, Benjamin Hart, Wm (x) Barbee.

\- - -

A-152 Will of BURGES HARRILSON. Dated 9 May 1772, proved --

wife: Elizabeth, gets "her maintanance"

son: Ezekiel "plantation I purchased of Wm. Chambers, Sr"
son: Elijah, 20 shillings

dau: "Elishaba Harrilson the wife of Elkanah Harrilson, plantation whereon he now lives"

dau: Drusilla Harrilson
dau: Jemima Harrilson land in Henrico Co., Va. "on Stoney Run which I purchased of James Allen (?)"

grandson: "I. Harrilson, the oldest son of Elijah Harrilson, land I purchased of my brother Paul Harrilson, lying on Stony (or Storey's) Creek"

Executors: Ezekiel Harrilson, Elkanah Harrilson.
Witnesses: Joe Johnson, William Stone, John (x) Harrilson.

\- - -

A-154 Will of WILLIAM REA of Little River, Parish of Saint Matthew. Dated 16 October 1769, proved May 1774.

wife: Catherine "money that is now in Joseph Allison and Patrick Rutherford's hands", etc

son: William grandson: David Rea.

sons-in-law: Michael Robbinson, John Mordah, James Mordah, Patrick Rutherford.

After wife's death, Joseph Allison is to have a slave.

Executors: Joseph Allison, William Rea.
Witnesses: Robert Willson, James Rea,Jr, Samuel Sample.

- - -

A-156 Will of ISAAC ALLEN. Dated 24 Nov 1773 ?, proved Jan 1772 ?

wife: Mary

"My children" names and number not stated.

Executrix: Mary Allen. Witnesses: John Rainey, Wm. Rainey.

- - -

A-158 Will of ALEX RUSSELL. Dated 10 Dec 1771, proved Jan 1772

wife: Jane sons: James, Alex

daughters: Margaret, Elenor, Elizabeth, Jane

friends: Eli McDaniel and wife.

Executors: "friends William Rogers and James Neville, guardians to see the same duly executed."
Witnesses: William Hannah, Nathaniel Lyon, Josiah Blaik.

- - -

A-160 Will of JOHN PRYOR. Dated 28 Sept 1771, proved Jan 1772.

wife: Margaret

son: Robert "tract in Granville County, 640 acres"
sons: John Henry Pryor, Abner

daus:Elizabeth Flournoy, Rhoda Stone, Leah Perkins, Mildred Womack, Lucy Tapley, Rachel Pope, Dorothy Pyror, Martha "when she comes of age"

grandchildren: John Pryor son of Green Pryor
Betty Green Pryor
grandson: John Pryor Smith "tract I purchased of Hosea Tapley".

Executors: son-in-law William Stone, wife Margaret, son-in-law David Womack.
Witnesses: Burgis Harralson, Joseph Hicks, Peter Rogers.

- - -

A-164 Will of DAVID PINKERTON,"yoeman" of St. Matthew's Parish.
Dated 27 Feb 1764, proved Jan / 1772
wife: Margaret

sons: John, William, David
daughters Martha and Mary, both under 18 years of age

step-daughter Agnes Trickey ? 5 shillings.

Executors: wife Margaret, son John.
Witnesses: George Miller, James Latta.

- - -

A-166 Will of JOSEPH BARNETT. Dated 18 April 1771, proved Jan 1773.
wife: Rachel is pregnant -"child wife is with" ..

son: Samuel daughters: Mary and Sarah Barnett.

Witnesses: John Barnett, Wm Miles, Thomas Barnett.

- - -

A-168 Will of HENRY LEA. Dated 14 Dec 1774, proved Aug 1774.

wife: Elizabeth "all parts of my estate given to me by her parents"...

daughter, Frances, is under age.

Executors: friends James Lea "my brother in law", Ann McNiel, Sr.
Witnesses; James Roberts, Thomas McNeill, John Lea.

- - -

A-169 Will of THOMAS DOBBINS. Dated 31 July 1774, proved Aug 1774
wife: Rachel
sons: Hugh -440 acres, John, 2nd son, 432 acres, Thomas, youngest son, plantation. The lands lie on Country Line Creek and Reedy Fork of Hico Creek.
daus: Margaret, Elizabeth Dobbin.
"My two little daughters Rachel and Nancy"

Executors: wife Rachel, son Hugh, friend Archibald Murphy.
Execs are to make a deed to Daniel Hall for "land he bought of my cousin Thomas Dobbins."
Witnesses: William Zachary, John Connor.

A-172 Will of JACOB BISHIND (BASON) Dated 11 Oct 1773, proved Aug 1774
wife: Catherine
daughter: Hannah son: Jacob.

Executors: wife Catherine, son John.
Witnesses: David Rainey, Jane Attcut (?).

- - -

A-174 Will of ISAAC WRITE of St. Mathew's Parish.

Dated 26 May 1772, proved Aug 1774. Wife: Mary

sons: Zacharias and Isaac, both under age.

"Rest of my estate to be equally divided amongst all my children: Providence, Zacarias, Mary and Isaac Write."

Executrix: wife Mary.
Witnesses: Bridger Haynie, Benjamin Ingram, Abraham Miles.

- - -

A-176 Will of JOHN PIKE. Dated 30 March 1771, proved Aug 1774.
Wife: Abigail

sons: John, Samuel, Nathan (youngest)

"My six daughters: Sarah Piggott, Anne Hughes, Susannah Lee, Elizabeth Stuart, Ruth Winner, Rachel Williams."

Executors: wife Abigail, son John.
Witnesses: Thomas Hill, Priscilla Pike, Obediah R..?..

- - -

A-177 Will of THOMAS CRABTREE. Dated 11 April 1774, proved Aug 1774.
Wife: Elizabeth

sons: William, John, James, Thomas

daughter: Mary

Executrix: wife Elizabeth.
Overseers of Will: friends Thomas Barton, John Connor.
Witnesses: Thomas Barton, John Connor, Elizabeth Connor.

- - -

A-179 Will of STEPHEN NORTON. Dated 3 July 1773, proved Aug 1774.
Wife: Jane

sons: John, William, Richard.

daus: Anne Norton, Margaret Norton, Elizabeth Norton.

Executors: Abam. Armstead, John Armstrong.
Witnesses: Wm. Bailey Smith, John Middlebrooks, Richard Boggass.

- - -

A-181 Will of JONATHAN WEST. Dated 1 June 1774,
proved Nov 1774.

Wife: Elenor

cousin: Jonathan West.

Sole Executrix: wife Elenor.
Witnesses: Josiah Black, James Tinnen.

- - -

A-182 Will of JOHN GRAY. Dated 19 Feb 1775, proved May / 1775

To Colonel Thomas Hart, land on Seven Mile Creek, beginning date 25 March 1752 from Lord Granville.

Executors: Col. Thomas Hart, Maj. David Hart, Nathaniel Hart.
Witnesses: John Riley, James Weeks, Henry Hastings.

- - -

A-184 Will of JOSEPH SUTTON. Dated 20 March 1775, proved -

Estate to Daniel Hughes, oldest son of Gabriel Hughes, for love and good will.

Executor: Gabriel Hughes. He is to keep estate in hand until Daniel arrives at 21 years of age.
Witnesses: Shrewood Parish, James Dickings, Sherwood James.

- - -

NOTE by Ruth Herndon Shields.

In reading this book you will no doubt notice the confusing dates given for the probate of the wills and other papers. We have copied the dates as given in the books. The books appear to have been copied from older books, or rebound, and the dates are badly confused.

For instance the wills probated at the November 1800 term of Court, precede the wills recorded at the Court of August 1800.

This book is intended solely as a <u>guide</u> to what is in the WILL BOOKS in Hillsborough. In citing these wills as proof it is advisable to get the full text of the will. Unless I have stated that the will is preserved in the State Archives, the original has been lost, and a copy can only be obtained from the Clerk of Court in Hillsborough. If the original is in Raleigh, a photostat or Xerox copy can be ordered from The Historical Commission, Raleigh, N.C.

Spelling of proper names in some of the wills was not uniform. Sometimes a name was spelled three different ways in the same will. In other cases the writing was so poor the name could only be guessed. Look for every variation of the name you are seeking.

A-185 Will of JOHN BURGESS. Dated 27 Feb 1775,
proved May 1775.

Wife: Elizabeth McConkey

After wife's death property to Lidy Breeze, Susannah Stone, Benjamin Williams. No relationship stated.

Executrix: wife Elizabeth.
Witnesses: Thomas Palmer, Edward Roberts.

- - -

A- 187 Will of JOHN BORING. Dated 6 Jan 1775,
proved May 1775.

Wife; Elizabeth

daughters: Ribecca, Nicy, Mary.

Executors: wife Elizabeth, James Boren (Boring).
Witnesses: James Currie, James Borin, Ann Green.

- - -

A-188 Will of JOSEPH BORRIN. Dated 11 Jan 1775,
proved May 1775.

Wife: Susannah

sons: James, William, Isaac, Joseph Jr, David (under age)

..."to be paid by oldest brother John when David comes of age."

relationship not stated: "john Borrin to have ..."

daughters: Susan, Becky, Phebe, Sara

cousin: Patty Clarke.

Executors: Charles Stephens, James Currie.
Witnesses: James Culberson, James Currie.

- - -

A-189 "ill of JOHN CAMPBELL, tailor. Dated 22 Feb 1761,
proved May 1775.

Wife: Margaret

sons-in-law: John Ferguson, Andrew Ferguson.

sons: Robert, David,
Joseph land adjoining James Stewart's line.

Testator owns land in Albemarle County, Virginia.

Witnesses: Samuel Bell, Thomas Dobbins.
Executors: wife Margaret and son-in-law John Ferguson.

- - -

A-191 Will of JOSEPH (or JONES?) PARKER. Dated 21 Oct 1771,
proved May 1775.

Wife: Rebecca

Children, named in this order:
Richard, Stephen, David, Powell, Francis, Abner, Winny, Sally, Betty. "My son Richard to come of age at 21".

Executors: Thomas Person, Edward Bumpass.
Witnesses: Robert Bumpass, William Fowler,
Grace Fowler, Joanna Person.

\- - -

A-194 Will of CHRISTOPHER MIER. Dated 17 August 1775,
proved Nov 1775.

Wife mentioned but name not stated.

"Eldest son George"

He seems to have other sons and daughters, but no names are given.

Executors: Adam I..?... , Jacob Grissom.
Witnesses: George Fogleman, George Cortner (?), Doolin Law.

\- - -

A-194 Will of GEORGE G. GIBSON. Dated 5 Nov 1775,
proved May 1775.

Wife: Mary

Sons mentioned, but number and names not stated.

Daughters mentioned, but number and names not stated.

Executors: Sherw'd Parrish, Thomas Gibson Liner.
Witnesses: Sherw'd Parrish, Joel (x) Gibson,
Lucreasy (x) Collons.

\- - -

A-196 Will of MOSES FARLEY. Dated 25 March 1776,
proved May 1776.

Wife: Sarah

son: Josiah. dau: Elizabeth. brother: John James Farley.

Executors: John James Farley, William Price.
Witnesses: George Vincent, David Penyman, Henry Burton.

\- - -

A-197 Will of JAMES SANDERS, SENIOR. Dated 28 Feb 1776,
proved May 1776.

Wife mentioned, name not given.

sons: James Sanders, Richard, William.

- continued-

A-197 Will of JAMES SANDERS, SR. continued -

daus: Sarah wife of William Trigg, Cassandra,
Susannah wife of Robert Terry,
Fanny wife of William Sanders the Elder.

grandson: Jeremiah Terry, son of daughter Susannah.

granddaughter: "Casandra's oldest daughter"..

Executors: son James, Richard Sanders, William Trigg.
Witnesses: Andrew Haddock, James Sanders, Robin Terry.

- - -

A-199 Will of ALEXANDER (x) COHARON (?). Dated 28 Oct 1775, proved May 1776.

Wife: Easter , unborn child

sons: eldest son John "land purchased of Barnabas Grims"
second son James "plantation purchased of Richard / Parsons"
Alexander, Samuel

daus: eldest Minny wife of Joseph Guy,
Jean, Easter, Esibal.

Executors: wife Easter, son John.
Witnesses: Ezicaia (x) Witt, John Moor.

- - -

A-200 Will of ARTHUR (x) STEPHENS. Dated 2 March 1776, proved May 1776.

"Three sons" mentioned, but names not given.

daughters: oldest Sarah, second Leviner,
third Elizabeth.

Executors: Joshua Johnston, Joel Johnston,
John McCane, Abraham Stephens.

- - -

A-201 Will of WILLIAM (x) BUMPASS. Dated 10 March 1776, proved May 1776.

Wife: Mary

father: Robert Bumpass.

Executors: Gabriel Davey, Mary Bumpass, Edward Bumpass.
Witnesses: Isaia Vanhook, Wm. Yarborough, James Davis.

- - -

A-202 Will of JAMES WATSON. Dated 5 Dec 1776, proved Aug 1777.

son: James
daughter: Helen Reed wife of William Reed

grandsons: James Reed, Robert Reed, William Reed, Watson Reed, James Watson.

granddaughters: ....?... Reed, Helen Watson, Rebecca Watson, ...?.. Watson.

Executors: son James Watson, William Johnston, James Morris, Nathaniel Rochester.
No witnesses. Will proved by William Courtney.

- - -

A-203 Will of LODOWICK CLAPP. Dated 25 July 1768, proved Feb 1778.

Wife mentioned but name not stated.

sons: John, others mentioned but names & number not stated.

Daughters mentioned but names & number not stated.

Executrix: wife.
Witnesses: John Graves, Lodowick (x) Swing, George Cortner.

- - -

A-205 Will of ROBERT HOLLOWAY. Dated 9 Nov 1776, proved Nov 1778.

Wife: Martha, his third wife.

sons: oldest Samuel, Stephen.

daus: Elizabeth Horner, Brigett, Mary Readen.

"Remainder of children of the body of Martha, my third wife ... namely: Priscilla, Susannah, Ann, Stephen, Rachell, Ruth, Jane, Litici (?)."

Executrix: wife Martha.
Witnesses: Joseph Baker, Mary Baker, John Baker.

- - -

A-206 Will of ANDREW McBRIDE. Dated 1 Oct 1778, proved Feb 1779.

Wife: Jane

Executrix: wife Jane.
Witnesses: John Steel, William Morrow.

- - -

A-207 Will of WILLIAM FORREST. Dated 8 Aug 1777, proved Aug 1778.

Wife: Lovina

sons: Shadrack, Gresham, Joel, William, Jesse.

Executors: Edward Gresham, Archer (Gresham ?), wife Lovina (this name may be Louisa).
Witnesses: Edward Gresham, Jr, Isaac Forrest.

- - -

A-207 Will of MARTIN LAY. Dated 15 July 1777, proved May 1779.

Wife: Catherreney

sons: Henry, George daughter: Mary.

Executors: Jacob Allbright, George Lay.
Witnesses: Henry Garhurt, Isaac (x) Sharp.

- - -

A-208 Will of JACOB CAIN. Dated 6 Aug 1779, proved - 1779.

Wife: Joanna is pregnant, unborn child mentioned.

Executors: wife Joanna, Jacob Allen.
Witnesses: James Fen (?), Wm. (x) Leathers, Wm. Johnston.
W (?)

- - -

A-209 Will of ROBERT ABERCROMBY. Dated 31 May 1779, proved Aug 1779.

sons: Charles, Robert.
daughter: Jenny Mebane.

Executors: sons Charles and Robert.
Witnesses: William Saxon, James (x) Desern. Enoch Liner (or Lewis ?).

- - -

A-210 Will of GEORGE (x) HILL. Dated 24 Jan 1779, proved Feb 1780.

Wife mentioned, name not stated.

son: Henry

"After wife's marriage estate to be "equally divided amongst every one of my children." (Names and number not stated.)

Executors: wife, James Wood, Joseph Wood.
Witnesses: Thomas Guin, Mealy (x) ..?.., James Wood.

- - -

A-211 Will of MELCHI (x) DANIEL. Dated 23 Jan 1779,
or McDANIEL proved Feb 1780.

Wife: Marget

"Remaining children" .. names and number not stated, (others may have died or married and left home ?).

Executors: Lewis Kirk, Richard Cate.
Witness: Benjamin (x) McCool (?).

- - -

A-212 Bill of Sale from TIMOTHY CAIN to JAMES CAIN, for negroes. Dated 20 Feb 1781, proved August 1781.
Witnesses: Jno. Kelley, Jno. Cabe.

- - -

A-212 Bill of Sale from TIMOTHY CAIN to MARY CAIN.
Dated 20 Feb 1781, proved August 1781.
Witnesses: Jno. Kelley, Jno. Cabe.

- - -

The following wills dated 1800 and earlier, are preserved in the Archives in Raleigh, N.C. Proved 1801 or later.

TESTATOR	DATE OF WILL	BOOK
Bird, James	1793	D-155
Brewer, Katy	1800	D-30
Curry, James, Sr.	1800	D-137
Deley, William	1794	D-105
Dunnagan, Sherwood	1800	D-22
Freeman, William	1800	D-43
Gant, John	1800	D-30
Guthrie, James	1800	D-40
Harvey, Isaac	1800	D-63
Kell, John	1800	D-28
McCracken, Jeremiah	1794	D-66
Moore, John	1800	D-27
Clendenin, William	1790	D-25
Newlin, John, Sr.	1799	D-162
Forest, Benjamin	1800	D-21
Rainey, David	1800	D-68
Rice, Jesse	1798	D-111
Robertson, John	1800	D-46
Smith, Adam	1798	D-59
Stalcop; John	1800	D-125
Tenning, Elizabeth	1800	D-53

- - - - -

A-213 Bill of Sale from JAMES FRAZER to Thomas Hart for twelve slaves. Dated 18 Nov 1780, proved Nov 1780.
Witness: Jesse Benton.

- - -

A-214 Power of Attorney from THOMAS HART to "trusty friends James Hogg and Jesse Benton." Dated 19 Nov 1780, proved Nov 1780.
Witness: Susannah Miller.

- - -

A-215 Will in Archives. Dated 10 Oct 1777, proved Nov 1780.

THOMAS CAPPES (indexed in Archives as CAPPER)

"dear and only daughter Nancy"

Executors: wife Ann, "trusty friends Tapley Patterson and James Trice, Jr."
Witnesses: Jos. Harwood, Eliz. Trice, John (x) Davis.

- - -

A-217 Will in Archives. Dated 31 March 1779, proved Aug 1781.

MICHAEL SYNNOTT

Servant Mary Humphreys gets "land on Gooseberry Mountain" as long as she "lives single" unmarried.

Nephew Richard Synnott of St Catherine's Parish in Wapping, London- land "on Crooked Run, the Waters of Eno River."

He mentions bond on wearing apparel & books from Thomas Barefield, Arthur Brown & Benjamin Cotton (bond & inventory in the care of Dr. Thomas Burke.)

Executor: William Johnston.
Witnesses: R'd Bennehan, Mich'l (x) McGee.

- - -

A-220 Will in Archives. Dated 21 June 1780, proved Aug 1781.

THOMAS LAPSLIE wife: Charity

son: Thomas Lapslie gets land "on waters of Back Creek" ... and "tract he now lives on .. Dodson's Cabin ..."

daus: Elizabeth and Charity, both minors.
sons: David and James, both minors.

Executors: wife Charity, son Thomas, friend Wm. Anderson.
Witnesses: Francis Wilkinson, David Anderson, Robert Anderson.

- - -

A-223 Will in Archives. Dated 15 Aug 1779, proved Aug 1781.

JAMES TRICE wife: Sarah

"... my father and his wife should live with my wife ..."

nephew: Charles Trice "son of Edward Trice my brother"

brother: John Trice "my stallion"

relationship not given: James Trice and Joseph Trice.

Loney Hunter "£ 50 and my watch, etc, for building a Meeting house."

Executors: brother Edward Trice, Robert Campbell.
Witnesses: Robert Campbell, Abraham Massey, Richard Leigh.

– – –

A-225 Will in Archives. Dated 24 Sept 1781, proved Nov 1781.

JOSEPH YOUNG father: John Young

Wife mentioned, name not stated, is pregnant ? he says "if my wife is now with child ..."

son: John.

Executors: wife, and friend Robert Agnew.
Witnesses: Wm. Galbreath, R. Galbreath.

– – –

A-226 Will in Archives. Dated 25 Nov 1780, proved Aug 1781.

THOMAS CLARK (Yoeman)

wife: Susanna "that legacy that William Clark deceased Father to Susannah Clark did bequeath to me at his decease."

daus: Sarah Clark, Mary Clark, Catherine Clark.

sons: Thomas, William and Abner (youngest, a minor) Clark.

He mentions "land situated on Broad River, S.C."

Executors: James Carson, James Carr, Jr.
Witnesses: Wm. Strain, John Ray, Wm. Williams.

– – –

A-229 Will in Archives. Dated 24 Nov 1780, proved Aug 1781.

WILLIAM WILSON wife: Mary dau: Mary

sons: Samuel and Gregory.

Executors: "trusty friends" Richard Holman & Thomas Round-/tree
Witnesses: John Wilson, James Wilson, Susanna (x) Farmer.

– – –

A-231 Will in Archives. Dated 2 April 1781, proved Aug 1781.

GEORGE WAGGONER wife: Mary

daus: Elizabeth and Ann (both minors)

father: Henry Waggoner "land adjoining his line and Robert McCaul's line".

Executors: Mary Waggoner, Robert Berry.
Witnesses: Step. Smyth, George Clower, James Waggoner.

- - -

A-233 Will in Archives. Dated 10 Feb 1781, proved Nov 1781.

JOHN TAPLEY PATTERSON wife: Sarah

son: Mann Patterson land on Capper's Branch of New Hope

only daughter: Milly (Amelia)

son: Page Patterson "plantation I bought of John Whatly and tract I bought of William Whatly"

Executors: wife, and "only and well beloved brother Mark Patterson."
Witnesses: Jos. Barbee, John Patterson, Baxter Boling.

- - -

A-235 Will in Archives. Dated 21 June 1781, proved Nov 1781.

HUGH CAINE daughter: Ann Caine "all her mother's and sisters' wearing apparel" etc.

son: William

sons: Hugh, James, Allan "land and plantation whereon I at present reside"

cousin: Elizabeth McKinley.

called nephews - "John Caine son of my son William"
"James Caine another child of my son William"
called nieces: "Ann Caine another child of my son William"
"Fanny and Margaret twins of my son William".

Executors: sons William and Hugh Caine.
Witnesses: Moses Leathers, Wm. Johnston.

- - -

A-237 Will in Archives. Dated 15 Sept 1781, proved May 1782.

PETER (x) NOE wife: Hannah, all estate

sons: John, Joseph, 5 shillings each.

daus: Kathereana Rightenhous, Susannah Ridge, 5 shillings each, Elizabeth Coons, Elizabeth Ragen, 5 shillings each.

Executrix: wife. Witnesses: Jno. Armstrong, Anne (x) Armstrong.

- - -

A-239 Bill of Sale (in State Archives) dated 20 April 1781, proved Feb Court 1782, from CHARLES WHITE to Alexander Carnes, for negroes. Witnesses: William Clark, Wm. Williams.

- - -

A-240 Will in Archives. Dated 20 March 1775, proved Feb 1782.

JOHN LUTTRELL wife Susanna - unborn child or children -

Three brothers Thomas, Hugh and William Luttrell.

"Lands purchased by Richard Henderson & Co. of the Cherokee Indians on the waters of the Mississippi".

No executor named.
Witnesses: Jesse Benton, Thomas Farrar, Nath'l Henderson.

- - -

A-241 Will in Archives. Dated 27 June 1781, proved Feb 1782.

ISAAC (x) SHARP wife: Philipina - unborn child

two oldest sons: John and Bostian

children: Peter, Christian, Elizabeth and Philipina, minors.

Executors: "beloved friends Nicholas Gibbs & John Albright."
Witnesses: Samuel Suther or Luther, Jacob Albright.

- - -

A-243 Will in Archives. Dated 3 March 1779, proved Feb 1782.

WILLIAM CLARK wife: Mary

son: William - land from place he is now living on "south end of tract adjoining Peter Waltons"

son: James - land adjoining Samuel Allis ? or Allen

son: John daughters: Susannah, Hannah.

Executors: sons James and William Clark.
Witnesses: Nath'l Rochestor, John Allison.

- - -

A-245 Power of Attorney from JOHN RUTLEDGE, Esq, of Charleston, S.C. to Col. William Blount of North Carolina, to collect debt owed to Rutledge by John Cruden, Esq. late of North Carolina. Dated 3 May 1784, proved May 1784.

Witnesses: John Rutledge, Jr., Samuel Gruben ?.

- - -

A-247 Will in Archives. Dated 9 June 1781, proved Aug 1782.

WILLIAM CARRIGAN (signed WILLIAM KARGIN)

wife: name not stated

four children, John, Joseph, Elie, Mary

"bond ... to be paid by Robert Nelson."

Executors: Robert Nelson, Robert Burnside.
Witnesses: Brice Collins, John Carrigan.

- - -

A-248 Will in Archives. Dated 25 March 1781, proved Aug 1782

JOHN MORDAK of the Parish of Saint Mathews

wife: Mary is pregnant unborn child

son: Robert, a minor.

Executors: Robert Gray, Mary Mordak.
Witnesses: James Mordak, Margaret (x) Griffin.

- - -

A-249 Will dated 25 Sept 1780, proved August 1782.

JAMES MULLINS or MULLON Only legatee, James Ross.

Witnesses: Richard Clayton, James (x) Kanady,
Margaret (x) Wilson.

- - -

A-250 Will in Archives. Dated 8 Sept 1780,proved Aug 1782.

MOSES (x) GWINN, Planter, of Parish of Saint Mathews
"very sick and weak"

wife: Elizabeth

daus: Jane, Mary, Elizabeth

son: Moses "plantation he now lives on" and "horse I got from my brother Joseph", etc

Executors: James Mordah, Elizabeth Gwynn.
Witnesses: James Mordah, Elizabeth Mordah.

- - -

A-252 Will in Archives. Dated 15 March 1780, proved Aug 1782.

THOMAS LINDLEY wife: Ruth Lindley
"far advanced in years"

son: William, 200 cares son: Jonathan, remainder of land

- continued -

Will of THOMAS LINDLEY continued

dau: Katherine White Ь 20

"All my other children to wit, Thomas Lindley, Ruth Hadley, William Lindley, John Lindley, Elinor Marriss, Deborah Newlin, Ь 20 each".

"Thomas Lindley, son of James Lindley, dec'd" Ь 10

grandson: Thomas Lindley (a minor) son of Thomas Lindley Ь 10
" Thomas Lindley (a minor) " " William Lindley Ь 10

To "friends of Spring Meeting two acres of land whereon the Meeting House now stands."

Executors: sons William and Jonathan Lindley.
Witnesses: Zacharias Dicks, John Carter, John Newlin.

- - -

A-255 Will in Archives. Dated 22 July, proved Aug 1782.

JOHN KING wife: Hannah

son: Thomas - land "beginning at a beach on Bolings Creek Nathaniel King's corner .. Ready branch .. to Charles King's line ... to Joshua Eason's line.."

son: William - land "joining land of Thomas Lloyd, Jr"

daus: Nancy, Elizabeth, Obedience, Hannah, Rebecca , all are under age except Nancy

son: Thomas King (a minor).

Executors: wife Hannah, son William.
Witnesses: John Hogan, Thos. Lloyd, Jr, Nathaniel King.

- - -

A-257 Will in Archives. Dated 20 April 1781,proved Aug 1782.

AMOS (x) THOMSON or THOMPSON wife: Martha

son: Littlebury Thomson

brother: Charles Thomson "all my Land in Donwoody County, Va."

Executors: Lewis Kirk, Richard Cate, brother Charles Thomson, Jesse Roper.
Witnesses: Hen. Hancock, Robert Peebles, Buckner (x) Floyd, Benjamin Tarver.

- - -

Footnotes to will of JOHN CHRISTMAS, on following page.

The will was proved by "James Pickhart and Wm. Richards."

Ann Peealer Christmas marriage bond to Nathaniel McLemore was dated 22 August 1786.

A-259 Will in Archives. Dated 1 July 1783, proved Nov 1783.

JOHN DEBOW, Minister of the Gospel. wife: Liney

son: Solomon (a minor) "tract of land lying on waters of Eno"
son: Stephen (a minor)

Guardian, in case of wife's death, Mr. Lake.

"To Liney Lake at her sixteenth year" ...

"to John De Hodge L for his education ... "

Executors: Liney Debow, Mr. Jacob Lake.
Witnesses: William Tate, John (x) Hodge, Joel Rice, Jos. Baker.

- - -

A-261 Will in Archives. Dated 12 Oct 1782, prpved Nov 1783.

EDWARD CARRIGAN wife: Margaret is pregnant - "unborn child"

Wife's father is living.

brothers: John and James

brother in law: John Paul.

Executors: brothers John and James.
Witnesses: John Carragan, James Carragan.

- - -

A-262 Will in Archives. Dated 19 Jan 1783, proved Nov 1783.

JOHN (x) RICE wife: Catrin dau: Hannah

"Son-in-law Jesse Towel and daughter Hannah" ...

grandsons: John Towel, Henry Towel

Executors: son-in-law Jesse Towel, nephew John Murry.
Witnesses: James Thomson, John Marduk, Prudence Marduk.

- - -

A-264 Will in Archives. Dated 11 Aug 1783, proved Nov 1783.

JOHN CHRISTMAS (planter) daus: Mary, Elizabeth, Heneritta

wife: Mary "plantation where I now live, with all land on S side of Cane Creek & below Mockasson branch"
dau: Ann Pickat ? or Peeler ?
sons: Thomas, John, William, Nathaniel
son: Richard - land on N side of Cane Creek - near mouth of Richland Branch with the land where Thomas Mason formerly lived.
young sons, all minors, Robert, James and Charles.
grandson Henry Christmas, son of John, dec'd, land in Warren County adjoining land formerly Charles Allen's"

Executors: wife Mary, sons Richard and Robert.
Witnesses: Richard Christmas, Wm. Richards, James J. Pickat.

A-268 Will in Archives. Dated 30 July 1780, proved Nov 1783.

HUGH MORROW of Cane Creek — wife: Sarah

children: James (a minor), Mary

Execs: wife Sarah, friend and neighbor John Murdock.

Witnesses: John Jenkinson, Richard Laughlin, Margaret Harper.

- - -

A-270 Will in Archives. Dated 6 March 1776, proved Nov 1782.

WILLIAM RIGGS — wife: Mary

sons: George, Thomas and James (minors), Henry, Samuel, John

daus: Ann, Jane (a minor), Mary "Barnaba Grymes' wife".

Executors: wife Mary and son George.
Witnesses: John Latta, George Riggs.

- - -

A-272 Will in Archives (indexed there as BERRY).
Dated 28 Sept 1782, proved Nov 1782

MICHEL BURY death bed will, witnessed by Samuel Ector and John Daley.
His accounts to be settled and residue given to John Dunnevin.

- - -

A-273 Will in Archives. Dated 17 Oct 1782, proved Nov 1782.

MATHEW SCOBY — wife: Jenit

Eldest son: David Scoby — son: Robert
Eldest daughter: Margaret Tait
He speaks of "the girls"...
Guardians: Robert Burnsides and Jno. Patton.

Executors: wife Jenit, and David Scoby.
Witness: Robert Burnsides, Jr.

- - -

A-275 Will in Archives. Dated 2 April 1783, proved May 1783.

BENJAMIN BLAKE (planter) — wife, name not stated

son: Benjamin Blake

daus: Martha Cain, Sarah Braswell, Rebecca Mason? or MASSEY?
Penelope Blake, Ann Blake, Bethana Blake, all minors.

grandchildren: Penelope, Mary, Ann, Obedience, Hardy Philips, children of Thomas Philips.
Sarah and Absalom Cane, children of Elisha Cane.
Trustee: "trusty friend, my near neighbor, Edward Trice".
Sole Executor: son Jones Blake.
Witnesses: Enoch Lewis, James Trice, William Trice.

- - -

Book A, page 277. Bill of Sale, dated 28 Aug 1782. Rec'd of RALPH WILLIAMS .. for a negro man, formerly the property of Thomas W. Knight or Parker.

John Ramsey — Comms. of Confiscated Property for
John Montgomery — the County of Chatham, N.C.
Zach. Harmon

"Transfer of right and property of above ... negro man Africa unto William Courtney ... this 28th day of Aug. 1782"

Witnesses: John Ramsey
Zach. Harmon
John Montgomery

RALPH WILLIAMS

Proved in Orange Court
August 1782

– – –

A-277 JOHN SEARS of North Carolina paid ... by John Booth of the said Province .. 100 pounds ... for all my Right of my father's Estate ... after my mother's death of both land and negroes and everything else ..." Dated 27 August 1781
Proved August 1782

signed: JOHN SEARS

Witnesses: John Partin, John Boothe, Junior

– – –

A-278 DEED OF GIFT , dated recorded August 1783

From SUKEY CASSELBURY to dau. Gilley, dau. Mary, dau. Rosy, dau. Elizabeth, dau. Ruth, dau. Dise, son Solomon, son David, granddaughter Patsy , "the third part of the Estate of Paul Casselbury Deceased. This Deed of Gift made to keep any person or persons from taking of any of this Estate for any debts or demands contracted by Anson Brown & Anson Brown shall deliver up all the estate to Paul Casselbury children or their guardians at his wife's death"

Witnesses: Thomas Roberts
Joseph Casslbury

Susanah (x) Casslbury
Anson Brown

– – –

A-279 Will in Archives. Dated 13 August 1781, proved August 1783.

EDWARD GANT — wife: Elizabeth

sons: John, Thomas

"land joining Luis Simmons"

daus: Cary, Sarah ("Sary")

Executors: brother John Gant,and wife Elizabeth.

Witnesses: William Rainey, Mary (x) Rainey

– – –

Book A, page 280. Will in Archives. Dated 4 Sept 1779
Proved May 1783

WILLIAM SMITH Wife: Mary Smith gets "Mansion House".

sons: Samuel, Robert, William, Cunningham, Jonathan
daus: Marget, Ann
"to my son Samuel my large Bible & my walnut chest"...

Executors: Thomas Tilford, wife Mary Smith, son Samuel.
Witnesses: John Robertson, James (x) Warnock, George Hamilton.

– – –

A-283 Will in Archives. Dated 14 Nov 1783, proved April '84

THOMAS BURKE wife: J ..?..

dau: Mary (under 21 years of age)

Executors: Willie Jones, James Hogg.
Witnesses: Jno. Williams, Alfred Moore.

(Burke owes Robert Little a balance on a plantation. Little has given a note to William Wylie.)

– – –

A-286 Will in Archives. Dated 17 May 1770, proved May 1784.

THOMAS BREAZIER wife: Hannah

sons Thomas, John and Aquilla get 1 shilling each

"2youngest sons James and Samuel my land and plantation"

daus: Elizabeth Jones, Sarah Pyle, Hanah Teague

"youngest daughters Mary Cassa Jean and Rachel" (no punctuation). "Until they marry or come of age"

Executors: John Pyle , Sen'r, William Cox
Witnesses: William Paine, Mary Paine, H.. Black, Wm. Cox.

– – –

A-288 Will in Archives. Dated 7 Feb 1784, proved May 1784.

RICHARD LEAK

dau: Elizabeth Terry, wife of James Terry

grandchildren: Richard Leak Terry, John Terry and others

dau: Mary Moore

"to Richard Leak Moore one negor now in the care of my daughter Mary Moore" John Moor, relationship not stated.

daus: Jean Harley, Susannah Campble

Richard Campble...

-continued-

A-288 Will of Richard Leak continued-

grandson: Walter Slatter (Slaughter ?)

"my grandson Walter Slatter's son Richard Slatter"

Testator has land in Richmond County upon P D (Pee Dee River

Executor: Walter Slatter.
Witnesses: Charles Clindenin, George Webb, John Pugh.

- - -

A-290 An agreement between Hannah King and William King, both of Orange County, Executors of the last will and testament of JOHN KING deceased of the one part and John King, Baxter King, Charles King, Nathaniel King, William Blackwood Richard Morris, Anne King and Elizabeth King as well on behalf of themselves or for Obedience King, Thomas King, Hannah King and Rebecca King minors all legatees of the aforesaid ... John King, Deceased. Jesse Buckner one of the legatees and the guardian of Thomas, Obedience, and Rebecca King, minors. After the death of Hannah King .. "to be equally divided amongst her children".

Witnesses: John Hogan, William (x) Partin

Proved May 1784

Dated 12 June 1783

(John King's will is recorded on page 255, Book A.)

- - -

A-292 There is another item concerning the Estate of John King, which names the same persons as those above.

- - -

Note by Ruth Herndon Shields.

Many of these signatures are given thus : John x Smith. Such a signature means that the person did not actually sign, but made "his mark". Not every person who signed a will or other paper with an x was illiterate. Many of these are death bed wills, others were made by old infirm, possibly blind, persons. In all the wills I personally abstracted I have copied "the mark" wherever used, as a matter of accuracy. But in checking the work of some of my helpers, I found that they did not make a note of it. Many, many of the witnesses signed with a mark, especially the women.

In every case where the original has survived, and is preserved in the State Archives in Raleigh, I have noted that fact. Photostats of these original wills can be obtained from the Archives. For those wills which have been lost, write to the Clerk of Court, Hillsboro, N.C.

Book A, page 293. This will is in N. C. Archives.

JOHN (x) TROUSDALE of Orange County, "Taylor"

wife : Elizabeth

Dated 3 August 1779
Proved February 1784

sons : William
James

daus : Margaret
Mary

Executors : sons William and John.

Witnesses : James Wilkins, Jno. T. Sharp, Wm. Phillips

- - -

Book A, page 294. Will in N.C. Archives.

ANDREW McBROOM

Dated 1 December 1783
Proved February 1784

wife : Mary

sons : Andrew
William

"my three daughters" , Jane, Rebecca and Mary.

John McCaleb (no relationship stated) is to live with wife.

Executors : "trusty friends Andrew McBroom and
John Armstrong ".

Witnesses : Jno. Armstrong, John Allison.

- - -

Book A, page 295 Will in Archives

JAMES McCANLIS

Dated 28 December 1783
Proved February 1784

wife : Jane

" amongst my children, to wit : John Cammons, Robert Lindsey, Elizabeth John, James, David & William McCanlis."

Executors : wife Jane, son David.

Witnesses : Jno. Armstrong
Thomas Jordan
Anne (x) Armstrong.

Book A, page 296 ,Will in Archives, indexed as BREESE.

THOMAS (x) BRUCE — Dated 1 June 1783, Proved February 1784

wife : Martha

sons : Richard
John
Robert
William

dau : Jannet Robeson

no relationship stated, possibly grandchildren :
"James Bruce & his sister Martha"
"William's son Thomas Bruce"
"Martha Robison & Rachel Robison".

Executors : wife Martha and son John.

Witnesses : Joseph Allison, John Berks.

- - -

Book A, page 298 Will in Archives

PHILIP DOSSETT — Dated 7 December 1783, Proved February 1784

wife : Selah Dossett

daus : Seney
Susannah

son : William

Executors : Benjamin Forrest
Stephen Forrest.

Witnesses : Jacob Allen , Blaton Wood
Joseph (x) Townsend.

- - -

Book A, page 300 Will in Archives

WILLIAM (x) EDWARDS,"son of John Edwards, Senior "

wife mentioned, name not stated — Dated 24 January 1784, Proved February 1784

" all my sons .".

Executors : Benjamin Davis , Sackfield Brewer.

Witnesses : Benjamin Lacy
John Durham
John Edwards.

- - -

Book A , page 301 DEED OF GIFT

STEPHEN KIRK to his son Jesse Kirk, two negroes.

Dated 22 October 1783, proved November 1784.

Witnesses : Wm. Kirk, Lewis Kirk, Jesse (x) Brown.

- - -

Book A, page 301 DEED OF GIFT

STEPHEN KIRK to his son Thomas Kirk, both of Orange County, one negro girl.

Dated 22 October 1783, proved November 1784.

Witnesses : Wm. Kirk , Lewis Kirk , Jesse (x) Brown.

- - -

Book A , page 304 POWER OF ATTORNEY

HADAWICK (x) DAVIS, spinster, to John Latta, both of Orange, to sell lands in Orange and Mecklenberg counties.

Dated 4 July 1782, proved August 1784.

Witnesses : John Davis, Robert Davis.

- - -

Book A , page 306

INVENTORY of Sundries sold by James Elliott, Administrator to BENJAMIN NICHOLSON, deceased. August 1784

- - -

- - -

Book A , page 307 Dated 5 July 1784
Recorded August 1784

INVENTORY of goods and chattels of FRANCIS BARTLETT deceased sold at public auction by Joseph Woody, Administrator.

Purchasers were : Joseph Woody , John Thompson, James Partin, Henry Paris, Caleb Williams, Rachel Phinney, Joseph Norman, Thomas Bradshaw, Samuel McMullen, Thomas Whitehead, Henry O'Daniel, Mary Pennel, Margaret McMullin, Mary Taylor, John Winnery, Robert Winnery, Samuel Stuart, John Morton, John Steel, Moses Payce, Catren Whitehead, William Paris, Wm. Bareckley, Elie McDaniel, John Payne, Molton Mubanks (?), James Roach.

- - -

Book A, page 309 BILL OF SALE

BOOTH PERRY of Granville Co., N.C. sells to Bernard Major of Dinwiddie Co., Va., his right in three negroes " now in the possession of Agnes Perry widow and relict of Peter Perry late of Dinwiddie Co., Va. "

Dated 17 June 1763, proved August 1784.

Witnesses : John Duke, John Bowie, Mary Bowie.

- - -

(This original paper is in the Archives.)

Book A, page 310 DEED OF GIFT from

SARAH MORGAN to son Hardy Morgan, both of Orange Co., N.C., four negroes ... money ... stock ... household furnishings.

Dated 15 January 1780, proved August 1784.

Witnesses : Claud Bailey, Thomas Bailey.

- - -

Book A, page 311 Will in Archives

WILLIAM LINDLEY

Dated 22 September 1784
Proved November 1784

wife : MARY

son Thomas (under 21) gets plantation testator now lives on, with the mill.

" 2 daughters, namely Ruth and Mary " (under 18)

son Samuel (under 21) " plantation formerly owned by Reubin Hollingsworth "

son William (under 21) "plantation that John Lindley formerly owned."

brothers : Jonathan, Thomas
John Lindley "plantation joining James Newlin's."

relationship not stated : "Susannah Maris and her brother William Maris " (both under age).

Executors : brothers Thomas and Jonathan Lindley.

Witnesses : Joshua Hadley, Henry Holloday, Mary (x) Holloday.

- - -

Book A, page 314 Will in Archives

ROBERT (x) SCOTT " of Orange Co., N.C., being now in
Culpeper Co., Va. "

Dated 5 September 1780 , proved in Orange Co., N.C. Nov. 1784
by Rawley Corbin

Proved in Culpeper Co., Va. 20 Nov 1780 by William Roberts.

wife : Mary Scott

"my beloved children , Jesse Scott, William Scott, Vaughan Scott, Molley Scott, John Scott, Henry Scott, Richard Scott".

Executors : wife Mary,
Fhannon (?) Viscrarser (?).

Witnesses : Rawley Corbin,
Wm. Roberts.

– – –

Book A, page 315 QUIT CLAIM DEED from

HARDY MORGAN to Sarah Morgan, both of Orange Co., N.C.

Dated 15 September 1784, proved November 1784.

Witnesses : Benjamin Yeargin, John Morgan
Joseph Harwood, John Owen.

– – –

Book A, page 316 Bill of Sale from WILLIAM HOOPER, SR. to his daughter Elizabeth, for a slave.

Dated 25 Sept 1784, proved the same day.

Witness: John Hogg.

– – –

A-316 Bill of Sale from WILLIAM HOOPER, SR. to his son Thomas Hogg Hooper, for a slave.

Dated 25 Sept 1784, proved the same day.

Witness: John Hogg.

– – –

Book A, page 319 Will in Archives

JOHN (x) HALL Dated 20 December 1784
Proved February 1785

wife : Jean Hall

dau : Rebecca

"remainder of my children, viz : William Hall, Robert Hall, Mary Hall, Sarah Hall, John Hall, Thomas Hall & Rachel Hall".

"father-in-law William Deal to live on plantation where he now lives for 1 shilling rent ".

Executors : "Thomas Rountree and William Rountree, both of Orange County. "

Witnesses : William Buchannon , Wm. McKie.

- - -

Book A, page 320 Will in Archives

MORDECAI (x) GWINN No date
Proved February 1785

wife : Elizabeth

"my three sons, John, Alexander and James " (all under age).

son : Edward

daus : Margaret
Mary
Jane
Sarah
Elizabeth.

grandsons : John Gwinn and Mordecai Gwinn.

Executors : wife, and son Edward.

Witnesses : Thomas (x) Moore , William Gwinn.

- - -

Book A,page 321 Will in Archives

ABEL (x) POCOCK Dated 25 October 1784
Proved February 1785

wife : Temperance Pocock

dau : Nancy Pocock (under age)

(continued - next page)

Will of Abel Pocock, continued

son : James Pocock.

Executors : John Butler, Henry Bunch.

Witnesses : John Butler , Henry Bunch
Betsy (x) Rebe Horn.

- - -

Book A, page 323 Will in Archives

GEORGE FOGLEMAN Dated 18 March 1785
Proved May 1785

wife : Catherine

sons : Henry, George, John, Peter

dau : Eve (unmarried)

"my daughters when they left me", names & number not stated.

Executors : Malachi Fogleman, Adam Starr.

Witnesses : Adam Smith, Peter Hume (?).

- - -

Book A, page 325 Will in Archives

THOMAS TELFORD Dated 20 October 1784
Proved May 1785

wife : Elizabeth

sons : Robert, Hugh, Thomas, all under age.
William and Samuel, under 17 years

daus : Rosannah and Elizabeth

Telford land is bounded by James Warnock, Samuel Smith and Cunningham Smith.

Executors : wife Elizabeth,
"sons Robert Telford and Hugh Telford".

Witnesses : David Macklin,
James Moore,
James Macklin.

Book A, page 329   Will in Archives

WILLIAM (x) CRAIGE   Dated 11 January 1785
Proved August 1785

wife : Abigail Craige

step-daughter : Elinor Black

daus : Joanna McMullin
Abigail Pasmore (Parmore ?)
Bathsheba Craton
Ruth Simmons
Mary Sheart.

relationship not stated : Rebecca Freeman.

Sole Executor : "my friend Samuel Freeman."

Witnesses : James Thompson , Jacob Manhill?

Book A, page 330   Will in Archives

WILLIAM (x) WATSON   Dated 15 December 1785
Proved August 1785

wife Ellenor Watson.

Executors : Thomas Barbee, Job Farmer.

Witnesses : David Drishall, John Green, Job Farmer.

Book A, page 330   Will not in Archives

HENRY (x) WAGGONER   Dated 1 July 1784
Proved May 1785

wife : Ketriana

sons : John Waggoner, Hemry Waggoner, Jacob Waggoner,
all under age , get " tract of land adjoining John
Brown, Alexander Torrentine and others" .

son : Stephen Smith

daus : Susannah Smith
Elizabeth Johns
Mary Waggoner , Judith Waggoner
Ketrin Waggoner, Uli Waggoner

granddaughters : "my son George Waggoner's children Mary
and Agnes Waggoner"

Executors : wife Ketrin, son Stephen Smith.

Witnesses : John Hall, William Buchanon, William Hannah.

Book A, page 333 Will in Archives. Dated 1780

WILLIAM JOHNSTON of Orange Co., N.C., Merchant, "only son and heir of Robert Johnston late of Harthwood (?) in the Parish of Lochmabin and Shire of Annandale in Scotland, deceased by Isabell his then wife."

mother : Isabell Johnston

"to the children of Catherine Gardner deceased late wife of Mr. Edward Gardner of the City of Lincoln in the Kingdon of Great Britain."

"my cousin Mary Robson, wife of Henry Robson, now or late of the County of Cumberland near Carlisle in the Kingdom of Great Britain, sister to the said Catherine Gardner."

Mary Harrison widow of James Harrison dec'd, near the town of South in the Shire of Lincoln in G. Britain.

"Elizabeth Robinson widow of Jno Robinson Esq. dec'd , late of City of Lincoln."

"Robert Read now of Lincoln"

"John Dixon Esq. of Lochmaben in shire of Annandale"

£ 100 to Seminary of learning.

William Johnston's deceased wife and children are buried at his plantation at Little River in Orange Co., N.C.

Trustees for the estate of "beloved daughter and only child Amelia Johnston (a minor) are : Edward Stabler, Esq. of Petersburg, Va., Samuel Johnston, Esq. of Edenton, N.C., James Hogg, Thomas Hart, Jno. Kinchen, Richard Bennehan.

"Mrs. Ann Hamilton, late of the City of Lincoln, widow of Hamilton Hamilton late of town of Kingston upon Hull in the shire of York... daughter of Wm. Alderman Fow."

"Mrs. Mildred Fenton wife of Thos. Fenton near the town of Leeds in the shire of York .. dau. of Jno. and Elizabeth Robinson."

" to Robert Burnett of the Parish of Morshall (?) and County of Withdall (Millsdale ?) in Scotland, brother to my said mother."

- continued on next page -

Will of WILLIAM JOHNSTON continued

"Mrs. Jane Craik of Moorshall Parish,sister to my said mother"

"my friend James Gibson of Kelton in the Shire of Galloway in Scotland"

Executors: friends James Hogg, Thomas Hart, John Kinchen,
Richard Bennehan. No witnesses.

- - -

A-337 Will in Archives. Dated 26 Aug 1785, proved Nov 1785.

JAMES (x) HARRIS wife: Hannah

daus: Mary Harris, Elizabeth Harris, Sarah Harris,
Susannah Harris, "Martha Hargrove wife of Henry Hargrove"

sons: Richmond, James, John, "lands and plantation on Flat River and Eno".

Executors: son Richard, friends Edward Harris and Richard Bennehan.
Witnesses: Susannah (x)Glen, Wm (x) Pettigrew, Harris Pettigrew.

- - -

A-339 Will in Archives. Dated 28 Sept 1784, proved Nov 1785.

WILLIAM (x) FOSSETT, farmer "sick and very weak"

wife: Margrete whole estate during her lifetime.

son: William -"the place he now lives on" - "£ 20 more than any of the rest "
daughter: Elenor ? (OLDS has this daughter as Eliza).

No executor named.
Witnesses: David Fossett, Richard Fossett, Jno. Umstead.

- - -

A-340 Bond between William McCauley, Chairman of the County Court of Orange County, N.C. and Matthew McCauley for apprenticeship of THOMAS KEE (10 years old) as a blacksmith.

Dated 3 March 1785. Witness: J. Benton, C.C.

- - -

A-341 Bond between Jno. Ray, Chairman of Orange County, N.C. County Court and Roswell Huntington. Dated 3 March 1785.

FRANCIS NASH (13 years old) is apprenticed to Roswell Huntington, silver and gold smith.

Signatures to Indenture: Archer Grisham, Roswell Huntington.
Witness: J. Benton, C.C.

- - -

A-342 Bond between Wm. McCauley, Chairman of Orange County, N.C. County Court, and John Steel, Sr. March 3, 1785.

BETSY COOK is apprenticed to "learn the art of a spinster".

Signatures to Indenture: Wm. McCauley, Jno. Steel.
Witness: J. Benton, C.C.

- - -

A-343 Deed of Gift from JOHN STEEL, SR to John Steel, Jr for wagon and gears, cattle, etc, etc.

Witnesses: Thomas Howard, Samuel Steel.

- - -

A-345 Power of Attorney from JOHN EVANS of Philadelphia, Pa. to JOHN LATTA, of Orange County, N.C. "trusty and esteemed friend", to collect from "John Kelly trader late of said county" and "William Jackson, trader of Hillsboro" ....

Dated 13 Jan 1786, proved Feb 1786.
Witnesses: William Gregson, Thos. Latta.

- - -

A-347 same as A-342 above - BETSY COOK apprenticed.

- - -

A-348 Deed from JAMES ARMSTRONG, Planter, to grandson THOMAS ARMSTRONG, of Lincoln County, Va. for one negro.

Dated 3 May 1786, proved May 1786.
Witnesses: Jacob Lake, Mary Lake.

- - -

A-349 Power of Attorney from JOHN TRICE to EDWARD TRICE, SR to execute deed of conveyance to Thomas Gwinn for land joining land of Edward Grisham, Sr & Edward Grisham, Jr.

Dated 7 Nov 1784, proved Feb 1785.
Witnesses: Thomas May, Thomas Lay, Robert Abercrombie.

- - -

A-350 Deed from JOHN MAY to "JAMES DESERN my son-in-law" for land on Elibees Creek ... joining lands of John Baker, John Vickers and ..... Grisham. "for love and affection..."

Dated 14 Feb 1785, proved Feb 1785.
Witnesses: Henry Bunch, George Grisham.

- - -

A-351 DEED for negroes and other chattels from

SAMUEL MAY to son Southerland and daughters Molly and Sally.

The negroes were willed to him or to his wife Izzabel by Thomas Stephens late of Virginia after the decease of Mary Stephens the widow and relict of the said Thomas Stephens, dec'd. Dated 26 May 1785, proved May 1785.

Witness: Jacob Richards.

- - -

A-352 DEED (Improvements and Rite of Entry) from PENELOPE DIXON to Joseph Buckingham.

Witnesses: Benjamin Piggott
Drury (x) Hunnycutt

Dated 3 May 1784
Proved Feb 1785.

- - -

A-353 DEED for negroes from ATHANISIUS ROBISON to

granddaughter Sarah Lindsay, son Nathaniel Robison, daughter Mary Lindsay.

Witnesses: Eli McDaniel
John Murry

Dated 25 May 1785
Proved May 1785.

- - -

A-354 DEED to plantation from GEORGE HORNER to son James Horner.

Witnesses: Thomas Hunter
George Horner, Jr.

Dated 17 Feb 1785
Proved May 1785

- - -

A-355 Will in Archives. Dated 31 March 1783, proved Feb 1785.

JOHN McCOLLOCH wife: Mary

sons: Robert, James, John.

Executors: John Armstrong, William Brayns.
Witnesses: Robert Idan (?), Sarah (x) Locklin, John Armstrong.

- - -

A-356 BOND (for Sheriff). Archibald Latta, Wm. Mebane, Alexander Mebane, Jr., Wm. McCauley, Matthew McCauley, Anthony Sharp, William Bell.

Archibald Lytle, Commissioner

Witness: A.Tatom
Dated 1 March 1785.

- - -

A-357 Will in Archives. Dated 9 Sept 1785, proved Feb 1786 ?

JOHN VAUGHAN wife: Catron.

Executors: wife and James Walker.
Witnesses: James Vaughan, Thomas (x) King.

A-358 Will in Archives. Dated 25 Dec. 1785, proved Feb 1786

WILLIAM NELSON wife: Ann

daus: Rachel, Rebeca, Ruth, Elinor, Hannah.

son: Samuel.

Executors: wife Ann, William Adams.
Witnesses: John Allen, Samuel Stout, Joseph Stout.

- - -

A-359 MEMORANDUM OF WILL. Recorded Feb 1786 ? Not dated.

JINNET TATE

sons: James, George

daus: Margaret, Elizabeth, Keturo, Polly, Agnes, Jinnet (a minor), Lettice (she gets a black mare "I had of Andrew Mitchell")
"The sum betwixt Samuel Nelson and me I leave betwixt his own two daughters to be divided equally betwixt them and one to his son David the overplus I paid to John Mitchell above his wife's dower I leave to his daughter Jinnet."

Bequests made to Andrew Mitchell's oldest son, and to "my daughter Polly".
Samuel Nelson is requested to take Jinnet and Margaret to raise.

Executors: son James Tate, Samuel Nelson.
Witnesses: Thomas Mulhollan, Jas. Mebane, Edward Willson.

- - -

A-361 Will in Archives. Dated 1 Nov 1785, proved

DAVID CRAIG wife: name not stated

Sons: William Johnston, John, David

daughter mentioned, but not named. Unborn child mentioned.

Executors: Friends William McCauley, John Craig, Samuel Craig.
Witnesses: Samuel Hunter, Aaron (x) Hunter, Wm.(x) Lagan

- - -

A-362 Will in Archives. Dated 3 May 1785, proved - no date.

ROBERT FOSSETT wife: name not stated

sons: George, Robert, Thomas

daus: Fanny, Elizabeth

grandsons: Robert, son of George; Edward, son of Thomas.

-continued-

A362, Will of Robert Fossett, continued -

Witnesses: John Walker, Hugh Crawford. No executor named.

- - -

A- 363. Not in Archives. Dated 1 March 1786, proved May 1786.

GEORGE ALLEN DEED OF GIFT to his

grandson George Mebane (a minor),"son of daughter Margaret, wife of James Mebane," and his

granddaughter Elizabeth Mebane,"sister of George Mebane ".

Witnesses: Absolom Tatom,Wm. McCauley, A. Lytle.

- - -

A-364 BILL OF SALE, from BENJAMIN CHAPMAN to William Newman.

Dated 26 June 1784, proved Nov 1785.

Witnesses: Bern M. Gurkin (?), Benjamin Newman.

- - -

A-365 BOND . ASA BLAKE of Wake County for James Blake's standing security for Asa Blake to the Administrators of Benjamin and Jones Blake.
Witness: Jno. G. Rencher. Dated 25 Nov 1785

- - -

A-366 BILL OF SALE from SAMUEL GUTHRIE of Gloucester Co., Va. to Edward Trice of "Orange County and State of Virginia."

Dated 8 October, no year given. Witnesses: John Butler
A. Tatom.

- - -

A-366 BILL OF SALE from WILLIAM RHOADS to Joseph Moore.

Dated 21 July 1786, proved Aug 1786.
Witnesses: Josiah Watts, John Moore.

- - -

A-367 DEED for a negro from JOHN EDWARDS to "friend Margaret Edwards, and at her death to her son Henry Edwards."
Dated 14 June 1785 Witnesses: John Durrum,
Sarah Durrum.

- - -

A-368 BILL OF SALE from JOHN MURRAY to John Elliott
Dated 6 July 1785, proved May 1786 Witness: David Pasmore.

A-369 Bond between Alexander Mebane, for County Court and John McVinch. Binding "JOHN RILEY, now of the age of 2 yrs" to John McVinch as a servant, until he becomes 21 yrs old.

Dated 24 Nov 1784. Witness: A. Tatom.

- - -

A-370 Agreement (Easement) , between Jesse Benton and William Shepperd of Hartford, both of Orange County, N.C.

Dated 4 June 1783. Witnesses: James Boswell, James Gooch.

- - -

A-371 Bill of Sale. John Stacy sells negroes to William Galbreath.

Dated 17 March 1786, proved Nov 1786.
Witnesses: Geo. Hodge, Lewis Jones.

- - -

A-372 Will in Archives. Dated 10 March 1786,proved Nov '86.

JOBE FARMER wife: name not stated

sons: Athniel Farmer, James Farmer

daus: Ann Farmer, Drucilla Farmer.

Executors: wife, and Daniel Green.
Witnesses: Daniel Green, Grisham Forrest, John (x) Edwards.

- - -

A-373 Bill of Sale from PHILIP PENDLETON to James G. Hunt, for a negro, "now in possession of Henry Thompson".

Dated 21 July 1786, proved Nov 1786.
Witness: Henry Thompson.

- - -

A-374 Bill of Sale from GRISCAL McCALLISTER to Mary Clark. Dated 25 March 1786, proved Nov 1786. Witness: John Ray.

- - -

A-375 Power of Attorney from JOSEPH BRAWNER to James Hester of Mecklinburgh County, Va. Dated 30 May 1787
Witness: J. Benton, C.C. proved May 1787.

- - -

A-376 Deed from WILL HOOPER to his daughter Elizabeth.
Dated 24 Oct 1787, proved --
Witnesses: Walter Alves, Wm. Watters (or Walters).

A-377 Bill of Sale from JOHN MURRY to James Neal, for a negro.

Dated 30 May 1787, proved May 1787.
Witnesses: Andrew Gibson, Tho. Johns.

- - -

A-377 Bill of Sale from WILLIAM SHEPPERD to John Williams, Esq. of Chatham County, for a negro.

Dated 1 March 1788. Witness: S. Pinto.

- - -

A-378 Deed of Gift from CARNES TINNEN to son Robert Tinnen.

Dated 4 Oct 1787, proved Feb 1788.
Witnesses: Jacob Lake, Wm. Tate.

A-379 Bond from ROBERT ABERCROMBIE to Charles Abercrombie.

Dated 5 Feb 1784, proved Nov 1788.
Witnesses: John Michaux, Harris Grisham.

- - -

A-380 Power of Attorney from JAMES WILLIAMS "late of Hillsbourough in North Carolina but now in Washington in the County of Wilkes and State of Georgia Esquire" to John Estes of Hillsborough, Esquire, and John Williams, Esq. of Chatham Co., N.C.

Witness: Thomas Watts.

Dated 6 Oct 1787, proved Aug 1788.

End of BOOK A.

BOOK B, page 1. Will in Archives. Dated 20 May 1785,

JOHN BUTLER wife: Anne

Executors: wife Anne, William Rainey, Esq.
Witnesses: Moses Crawford, Wm. Shannon.

- - -

B-2 Will in Archives. Dated 10 Jan 1787

DANIEL HOGAN wife: name not stated

sons: Thomas Lloyd Hogan; another son, name not stated.

daughters, names and number not stated.

Executors: "well-beloved-friends" John Hogan and William McCauley.
Witnesses: Henry Morras, Sam Craig, Alec Piper.

- - -

B-3 Will in Archives. Dated 17 Oct 1785, proved --

SARAH MORGAN Sons: John Morgan, Hardy Morgan

daus: Anne Hart, and Sarah Yeargan, wife of Benjamin.

granddaughter: Charlotte Yeargin

"the surviving children she (Sarah Yeargin) has by Ben Yeargin".

Executors: Benjamin Yeargin, Daniel Hogan.
Witnesses: Robt. Campbell, Nicholas Quesenbury, Dan Boothe.

\- - -

B-5 Deed of Gift from JOHN SHEELS to his wife Mary Sheels, for 1 negro girl. Witness: John Nichols.
Dated 2 March 1787, proved ...

\- - -

B-6 Will in Archives. Dated 4 August 1786, proved ..

WILLIAM STROUD wife: Elizabeth

sons: John Stroud, Anderson Stroud, Wm. Stroud, Marshal Stroud, Thomas Stroud, Dickson Stroud.
dau: Margaret Douglass
daus: Mary Thrift, Salley King, Fanney Howell, Eliz. Stroud.

Executors: wife Elizabeth, and "trusty friend John Hogan".
Witnesses: William Willis, William Buckner, Mary Buckner.

\- - -

B-11 Power of Attorney from ABSOLOM TATOM of Hillsboro, N.C. to Charles Taylor. Dated 2 April 1785.

\- - -

B-13 Will in Archives. Dated 10 March 1786, proved ..

JOB FARMER wife: name not stated

sons: Nathaniel Farmer, James Farmer.

Anne Farmer, Drucilla Farmer

Executors: wife, and Daniel Green.
Witnesses: Daniel Green, Gresham Forrest, John Edwards.

\- - -

B-14 JAMES (or FAMUS) S...?..(impossible to read) , assigns his right in a tract of land to "Eliza Simons relict of Henry Simons deceased." Dated 24 Sept 1782, proved ..
Witnesses: Ralph Jackson, Eliza Williams.

\- - -

B-15 Will of RICHARD HOPSON. Dated 12 Dec 1786, proved ..

Wife: Elizabeth Hopson

sons: Younger Hopson, Mar/tin Hopson, Daniel Hopson.

daus: Sarah Hopson, Mary Hopson

sons-in-law: Ephriam Barcor, Isaac Kirk, William Baucom.

Executors: wife Elixabeth, John Jenkins.
Witnesses: Nathan Almond, George Taylor.

\- - -

B-17 Will in Archives. Dated 5 July 1787, proved ..

NICHOLAS HOLT wife: Eve

sons: Francis Holt, John Holt, Nicholas Holt, James Holt.

dau: Rachel Holt

grandson: Michael Holt

Executors: Francis Holt, Nicholas Holt.
Witnesses: Michael Holt, Joshua Holt.

\- - -

B-19 Power of Attorney from MICHAEL SAMPSON of Wilmimgton, Merchant, to Joseph Dickson.
Dated 1 Feb 1787, proved .. Witness: T. Benton, C.C.

\- - -

B-20 Will in Archives. Dated 18 July 1877, proved ..

ANDROSS RANDALL Wife: Catherine

daughter, Mary Randall. No executor named.

Witnesses: Robert Cate, Joseph Cate, Thomas Cate.

\- - -

B-22 Will in Archives. Dated 18 June 1787, proved ..

WILLIAM WILLIAMS wife: Elizabeth

son: William gets land given to testator by the State of N.C. for his services "as Captain in the Continental line of this State."

brother: Sam Williams
nephew: William Williams, son of Sam.

His wife gets house and lot in town of Hillsborough, and land which he purchased from Jacob Richards in Orange Co.
Executors: wife Elizabeth, George Doherty.
Witnesses: J.Watts, Will Lytle.

\- - -

B-25 Deed from PATRICK McCOLLOCH to John Woods, son of Hugh Woods, for 100 acres of land after the death of Patrick McColloch and his wife. Dated 20 August 1785. Witnesses: Andrew Patterson, John Elliott.

- - -

B-26 Will in Archives. Dated 31 Oct 1787, proved --

JOHN SHEELS wife: Mary Cumming

Executrix: wife Mary Cumming.
Witnesses: Wm. McCauley, Will Lytle, A. Tatom.

- - -

B-28 Will in Archives. Dated Dec 1787, proved --

THOMAS PRATT Nephews and nieces are the chief legatees.

nephew: James Pratt Ŀ 100 "hard money", etc
" George Pratt Ŀ 100 "hard money",Gilt Stock Buckle, 1pr Shoe Buckles
nieces: Peggy Pratt, Lucy Pratt, money, etc.

relationship, if any, not stated to: James Grant, David Ray, John McWhitney, Walter Alves, Samuel Benton.
"James Taylor son of Frederick Taylor" Ŀ 25."paper money".

Executor: David Ray. Witnesses: John McWhitney, Mary (x) Pratt.

- - -

B-32 Will in Archives. No date.

CHRISTIAN GRADY Heirs are Isaac Gaddes and his wife.

Executor: James Hogg. Witnesses: Wm. Parks, Elizabeth Parks.

- - -

B-32 Will in Archives. Dated 25 March 1779, proved --

JAMES FEW wife: Frances

son: James

"My three daughters Elizabeth, Ann and Bethiah".

Executrix: wife Frances.
Witnesses: John Wood, Ann Wood, John Flinthem.

- - -

B-34 Will in Archives. Dated 8 Nov 1787, proved --

ARCHIBALD HAMILTON nephew: Joseph Hamilton

"First son, Joseph Hamilton ....

The will is unfinished, and unsigned - no witnesses.

- - -

B-35 Will in Archives. Dated 21 April 1786, proved --

JOHN (x) REED wife: Lydia Reed

His property is on Stagg's Creek and Hico Creek.

daughters: Rebecca Reed, Jemimah Reed.

Executor: Henry Cole.
Witnesses: Thomas Cole, Wm. McMennamy, John McMennamy.

B-36 Will in Archives. Dated 26 Oct 1788, proved --

JAMES (x) VAUGHAN second wife: Mary Vaughan

Son, Grief Evand Vaughan and daughter Susannah Selton, given "one shilling apiece".

Children of second wife: John Vaughan, Sarah, Peggy, Betsey, Polly, to receive all property.

Executors: Mary Vaughan, James Walker.
Witnesses: Wm. Smallwood, Julius King.

B-37 Will in Archives. Dated --, proved --

SAMUEL PARKS wife: Mary Vaughan Parks

sons: Thomas, Samuel, Alexander, John, James

daus: Tine, she has a son William , name not stated.
Nancy," " " " Alexander, name not stated.

The Executors are ordered to sell 100 acres of land adjoining James Bracken on Stony Creek.

Executors: wife Mary, John Robinson, William Rainey.
Witness: William Rainey.

B-38 Agreement between THOMAS KING and JEREMIAH EDGE, both of Orange County, N.C. Dated 14 October 1788.

THOMAS KING proposes to leave wife Sophia and children, to travel. Under this agreement he binds himself to Jeremiah Edge. Agrees to divide personal and real property (land bought of John Duke and taken up in parternership with Jeremiah Edge.) Edge is to look after King's wife and children. Witnesses: Archibald Harris, John Duke.

B-39 Will in Archives. Dated 6 July 1788, proved --

JOSIAH WATTS wife: Susannah daughter: Susannah

Partners in business: Courtney Watts, Wm. Lytle, Esq.

- continued -

B-39 Will of JOSIAH WATTS continued -

Executors: brother Thomas Watts, John Grant Rencher.
Witnesses: Vincent P. Williamson, William Courtney.

- - -

B-40 Will in Archives. Dated 1 July 1788, proved

THOMAS SEARES wife: Elizabeth Seares

sons; William, Joseph, Thomas, John, Henry

daus: Elizabeth, Mary Surls (?)

Executors: Elizabeth Seares, Thomas Seares, John Seares.
Witnesses: Wortham Glenn, Henry Seares, Elizabeth (x) Seares.

- - -

B-41 Will in Archives. Dated 13 July 1786, proved ..

PETER (x) HENDRICKS wife: Amy

sons: Isaac, Abraham, William

daus: Ann Hendricks, Mary Hendricks Balander, Eliz. Hendricks

Executrix: Amy Hendricks.
Witnesses: John Cabe, Thomas Reding.

- - -

B-42 Will in Archives. Dated 22 August 1787, proved ..

WILLIAM (x) LOGAN Wife: Agnes

son: John Logan daughter Elizabeth
grandson: William Logan.

Executors: John Hart, Senior; James Hart.
Witnesses: William Hart, John Hart Jr.

- - -

B-50 Will of NATHANIEL (x) LEWIS. Dated 11 Nov 1788, proved ..

Wife: Elizabeth

sons: John Lewis, William Lewis

daus: Lydia, Sarah, Rebeccah, Mary

Executors: wife Elizabeth, son John.
Witnesses: John Wood, Anne Wood.

- - -

B-54 Will in Archives. Dated 25 Oct 1785, proved ..

JAMES PAULL wife: Elizabeth

sons: James, William, John.

dau: Rachel. grandau: Elizabeth Carregan.

Executors: Elizabeth Paull, John Paull.
Witnesses: Margaret Collins, Joseph Collins, Jesse Benton.

- - -

B-57 Will in Archives. Dated 19 Jan 1789, proved ..

JEAN (x) BOWLING

Sons: Archibald, Abraham, Alexander, and Andrew Bowling.

daus: Isabel Butler wife of John Butler,
Susannah Boswell, Elizabeth Bowling.

relationship not stated: Nancy Flintom.

Witnesses: Sam'l Wray, William Nunn, Joseph Hart.

- - -

B-63 Will in Archives. Dated 20 April 1789, proved ..

ELI McDANNELL (signed McDANIEL). wife: Margaret

son John, land on Quaker Road adjoining Peter Woolf and
Samuel Campbell- bought of C. Lytle.

son James, land formerly occupied by Daniel McVey, and also
land bought from James Williams.

son Eli, land adjoining above tracts.

daus: Elizabeth, Susannah, and two younger ones not named.

Executors: wife Margaret, son John.
Witnesses:Ruth Christmas, Robert Scoby.

- - -

B-65 Will in Archives. Dated 15 March 1789, proved ..

ADAM MARLEY wife: Rosannah

sons: Robert, Adam, and Samuel Marley.

grandsons: Robert Marley son of Adam, Adam Marley son of / Robert.

" I give to my beloved son Adam Marley Mary Douglas Hannah
White Nancy Hall Robert Marley's son Adam, and my son Adam
Marley's son Robert .." (No punctuation given.)

- continued -

B-65 Will of ADAM MARLEY continued -

Executor: Samuel Marley.
Witnesses: Arthur Lovins, John Stark, Alexander Robbs.

- --

B-70 Will of JOSEPH ALLISON. Dated 7 April 1789, proved ..

Wife: Elizabeth

Sons: David Allison(land on Duck River),Joseph Allison.

daus: Margaret, Mary, Sarah, Nancy Allison.

sons-in-law: John Thompson, Asiriah Thompson, Samuel Woods.

Executors: Elizabeth Allison, David and John Thompson.
Witnesses: John Wilson, Sarah (x) Gomage.

- - -

B-72 Will of WILLIAM CLARKE. Dated 25 July 1789, proved ..

Heir: "George Daniel, for his trouble and care of me".

Executor: Samuel Daniel.
Witnesses: William Findley, John Daniel, Mary Castlebury.

- - -

B- 73 Will in Archives. Dated 3 Sept 1788, proved ;;

STEPHEN TATOM wife: Mornin

sons: Stephen and John lands on Camp Creek.
William, 1 shilling.

daus: Sarah, Anna, Elizabeth, Francis, Tizia, Mary, Jemima.

Executors: "trusty friends Towland Gooch and John Wilburn".
Witnesses: Fowler Jones, William (x) Tatom.

- - -

B 74-77. Will in Archives. Dated 9 June 1789, proved ..

CHARLES JOHNSTON wife: Martha Johnston

son: George

sons-in-law: John Freeland, Chaldous (?) Bailey,
Samuel Craig, John Strayhorn, Matthew McCauley.

grandsons: William Craig, John McCauley.

Charles McCauley and Charles Strayhorn mentioned, but no relationship stated.

- continued -

B-74-77 Will of CHARLES JOHNSTON continued -

He says "all my children" , but does not give names.

Executors: "trusty and well-beloved friends, Samuel Craig
and William McCauley."
Witnesses: Wm. Blackwood, Joseph Blackwood, James Blackwood.

- - -

B-78 Will in Archives. Dated 1 May 1789, proved ..

JAMES DIXON wife: Nancy

sons: James, Stewart, Robert, William, Thomas, "my five sons"

daus: Polly, Margaret.

Executors: wife Nancy, and Stewart.
Witnesses: James Freeland, Joseph Hodge.

- - -

B-79 Will in Archives. Dated 12 Dec 1786, proved Feb 1790 ?

JOHN FOUST wife: Barbara Foust

sons: Philip, John, Jacob, Christian, and George each get
5 shillings.
" 3 youngest sons George, Peter and Daniel Foust" get
all his real estate.

daus: Barbara Clap, and Judith Clap, get 5 shillings each.

Executors: " two sons George and Peter Foust".
Witnesses: Joseph Stout, Samuel Stout, Jacob Marshall.

- - -

B-81 Bill of Sale from JOHN McDANIEL of Cane Creek Settlement of Orange Co.,and Mary his wife, to Daniel Foust.

Dated 20 Jan 1790 Witnesses: John Murray (?), James Neal.

- - -

B-82 Will in Archives. Dated 19 March 1789, proved 1790.

THOMAS (x) ASPEN wife: Sarah

Relationship, if any, to Souths and Paschalls not stated

"Benjamin South is to pay her (Sarah) 3 pounds a year and William Paschall 2 pounds a year, then I will my plantation to William Paschall during his life and his wife's life, and at their demise to William Paschall's son Thomas".

- continued -

B-82 Will of Thomas Aspen continued -

"Benjamin South and his wife"...
"Dilly South and Gemima South"...

Executors: "Trusty friends John Armstrong and John Woods."
Witnesses: Jno. Armstrong, Jno. Allison.

- - -

B-84 Bill of Sale from VINCENT PETER WILLIAMSON of town of Hillsborough, N.C. to Charles Holeman of Caswell Co., N.C.

For Lots #70, 71, 89, 90, dwelling house, one negro woman, gray horse, etc. Dated 25 Feb 1790

Witnesses: William Cumming, Will Rountree.

- - -

B-85 Bill of Sale from ROBERT ASHLEY to Jeremiah Edge, both of Orange Co., N.C. Witnesses: Wm. Smallwood, Wm. Dyar.

- - -

B-85 Will in Archives. Dated 11 June 1789, proved Feb 1790.

ANTHONY STANFORD wife: Elizabeth

sons: Charles, Robert, James and William Stanford.

daus: Agnes, Jean, Martha, Elizabeth, Mary, Margaret.

granddau: Fanny King.

Executors: "my wife Elizabeth and my son James".
Witnesses: Daniel (x) Hanley, J. Galbreath.

- - -

B-87 Bill of Sale from GEORGE DOHERTY to James Hogg, Esq., both of Orange Co., N.C. Dated 2 Jan 1790, recorded Feb '90. (James Hogg is guardian for Polly Burke.)

Witnesses: Theopilus Thompson, Wm. Comb, Walter Alves.

- - -

B-89 Deed of Gift from ELIZABETH PAUL of Orange Co., N.C. "for love" .., "to my son James Paul of Washington Co., Ga." and for 1 shilling paid, a negro boy named Peter.

Dated 30 Nov 1789, proved May 1790.
Witnesses: Robert Faucet, Jacob Walters.

- - -

B-90 Will in Archives. Dated 17 March 1789, proved May 1790.

ROBERT NELSON wife: Mary

"to my two sons James and Robert the plantation whereon I now live " .. " but my wife to have the benefit until they arrive to the age of 17 and 16 years". - continued -

B-90 Will of ROBERT NELSON continued -

"daughter Jean Scott one lot in the town of Randolph Courthouse in the County of Randolph."

Witnesses: John Umstead, Peter Wrightman.

- - -

B-92 Will in Archives. Dated 27 Sept 1789, proved May 1790.

ZACHARIAH ALLEN wife: name not stated

sons: George; William;
James gets land in "Lincorn County on S. Side of Catawba (River)."
John, under age.

"rest of my children, Mary Jean, Sarah, Robert Ruth Lovda(?) Joseph & Zachariah." (punctuation very poor.)

Executors: "my worthy friends John Thomson son of Thomas and James Allen."

Witnesses: James Allen, Daniel McDaniel.

- - -

B- 93 Will in Archives. Dated 29 March 1790, proved May 1790.

CHRISTIAN (x) HUFFMAN

brother: Peter Huffman

"friend and brother Jesse Acock"

Elizabeth Huffman, no relationship stated.

"I give and bequeath to Suffice (?) Ingle, if her mother swears her to me one shilling, if not nothing."

"my brothers and sisters" mentioned, but not named.

Executors: friends George Clap and Barney Troxler.
Witnesses: Michael Charles, Jacob Clap.

- - -

B-94 Deed of Gift for 1 negro girl from SAMUEL DANIEL to his son John Daniel, for love.

Dated 17 Feb 1790, proved May 1790.
Witnesses: Edward Trice, Robert T. Daniel.

- - -

B-95 Will in Archives. Dated 11 Sept 1789, proved May 1790

JOHN (x) HOLSTEIN

brother: Jacob Holstein "land on Adcock Creek in Granville County, N.C."

B-95 Will of JOHN HOLSTEIN continued -

brother-in-law : Henry Streider "land in Granville on Adcock Creek".
"three sisters Mary, Susannah and Barbaryman".

Executors: Henry Streider, Jacob Holstein.
Witnesses: William Jacob, George (x) Streider.

\- - -

B-97 Will in Archives. Dated 28 Jan 1790, proved Aug 1790.

ANDREW PATTEN (or PATTON)

wife: Margaret " to receive an equal part with the children who are boys and girls."

"to sons Robert and Thomas all my Cumberland lands- one survey."
"to sons John and Andrew land in Orange County."

daughter; Sarah Hughes.

He speaks of "wife and younger children."

Executors: "friends Joseph Thompson and James Hughes."
Witnesses: Henry Campbell, Robert Tinnen, John Thompson.

\- - -

B-98 Deed of Gift from THOMAS (x) BIBINGS "to the two children Robert Carter and Thomas Bebins junior" , horse, cow, etc. No relationship stated. Witness: Joseph Sharp.

Dated 15 August 1790, proved August 1790.

\- - -

B-99 Will in Archives. Dated 25 Aug 1790, proved -- 1790.

SAMUEL McCADDAMS or McADAMS. wife: Catherine.

mother: Sarah McCaddams. brothers: Joseph and William.

dau: Mary

"my children, Sarah, Catherine, Ellender, John, Joseph, and William."

Executors: "my trusty friends John Sloss and Andrew Murdock."
Witnesses: Thos. Mulhollan, Jno. Unstead, Alex. Kirkpatrick.

\- - -

B-100 Will in Archives. Dated 24 Nov 1789, proved .

ARTHUR MANGUM wife: Lucy

sons: William Mangum, Arthur Mangum - continued -

B-100 Will of Arthur Mangum continued -

daus: Sally Bobitt, Clarey, Chaney.
Holley "land adjoining John Mize's and James Bobbitt's and William Mangum's."

Executors: "trusty friends John Carrington and William Mangum, junior."

- - -

B-102 Will in Archives. Dated 6 July 1782, proved Oct 1790.

JACOB CANTRELL wife: Mary

daus: eldest Margaret Cantril, Jane, Hannah, Sarah, Susannah.

sons: Zebedee Cantril, Thomas Cantril, Joseph Cantril.

Sole Executor: wife Mary.
Witnesses: John Hinslee, Rachel (x) Robinson.

- - -

B-105 Will in Archives. Dated 20 Feb 1790, proved Nov 1790.

JOHN JENKINS wife: Mary

Children listed in the order they are named in the will.
daughters, Nancy Fennel, Patty Allen,
sons, Sanford Jenkins, John, Thomas, Mansfield Jenkins,
daughters Betsey, Polly, Patience, Catherine Jenkins.

"granddaughter Higgerson" (under 18 years of age). See below.

Executors: wife Mary Jenkins, and friends William Merritt and Joseph Fennel.
Witnesses: William Halliburton, Massey Chrismus Medearis, William Merritt.

- - -

B-124 The will of JOHN JENKINS exactly as above, except that the granddaughter is called Polly Higgerson.

- - -

B-107 Will in Archives. Dated 3 Nov 1790, proved Nov 1790.

JOHN (x) ALBRIGHT wife: Hester (is pregnant ?)

sons: John Christian plantation on Beaver Creek joining John Clap.
"If I should have more sons than the one mentioned ...."

daughters: Elizabeth, "rest of her sisters..."

Executors: brother William Albright, neighbor Adam Smith.
Witnesses: William Harp, Jacob Clap.

- - -

B-109 Receipt. ROBERT RAY, Junior and JOHN RAY, sons of Robert Ray, Senior, do acknowledge that we have received our full part of the real estate of Robert Ray, our father.

Dated 31 Dec 1789. Witnesses: Joseph Clendenning,
Thomas Holgan.

- - -

B-110 Bill of Sale from NORMAN BIGELOW to John Umstead, both of Orange Co., N.C. for "one negro fellow".

Dated 9 Feb 1791, proved Feb 1791. Witness: James Grant.

- - -

B-111 Bill of Sale from JAMES WIRES of Chatham Co., N.C. to George Foust of Orange Co., N.C., for "one negro man".

Dated 8 Nov 1790, proved Nov 1790. Witness: Jno. Ray.

- - -

B-112 Will in Archives. Dated 18 Sept 1790, proved Feb 1791.

SAMUEL CRAIG wife: Mary

sons: William Craig, David Craig, Samuel Craig, all under 20.

dau: Martha , for others, see below.

"My children together with my wife to wit Martha, Margaret, Elizabeth, Jenney, Issabel, and my wife."

Executors: wife Mary, "trusty friend George Johnston."
Witnesses: Wm. McCauley, John Craig, Matthew McCauley.

- - -

B-114 Bill of Sale from HENRY STEPHENS to John Ross, both of Orange Co., N.C. Witness: Thomas Mulhollan.
Dated 30 Jan 1791, proved Feb 1791.

- - -

B-116 Bill of Sale from HARDY SANDERS of Wake Co., N.C. to John Grant Rencher of Orange Co., N.C., for a negro girl.

Dated 3 March 1790, proved Feb 1791. Witness: Joseph Taylor.

- - -

B-117 Power of Attorney from JOHN MORGAN to "trusty friend John Grant Rencher" to manage his plantation. He speaks of "my children" but they are not named.

Dated 3 March 1791 ?, proved Feb 1791.
Witnesses: Henry (x) Sears, Jacob Flowers, Jr., Mark Morgan.

- - -

B-119-120 Power of Attorney. JOHN LATTA of Orange Co., N.C. Attorney for John Evans of Philadelphia to prosecute a suit against Orange County merchants, deputizes his "worthy friend Johnathan Lindley" to act for him under this Power of Attorney. Feb 1791.

- - -

B-120 Will in Archives. Dated 6 Jan 1791, proved Feb 1791.

WILLIAM RHODES wife: Mary

"My three children Hannah Rhodes, Elizabeth Rhodes, Alexander Rhodes."

Executors: wife Mary, brother Aquilla Rhodes.
Witnesses: Richard Rhodes, Thomas Rhodes, Henry Burch? or - Bunch.

- - -

B-121 Will in Archives. Dated 25 Nov 1790, proved Feb 1791.

JOHN ARMSTRONG wife: Margaret

son: William, land on Haw River joining John Holmes, Moses Crawford and Richard Christmas.

daus: Elizabeth (under 18 years), Mary, Margaret, Rachel.

Executors: wife, and Richard Christmas.
Witnesses: Richard Goff, William Trousdale.

- - -

B124 Will of JOHN JENKINS, already given on page B-105.

- - -

B-126 Will of JACOB DEBLEY. In Archives. Dated 17 May 1790, proved Feb 1791.

Wife: Margery Debley

"boys Jacob, James and John Debley, my three sons."

daus: Mary Debley, Fanny Debly.

The children are all minors. Sons are to be apprenticed to trades when they reach 14 years of age.

Executors: John Steele, John Thompson.

Witnesses: William Clendennin, William Morrow.

- - -

B-128 Will in Archives. Dated 10 July 1790, proved May 1791.
JOHN PATTERSON, Senior wife: Margaret

sons: David, Isaac, William, James, John.

daus: Jean, Margaret Abbott, Mary Patterson, Agnes.

Executors: wife Margaret, son David.
Witnesses: Jacob ...?.., Nathaniel Matthews.

- - -

B-130 Bill of Sale from JOHN MITCHELL to James Comb of Orange Co., N.C., for 4 negroes.
Dated 30 Nov 1791, proved May 1791 (dates that way in book).
Witnesses: John McKerrall, Mary Comb.

- - -

B-130 Bond. Dated 1 Sept 1789, proved May 1791.

JOHN RICE of Davidson Co., N.C. and JESSE BENTON of Orange Co., N.C. bound unto ROBINSON MUMFORD of Orange Co., N.C. Eleven hundred pounds. John Rice purchased "15,000 acres of land situate on the Western waters"from Robinson Mumford.

Witnesses: James Mumford, John Umstead.

- - -

B-132 Will in Archives. Dated 25 Dec 1789, proved May 1791.

NATHANIEL PATTERSON wife: Issabel

daus: Jenny Ward, Margaret Swift, Susannah Ray,
Elizabeth Baker, Mary

"John Ward son of my daughter Margaret Swift deceased".

Executors: wife Issabel, son William, "John Ray my son-in-law", Issabel Ray (relationship not stated).

Witnesses: William Hodges, Jr., Andrew Murdock.

- - -

B-136 Will in Archives. No date, proved Aug 1791.

SAMUEL (x) TOLBY (this will is indexed in the Archives as TALLEY.)
wife: Elizabeth

no relationship stated: Elizabeth Faddis.

son: William Hitchcock Tolby
daus: Milly Whitaker, Mary Kennady, Elizabeth Rhodes.

Executors: James Kennady, Richard Rhodes.
Witnesses: A. Tatom, Wm. Strayhorn.

- - -

B-136 Will in Archives. Dated 8 April 1789, proved Aug 1791.

ALEXANDER (x) CARSON wife: name not stated.

sons: Robert Carson, Samuel Carson.

grandson: Alexander Carson. grandson: David Clenny.

daus: Elizabeth, Mary Carson, Alice Clenny wife to Wm. Clenny

Executors: wife, and John Grant Rencher.
Witnesses: Wm. McCauley, Wm. Ansley, Henry McCollum.

- - -

B-141 Will in Archives. Dated 2 August 1791, proved August 1791.

WILLIAM COMB wife: Ann

sons: James (under 21), John

daus: Mary Comb, Nancy Comb, Betty Mitchell, Ellender Trice.

granddau: Sarah Miller.

Executors: wife Ann, sons James & John, daughters Mary & Nancy Comb.

Witnesses: John Turrentine, Caleb Harvey.

- - -

B-143 Bill of Sale from WILLIAM HALL of Orange Co., N.C. to William Watters, for 7 negroes.

Dated 26 May 1786, proved August 1791.
Witnesses: John Hall, James Grange (?).

- - -

B-144 Will in Archives. Dated 21 Oct 1790, proved Aug 1791.

JESSE BENTON wife: Nancy

This will is four pages long.

Testator has several children, all minors, but their names are not given.

Executors: wife Nancy, Colonel Alfred Moore, William Walters, Absolom Tatom.

Witnesses: S. Benton, A. Benton.

- - -

B-149 Bill of Sale from ABNER NASH of Craven Co., N.C. to

William Nash of Orange Co., N.C. for 2 negroes.
Dated 25 March 1791, proved Aug 1791. Witness: And. Murdock.

- - -

B-149 Deed of Gift from ABNER NASH of Craven Co., N.C. to William Nash of Orange Co., N.C., for a negro boy "for love".

Dated 25 March 1791, proved Aug 1791.
Witness: Andrew Murdock.

- - -

B-149 Will in Archives. Dated 2 June 1791, proved Feb. 1792.

WILLIAM HAMILTON

son: Joseph Hamilton

daus: Elizabeth, Jean, Margaret, Nancy.

Executors and "trustees for my daughters": son Joseph, and Thomas Bradford.
Witnesses: William Bradford, Thomas Bradford.

- - -

B-151/Receipt entered on book 18 Feb 1792 from "John Craven, late Treasurer of the Board of Trustees of The University of North Carolina." (Long document.)

- - -

B-152 Will in Archives. Dated 28 July 1791, proved 179-

JOHN RILEY (or RIELEY) wife: Mary

sons: William, Robert, Samuel

daus: Jane Riley, Mary Donaldson, Nancy, Elizabeth.

Executors: "trusty friends John Armstrong and Mary Ruby (?)"
Witnesses: John Armstrong, James Riggs.

- - -

B-154 Will in Archives. Dated 10 April 1791, proved 179-

THOMAS LOVE only heir: Peggy Love, relationship not given.

Executors: Thomas Love, James Love.
Witnesses: Joseph Armstrong, William Love.

- - -

B-156 Will in Archives. Dated 28 July 1791, proved 179-

JACOB ALBRIGHT, SENIOR wife: Catherine

sons: George, John, Jacob, Joseph, Henry, Daniel.

daus: Sophia, Catherine.

Executors: son John Albright, Strudwick Clap.
Witnesses: William Ray, Boston Sharp.

- - -

B-160 Will in Archives. Dated --, proved Feb 1792.

ELIZABETH PAUL daus: Margaret Reddin, Elizabeth Gray.

grandchildren: Elizabeth Carrigan, William Reddin,
James Gray, James Paul, Elizabeth Gray,
Elizabeth Paul.

Executor: Enoe Robert Fassetts.
Witnesses: Francis Wilkinson, Samuel McCracken.

- - -

B-162 Will in Archives. Dated 9 Feb 1792, proved Feb 1792.

DANIEL (x) SULLIVAN wife: Margaret

sons: "oldest son Joseph Sullivan", Ben Sullivan,
Isaac,Daniel, John, "youngest son Edmund Sullivan".

daus: "oldest daughter Mary", Sarah, Margaret.

Witnesses: George Spous, John Melvin, Edmund (x) Melvin.

- - -

B-166 Will in Archives. Dated 17 Jan 1792, proved May 1792.

CHRISTOPHER BARBEE wife: Dicy Barbee (she is pregnant)

Daughters mentioned, but names not given.

Executors: "loving friends Goin Barbee and Joseph Barbee".
Witnesses: Goin Barbee, Ephriam Beasley, Ransom (x) David.

- - -

B-168 Will in Archives. Dated 9 Jan 1792, proved Feb 1792.

ENOCH DAVIS sons: Abraham Davis, John Davis.

"loving son William Eavins"

dau: Ellenor Darker he mentions "four daughters"...

Sole Executor: son Abraham Davis.
Witnesses: Stephen Merritt, Mary (x) Houge.

- - -

B-170 Will in Archives. Dated 7 Feb 1792, proved May 1792.

THOMAS LLOYD sons: Thomas Lloyd, Frederick Lloyd.

daus: Sarah Hogan, Mary Hogan

sons-in-law: John Hogan,John Maxeden,Adlai Osborne,

grandchildren: Thomas Hogan, John Hogan,William Hogan,
James Hogan, Alexander Hogan,
Margaret Lloyd Hogan,
Thomas Lloyd son of Stephen Lloyd. -continued-

B-170 Will of THOMAS LLOYD continued -

Executors: "trusty friends John Hogan and Baxton King".
Witnesses: Benjamin Howell (?), Wm. Forester, Wm. Brasher.

- - -

B-174 Will in Archives. Dated 10 Sept 1791, proved May 1792.

JEAN (x) HALL

sons: William Hall, John Hall, Robert Hall, Thomas Hall.

daus: Rebecca Kell, Mary Nichols, Sarah Hall, Rachel Hall.

Executors: Thos. Rountree, Robert Hall.
Witnesses: Charles Rountree, Lydia Rountree.

- - -

B-177 Will in Archives. Dated 11 Feb 1792, proved May 1792.

JAMES ROACH wife: Ann Roach

son: Absolom

He has sons under age, names and number not stated.

He has 3 daughters under 18. His mother is living.

Executors: wife Ann, Absolom Roach, John Thompson (miller).
Witnesses: James Thompson, Wm. Thompson, Wm. (x) Roach.

- - -

B-180 Will in Archives. Dated 7 June 1788, proved May 1792.

JOHN CONNER wife: Elizabeth

"James Watson and Margaret his wife"
"Said Watson's children"... James Watson, Jr.

No executor named. Witnesses: William Railey, James Railey.

- - -

B-182 Will in Archives. Dated 6 April 1792, proved May 1792.

THOMAS HORN, SENIOR sons: Thomas Horn, James Horn.

"Joshua Horn Senior, "young Henry Horn son of Joshua Horn",
"Nelly Horn daughter of James Horn .. and her mother Margery"
William Horn Senior and John Horn 1 shilling each.

No executor named. Witnesses: John Adams, Thomas Holloway.

- - -

B-185 Deed of Gift from MARK MORGAN of Orange Co., N.C. to "three sons Mark Morgan, John Morgan and Solomon Morgan of the same county"... for love ... certain tracts of land.

Dated 31 May 1792, proved May 1792.
Witnesses: John Scott, Phillip Allan, Albert Sears, William Goodwin.

- - -

B-188 JOHN SHAW and SEANY SHAW renounce title to land on Bolings Creek in Orange County, conveyed to Seany Jones in "her infancy" by John Boothe. Seany is now John Shaw's wife.

Dated 18 March 1792, proved May 1792;
Witnesses: James Trice, Mark Barbee, Zachariah Boothe.

- - -

B-199 Will in Archives. Dated 10 Aug 1792, proved Aug 1792.

JUDITH (x) STAGG

All her property to grandchildren Charles and Celia Stagg.

Witnesses: James Hogg, Gavin Alves.

- - -

B-191 Will in Archives. Dated 24 Feb 1792, proved Nov 1792.

JAMES WOODY wife: Rebecca Woody.

"two youngest brothers Joseph and Lewis Woody", both under 21.

Executors: Johnathan Lindley, James Woody.
Witnesses: Ezekiel Hornaday, Peter Duks, Zachariah Duks.

- - -

B-193 Will in Archives. Dated 5 June 1792, proved 1792.

ISAAC SEBASTION or SURBASTEN. wife: Sarah

"Estate to support wife and her family".

Executor: "Friend Stephen Conger".
Witnesses: John Eubanks, Samuel Williams.

- - -

B- 194 Will in Archives. Dated 24 Aug 1786, proved 1792.

CATHERINE LOCKHART of the town of Hillsborough, N.C.

son: William Lockhart

daus: Catherine Roads, Jean Holt, Sarah Parker, Elizabeth Mucklejohn, Mary (?) Smith.
Executors: son William, son-in-law James Parker.
Witnesses: John Allison, William Kennedy, Martin Palmer.

- - -

B-197 Will in Archives. Dated 17 May 1792, proved Nov 179-

JOHN WOODS wife: Margaret Woods

sons: Matthew; John and Richard, both under 21.

daus: Margaret Woods, Nancy Woods, Sarah Woods, Hannah Kirkpatrick.
He speaks of "my two young daughters".."youngest daughters".

son-in-law: Samuel Kirkpatrick.

Executors: wife Margaret, son Matthew.
Witnesses: Abe Allen, Reubèn Smith, Thomas Bradford.

- - -

B-204 to 208. Will in Archives. Dated 1 May 1792, proved Aug 1792.

FRANCIS CHILD wife: Frances

"My 3 sons Samuel (eldest), Wilson and Francis." All are under 21 years of age.

daughter-in-law: Fanny McKerall

"My natural son James Floyd".

Executors: wife Frances, Robert Freeman, Jno. Casey.
Witnesses: Jno. Casey, David Sloan, Will McKerall.

Codicil appoints " friends John Haywood and William Watters Esquires" .. " guardians to my three sons Samuel, Wilson and Thomas". Same witnesses as the will.

- - -

B-209 Will in Archives. Dated 19 June 1792, proved Aug 1792.

MARY (x) WALTON

daus: Mary Collins, Jemima Ward, Keziah Bane.

She mentions "my late husband Nathaniel Walton". (He died in 1786 ?).

Sole Executor: son-in-law Thomas Bane.
Witnesses: Thomas Armstrong, William Clarke.

- - -

B-211 Bill of Sale from HENRY (x) WHITE to William Nash, both of Orange Co., N.C., for 1 negro girl.

No date, proved Feb 1793.

Witnesses: Michael Holt, Jr., Robert Mitchell.

- - -

B-211 Bill of Sale from HENRY (x) WHITE to William Nash, for a slave, Kesiah and her daughter Lucy.

Dated 21 Aug 1793 ?, proved Feb 1793.

- - -

B-212 Bill of Sale from WILLIAM NEWMAN to William Nash, both of Orange Co., N.C., for 4 negroes.

Dated 10 Nov 1792, proved Feb 1793. Witness: S. Benton.

- - -

B-213 Power of Attorney from CHARLES MILLIKEN to Alexander Hatch. Dated 18 Jan 1793, proved Feb. 1793.
Witness: John Thompson.

- - -

B-215 Deed of Gift from THOMAS TRICE to his daughter Ann House and son-in-law House, for love.. 200 acres of land during their lives, then to his granddaughter Betsey House.

Dated 26 Feb 1793, proved Feb 1793.
Witnesses: Daniel Carlton, Sam'l Daniel.

- - -

B-216 Will in Archives. Dated 30 April 1789, proved Feb '93.

ALEXANDER MEBANE wife: Name not stated

sons: William, Alexander, James, John

daus: Jennett Anderson, Ann Morrow, Margaret Murdaugh.

granddaughter: Margaret Anderson.
grandson: Alexander Anderson.

Executors: Alexander Mebane, James Mebane.
Witnesses: Thos. Mulholland, Edward Wilson, William Wilson.

- - -

B-220 Will in Archives. Dated 2 March 1792, proved Feb 1793.

ROBERT RAY wife: Hannah Ray

"Eldest daughters Isabella, Fanny, Margaret, Silly, Mary, Martha and Nancy".

sons: Robert, John, Matthew (under 21).

dau: Kassey under 21. step-daughter: Ann Massey.

"granddaughter Rebecca daughter of Robert".

Executors: wife Hannah, William Clendennin.
Witnesses: Jas. Freeland, Joseph Pindar, Matthew Hunter.

- - -

B-222 Will in Archives. Dated 13 March 1792, proved Feb 1793.

WILLIAM (x) JAMISON, SENIOR   wife: Rachel

daus: Rachel Jamison, Mary Parks, Margaret Lindsey.

sons: John, Ellis, Thomas, William.

Executor: friend Sterling Harris.
Witnesses: Theopilus Thompson, Sterling Harris.

- - -

B-224 Bill of Sale from PETER BURTON of Mecklenburg Co., Va. to Abraham Thompson of Orange Co., N.C. for 1 negro girl.

Dated 24 Aug 1791, proved May 1792. Witness: John Thompson.

- - -

B-228 Bill of Sale from JOSEPH BRADFORD of St. Asaph's Parish, Orange Co., N.C. to Benjamin Piggott of Orange Co.

Dated 21 May 1792, proved May 1792.
Witnesses: Jas. Stoneman, Jos. Stoneman, Lewis Hornaday.

- - -

B-229 Will in Archives. Dated 29 Dec 1791, proved Feb 1792.

JAMES WALKER   Wife: Elizabeth

"My five children that I had by my first wife (viz) Ann Cimbol, Sanders Walker, Lydia Wright, Jeremiah Walker and William Walker.".

"My three children that I had by my second wife Sarah Colbert, Elizabeth Horton, James Walker."

Sole Executor: James Walker.
Witnesses: Thomas Latta, Samuel Garrard.

- - -

B-231 Inquest on the body of PETER NOE. 7 November 1787. Jurymen were : Joel Burrow, farmer, Nicholas Coonee, Frederick Kimbrough, Jacob Jones, Philip Burrow, Philip Eulice (?), Abraham Jones, Conrad Kimbrough, Joshua Holt, Martin Shofner, Henry Kimbrough. They found that Peter Noe died from natural causes.

- - -

B-233 Bill of Sale from GRAHAM BELL to William Nash for a slave. Dated 20 April 1793, proved May 1793.
Witness: J. Estes.

- - -

B-234 Will in Archives. Dated 4 Jan 1793, proved May 1793

PETER (x) EFLAND wife: Catherine

son: Daniel Efland 5 shillings.

"To my son John Efland, Catherine Noe, Mary Gibbs, Elizabeth Nance, Sarah Graves and Philis Sharp an equal share."

Executors: "friends John Albright and Obed Green."
Witnesses: John Bullock, James Holmes.

- - -

B-236 Will in Archives. Dated 10 Oct 1791, proved Aug 1793.

GEORGE DOHERTY

"to my wife Mary, and her three daughters Polly W. Burke, Frances Daugherty and Nelly Daugherty, share and share alike"

Executors: wife Mary, James Gillespie Esq. of Duplin County.
Witnesses: James Grant, John Casey.

- - -

B-237 Will in Archives Dated 6 May 1793, proved Aug 1793

WILLIAM LEWIS

All estate "to my brothers James, Howell, Robert, Charles, Nicholas and my sister Jane Mereweather Lewis."

Executors: brothers James, Howell and Robert Lewis.
Witnesses: Eliza Ridley, Charles Lewis, Thos. Hines.

- - -

B-238 Quit-claim-deed from JOSHUA (x) HORN to Jesse James and his wife, formerly Betsey Horne.

Dated 27 Aug 1793, proved Aug 1793. Witness: James H. Keys

- - -

B-239 Power of Attorney from JAMES WILLIAMS of Wilkes Co., Georgia to John Willis Esq. of Orange Co., N.C. to sell land on the Allamance in Orange Co., N.C.

Dated --, proved August 1793.
Witnesses: S. Benton, A. Tatom, John Taylor.

- - -

B-240 Will in Archives. Dated 11 Dec 1792, proved Aug 1793.

JAMES ROSS wife: Margaret

daus: Jane Smith, Levinia Minnis. - continued -

B-240 Will of JAMES ROSS continued -

Executors: wife Margaret, Levinia Minnis, John Minnis.
Witnesses: A. Tatom, John Casey, John Allison.

- - -

B-241 Will in Archives. Dated 12 Jan 1791, proved Aug 1793.

ROBERT ANDREW wife: Sarah

sons: Robert, David, Thomas and William Andrew.

"grandson Robert Andrew, son of John Andrew Deceased."

"My four daughters, namely Jane, Katherine, Ann and Sarah."

Executors: sons William and Thomas Andrew.
Witnesses: John Carter, James Woody.

- - -

B-243 Indenture. HERMAN (x) HUSK binds himself to John Sloss Esq. as a servant for 1 year

Dated 31 Aug 1793, proved Aug 1793. Witness: Andrew Burke.

- - -

B-245 Power of Attorney from SAMUEL STRUDWICK of the State of N.C., Planter, to Henry Shepperd of the State of N.C. " to receive such sums as may be due me from Michael Wooley, Robert Christmass, or any other persons, of, in, or belonging to the State of Georgia in America."

Dated 24 Nov 1793, proved Nov 1793.
Witnesses: Wm. Shepperd, W.F.Strudwick

- - -

B-246 Power of Attorney from D. WITHERSPOON to William Nash Esq. to sell land on Flat River in Orange County, N.C

Dated 22 Oct 1792, proved Nov 1793. Witness: Wm. Courtney.

- - -

B-247 Bill of Sale from JOHN BILLUPS and RICHARD K. CARROLL to John Scott, for 1 negro and her child.

Dated 30 July 1791, proved Nov 1793.
Witnesses: John Ray, George Ray.

- - -

B-248 Bill of Sale from ENOCH LEWIS to John Scott, both of Orange Co., N.C. for 1 negro boy.

Dated 25 Feb 1793, proved Nov 1793.
Witnesses: John Dannel, Ezekiel Trice.

- - -

B-249 Bill of Sale from JAMES G BOHUN of Warren Co., N.C to Michael Shofner, for a negro boy. Dated 17 Feb 1794. Witness: Augustine Willis.

- - -

B-249 Will in Archives Dated 18 Feb 1794, proved 179-

JAMES HUNTER wife: Christian

relationship not stated: James Hunter Andrew, Richard Hunter.

brother: Andrew Hunter.

Sole Executrix: wife.
Witnesses: Reuben Harris, James Walker, Priscilla (x) Montgomery.

- - -

B-251 to 254 Will in Archives. Dated 20 Aug 1793, proved Nov 1793

JOHN STEEL wife: Mary

daus: Agnes (youngest), Elizabeth Steel, Mary Steel (2nd), Sarah. All the daughters are under 16 years of age

son: Joseph Steel under 20 years of age.

"right of Margery Carrigan's third"...

Executors: "wife Mary and trusty friend Joseph Hodge."
Witnesses: Wm Steel, John Pickard, Charles Clendennin.

- - -

B-255 Will in Archives Dated 27 Feb 1793, proved Nov 1793

PHILIP (x) SNOTERLY wife: Elizabeth

sons: Henry, Jacob

"3 youngest daughters Susannah, Rachel Catherine" all under age. No other daughters are named.

Executors: "Trusty friends Peter Foust and Jacob Antony".
Witnesses: William Ray, Henry (x) Lay.

- - -

B-257 Will in Archives. Dated 15 Jan 1774, proved Nov 1793

GEORGE GOBEL (COBLE ?) sons: Henry, David.

Witnesses: George Cortner, Solomon Ly..?.., Simeon Anderson.

Codicil dated 25 Feb 1786 names same heirs.
Witnesses: David Thornburg (?), ...?..

The above will is indexed in OLDS as COBLE.

B-259 Will in Archives. Dated16 July 1793, proved Feb 1794

RICHARD CATE wife: Emelia

"My eight children .. James, Jesse, Richard, Thomas,John, Martha, Susannah, Emilia"

son: Benjamin dau: Martha Hastin (Hastings ?)

Several tracts of land are devised. One tract joins Charles Kelly, Another, "100 acres which I purchased from James Crawford". "50 acres on Cain Creek". "Land purchased from Thomas Moore", "tract bought of Richard Tinnen on E. side of Cain Creek", "my mill on west side of Cain Creek".

Executors: Sackfield (?) Brewer, brother John Cate,
son James Cate.

Witnesses: Bernard Cate, Lewis Kirk.

- - -

B-262 Will in Archives. Dated 3 March 1790, proved Feb 1794

DANIEL (x) HANLEY wife: name not stated

daus: Ester and Susannah, both under age.
Ann Linnin, Elizabeth, Grace, Ruth,

"My only son William"...

grandson: "Grace's son Daniel".

Testator devises "lands on the Cumberland".

Executors: Alexander Mebane, James Mebane.
Witnesses: William Allen, Daniel Mason.

Codicil dated March 3 1790. "If son dies without heir, daughters are to share equally in estate".

Witnesses to codicil: Henry Beason, Daniel Mason.

- - -

B-264 Bill of Sale from JOHN WILLS of Orange Co., N.C, to William Falkner of Warren Co., N.C. for slaves, etc.

Dated 16 Sept 1793, proved Feb 1794.

- - -

B-265 Bill of Sale from WILLIAM O'NEAL to Thomas Cole, both of Orange Co., N.C., for slaves.

Dated 26 Nov 1793, proved Feb 1794.
Witness: William Nash.

- - -

B266 Deed of Gift from THOMAS DABNEY of Caswell County to his niece Barshaba Crumbie of Orange County, for love , "Fifty pounds in property on or before she comes to age of 21 years". Dated 15 Nov 1793, proved Feb 1794.

Witnesses: Frances Moreland, John Wood.

- - -

B-267 Will in Archives. Dated 30 Aug 1793, proved Feb 1794.

ISRAEL (x) STANTEFER wife: Cassander

sons: Ephriam eldest, Joshua.
Isarel "100 acres of land called by name of William Baker's place."
Benjamin Stantefer.

daus: Sarah Rhoades, Rossaner Rhodes, Casander Hendon.
"to daughters Mary Stantefer and Elizabeth Stantefer land adjoining Thomas Guyns, John Cabe's, William Tesmon (?)."

granddaughter: "Sarah Rhoades daughter Cassandra."

grandson: Israel Turner "son of Ruth Turner, wife of Wm. Turner, 88 acres on the north side of William Pickett's cart road joining on Benjamin Peeler's land."

Executors: wife Casander, son Joshua.
Witnesses: Joshua Standeford, Mary (x) Stantefer, Henry Bunch.

- - -

B-270 Bill of Sale from EDWARD WILSON to William Wilson, both of Orange Co., N.C. for ..."three entries of land ... in the Hawfields in Orange County... adjoining lands of Samuel Strudwick." Dated 23 Sept 1793, proved Feb 1794.

Witnesses: James Tate, George Tate.

- - -

B-271 Deed of Gift from LEWIS KIRK to granddaughter Martha Williamson Kirk, both of Orange Co., N.C., for love, a "Negro girl Agnes, one year old."
Dated 2 Dec 1793, proved Feb 1794.

Witnesses: Nathaniel Christmas, Reubin Smith.

- - -

B-272 Deed of Gift from EDWARD WILSON to "my loving daughter Mary Wilson", both of Orange Co., N.C. "All goods and chattels now being in my dwelling house". A signed inventory is given. Dated 23 Sept 1793, proved Nov 1794.

Witnesses: James Tate, George Tate.

- - -

B-274 Will in Archives. Dated 24 Oct 1793, proved Feb 1794.

JOHN MOORE, JUNIOR. wife: Name not stated.

"Only son Asahel, plantation whereon I now live with an obligation for 900 acres of land in Cumberland".

dau: Elizabeth.

Executors: "trusty friends James Moore and David Turrentine".
Witnesses: Jno. Umstead, Samuel Turrentine, James Turrentine.

- - -

B-275 Will not in Archives. Dated 20 Oct 1793, proved Feb 1794.

JOHN LINDSEY wife: Mary Lindsey

"Three sons Athanatious Lindsey, John Lindsey, Caleb Lindsey".

dau: Dille Lindsey.

"All my children that are not married"...

Executors: son Athanatious Lindsey,
son-in-law Henry Edwards.
Witnesses: David Durham, Benjamin Davis, ..(torn) Lindsey.

- - -

B-277 Quit-claim-deed from DAVID BRADFORD to George Bradford "parcel of land bequeathed by George Bradford's father Davis Brandford to George Bradford (name is spelled 3 ways in deed). Speaks of land forming Andrew Pattin's line.

Dated 25 Feb 1794, proved Feb 1794.
Witnesses: John Armstrong, John Allison.

- - -

B-279 Will in Archives. Dated 15 June 1790, proved Nov 1795 ?

ANDREW MITCHELL son: James Mitchell

"All my children", names and number not stated.

Executors: Sam'l Woods, James Carr.
Witnesses: Wm. McCauley, George Long.

- - -

B-281 Bill of Sale from WILLIAM BAYLEY or BEEZELY ? of Chatham Co., N.C. to James Motley (Moseley ?) of Oring (Orange) Co., for a negro. Dated 22 Nov 1794, proved Nov 1794.

Witnesses: Ephriam (x) Beasley, Thomas Hopson.

- - -

B-282 Bill of Sale from JOHN FAIRMAN of town of Hillsbor - ough, Orange Co., N.C. to Joseph Dixon, for 2 negroes. Dated 25 Nov 1794. Witnesses: A. Tatom, Walter Alves.

- - -

B-280 Will not in Archives. Dated 2 November 3 o'clock A.M. no year.

ARCHIBALD LYTLE

"All to my brother William Lytle to dispose of".

"Step-mother Sarah Lytle to have use of plantation she lives on during her life for the use of her children."

Witnesses: George Doherty, Jno. Hawkins.

- - -

B-284 Deed of Gift from PATERSON (x) DANIEL to brother Roger Daniel a tract of land, 100 acres, for love, adjoining lands of Roger Daniel, Christopher Daniel, John Daniel, Thomas Trice, and Joseph Bough".. about 13 miles from the town of Hillsborough. No date, proved 1794 ?

Witnesses: Francis Nash, J or I. Walker.

- - -

B-285 Power of Attorney from FRANCIS STRUDWICK to Henry Shepperd, both of Orange Co., N.C. "to demand and receive money or negroes " due from (blank) Patterson of the State of South Carolina. Dated 27 Oct 1794, proved 179-

- - -

B-286 Power of Attorney from MARTHA STRUDWICK of N.C. (sole Executrix of Samuel deceased) to Henry Shepperd of N.C. to sue for "money due to me from Michael Watley or Robert Christmas, or any other person or persons in the state of Georgia in America". Dated 27 Oct 1794, proved 179-

Witnesses: Wm. Shepperd, Morgan Hart (?).

- - -

B-287 Bill of Sale from WILLIAM FALKENER of Warren Co., N.C. to James F. Brehan of Warren Co. Falkener sells stock of hogs which he bought from John Wills of Orange Co., N.C. in a bill, dated 16 Sept 1793.

Dated 28 Jan. 1795, proved Feb 1795.

- - -

B-288 Bill of Sale from JOHN FAIRMAN to Thomas O'Harro, both of Orange Co., N.C., for slaves.
Dated 3 Dec 1794, proved Feb 1795.

Witnesses: Joseph Dixon, James Coghlin.

- - -

B-289 Will in Archives. Dated 10 Sept 1794, proved Feb 1795.

WILLIAM SHANNON

Estate to "Loving cousins Thomas and Robert Shannon".

Sole Executor: "My trusty friend Richard Christmas."
Witnesses: Moses Crawford, Rachel Crawford.

- - -

B-290 Will in Archives. Dated 5 March 1793, proved Feb 1795.

GEORGE MILLER sons: Jesse Miller, James Miller.

daus: Sarah Ray, wife of John Ray
Lydia, widow of Joseph Ray, deceased
Mary, wife of Zachariah Dickey

grandsons: Joseph Miller, son of Wm. and Ann Miller.
George Ray, son of John and Sarah Ray.
George Ray, son of Lydia and Joseph Ray deceased.
George Miller, son of Martha and Jesse Miller.
George Dickey, son of Mary and Zachariah Dickey.

Sole Executor: son James Miller.
Witnesses: James Jackson, James Ray, Jean (x) Turentine.

- - -

B-292 Will in Archives. Dated 26 Nov 1794, proved Feb 1795.

HENRY (x) DUNWEDDEE wife: Elizabeth son: John

daus: Nancy Long, Sarah Gresham.

grandsons: Absolom and James, sons of John Dunweddee,
John Jackson.

Executors: Josiah Warren, John Redman.
Witnesses: Jonathan (x) Dollar, Tho. Gresham,
Maryan (x) Gresham.

- - -

B-294 Bill of Sale from WILLIAM G. SMITH of State of New York, to DANIEL MAY, Senior, for negroes.
Dated 12 Aug 1794, proved Feb 1795.

Witnesses: Francis Nash, ...?... Patterson.

- - -

B-294 Bill of Sale from HENRY WHITE to Adam Smith, for a negro. Dated 9 July 1794, proved Feb 1795.

WITNESSES: ...?.. Patterson, Joshua Holt.

- - -

B-296 Bill of Sale from JOHN STROUD to Obed Green, for a negro. Dated 15 Aug 1794, proved Feb 1795.

Witnesses: James Patterson, Thos. Whitehead.

- - -

B-297 Bill of Sale from JOHN ELLIFF (ELLIS ?) to Thomas Cole, for a negro. Dated 20 Nov 1794, proved Feb 1795.

Witnesses: Absolom Holt, Jeremiah Holt.

- - -

B-298 Bond. JAMES MEBANE agrees to sell to Thomas Lloyd, Sr a tract of "land on which Col. Hogan now lives"

Dated 5 Jan 1795, proved Feb 1795.
Witnesses: B. Stanford, R. Morris, Isaac Blackwood

- - -

B-299 Power of Attorney from ZACHARIAH BOOTHE of Hancock Co., Ga. to friend William Trice of Orange Co., N.C. to make lawful deed to James Trice of lands in Chatham Co., N.C. on the waters of White Oak. Dated 7 Nov 1794, proved Feb 1795.

Witnesses: Jas. Trice, Edward Trice.

- - -

B-300 Bill of Sale from JOSEPH HODGE, Sheriff of Orange Co., N.C. John Allison of town of Hillsborough. "Allison was in debt to the estate of William Armistead.)

Dated 17 Oct 1795, proved Nov 1795. Witness: John Kelly.

- - -

B-301 Receipt to JOHN RAY, Administrator of William Jameson deceased, for the just and full sum of Thirteen hundred and twenty-nine pounds, Eleven shillings and ten pence in full of his administration upon the Estate of William Jameson deceased, by me Jean Jameson, Guardian of Margaret Jameson, John Jameson, Mary Jameson, Jean Jameson, William Jameson and Robert Jameson. I say rec'd the above sum by me.

Jean (x) Jameson

Witness: Andrew McBroom.

This is the last entry in WILL BOOK B.

- - - - - - -

Book C, page 1. Will in Archives. Dated 3 Feb 1794
proved May 1794.

THOMAS (x) MORTISE wife: Mary Mortise

daughter, name not stated.

Witnesses: John Adams, Joseph Hastings.

- - -

C-2 Will in Archives. Dated 20 Jan 1794, proved May 1794.

GRIZZEL McCALLISTER

Heirs named as follows, relationship not stated to some of them. David Allison, John Allison son, Margaret Allison, Grizzle Thompson, Mary Clark daughter, Jane Allison, James Donaldson, Elizabeth Allison, Sarah Allison.

Sole Executor: David Allison.
Witnesses: James Mordah, Elizabeth Allison.

- - -

C-3 Power of Attorney dated 24 May 1794 from Ezekiel Mace, John Darris & Angel his wife ... The said John Darris in right of his wife heretofore Angel Mace ... the said Ezekiel Mace and Angel Darris being the only surviving children of Josias Mace heretofore of Dorchester County, Md, deceased ... do constitute Edmond Brannock of Dorchester Co. Md. their lawful att'y to sell their share of the property of John Brannock of Maryland known as Grace Ridings ... which Josias Mace purchased of Lewis Woolford and Mary his wife ...
Witnesses: Hardy Hurdle, Stephen Mareign, Jacob Etterton, Alex. Robbs.

- - -

May Court 1794 the heirs deputize "Our uncle Alex. Robbs to act for us and to sell property in Dorchester Co., Maryland known as Buttons Intent" ... this 24 May 1794.

Witnesses: Hardy Hurdle, Stephen Maragn, Jacob Mortise.

- - -

C-8 Bill of Sale dated 12 October 1792

JOHN GREGORY & PETER BURTON deliver to MRS. FRANCIS CHILD one negro boy, 14 years old, for 160 Spanish dollars.
Witness: John Casey.

- - -

C-9 Bill of Sale dated 16 Feb 1793 from
MITCHELL RUSSOM to MRS. FRANCES CHILD, Exec'x of Francis Child, dec'd, for slaves. Witness: John McKerral.

- - -

C-9 Bill of Sale dated 16 Feb 1793 from HENRY WHITE to MRS. FRANCES CHILD, Exec'x of the will of Frances Cdild, dec'd, for five slaves. Witness: John Casey.

- - -

C-10, C-11, and C-12 have other transactions concerning MRS. FRANCES CHILD. JOSEPH NICHOLS sells .... etc.

C-13 Deed of Gift from RICHARD RHODES "for love and good will to the Church and the Gospel..." He gives two acres for a meeting house on Kennady's .. Date 18 Jan./1794

C-14 Deed. Dated 25 Dec 1794? from GEORGE RIDENS to John Tilley, for land, etc. Witness: Wm. Hopkins.

- - -

C-16 Bond. Dated 20 Feb 1794, proved Aug 1794.

THOMAS HORNE, SR to Stephen Carroll & Henry Bunch a bond that said Carroll & Bunch joined with Thos. Horne to give to John Latta for 125 pounds for which I make over my tract of 250 acres. Signed: Thomas Horne, Sr.
Witnesses: Wm. Horn, John Riley.

- - -

C-17 Bill of sale dated 26 August 1794. AMBROSE GREGORY of Mecklenburg Co., Va. sells to William Nash of Orange Co., N.C. two negro boys. Witness: Jas. Philips.

- - -

C-18 HARDY MORGAN "for the good will that I have for my friend & neighbor JAS. PATTERSON of Chatham Co.,N.C. give him the privilege of cutting all large pine trees for sawing to Sam'l Allen's line .. to land adjoining Christopher Barbee's. Dated 18 Nov 1793,
Witness: John McCauley,Jr. proved August 1794.

- - -

C-20 Bill of sale. Dated 4 April 1794, proved Aug 1794.

JOHN WILLIS sells to JAMES G. BRECKON of Warren Co., N.C. household furniture, etc.
Witnesses: Thos. Glasier, Will Kirkland.

- - -

C-19 Will in Archives. Dated 24 July 1794, proved Aug 1794.

THOMAS (x) HULGAN wife: Fanny

sons: Robert, Stephen

daughters: Margaret Neely, Rosannah, Mary.

Executors: wife Fanny, William Ray, John Ray.
Witnesses: Samuel Mebane, Steward Dickson.

- - -

C-21 Will in Archives. Dated July 1794, proved Aug 1794.

JAMES THOMPSON He speaks of "my seven children" ...

son: James gets one fourth "of tract I purchased of Stephen Hart" and "land purchased from Robert Burnside"
son: Joshua (he is under 21) gets land purchased of Thomas Norris, and land purchased of James Riley.
son: John (he is under 21)

daughters: Ellinor, Martha , both under 18 years of age. Sarah Lindley, Elizabeth Hadley.

- continued -

C-21 Will of JAMES THOMPSON continued -

son-in-law: Owen Lindley

brother: Joseph

no relationship stated to William Rily.

Executors: Samuel Chambers brother-in-law, and brother
Joseph Thompson.
Witnesses: Will Raily, Jno. Bowle, Sarah Chambers.

- - -

C-25 Deed dated 7 Nov 1793, proved Aug 1794.

GOIN BARBEE of Wake County, N.C. "for 100 pounds paid to me by JOHN BARBEE, sell him land in aforesaid county, being part of land surveyed for John Barbee, Sr containing 263 acres on N. East (Creek)". Witnesses: Phebe Barbee, Benj. Barbee.

- - -

C-26 Deed dated 27 Nov 1793, proved Aug 1794.

GOIN BARBEE of Wake County, N.C. sells to BENJAMIN BARBEE land "surveyed for John Barbee, Sr" ..."lying on prong of the N. East of New Hope (Creek)". Witnesses: Jos. Burnett, John Barbee.

- - -

C-28 Will in Archives. Dated 24 Dec 1793, proved Aug 1794.

JOSEPH CATE wife: Ann

sons: Solomon, Charles, Steven

daughters: Esther, Sall

Testator's property is on Cane Creek. Neighbors mentioned are John Cate, Thomas Baskett, Thomas Durham, W. or Mr. Brewer.

Executors: wife Ann, brother Thomas.
Witnesses: John Cate, Elizabeth Cate, John Workman.

- - -

C-30 Indenture between MARY STONE and KENNETH ANDERSON .... Dated 13 Feb 1794. Witnesses: Thos. Smith, Ruben Smith.

- - -

C-33 through C-48 are blank.pages.

- - -

C-49 Bill of Sale dated 12 Feb 1793, proved Nov 1794.

FRANCES CHILD, widow of Francis Child, sells to Miss Frances McKerrall, a negro woman ..... Witness: John McKerrall.

- - -

C-50 Bill of Sale dated 12 July 1794.

JOHN BILLUPS & WM. G. GOOCH sell to MRS FRANCES CHILD three sleves, etc. Witness: John McKerrall.

C-50 Bill of Sale dated 10 May 1793. JOHN McKERRALL sells to MRS. FRANCES CHILD, one negro woman. Witness: Jos. Dixon.

\- - -

C-52 is blank.

C-53 Will in Archives. Dated 10 Feb 1794, proved Aug 1795.

JAMES BURCH wife: Mary

sons: John, George, William, James Johnston.

daughters: Sareh, Agnas.

Executors: wife Mary and son John.
Witnesses: John Kennedy, Caleb Burch, John Sloss.

\- - -

C-56 Will in Archives. Dated --, proved August 1795.

ANNE HOOPER

sons: William, Thomas

daughter: Elizabeth Watters or Walters.

grandson: Henry Walters.

Executors:sons William and Thomas, and daughter Elizabeth.
Witnesses: Gavin Alves, Sam'l Benton.

\- - -

C-53 to 56 Will in Archives. Dated 3 July 1795, proved Aug / 1795

ALEXANDER MEBANE

wife: Ann, has property in Philadelphia.

sons: John Alexander, William, Robert, James.

daus: Jannet Stanford, Mary Hodge,
Sarah, Fanny, Susannah, Elizabeth, Nancy.

grandchildren: Arriana and Mary Stanford.

Executors: son James, brother James, and Robert Hodge.
Witnesses: Wm. Hodge, John Matthews.

\- - -

C-57 Will in Archives. Dated 20 Aug 1778, proved Aug 1795.

THOMAS SMOTHERS wife: Susannah

sons: William, John, James, Thomas - continued -

C-57 Will of THOMAS SMOTHERS continued -

daus: Sarah Smothers, Rebecca Sumner or Summer,
Elizabeth Pickard, Mary Smothers.

Executors: wife Susanna and Alex. Summers ?.
Witnesses: John Daniely, Jonathan Clampit.

- - -

C-58 Will in Archives. Dated 27 Feb 1793, proved Aug 1795.

JOHN SHY wife: Martha

"Brother Ike and his heirs ..."

Executors: wife Martha and Robert Harrison.
Witnesses: Samuel Hill, Caleb Harvey.

- - -

C-59 Will in Archives. Dated 7 March 1794, proved Aug 1794.

JOHN MOORE wife: Elizabeth

sons: James, Henry

daughters: Elizabeth, Martha

grandson: Ashahel Moore

cousin: Martha Moore.

Executors: James Moore, Charles Robinson.
Witnesses: James Watson, Henry Moore, Margaret Watson.

- - -

C-61 Will in Archives. Dated 21 Feb 1793, proved Nov 1795.

JOSEPH BUCKINGHAM wife: Margery

brothers: James, William

"To my brother James Buckingham's son Joshua Buckingham" half of estate.

"To my brother William Buckingham's son William" 40 sh.

"brother-in-law's son Jeremiah Piggott's son Jeremiah ..."
"brother-in-law Jeremiah Piggott's daughter Rachel"...

no relationship stated to: Barbara Carter.

Executors: wife Margery, Joshua Buckingham.
Witnesses: Benj. Piggott, Mary Piggott, John Piggott.

- - -

BOOK C, page 62 Will in Archives. Dated Nov. 1795,
Proved Nov. 1795

PHILLIP WALKER

names wife and children, but names are not given.

Executors: John Trusdale, John Walker.

Witnesses: John Walker, Wm. Walker.

- - -

C-62 Will in Archives. Dated 22 June 1795. Proved Nov. 1795

BENJAMIN THOMPSON wife: Sarah

sons: Robert, Richard, Stephen, Samuel.

dau: Frances Thompson

Executors: wife Sarah, and Caleb Harvey.

Witnesses: Caleb Harvey, Joseph Anderson.

- - -

C-64 Will in Archives. Dated April 1795, Proved Nov. 1795

ATHENATIUS ROBERTSON wife: Dilley

Son: Nathaniel dau: Mary Lindsay

grandson: Athenatious Lindsay.

Executors: John Snipes and grandson Athenatious Lindsay.

Witnesses: Thos. Snipes, Wm. Snipes, Alex. Hatch.

- - -

BOOK C, page 65 Will in Archives. Dated 27 August 1795
Proved November 1795

ALEXANDER McCRACKEN

wife: Abigail

sons: Samuel (eldest), Thomas, John, William,
Robert, Alexander.

daus: Mary Andrew, Hannah Tinnen,
Abigail Davis, Ruth Chamness.

-continued on next page-

Will of Alexander McCracken continued

Executors: son Samuel McCracken, Francis Wilkinson.

Witnesses: David Gilston, Samuel Chambers, Thomas Bradford.

- - -

C-67 Will in Archives. Dated Oct. 7, 1795, proved Nov. 1795.

TENTS MASSEY wife: Ruth

son: James dau: Mary

Executors: wife Ruth, and "my mother Hannah Ray".

Witnesses: Eli Harvey, Nathan Hicks.

- - -

C-68 Will in Archives. Dated 2 July 1795, proved Nov 1795.

SAMUEL CLENEAY (spelled Clenny in Probate.)

sons: William, Samuel, Johnathan.

3 daughters to get "claim of land on the western waters", their names not stated.

Sole Executor: son-in-law William Belvin.

Witnesses: John Wood, Ann Wood, Rebecca Wood.

- - -

C-69 Will in Archives. Dated 9 Dec. 1795, proved Feb. 1796.

MATHEW DURHAM wife: Susanna Durham

son: Mark Durham no Executor named.

Witnesses: Wm. Stroud, Lysias Durham.

- - -

C-70 Will in Archives. Dated 17 March 1794, proved Feb 1796

THOMAS THOMPSON of Eno, Orange Co., N.C. wife: Ann

son: Samuel "150 acres of land on which he now lives joining Maddon's and Chamberlan's lands."

-continued - next page

Will of Thomas Thompson continued

son: Abraham "home tract oh which I now live"

grandson: John Debow.

Sole Executor: son Abraham.

Witnesses: Jacob Lake, Wm. McMun.

- - -

C-71 Will in Archives. Dated 30 July 1795, proved Feb 1796.

JAMES CLARK wife: Elizabeth

"son William Clark deceased's sons James Clark, Thomas Clark, William Clark, Jesse Clark, Joseph Clark".

"dau. Elinor wife of John Clark"

Dau: Catrenah

son: James Clark gets "plantation where I now live".

"granddaughter Sarah that now lives with me"...

Executors: "my son James Clark", and"my friend John Ray".

Witnesses: Jesse Clark, Thomas Clark.

- - -

C- 73 POWER OF ATTORNEY Dated 1 Dec 1795, proved Feb. 1796.

From DAVID LYNCH of Orange Co. to his brother Jesse Lynch.

Witnesses: Empson Bird, J.P., William Bird

- - -

C-73 POWER OF ATTORNEY dated 19 Sept 1795, proved Feb 1796

From JOHN HOGAN to "trusty friend" John Grant Rencher, both of Orange Co., N.C. To empower said attorney to convey 100 acres of land to Baxter King.

Witnesses: Thomas Lloyd, John Kimbel.

- - -

BOOK C, page 75 Will in Archives. Dated 8 December 1795
Proved February 1796

JOHN ALLISON wife: Martha

son: Joseph Allison , 20 shillings
James Allison " 240 acres of the entry joining David Allison's tract "

John Allison, Charles Allison, Hamilton Allison.

daus: "Jennet wife of James Ray"
"Mary wife of Thomas Curtis"
"Martha wife of Samuel Garat"
Grisel Allison, Agnes Allison, Elizabeth Allison.

Executors: wife Martha, and son Joseph Allison

Witnesses: John Ray, Andrew McBroom.

- - -

C-76 Will in Archives. Dated 2 Sept. 1795, proved Feb 1796

JAMES (x) HUTCHINSON wife: Margaret

sons: Samuel, James, Ross

daus: Margaret Kelly, Jane Lynch.

Executors: wife Margaret, and son James.

Witnesses: William Mebane, John (x) McCrory
Judah (x) Griffith.

- - -

C-78 Will in Archives Dated 17 Dec. 1795, proved Feb 1796

ALEXANDER (x) CHISENHALL wife: Celah

sons: Samuel Chizenall, Reuben Chizenall, John Chizenall.

daus: Elizabeth Ridgeway, Sarah Manning
Markey Wood.

Executors: wife Celah and son Samuel.

Witnesses: William Ansley, John (x) Reaves.

- - -

BOOK C, page 79 Will in Archives. Dated --- , proved Feb. 1796.

MARY (x) PATTERSON

All her estate " to be equally divided among the surviving children of John Couch and Betsey his wife deceased ".. "The names of the several children now living being Mary Couch, Letitia Couch, July Couch, Elenor Couch, Elizabeth Couch". (They are all under 18 years of age.)

Executors: "Worthy friends Robert Campbell, Roger Daniel, and John Couch."

Witnesses: Robert Campbell, Roger (x) Daniel.

- - -

C- 80 Will in Archives. Dated 29 Feb. 1796, proved May 1796.

THOMAS MULHOLLAND wife: Martha

daus: Mary
Elizabeth "lands in Cumberland and this county".

"As to my four sons Hugh, John, Thomas and Henry, I leave my whole Mumford lands" Hugh gets surveying instruments.

Executors: wife, and son Hugh.

Witnesses: John Umstead, Samuel Nelson, John Nelson.

- - -

C-81 Will in Archives. Datedl8 July 1796, proved Aug. 1796.

JOHN LACKEY

wife: Elizabeth gets all his estate "to raise and school my children." The number of children is not stated, no names given. He mentions " my sons". All the children are under 21 years of age.

Executors: wife Elizabeth and son Robert Lackey.

Witnesses: John Moody (Woody ?), Hugh Lackey.

- - -

C-82 Will in Archives. Dated 22 March 1796, proved Aug/
1796

JAMES HALL wife: Mary Hall

son: Levi, blacksmith tools, etc
son: Jehu, plantation, etc.

daughters: Mary Garrison, Lydia Faucette, Tamar Server, Deborah Davis, Margaret Garrison, Elizabeth Hall, Phebe Anderson.

Executor: son Jehu Hall.
Witnesses: Hardy Hurdle, Isaac Hall, Garrit Garrison.

- - -

C-83 Bill of Sale from ROBERT SCOBY to ROBERT TINNEN, both of Orange Co.,N.C., for one negro boy.
Dated 13 Nov 1795, proved Aug 1796.
Witnesses: Jo. Moore, William Fitch.

- - -

C-84 Will in Archives. Dated 15 Oct 1795, proved Aug 1796

JOHN MURDOCK wife: Ann

son: William daughter: Prudence "one loom"

grandsons: John Murdock, John Ray

William Pain and his wife Rebecca 5 shillings.

"My son-in-law Robert Ray and his wife Elinor ..."

Executors: wife Ann and son William.
Witnesses: John (x) Thompson, Levi Thompson.

- - -

C-85 Will in Archives. Dated 8 May 1796, proved Aug 1796

GEORGE HERNDON wife: Sarah

sons: James, George, Zachariah, Reuben, Edmund, Lewis.

daus: Mary Roberts, Ruth Roberts, Salley McCoy, Betty Cole, Ester Barbee, Delilah Rhodes, Maryanne Trice.

grandson: George Roberts.

Executors: wife Sarah, Zachariah Herndon, James Herndon
Witnesses: Joseph Booth, Jos. Bilbo, David (x) George.

- - -

C-88 Will in Archives. Dated 6 April 1794, proved Nov /
1796

JAMES (x) ARMSTRONG Slave Cicero is set free.

son: William Armstrong

- continued -

C-88 continued -
daughters: Sarah Allen, Susannah Lloyed.
"To the heirs of my daughter Mary Mebane..."
"To the heirs of my daughter Elizabeth Lapsley...

grandsons: Thomas, James & Wm. Armstrong, all under age.
granddaughter: Mary Tinnen.

Executors: "well beloved friends John Taylor and Robert Faucette". Witnesses: William Elliott, Robert Taylor.

- - -

C-90 Will in Archives. Dated 12 Sept 1796, proved Nov 1796.

JOHN (x) BOYLE wife: Martha Boyle

sons: John Boyle and William Boyle each 500 acres of land "lying in Cumberland in company with Jesse Benton and Charles Parate."

grandson: "John Boyle son to my son James" 500 acres.
"To each of my grandsons and daughters a Bible."

Executors: sons James and John Boyle.
Witnesses: Samuel Thompson, Wm. Boyle, James Boyle.

- - -

C-91 Will in Archives. Dated 30 -- 1793, proved Nov 1796.

THOMAS SEARLES wife a legatee, name not stated.

sons: Coventon Searles "100 acres lying in Wake Co., N.C. where he now lives".
Henry, 100 acres in Orange joining George Herndon.
Ephriam, land in Orange.
Francis "100 acres in Orange joining Joseph Clark".
Edward Searles.

daughters: Winney Searles,Betty Searles,Peggy Cook.

Executors: sons Henry and Francis Searles, "son-in-law Joseph Searles".
Witnesses: Dan Green,Bartholomew (x) Stovall, Othniel (x) Farmer.

- - -

C-92 Bill of Sale from JOHN TAYLOR, Esq. of Orange to WILLIAM LYTLE, Esq. and ANDREW GIBSON, one bay mare and seven negroes. Dated 28 Feb 1797, proved Feb '97.

- - -

C-93 Will in Archives. Dated 9 Nov 1796, proved Feb 1797.

WILLIAM BELVIN

Wife Magdalene "lot I now live on in Hillsboro (#29)" etc.

Executors: wife Magdalene and William Whitted, Jr.
Witnesses: Wm. Courtney, John Faddis, Wm. Whitted, Jr.

- - -

Book C, page 94. Will in Archives. Dated 17 Feb 1797, proved May 1797.

JOHN KING

sons: Thomas King (oldest), Edward King, Armour King, William King, get $1 each.

John King gets estate.

Sole Executor: son John King.

Witnesses: Thomas Bradford, D. Bradford.

- - -

C-94. Will in Archives. Dated 6 March 1797, proved May 1796.

JOHN FOSSETT (signed John Faucette) wife: Pherebe

son: Thomas Fossett "plantation joining Jpseph Hastings"

dau: Polly Fossett.

Executors: Thomas Cate, Ezra Cate, "my brother Sam Fossett".

Witnesses: Richard (x) Fossett, Thomas (x) Faucette.

- - -

C-96 POWER OF ATTORNEY from JEMIMA (x) BARBEE to Benjamin Barbee, both of Orange. Dated 23 April 1794, proved May 1797.

Witnesses: George Herndon, George (x) Holder.

- - -

C- 97 Will in Archives. Dated 1 April 1797, proved May 1797.

JAMES K.D.BYRN wife: Mary

sons: Thomas Byrn, James Byrn, Absolom Byrn, Resin Byrn.

daus: Elizabeth, Mary.

Some of the children are under age.

EXECUTORS: wife Mary and son James.

Witnesses: William Ray, James H. Ray.

- - -

BOOK C, page 98 Will in Archives. Dated 22 April 1797
Proved May 1797

HARDY MORGAN

wife: Sarah " and if she should have an heir or heirs"

sons: Samuel and Allen

Executors: wife Sarah, John Daniel.

Witnesses: John Daniel, C.P.Patterson.

- - -

C-100 Will in Archives. Dated 1 August 1797, proved August 1797.

ROBERT BARNHILL wife: Margaret

sons: "eldest son James"
John - "plantation whereon he lives"

Sole Executor: wife Margaret

Witnesses: Thomas Johnston, George Fausett.

- - -

C-101 Will in Archives. Dated 6 June 1794, proved Aug. 1797.

WILLIAM O'NEAL

wife: Elizabeth "all my estate during her life".

relationship not stated:

" William O'Neal Perkins and his brothers and sisters.".
" Thomas H. Perkins and Mary his wife and children"...

Executors: "Trusty Friends Thomas H. Perkins and Elizabeth O'Neal."

Witnesses: Andrew Gibson, Joseph Culbertson, Robert Dickson.

- - -

C-102 MORTGAGE from THOMAS CONNALLY,SR. to John McCawley on "negro man Jack" Dated 3 Feb. 1796, proved August 1797.

Witnesses: George Johnston, Alexander Borland.

- - -

Book C, page 103 Will in Archives. Dated 11 March 1795
proved August 1797

CONRAD LONG wife: Catey

"2 sons Jacob and Conrad"

sons Henry and Casper

daus: Mary, Elizabeth

Executors: wife Catey, son Henry.

Witnesses: William Rainey, Mary (x) Rainey.

- - -

C-104 Will in Archives. Dated 27 May 1797, proved Nov. 1797

WILLIAM (x) RODGERS of the Hawfields

wife: Elizabeth

sons: Abraham Rodgers, Theopelous Rodgers, Nathan Rodgers

daus: Rachel Garner, Morning Perkins, Wilthy Bryant, Jemima Green, Leasey Rodgers, Laney Rodgers, youngest

Executors: wife Elizabeth, son Theopelous.

Witnesses: Thomas Bradford, Moses Cate.

- - -

C-105 BILL OF SALE from SAMUEL DANIEL of Orange Co., N.C. to John Daniel for a "negro woman and her sucking child". Dated 12 Sept. 1797, proved Feb. 1798.

Witnesses. Thomas Trice, Robert T. Daniel.

- - -

C-106 BILL OF SALE from SARAH (x) MURRELL "of the county of Orange, N.C., late of the State of Virginia, Granville Co., to Robert Tinnen of Orange Co., N.C." .. one negro girl. Dated 16 August 1797, proved Feb. 1789.

Witnesses: Thomas Armstrong, John Paul.

- - -

C-107 Will in Archives. Dated 18 Jan 1797, proved Feb 1798.

JOHN (x) FANN wife: Elizabeth

"Five youngest daughters, Rebecca, Patsey, Tabby, Anne and Betsy Fanns..."

"Three youngest sons, Elijah, Willie and Rawley Fanns..." all three are under age.

"My elder children"...(not named except for son Macky) have received their parts."

Executors: wife Elizabeth, and friend John Wilson.
Witnesses: John Walker, Mack Fann, William Dodd.

- - -

C-109 Will in Archives. Dated 19 Nov 1794, proved Feb 1800.

WILLIAM BROWN wife: Hannah

sons: Joel Brown, William Brown

daughter: Deborah Brown

..."sons who are living at wife's decease ..."
..."daughters who are living at wife's decease ..."
"I give five shillings to each of my married children."

Executors: son Joel Brown, friend Jacob Marshall.
Witnesses: William Brown, Jacob Brown, William Stout.

- - -

C-110 Will in Archives. Dated 23 May 1786, proved Feb 1800.

THOMAS (x) WOOD of Eno River. wife: Mary

dau: Lydia Good	son: Henry Wood
son: Edward Wood	dau: Meley Gwin
" william Wood	" Theaney Wallace
" Blayton Wood	" Mary Woods
dau: Sarah Forrest	" Elizabeth Acory

All the above children are to receive one shilling each.

..."sons James Wood and Joseph Wood all the remainder."

Executors: sons James and Joseph.
Witnesses: James Alston, Elias Turner, Frederick Geer.

- - -

C-111 Will in Archives. Dated 19 Nov 1799, proved Feb 1800

ELIZABETH SHARP "of the Town of Hillsboro, N.C."

Daughter Elizabeth to receive entire estate.

Sole Executrix: daughter Elizabeth.
Witnesses: I or J Casey, Catlett Campbell, James Yarborough.

- - -

C-112 Will in Archives. Dated 11 Feb 1797, proved Feb 1798.

GEORGE HOLT

wife Cise receives half his estate. She appears to be his second wife, as he provides for "paling of my grave where my wife now lieth."

£ 5 for repairing the meeting house at Joshua Holt's.

relationship not stated: Elizabeth O'Neal receives half estate.

No executor named.

Witnesses: Wm. Rainey, Harmon (x) Lowe.

- - -

C-113 Will in Archives. Dated 7 July 1797, proved Feb 1798.

ISAAC FORREST wife a legatee, her name not stated.

sons: Silous and William, both under age.

"my 3 daughters, Mary, Sarah and Milly"...

Executors: brother Shadrack Forrest, and James Curry.

Witnesses: Thornberry Anderson, Silas Forrest, Philon Forrest.

- - -

C-114 Will in Archives. Dated 6 April 1773, proved May 1798.

JAMES (x) TINNEN wife: Elizabeth

other legatees, relationship not stated:
"Alexander, son of John Tinnen", "Cearns Tinnen's son Robert", "Robert Tinnen's son Robert" and "to his brother Cearns", "James Tinnen the son of Robert Tinnen". Sarah Johnston.

Executors: wife Elizabeth and John Thompson Miller.

Witnesses: John Reading, Arch'd Campbell, William Campbell.

- -

C-115 Power of Attorney from JAMES SHEPPARD of Washington Co., Ga. to William Francis Strudwick of Orange Co., N.C. to receive a negro from Andrew Murdock of Orange Co., N.C.

Dated 31 Oct 1797, proved May 1798.
Witnesses: Jarret Groce, H. Shepard.
The above P of A had been recorded in "Lyncoln County, Ga."

- - -

C-117 Will in Archives. Dated 31 March 1798, proved May 1798.

RAINEY PHILLIPS

wife Mary gets "estate to raise my children"

stepson: Henry stepdaughter: Leander

dau: Polly "100 acres on N. Side of Haw River bought of / Widow Parks"

dau: Rachel son: Ben Rainey
" Hannah Johnston dau: Lucretia.

Executors: wife, and brother William Phillips.

Witnesses: Sarah Phillips, William Madray.

- - -

C-118 Will in Archives. Dated 8 Feb 1798, proved May 1798.

ZACCHEUS TATE (no wife mentioned)

Heirs given in the order in which they occur in the will.
Most of the children are under age.

son: John Tate granddaughter: Jean Mechum Tracy

daus: Jean Tate, Lydia Tate, and Udose Tate

sons; Zaccheus Tate, Velentine Tate, Uriah Tate,
Zephaniah Tate, Uzziah Tate, Zenas Tate,
Simpson Tate (he is married).

dau: Sally Spruce wife of Quinton Spruce.

Executor: son John Tate.

Witnesses: Wm. Brackin, James McClary.

- - -

C-120 Will in Archives. Dated 20 Aug 1798, proved Aug 1798.

ABIJAH (x) MASSEY wife: Jemima

"my children" number and names not stated.
He mentions a tract of land bought from John Conally.

Executors: brother Abner Massey,
"William Pendergrass my Honorable Father-in-Law".
Witnesses: Matthew McCauley, Jobe (x) Pendergrass,
John Pendergrass.

- - -

Book C, page 122 "Petersburg 12th June 1798

Mr. John McKerall, Sir- In consequence of Mr. Kirkland's agreement with you to collect the debts of William McQuiston assigned to me as attorney for Miss Watson sister to the late Andrew Watson, I hereby confirm Mr. Kirkland's appointment of of you as collector." ...
Witness: Wil. Kirkland CHARLES DUNCAN

Recorded November 1798.

- - -

C-122 Will in Archives. Dated 27 May 1798, proved Nov 1798.

JOHN PIPER daughter: Mary Brown

relationship not stated: Sarah Findley, Ruth Brown, Jemima Cabe
son: John Piper

"my daughters"mentioned, no names.

Sole executor: John Piper

Witnesses: Samuel Piper, Wm. Cabe, Stephen Scarlet.

- - -

C-124 Will in Archives. Dated 28 Oct 1798, proved Nov 1798.

THOMAS (x) SMITH wife: Sarah

son: Abraham

"3 daughters, Elizabeth, Mary and Hannah"

Executor: Alexander Boling.

Witnesses: Thos. Reding, John Whitaker.

- - -

C-126 Will in Archives. Dated 6 April 1798, proved Nov 1798.

GEORGE RIGGS wife: Sarah

sons: William Riggs, James Riggs

"my six daughters, namely Mary Newton, Jane Eakins, Sarah Montgomery, Ann Cell (?), Susannah Watson & Elizabeth Watson."

"my three daughters namely Margaret Riggs, Agnes Riggs, and Rachel Riggs."

grandson: James Woods

"my daughter Elizabeth's two eldest children", names not stated

Executors: wife Sarah and John Latta, Senior.

Witnesses: John Latta, Elizabeth (x) Latta, Eliz. Latta, Jr.

- - -

Book C, page 127 Will in Archives. Dated 30 Nov 1798,
proved Feb 1798.

DAVID CARSON

father: James Carson receives all estate.

"to my beloved son known by the name of Ecklon Woods" $100 if he lives to become 21 years old.

Sole executor: father James Carson.

Witnesses: Robert A. Carson, Moses Carson.

– – –

C-128 Will in Archives. Dated 7 Jan 1799, proved Feb 1799.

JOHN PATTON wife a legatee, name not stated.

sons: William, John

daus: Jean, Mary

Executor: Matthew Patton.

Witnesses: Joseph Clendennin, John McDaniel.

– – –

C-129 Will in Archives. Dated 4 Sept 1791, proved Feb 1799.

JONATHAN HILL wife: Rezzy

"my three younger children "

son: Elzy Hill.

Sole executrix: wife Rezzy.

Witnesses: John Hervey, John Starr.

– – –

C-131 Will in Archives. Dated 18 March 1793, proved
Feb 1799.

HENRY (x) PARISH wife: Mary

sons: Henry Parish, William Parish

dau: Tenah Sanders.

Executors: wife Mary, and Moses Cox.

Witnesses: Jno. Thompson, Joseph Woody,
Thomas McMullin, Robert Thompson.

– – –

Book C, page 132 Will in Archives. Dated 3 Sept 1798,
proved Feb 1799.

ABRAHAM MASSEY

wife: Gwen Massey

sons: Daniel, Enoch, Thomas, Abner.

daus: Anne, Mary, Lydia Herndon.

Executors: Abner Massey, Daniel Massey.

Witnesses: Bethier Bragg, John Bragg, James Trice.

- - -

C-134 Will in Archives. Dated 29 Dec 1795, proved May 1798.

JOHN (x) LOWRY

"to Thaipiah Henderson daughter of Margaret Henderson"...

Witnesses: John Daniely, James Ross, Thomas Phillips.

"N.B. I the said JOHN LOWRY further appoint the above said Margaret Cleft Executrix."

Mary Cleft qualified as Executrix.

- - -

C-135 Will in Archives. Dated --- proved May 1799.

WILLIAM DUNNAGAN, SENIOR   wife: Sarah

This is a very poorly worded will, relationships not clear.

son: William

sons ? Ashby Dunnagan, Sherod.

dau: Peggy.

He has married children, and unmarried daughters.

He mentions "the three boys" ... "all the girls".

Executors: Ashby Dunnagan, William Dunnagan.

Witnesses: Alex. McMullan
Winnifred (x) McMullan.

- - -

Book C, page 136 Will in Archives. Dated 2 Dec 1798,
proved May 1799.

BENJAMIN (x) CATE

wife: Mary to receive 1/6th part of estate.

He is to "be buried at the Reading House".

"5 sons viz: John Cate, Timothy Cate, Jesse Cate, William Cate and James Cate."

dau: Mary Cate, under age

"to Henry Hunt's oldest boy Elijah Hunt"...
"to David Nutt's oldest son John Nutt"...

Executors: brother Richard Cate, William Cain, merchant.

Witnesses: Alex'r McMullan, Edward Wortham,
William (x) Cate.

- - -

C-137 Will in Archives. Dated 30 April 1799, proved
May 1799.

SUSANNAH (x) DURHAM

sons: Matthew Durham, Lysias Durham, Mark Durham.

dau: Mary Mechum

"daughter Jane's children Susannah Piper and Sarah Piper".

Executor: Lysias Durham.

Witnesses: Alexander Hatch, Frances (x) Durham, Oney Hutson.

- - -

C- 139 Will in Archives. Dated 8 Dec 1793, proved May 1799.

JAMES (x) MORDAK wife: Elizabeth

son: James Mordak

daus: Ketren, Mary Behanon, Ann Mordak.

son: William Mordak

grandson: William Riggs.

Executors: wife Elizabeth and son William.

Witnesses: Wm. Bowls, Fanney (x) Bowls.

- - -

Book C, page 140 Will in Archives. Dated -- proved May / 1799.

JAMES NELSON

brothers: John, Abraham and Archer Nelson

sisters: Elizabeth Waldrop and Milly Meredith.

"to John Nelson Rencher and Sarah Rencher son and daughter of Jno. G. Rencher and Nancy Rencher."
"to James son of above"...

"to Sarah Nelson daughter of Archer"...
"Nelly Nelson daughter of Archer"...

sister: Nancy Rencher

"Lydia and Elizabeth Harold daughters of Edy Harold"...

"my honored father" . . .

Executors: George Johnston, Alexander Bowland.

Witnesses: James Strayhorn, Adam (x) Stowers.

\- - -

C-142 Will in Archives. Dated 1 Aug 1799, proved Aug 1799.

EDWARD GAINS wife: Susannah

sons: Thomas Gains, Joseph Gains, Francis Gains, Solomon Gains, Broadus Gains, Wilson Gains.

daus: Susannah Gains, Elizabeth Gains, Mary Gains, Nancy Gains.

Executors: wife, and son Thomas.

Witnesses: Isaac Rainey, Asa (x) Kent, Rob't (x) Pinkerton.

\- - -

C-144 Will in Archives. Dated 17 Oct 1796, proved Aug 1799.

JOSHUA WYATT wife: Elizabeth

sons: Joshua Wyatt, Frederick Wyatt get land bought of / Isaac Dorris

daus: Elizabeth Wyatt, Mary Simpson.

Executors: wife Elizabeth, sons Joshua and Frederick.

Witnesses: Will Wilkins, Mary (x) Wilkins.

\- - -

Book C, page 145 BILL OF SALE from JOHN TROUSDALE to Joseph Allison, for one negro. Dated 12 Aug 1797, proved Aug. 1799. Witness: John Campbell.

– – –

C-146 Will in Archives. Dated 17 April 1799, proved Aug 1799.

FRANCES THOMPSON

daughter Margaret "half of estate left me by my father Benjamin Thompson at the decease of my mother Sarah Thompson."

son: Anderson (under age) other half of estate.

Executors: brothers Robert and Richard Thompson.

Witnesses: Samuel Thompson, Caleb Harvey.

– – –

C-147 Will in Archives. Dated 9 Feb 1799, proved Aug 1799.

JOHN MOORE wife: Mary

4 oldest sons: James, John, Nathan, Alfred (a minor), get land on waters of Laughlens Creek.

daus: Mary, Martha, Sarah

Executors: wife Mary, son James.

Witnesses: James Boyle, Lem'l C. Jepson, Robert Moore.

– – –

C-149 Will in Archives. Dated 23 Jan 1798, proved Aug 1799.

MICHAEL HOLT wife: Jean

children by first wife...

son: Joseph Holt
daus: Margaret Powell, Elizabeth Smith

dau: Sarah Hardin
sons: Joshua Holt, Isaac Holt
daus: Mary Thompson, Catherine Holt
sons: Michael Holt, William Holt.

Executors: wife Jean, sons Isaac and Joshua.

Witnesses: J. Scott, Wm. Rainey, John Holt.

– – –

C-153 Deed in Archives, dated 19 Aug 1799, proved Nov 1799.

From HENRY COOK, SR to "my three children Ann Cook, Augustin Cook and Hamlin Cook" five negroes.
Witness: Hardress Hawkins.

- - -

C-153 Will in Archives. Dated 29 May 1781, proved Nov 1799.

JOHN ESTES of the Town of Hillsborough.

To wife Eliza "all my estate".

Executors: wife Eliza, Col. Robert Rowan of Cumberland Co.
Witnesses: Francis McKerall, A. Tatom.

- - -

C-154 Bond from THOMAS MULHOLLAND to DAVID ENGLISH on land joining lands of John Parks, James McCanlis and Thomas Person. Witnesses: Jno. Armstrong, J. Baldridge.

- - -

C-155 Will in Archives. Dated 17 Oct 1799, proved Nov 1799.

CONRAD MESSER SMITH

sons: Leonard, Stephen, Conrad, Phette.

daus: Elizabeth Cates, Mary "10 sh. to disinherit her".

Witnesses: Jno. McMullan, Alexander Turrentine.
Executor named by the Court, Samuel Turrentine.

- - -

C-156 Will in Archives. Dated 28 Jan 1799, proved Nov 1799.

ENOCH LEWIS

Bequests to: John Moore, Joseph Trice,
Abner Massey "land lying on Crooked Creek waters of New Hope", Gwen Massey-see note below, Thomas Massey, Enoch Massey, Ann Massey dau of Gwen Massey, Mary Gray wife of Thomas Gray, Daniel Massey, Lydia Herndon -see note below.

Executors: "trusty friends John Moore and Abner Massey".
Witnesses: Thomas Trice, Mann Patterson, James Trice.

Note by Ruth Herndon Shields. Notice that these are the same Massey heirs named in the will of Abraham Massey, C-132. Gwen Massey was the sister of ENOCH LEWIS. Lydia Massey married Benjamin Herndon, and thus became my great-great-great-grandmother. Her descendants are given in PART FOUR of THE HERNDON FAMILY OF VIRGINIA by Dr. John Goodwin Herndon.

Also in the same book are the descendants of George and his wife Sarah Herndon (see C-85) my great-great-great-grandparents in my father's maternal line.

- - -

C-157 Will in Archives. Dated 18 Oct 1799, proved Nov 1799.

GEORGE LOY wife: name not stated.

sons: John, Jacob, George, Henry, William

daughter: Sally
daus: Elizabeth Moser, Caty Albright,
Margaret Clapp, Rachel Albright.

Executors: wife, and son John.
Witnesses: Michael Holt, John Loy.

- - -

* * C-159 Will in Archives. Dated 5 May 1799, proved Nov 1799.

JOHN BARBEE wife: Sarah (she was Sarah Patterson)

Three sons Mark, Young, William, get 440 acres in Chatham County near Torrinton's (Farrington's ?) Mill.

Relationship not stated, but we know from deeds that they are children: Joseph, Patt/ (Martha), John, Sylve, Edie, have had their parts.
"rest of my children Sally, Elizabeth, Rosanna and Theina"..

granddaughter: Frances (under age) sirname not stated.

Executors: wife Sarah Barbee, brother Christopher Barbee.
Witnesses: Mark Patterson, James Rainey, Syntha Rhodes.

- - -

C-161 Will in Archives. Dated 16 July 1799, proved Feb 1800.

JOSEPH COURTNEY

wife: Hannah, receives land "lately belonging to my brother Wm. Courtney which he purchased from Wm. Courtney, Sr". And other lands bounded by lands of Gilbert Strayhorn. Bond on Robert Glenn of Person County.

father: William Courtney

Executors: Major Absolom Tatom, William Whitehead, Jr.
Witnesses: Robert Bell, Abner Tapp.

- - -

C-162 Bill of Release, dated 2 Nov 1799, proved Feb 1800.

From JOHN McRAE to Capt. JOHN CARRINGTON. He relinquishes all property involved except land sold to Col. William Hunt of Granville County.

Witnesses: Wm. Hunt, Duncan McRae, George Jimmason.

- - -

C-163 Will in Archives. Dated 7 March 1799, proved Feb 1800

DAVID COPELAND, SENIOR wife: Elizabeth

sons: David, Douglass, Hugh, John.

daughter: Elizabeth Nunn.

Executors: sons David and Douglass Copeland.
Witnesses: John Wood, Isaac Holden, John Holden.

– – –

C-164 Will in Archives. Dated 19 March 1799, proved Feb / 1800

WILLIAM WARD wife: Susannah

sons: Stephen, Anthony, William, Thomas, James

daughters: Susanna Pike, Sarah Clark,
Priscilla Ferree, Esther Wells.

son-in-law: Daniel Ferree land joining Adam Coble.

Executors: wife Susanna, son Stephen.
Witnesses: Jacob Marshill, Jesse Hinshaw, Jr.

– – –

C-166 Will in Archives. Dated 29 Nov 1799, proved Feb 1800.

BENJAMIN PEELOR

wife: Christiana "land known by the name of my Anthony place, as also Boney tract."

son: Samuel receives "lands bounded by lands of Jno. Holt, Thos. Browning and William Pickett."

sons: Pleasant, Allen, Abner.

daughters: Franky, Polly, Esther.

son: Benjamin receives "place where Thomas McFarland lives and Mark Browning's place."

Executors: wife Christiana, friend Jno. G. Rencher.
Witnesses: J.G.Rencher, Christian Peelor.

– – –

END OF BOOK C

D-1 Will in Archives. Dated 18 Jan 1794, proved May 1800.

HUGH WOODS wife: Mary Woods

sons: Joseph Elihugh, John

daus: Susanna wife of James Faucette,
Sarah, Elizabeth, Mary Ann

granddau: Milly, dau. of George Riggs & wife Rebecca.
grandson: Hugh, son " " " " " "

Executors: wife Mary, and son-in-law James Faucett.
Witnesses: David Turrentine, James Grimes, Hugh Montgomery.

- - -

D-3 Will in Archives. Dated 22 July 1799, proved May 1800.

FREDERICK MOSIER, SR.

sons: John, Frederick, Jacob, Michael,
Abraham, Phillip, Nicholas.

daus: Caty Kimbro, Barbara Huffman, Lizy Sharp,
Eve Sharp, Magdalene Bulcher.

Executors: son Phillip and son-in-law Peter Sharpe.
Witness: Richard Cochran.

- - -

Note by Ruth H. Shields. Here are a few genealogies I happen to know about, that have information about families of Caswell, Chatham, Orange and Wake Counties of N.C. Some of them are out of print, I give information on those I know about.

BROOKS and Kindred Families by Ida Brooks Kellam (1950)
Much information on Chatham and neighboring counties.

WILLIAMS and MURPHY Records by R. Murphy Williams (1949)

The ALSTONS and ALLSTONS of North and South Carolina
by Joseph A. Groves, M.D. First published in 1902.
Re-issued in 1957. Price $10.00 order from
The Seeman Printery, Inc., Durham, N.C.

HAPPY VALLEY, by Thomas Felix Hickerson of Chapel Hill,N.C.

The NEVILLE family of Orange County is given in
Historical Southern Families, Vol 2, by John B. Boddie.

HERNDONS of The American Revolution, Part Four
by John Goodwin Herndon has Caswell and Orange families.

Descendants of William and Sarah (Poe) Herndon
of Caroline County, Va. and Chatham County, N.C.
Price $10.00, order from Mrs. C. W. Shields, Chapel Hill.

D-4 Will in Archives. Dated 22 July 1799, proved May 1800.

DEBORAH TURRENTINE

sons: Samuel, Daniel, James, Alexander.

daus: Elizabeth Baldridge, Martha Baldridge, Jean Watson.

Executors: sons Samuel and Alexander Turrentine.
Witnesses: James Roark, William Roark, Thomas Wilson.

- - -

D-5 Will in Archives. Dated 9 April 1800, proved May 1800.

URIAH SPRINGER wife: Margaret Springer.

sons: George, Adam, David.

daus: Mary, Eve Porter.

Executors: Stephen Ward, John Whiter.
Witnesses: Ebenezer Doan, John Bullack.

- - -

D-6 Will in Archives. Dated 6 March, proved May 1800.

ROBERT TURNER wife: Mary Turner

son: James Turner. daus: Eliza Agnew, Jane, Sarah.

Executors: wife Mary Turner, and John Agnew.
Witnesses: Hardy Hurdle, Thomas Rippy, Joseph Rippy.

- - -

D-7 Will in Archives. Dated 20 June 1800, proved Nov 1800.

EDWARD TRICE daus: Ruth Higgins, Betsy.

sons: John, Harrison, William, George,
Andrew, Charles, Zecel (Ezekiel).

Executors: wife Tabitha, and William Trice and John Moore.
Witnesses: John Moore, Enah Massey, Martha Casselberry.

- - -

D-9 Will in Archives. Dated 25 Sept 1800, proved Nov 1800.

ELIZABETH STROUD

Leaves property to children to wit - " Margaret Douglass, John Stroud, the children of Fanny Howell, Mary Thrift, Sally King, Anderson Stroud, William Stroud, Elizabeth Rane, Marshall Stroud, Dixon Stroud."

Executors: John Stroud, Anderson Stroud.
Witnesses: John King, Nancy Hogan, Elizabeth King.

- - -

D-10 Will in Archives. Dated 25 Jan 1794, proved Nov 1800.

JAMES FRUIT or FRUTH wife: Grizel (spelled Girzel)

son: John

daus: Elinor, Jennett, Hannah, Nancy, Mary.

Executor: John Fruth
Witnesses: Moses Crawford, Ann Crawford.

- - -

D-11 Will in Archives. Dated 9 Nov 1800, proved Nov 1800.

ENOCH BRADLEY, Blacksmith. wife: Rachel Bradley.

sisters: Mary Jackson, Ann Hill.

To "brother Charles Bradley and his 3 sons, George, Enoch, and Josiah".
To " sister Mary's 6 children: Jain Morgan, Baldwin, Ruth, John, Sarah and Deborah."
To " sister Ann Hill's 3 children - Elizabeth, Hannah, and Samuel."
"To sister Elizabeth Collin's children, namely, John, Catherine, Enoch, Mary Brice, Elizabeth, Jain, Joseph, and Margaret."
"To Nathaniel Carter's son Enoch."
"To Robert Green's son Enoch."

Sole Executor: James Newlin.
Witnesses: George Maden, John Newlin.

- - -

D-12 Will in Archives. Dated 9 Sept 1799, proved Nov 1800.

JOHN MURRAY wife: Jean Murray

sons: Thomas, John, Joseph.
daus: Rebekah, Mary, Elizabeth, Jean, Lydia.

Executors: wife Jean, and friend Jesse Towel.
Witnesses: Nathan Dicks, Isaac Harvey, Jacob Marshall.

- - -

D-14 Will in Archives. Dated 13 Feb 1800, proved Aug 1800.

JAMES ANDERSON wife: Jennet

sons: John, William.

daus: Margaret, Elizabeth Clendenning, Jennet Achles. (Eccles)

Executors: Benjamin Roney, Samuel Mebane.
Witnesses: Benjamin Roney, Samuel Mebane.

- - -

D-15 Will in Archives. Dated 4 March 1800, proved Aug 1800.

JACOB BEASON sons: John, Frederick, Joseph.

daus: Margaret, Hannah, and Catherine.

Executors: brother Henry Beason, brother-in-law Aron Sharpe.
Witnesses: W. Mebane, Richard Bull, Thomas Dixon.

- - -

D-16 Will in Archives. Dated 20 June 1800, proved Aug 1800.

JOHN HARVEY wife: Mary

sons: David, Absolom, Jonathan. daus: Mary, Alice.

"To John Harvey son of Jonathan Harvey"

Executors: son David, "true friend Wm. Fausett".
Witnesses: Levi Hall, James Hall.

- - -

D-18 Will in Archives. Dated 4 Jan 1799, proved Aug 1800.

WILLIAM GALBREATH wife

sons: Walter, William (2nd son), John ("3rd and youngest").

daus: "Cathron (oldest) now MacKieney",
"Elizabeth, now Cunningham".
"Mary, now Dickson".
Ann.

sons-in-law: Francis McKieney, Matthew Cunningham.

grandsons: Wm. McKieney, Wm. Dickson, Wm. Galbreath.

No Executor named. Witnesses: Mac Cunningham, Wm. Kirk.

- - -

D-20 Will in Archives. Dated 12 Jan 1789, proved Aug 1800.

GEORGE LAWS, SENIOR.

sons: William, George. daus: Elizabeth, Sarah Harris.

grandson: George Laws, son of William Laws.
granddaus: Nancy Laws daughter of Wm. Laws.
Mary Laws daughter of George Laws.
Betty Edge
son-in-law: Jeremiah Edge.

Executors: sons George Laws and William Laws.
Witnesses: Joseph Guess, Wm. Madison, Richard Bohannon.

- - -

For 19 other wills recorded in Book D see A-212-

MARRIAGES FOUND IN ORANGE COUNTY , N.C. WILLS RECORDED IN WILL BOOKS A, B, AND C, WHICH DO NOT APPEAR IN THE ORANGE COUNTY MARRIAGE RECORDS.

Not all of these marriages took place in Orange County. All we can be certain of is that some time befors the will was written in which they are mentioned, such marriages took place.

The date of the will in which they are given, and the date of the will, follows the name of the bride and groom. The last name in the line is the name of the person making the will. Anyone wishing to obtain a copy of one of these wills can write to the CLERK OF COURT, Hillsboro, N.C.

These marriages are presented first with the name of the bride indexed. They are then given with the name of the groom alphebetized.

BRIDE	GROOM	DATE OF WILL	TESTATOR
Abercromby, Jenny	...... Mebane	May 1779	Rob. Abercromby
Allen, Margaret	James Mebane	Mar 1786	George Allen
Anderson, Jennett	..... Achles	Feb 1800	James Anderson
Bond found -Jean Anderson 5 March 1792 John Eccles			
Asten, ...	Peter Downey	Nov 1766	Wm. Asten
" , ...	Archibald McLeroy	" "	" "
Berry, Margaret	James Morrow	Apr 1761	Thomas Berry
Blake, Martha	Elisha Cain	Apr 1783	Benj. Blake
" , Rebecca	...... Mason	" "	" "
" , Sarah	...... Braswell	" "	" "
Bohannon, Frankey	...... Boyd	.. 1760	Duncan Bohannon
Bowling, Isabel	John Butler	Jan 1789	Jean Bowling
" , Susannah	.... Boswell	" "	" "
Bowls, Elizabeth	.... Murdak	1798	Thomas Bowls
Breazier, Eliz.	.... Jameson	May 1770	Thos. Breazier
" , Hannah	.... Teague	" "	" "
" , Sarah	.... Pyle	" "	" "
Breese, (or Bruce) Jannet	..... Robeson	Feb 1784	Thos. Breese
Carson, Alice	Wm. Clenny	Apr 1789	Alex. Carson
Bond found - Alce Cearson 26 August 1787 William Clenny			

BRIDE	GROOM	DATE OF WILL	TESTATOR
Christmas, Ann	..... Pickat(?)	Aug 1783	John Christmas
Coharon, Minny	Joseph Guy	Oct 1775	Alex Coharon
Comb, Betty	.... Mitchell	Aug 1791	Wm. Comb
" , Ellender	.... Trice	" "	" "
Cox, Catherine	Elizor Hunt	Jan 1767	William Cox
" , Marjory	Isaac Nichols	" "	" "
" , Martha	Wm. Terrell	" "	" "
" , Mary	James Lindley	" "	" "
" , Rebecca	..... Dixon	" "	" "
Craige, Abigail	..... Pasmore	Jan 1785	William Craige
" , Bathsheba	..... Crayton	" "	" "
" , Joanna	..... McMullin	" "	" "
" , Mary	..... Sheart	" "	" "
" , Ruth	..... Simmons	" "	" "
Davis, Ellenor	..... Darker	Jan 1792	Enoch Davis
Deal, Jean ?	John Hall	Feb 1775	John Hall
Dixson, Anne	Caleb Bailey	Dec 1769	Joseph Dixson
Donaldson, Margaret	Wm. Ray	Mar 1770	Rob. Donaldson
Dunweddee, Nancy	... Long	Nov 1794	Henry Dunweddee
" , Sarah	.... Gresham	" "	" "
Durham, Jane	.... Piper	Apr 1799	Susannah Durham
Foust, Barbara	.... Clap	Dec 1786	John Foust
" , Judith	.... Clap	" "	" "
Galbreath, Cathron	Francis McKieney	Jan 1799	Wm. Galbreath
Geer, Mary	.... Burnett	Aug 1769	John Geer
George, Mary	.... Hinsford	Feb 1770	Joseph George
" , Catherine	.... Riddle	" "	" "
Greason, Marg't	.... Lowe	Sep 1768	Isaac Greason
" , Unitie	.. Lionburger	" "	" "
Hadley, Mary	.... Piggott	Sep 1760	Joshua Hadley
" , Ruth	.... Marshal	" "	" "
" , Sarah	.... Ford	" "	" "

BRIDE	GROOM	DATE OF WILL	TESTATOR
Hall, Rebecca	..... Kell ?	Sep 1791	Jean Hall
Hanley, Ann	..... Linin ,or Tinin ?	Mar 1790	Daniel Hanley
Harrison, Anne	(John ?) Ware	May 1773	Andrew Harrison
" , Milley	(Wm ?) Moore	" "	" "
" , Lenora ?	..... Burks	Jun 1773	Nath. Harrison
" , Unity	..... Callahan	" "	" "
Hendricks, Mary	... Balander	Jul 1786	Peter Hendricks
Herndon, Eliz.	(Wm.) Cole	May 1796	George Herndon
" , Mary	.... Roberts	" "	" "
" , Maryanne	(Ezekiel) Trice	" "	" "
" , Ruth	.... Roberts	" "	" "
" , Sally	(Henry) McCoy	" "	" "
Holloway, Eliz.	.... Horner	Nov 1776	Rob. Holloway
" , Mary	.... Readen	" "	" "
Holt, Eliz.	.... Smith	Jan 1798	Michael Holt
" , Margaret	.... Powell	" "	" "

(Two of Michael Holt's daughters were married in Orange Co. Mary in 1787, Sarah in 1785.)

BRIDE	GROOM	DATE OF WILL	TESTATOR
Hooper, Eliz.	..... Walters or Watters	Apr 1793	Anne Hooper
Hulgan,Marg't	..... Neely	Jul 1794	Thomas Hulgan
Jamison, Mary	.... Parks	Feb 1793	Wm. Jamison
" , Margaret	.... Lindsey	" "	" "
Jenkins, Nancy	.. Fennell (Ferrell ?)	1790	John Jenkins
" , Patty	.. Allen	Feb 1790	" "
Johnston, ...	Chaldous ? Bailey	Jun 1789	Chas. Johnston
" , ...	Samuel Craig	Jun 1789	" "
" , ...	John Strayhorn	" "	" "
Jones, Seaney	John Shaw	March 1792, Deed, B188	
Larkin, Eliz.	.... Boring	Aug 1792	Alex. Larkin
" , Mary	Mordecai Moor	" "	" "
Laws, ...	Jeremiah Edge	Jan 1798	Geo. Laws, Sr.
" , Sarah	.... Harris	" "	" " "
Leak, Eliz.	James Terry	Feb 1784	Richard Leak
" , Mary	..... Moor	" "	" "
" , Jean	..... Harley	" "	" "
" , Susannah	..... Campbell	" "	" "
" , ...	..... Slatter	" "	" "

BRIDE	GROOM	DATE OF WILL,TESTATOR
Lindley, Deborah	.... Newlin	Mar 1780 Wm. Lindley
" , Elinor	.... Mauriss (Morris?)	" " "
" , Katherine	.... White	Mar " " "
" , Ruth	.... Hadley	" " " "
Lloyd, Mary	(John?) Hogan	Feb 1792 Thomas Lloyd
Lockhart, Cath.	..... Roads	Aug 1786 Cath. Lockhart
" , Elizabeth	.. Mucklejohn	" " " "
" , Jean	..... Holt	" " " "
" , Mary	..... Smith	" " " "
" , Sarah	James Parker	" " " "
Mace, Angel	John Dorris	May 1794 Power of Att'y
Mangum, Sally	.... Bobitt	Nov 1789 Arthur Mangum
Massey, Lydia	(Benj.) Herndon	1798 Abr. Massey
" , "	" "	Feb 1799 Enoch Lewis
McCallister, Marg't	Andrew Patent (or Poteat?)	Jul 1768 John McCallister
McCracken, Abigail	.... Davis	Aug 1795 Alex. McCracken
" , Hannah	.... Tinnen	" " " "
" , Mary	.... Andrew	" " " "
" , Ruth	.... Chamness	" " " "
Mebane, Ann	.... Morrow	Apr 1789 Alex. Mebane
" , Jennett	.... Anderson	" " " "
" , Margaret	.... Murdaugh	" " " "
" , Jennett	.... Stanford	Jul 1795 " "
Miles, or Meler, or Mills, Hannah	.... Slade	Mar 1766 Thomas Miles
" ,......	.... Pottiett ?	" " " "
Miller, Lydia	Joseph Ray	Mar 1793 George Miller
" , Mary	Zach. Dickey	" " " "
" , Sarah	John Ray	" " " "
Mordak, Mary	.... Behanon	Dec 1793 James Mordak

(Probably Mary Murdock who m 17 June 1786 Thos. Buchanon.)

BRIDE	GROOM	DATE OF WILL,TESTATOR
Morgan, Anne	..... Hart	Jan 1787 Sarah Morgan
" , Sarah	..... Yeargan	" " " "
Mosier, Barbara	..... Huffman	Apr 1796 Frederick Mosier
" , Caty	..... Kimbro	" " " "
" , Lizy	..... Sharp	" " " "
" , Magdalene	..... Bulcher	" " " "

(Their sister Eve m in Orange 31 Aug 1795 Peter Sharp.)

BRIDE	GROOM	DATE OF WILL, TESTATOR
Nelson, Jean	.... Scott	Mar 1790 Robert Nelson
Parish, Tenah	.... Sanders	Mar 1793 Henry Parish
Patterson, Jenny	.... Ward	Dec 1789 Nath. Patterson
" , Margaret	.... Swift	" " " "
" , "	.... Abbott	Jul 1790 John Patterson
Phillips, Hannah	.... Johnston	May 1798 Rainey Phillips
Pike, Ann	.... Hughes	Mar 1771 John Pike
" , Elizabeth	.... Stuart	" " " "
" , Rachel	.... Williams	" " " "
" , Ruth	.... Winner	" " " "
" , Sarah	.... Piggott	" " " "
" , Susannah	.... Lee	" " " "
Pryor, Elizabeth	.... Flournoy	Sep 1771 John Pryor
" , Leah	.... Perkins	" " " "
" , Lucy	.... Tapley	" " " "
" , Mildred	David Womack	" " " "
" , Rachel	.... Pope	" " " "
" , Rhode	William Stone	" " " "
Rea, ...	James Mordah (k?)	Oct 1769 William Rea
" , ...	John Mordah (k?)	" " " "
" , ...	Michael Robbins	" " " "
" , ...	Patrick Rutherford	" " "
Rice, Hannah	Jesse Towell	Jan 1783 John Rice
Riggs, Ann	.... Cell (?)	Apr 1798 George Riggs
" , Eliz.	.... Watson	" " " "
" , Jane	.... Eakins	" " " "
" , Mary	.... Newton	" " " "
" , Mary	Barnaba Grymes	Mar 1776 William Riggs
Riley, Mary	.... Donaldson	July 1791 John Riley
Robbinson, Esthy	.... Thompson	Apr 1774 Alex. Robbinson
" , Ellenor	John Ceasey	" " " "
Robertson, Mary	.... Lindsay	Apr 1795 Ath. Robertson
Robison, Mary	.... Lindsay , deed,	May 1785 Athanasius Robison
Ross, Jane	.... Smith	Dec 1792 James Ross
" , Levinia	(John?) Minnis	" " " "
Sanders, Fanny	Wm. Sanders,Sr	Feb 1776 James Sanders Sr
" , Sarah	William Trigg	" " " " "
" , Susannah	Robert Terry	" " " " "

BRIDE	GROOM	DATE OF WILL	TESTATOR
Scoby, Margaret	.... Tait	Oct 1782	Matthew Scoby
Seares, Mary	.... Surls	Jul 1788	Thomas Seares
Smith, Elizabeth	.... Cates	Oct 1799	Conrod M. Smith
Smothers, Eliz.	.... Pickard	Aug 1778	Thomas Smothers
" , Rebecca	.... Sumner	" "	" "
Springer, Eve	.... Porter	Apr 1800	Uriah Springer
Stantefer,Casander	... Hendon	Aug 1793	Israel Stantefer
" , Rossaner	..... Rhodes	" "	" "
" , Sarah	..... Rhoades	" "	" "

(Ruth Stantefer m in Orange 14 Aug 1781 William Turner.)

BRIDE	GROOM	DATE OF WILL	TESTATOR
Stanford, ... ?	..... King ?	Jun 1789	Anthony Stanford
Stroud, Margaret	..... Douglass	Aug 1786	Wm. Stroud
" , Mary	..... Thrift	" "	" "
" , Salley	..... King	" "	" "

These 2 Stroud marriages also found in will of Elizabeth Stroud, Jan 1794.

BRIDE	GROOM	DATE OF WILL	TESTATOR
Thomas, Ann	..... Wilks	Mar 1769	Owen Thomas
" , Mary	.... Hart, or Hard	" "	"
Thompson, Eliz	.... Hadley	Jul 1794	James Thompson
" , Sarah	Owen Lindley	" "	" "
Tolby or Talley, Elizabeth	(Richard?) Rhodes	Aug 1791	Samuel Tolby ?
" , Mary	(James?) Kennady	" "	" "
" , Milly	..... Whitaker	" "	" "
Turner, Eliza	(John ?) Agnew	Mar 1800	Robert Turner
Turrentine, Eliz	.. Baldridge	Jul 1799	Deb. Turrentine
" , Martha	.... Baldridge	" "	" "
" , Jean	.... Watson	" "	" "
Wade, Eliz.	.... Talley	Jan 1757	Joseph Wade
" , Lucy	Joseph Powel	" "	" "
" , Mary	.... Strawther	" "	" "
" , Sarah	.... Fountain	" "	" "
" , Susannah	.... Hart	" "	" "
Waggoner, Eliz.	.... Johns	Jul 1784	Geo Waggoner
" , Susannah	.... Smith	" "	" "
Walker, Ann	.... Cimball	Dec 1791	James Walker
" , Elizabeth	.... Horton	" "	" "
" , Lydia	.... Wright	" "	" "
" , Sarah	.... Colbert	" "	" "

BRIDE	GROOM	DATE OF WILL, TESTATOR
Watson, Helen	William Reed	Dec 1776 James Watson
Wood, Elizabeth	.... Acory	May 1786 Thomas Wood
" , Lydia	.... Good	" " " "
" , Meley	.... Gwin	" " " "
" , Sarah	.... Forrest	" " " "
" , Theaney	.... Wallace	" " " "
Woods, Rebecca	George Riggs	Jan 1794 Hugh Woods
" , Susanna	James Faucette	" " " "
Wyatt, Mary	..... Simpson	Oct 1796 Joshua Wyatt

GROOM,	BRIDE	DATE OF WILL, TESTATOR
Abbott, ...	Margaret Patterson	Jul 1790 John Patterson
Achles, ...	Jennett Anderson	Feb 1800 James Anderson
Acory, ...	Elizabeth Wood	May 1786 Thomas Wood
Agnew, John (?)	Eliza Turner	Mar 1800 Robert Turner
Allen, ...	Patty Jenkins	Feb 1790 John Jenkins
Anderson, ...	Jennett Mebane	Apr 1789 Alex. Mebane
Andrew, ...	Mary McCracken	Aug 1795 Alex. McCracken
Bailey, Caleb	Anne Dixson	Dec 1769 Joseph Dixson
" , Chaldous ?	..... Johnston	Jun 1789 Chas. Johnston
Balander, ...	Mary Hendricks	Jul 1786 Peter Hendricks
Baldridge, ...	Eliz. Turrentine	Jul 1799 Deb. Turrentine
" , ...	Martha Turrentine	" " " "
Behanon, ...	Mary Mordak	Dec 1793 James Mordak
(Probably Thomas	Buchanan who m 17	June 1786 Mary Murdock.)
Bobitt, ...	Sally Mangum	Nov 1789 Arthur Mangum
Boring, ...	Elizabeth Larkin	Aug 1772 Alex. Larkin
Boswell, ...	Susannah Bowling	Jan 1789 Jean Bowling
Boyd, ...	Frankey Bohannon	1760 Duncan Bohannon
Braswell, ...	Sarah Blake	Apr 1783 Benj. Blake
Bulcher, ...	Magdalene Mosier	Apr 1796 Fred. Mosier

GROOM	BRIDE	DATE OF WILL, TESTATOR
Burks, ...	Lenora? Harris	Jun 1773 Nath. Harris
Burnett, ...	Mary Geer	Aug 1769 John Geer
Butler, John	Isabel Bowling	Jan 1789 Jean Bowling
Cain, Elisha	Martha Blake	Apr 1783 Benj Blake
Callahan, ...	Unitie Harris	Jun 1773 Nath. Harris
Campbell, ...	Susannah Leak	Feb 1784 Richard Leak
Cates, ...	Elizabeth Smith	Oct 1799 Conrod M. Smith
Ceasey, John	Ellenor Robbinson	Apr 1774 Alex. Robbinson
Cell ?, ...	Ann Riggs	Apr 1798 George Riggs
Chamness, ...	Ruth McCracken	Aug 1795 Alex. McCracken
Cimboll, ... (Kimball ?)	Ann Walker	Dec 1791 James Walker
Clap, ...	Barbara Foust	Dec 1786 John Foust
" , ...	Judith Foust	" " " "
Clenny, William	Alice Carson	Apr 1789 Alex. Carson
Colbert, ...	Sarah Walker	Dec 1791 James Walker
Cole, (Wm.)	Eliz. Herndon	May 1796 George Herndon
Craig, Samuel	.... Johnston	Jun 1789 Chas. Johnston
Crayton, ...	Bathsheba Craige	Jan 1785 William Craige
Darker, ...	Ellenor Davis	Jan 1792 Enoch Davis
Darris, John	Angel Mace	May 1794 deed, Will Bk. C
Davis, ...	Abigail McCracken	Aug 1795 Alex. McCracken
Dickey, Zach.	Mary Miller	Mar 1793 George Miller
Dixon, ...	Rebecca Cox	Jan 1767 William Cox
Donaldson, ...	Mary Riley	Jul 1791 John Riley
Douglass, ...	Margaret Stroud	Aug 1786 Wm. Stroud Jan 1794 Eliz. Stroud
Downey, Peter	..... Asten	Nov 1766 William Asten
Eakins, ...	Jane Riggs	Apr 1798 George Riggs

GROOM	BRIDE	DATE OF WILL,	TESTATOR
Edge, Jeremiah	.... Laws	Jan 1798	George Laws,Sr.
Faucette, James	Susanna Woods	Jan 1794	Hugh Woods
Fennell, ... (or Ferrell)	Nancy Jenkins	Feb 1790	John Jenkins
Flournoy, ..	Elizabeth Piper	Sep 1771	John Piper
Ford, ...	Sarah Hadley	Sep 1760	Joshua Hadley
Forrest, ...	Sarah Wood	May 1786	Thomas Wood
Fountain, ...	Sarah Wade	Jan 1757	Joseph Wade
Good, ...	Lydia Wood	May 1786	Thomas Wood
Gresham, ...	Sarah Dunweddeed	Nov 1794	Henry Dunweddee
Grymes, Bannaba	Mary Riggs	Mar 1776	William Riggs
Guy, Joseph	Minny Coharon	Oct 1775	Alex. Coharon
Gwin, ...	Meley Wood	May 1786	Thomas Wood
Hadley, ...	Ruth Lindley	Mar 1780	Wm. Lindley
" , ...	Eliz. Thompson	Jul 1794	Jas. Thompson
Hall, John	Jean ? Deal	Feb 1775	John Hall
Harley, ...	Jean Leak	Feb 1784	Richard Leak
Harris, ...	Sarah Laws	Jan 1798	Geo. Laws Sr.
Hart or Hard,.	Mary Thomas	Mar 1769	Owen Thomas
Hart, ...	Susannah Wade	Jan 1757	Joseph Wade
Hendon, ...	Casander Stantefer	Aug 1793	Israel Stantefer
Herndon, Benj.	Lydia Massey	[illegible] 1798	Abr. Massey
" "	" "	Feb 1799	Enoch Lewis
Hinsford, ...	Mary George	Feb 1770	Joseph George
Holt, ...	Jean Lockhart	Aug 1786	Cath. Lockhart
Horn, James	Margery ...	Apr 1792	Thos. Horn,Sr.
Horner, ...	Eliz. Holloway	Nov 1776	Rob. Holloway
Horton, ...	Eliz. Walker	Dec 1791	James Walker

GROOM	BRIDE	DATE OF WILL, TESTATOR
Hart, ...	Ann Morgan	Jan 1787 Sarah Morgan
Huffman, ...	Barbara Mosier	Apr 1796 Fred. Mosier
Hughes, ...	Ann Pike	Mar 1771 John Pike
Hunt, Elizor	Catherine Cox	Jan 1767 William Cox
Jameson, ...	Eliz. Breazier	May 1770 Thos. Breazier
Johns, ...	Eliz. Waggoner	Jul 1784 Geo. Waggoner
Johnston, ...	Hannah Phillips	May 1798 Rainey Phillips
Kell, ...	Rebecca Hall	Sep 1791 Jean Hall
Kennady, (James?)	Mary Tolby or Talley	Aug 1791 Samuel Tolby ?
Kimbro, ...	Caty Mosier	Apr 1796 Fred. Mosier
King, ...	.... Stanford	Jun 1789 Anthony Stanford
" , ...	Salley Stroud	Aug 1786 Wm. Stroud
"	" "	Jan 1794 Eliz. Stroud
Lee, ...	Susannah Pike	Mar 1771 John Pike
Lindley, James	Mary Cox	Jan 1767 William Cox
" , Owen	Sarah Thompson	Jul 1794 Jas Thompson
Lindsay, ...	Mary Robertson	Apr 1795 Ath. Robertson
" , ...	Mary Robison, deed, May 1785, Athanasuis / Robison.	
Lindsay, ...	Margaret Jamison	Feb 1793 Wm. Jamison
Linin, .. (or Tinin ?)	Ann Hanley	Mar 1790 Daniel Hanley
Lionburger, ..	Unitie Greason	Sep 1768 Isaac Greason
Long, ..	Nancy Dunweddee	Nov 1794 Henry Dunweddee
Lowe, ...	Margaret Greason	Sep 1768 Isaac Greason
Marshel, ...	Ruth Hadley	Sep 1760 Joshua Hadley
Mason, ...	Rebecca Blake	Apr 1783 Benj. Blake
Mauriss, ... (Morris ?)	Elinor Lindley	Mar 1780 Wm. Lindley
McCoy, (Henry)	Sally Herndon	May 1796 George Herndon

GROOM	BRIDE	DATE OF WILL,	TESTATOR
McKieney, Francis	Catherine Galbreath	Jan 1799	Wm. Galbreath
McLeroy, Archibald	...... Asten	Nov 1766	Wm. Asten
McMullin, ...	Joanna Craige	Jan 1785	Wm. Craige
Mebane, ...	Jenny Abercromby	May 1779	R. Abercromby
" , James	Margaret Allen	Mar 1786	George Allen.
Minnis, John ?	Levinia Ross	Dec 1792	James Ross
Mitchell, ...	Betty Comb	Aug 1791	Wm. Comb
Moor, Mordecai	Mary Larkin	Aug 1772	Alex. Larkin
" , ...	Mary Leak	Feb 1784	Richard Leak
Moore, (Wm.?)	Milley Harrison	May 1773	And. Harrison
Mordah (Murdock ?) James	...... Rea	Oct 1769	Wm. Rea
John	...... Rea	" "	" "
Morrow, James	Margaret Berry	Apr 1761	Thomas Berry
" , ...	Ann Mebane	Apr 1789	Alex. Mebane
Mucklejohn, ..	Eliz. Lockhart	Aug 1786	Cath. Lock-/hart.
Murdak, ...	Eliz. Bowls	1798	Thomas Bowls
Murdaugh, ...	Margaret Mebane	Apr 1789	Alex. Mebane
Neely, ...	Margaret Hulgan	Jul 1794	Thomas Hulgan
Newlin, ...	Deborah Lindley	Mar 1780	Wm. Lindley
Newton, ...	Mary Riggs	Apr 1798	George Riggs
Nicholas, Isaac	Marjory Cox	Jan 1767	Wm. Cox
Parker, James	Sarah Lockhart	Aug 1786	C. Lockhart
Parks, ...	Mary Jamison	Feb 1793	Wm. Jamison
Pasmore, ...	Abigail Craige	Jan 1785	Wm. Craige
Patent (Poteat?), Andrew	Marg't McCallister	Jul 1768	John McC.
Perkins, ...	Leah Pryor	Sep 1771	John Pryor
Pickard, ...	Eliz. Smothers	Aug 1778	Th. Smothers
Pickat, ... (Pickett ?)	Ann Christmas	Aug 1783	J. Christmas

GROOM	BRIDE	DATE OF WILL, TESTATOR
Piggott, ...	Mary Hadley	Sep 1760 Joshua Hadley
" , ...	Sarah Pike	Mar 1771 John Pike
Piper, ...	Jane Durham	Apr 1799 Susannah Durham
Pope, ...	Rachel Pryor	Sep 1771 John Pryor
Porter, ...	Eve Springer	Apr 1800 Uriah Springer
Pottiett, ...	... Miles, Meler, or Mills	Mar 1766 Thos. Miles ?
Powel, Joseph	Lucy Wade	Jan 1757 Joseph Wade
Powell, ...	Margaret Holt	Jan 1798 Michael Holt
Pyle, ...	Sarah Breazier	May 1770 Thos. Breazier
Ray, John	Sarah Miller	Mar 1793 George Miller
" , Joseph	Lydia Miller	" " " "
" , William	Marg't Donaldson	Mar 1770 Rob. Donaldson
Readen, ...	Mary Holloway	Nov 1776 Rob. Holloway
Reed, William	Helen Watson	Dec 1776 James Watson
Rhoades, ...	Sarah Stantefer	Aug 1793 Israel Stantefer
Rhodes, (Richard?)	Elizabeth Tolby (or Talley)	Aug 1791 Samuel Tolby ?
Rhodes, ... /	Rossaner Stantefer	Aug 1793 I. Stantefer
Riddle, ...	Catherine George	Feb 1770 Joseph George
Riggs, George	Rebecca Woods	Jan 1794 Hugh Woods
Roads, ...	Cath. Lockhart	Aug 1786 Cath. Lockhart
Robbins, Michael	.... Rea	Oct 1769 William Rea
Roberts, ...	Mary Herndon	May 1786 George Herndon
" , ...	Ruth Herndon	" " " "
Robeson, ...	Janet Breese (or Bruce)	Feb 1784 Thos. Breese
Rutherford, Pat.	..... Rea	Oct 1769 William Rea
Sanders, Wm. Sr.	Fanny Sanders	Feb 1776 James Sanders
" , ...	Tenah Parish	Mar 1793 Henry Parish
Scott, ...	Jean Nelson	Mar 1790 Robert Nelson
Sharp, ...	Lizy Mosier	Apr 1796 Fred. Mosier

GROOM	BRIDE	DATE OF WILL, TESTATOR
Shaw, John	Seaney Jones	Mar 1792 deed
Sheart, ...	Mary Craige	Jan 1785 Wm. Craige
Simmons, ..	Ruth Craige	" " " "
Simpson, ...	Mary Wyatt	Oct 1796 Joshua Wyatt
Slade, ...	Hannah Miles, (or Meler, Mills)	Mar 1766 Thos. Miles ?
Slatter, ...	...... Leak	Feb 1784 Richard Leak
Smith, ...	Eliz. Holt	Jan 1798 Michael Holt
" , ...	Mary Lockhart	Aug 1786 Cath. Lockhart
" , ...	Jane Ross	Dec 1792 James Ross
" , ...	Sus. Waggoner	Jul 1784 Geo. Waggoner
Stone, William	Rhode Pryor	Sep 1771 John Pryor
Strawther, ...	Mary Wade	Jan 1757 Joseph Wade
Strayhorn, John	.... Johnston	Jun 1789 Chas. Johnston
Stuart, ...	Elizabeth Pike	Mar 1771 John Pike
Sumner, ...	Rebecca Smothers	Aug 1778 Thos. Smothers
Surls, ...	Mary Seares	Jul 1788 Thomas Seares
Swift, ...	Marg't Patterson	Dec 1789 Nath. Patterson
Tait, ...	Margaret Scoby	Oct 1782 Matthew Scoby
Talley, ...	Elizabeth Wade	Jan 1757 Joseph Wade
Tapley, ...	Lucy Pryor	Sep 1771 John Pryor
Teague, ...	Hannah Breazier	May 1770 Thomas Breazier
Terrell, Wm.	Martha Cox	Jan 1767 William Cox
Terry, James	Elizabeth Leak	Feb 1784 Richard Leak
" , Robert	Sus. Sanders	Feb 1776 James Sanders
Thompson, ...	Esthy Robbinson	Apr 1774 Alex. Robbinson
Thrift, ...	Mary Stroud	Aug 1786 Wm. Stroud
"	" "	Jan 1794 Eliz. Stroud
Tinnen, ...	Hannah McCracken	Aug 1795 Alex. McCracken
Trice, ...	Ellender Comb	Aug 1791 William Comb
" , (Ezekiel)	Maryanne Herndon	May 1796 George Herndon

GROOM	BRIDE	DATE OF WILL	TESTATOR
Trigg, William	Sarah Sanders	Feb 1776	James Sanders
Towel, Jesse	Hannah Rice	Jan 1783	John Rice
Wallace, ...	Theaney Wood	May 1786	Thomas Wood
Walters, ...	Elizabeth Hooper	1795 Power of Attorney	
Watters, ...	" "	Apr 1793	Anne Hooper
Walton, Nath.	Mary ...	Jun 1786	Mary Walton
Ward, ...	Jenny Patterson	Dec 1789	Nath. Patterson
Ware, (John ?)	Anne Harrison	May 1773	Andrew Harrison
Watson, ...	Elizabeth Riggs	Apr 1798	George Riggs
" , ...	Jean Turrentine	Jul 1799	Deb. Turrentine
Whitaker, ...	Milly Tolby (or Talley)	Aug 1791	Samuel Tolby ?
White, (Wm.)	Katherine Lindley	Mar 1780	Wm. Lindley
Wilks, ...	Ann Thomas	Mar 1769	Owen Thomas
Williams, ...	Rachel Pike	Mar 1771	John Pike
Winner, ...	Ruth Pike	Mar 1771	" "
Womack, David	Mildred Pryor	Sep 1771	John Pryor
Wright, ...	Lydia Walker	Dec 1791	James Walker
Yeargan, ...	Sarah Morgan	Jan 1787	Sarah Morgan

- - - - - - - - - - - - - - - -

SUGGESTION : One way to prove where a marriage took place is to learn where the person who made the will lived at the probable time of the marriage.

Land Grants and deeds are the best source of information. Orange County was formed in 1752 almost entirely from Granville. Granville was formed from Bertie in 1746. Bertie was formed from Chowan in 1722. Thus a person who settled in Orange at the time of its earliest formation, may have a grant or deed in either or all of those counties.

The Secretary of State has a wonderful record of all the North Carolina Land Grants in his office at Raleigh, N.C.

- - - - -

INDEX

See page 28

INDEX

INDEX

INDEX

INDEX

INDEX

INDEX

INDEX

INDEX

INDEX

INDEX

INDEX

INDEX

INDEX

INDEX

INDEX

INDEX

INDEX

INDEX

INDEX

INDEX

INDEX

- - - - - - -

ABSTRACTS OF WILLS

RECORDED IN

ORANGE COUNTY NORTH CAROLINA

1800 - 1850

Compiled by

Ruth Herndon Shields

TABLE OF CONTENTS

- - - - - - - - - - -

ORANGE COUNTY was formed in 1752, largely from Granville, partly from Bladen and Johnston Counties.
From ORANGE COUNTY were taken:
all of Chatham, Guilford and Wake in 1771
all of Caswell in 1777 (Person was formed from Caswell 1792)
all of Alamance in 1849, part of Durham in 1881.
The eastern halves of Randolph and Rockingham Counties were formed from that part of Guilford which was taken from ORANGE.

- - - - - - - - - - -

FOREWORD

Abstracting the wills of Orange County to 1850 has been a project of the Genealogical Records Committee of Davie Poplar Chapter NSDAR for the last four years. Work was begun in 1955 with Mrs. Robert Lester as chairman, and Mrs. B.B.Lane as our Regent. Knowing how valuable these abctracts would be to the thousands of descendants of Orange County pioneers, I undertook publication of them. The volume for 1752-1800 was completed in 1957.

For the sake of historical accuracy, whenever a will was signed with a "mark", I have noted the fact. Some of the committee did not do this. I personally abstracted all of Book D, Book E from page 251 to the end, and parts of Book F. Writing of some of the clerks was poor, and their capital letters impossible to decipher. Dozens of the abstracts have been checked with the original wills in the Archives.

I was amazed to find that with the exception of nine wills (see page 221) every will listed in this book is preserved in the Archives in Raleigh. Photostats can be ordered through the Archives at about $1 per page.

My grateful thanks to each and every member of the committee who labored so long and patiently on this project, but most of all to Mrs. Lester and Mrs. Lane who were untiringly faithful.

Since marriage bonds were not required to be returned until about 1782, I listed all marriages mentioned in the wills up to 1820. This list was ckecked against the collected marriage bonds of Orange County, and seventy were found that are not listed in the collected bonds. They will be found on page 268. Many of these marriages may have taken place in other counties.

Ruth Herndon Shields (Mrs. C.W.) Chairman
Genealogical Records Committee, Davie Poplar Chapter, NSDAR
Chapel Hill, N.C.
November 17, 1958

ABSTRACTS OF WILLS, ORANGE COUNTY, N. C. 1800 - 1850

Book D, page 22 Will in Archives. Dated 7 Jan 1800,
proved Aug 1800

SHERID DUNNAGAN

Wife: Dice gets whole estate "to support the children until the youngest child is 21 years of age"

Sons: William, Sherid

"Two daughters Amelia and Mary"

Executors: wife, and her brother George Carington.
Witnesses: George Newton, Edward Worsham

- - -

D-23 Will in Archives. Dated 4 Nov 1800, proved Feb 1801.

BENJAMIN (x) FORRESTER Wife: Sarah

Sons: Ila gets land after mother's death
Edmund,(10 shillings), Josiah, Benjamin

Daus: Jemimah Woods wife of Harris Woods
Drucilla Dosset wife of William Dorset
Nancy, Betsy, Milly

Executors are to sell 50 acres of land joining George Carington and John Gains.

Executors: "friends James Woods and Joseph Woods".
Witnesses: Walter Alves, William Bennehan.

- - -

D-24 Paper dated 26 Feb 1801. THOMAS BROOKS of the Town of Hillsborough revokes a Power of Attorney made in the year 1784 to his son And'w Brooks, which was never used.

- - -

D-25 Will in Archives. Dated 17 June 1790, proved Feb 1801.

WILLIAM CLENDENNIN Wife: Mary

Sons: Younger, William, John, Joseph

Daus: Polly, Rebecca, Ann, Fanny, Jenny

"My niece Ann, daughter of John Clendenning deceased"

Sons: James and Fisher get 200 acres of land.

"Two youngest sons William and John the home plantation after they arrive at lawful age" They are to be bound out to trades.

Executors: John Thompson, Esquire, and Andrew Murdock.
Witnesses: James Johnston, John Johnston.

- - -

D-25 Will in Archives. Dated 6 May 1800, proved Feb 1801

JOHN MOORE Wife: Mary Moore

Legacies " to each of my children as they shall arrive at lawful age." (Their names and number not stated.)

Executors: "brother James Moore and my trusty friend James Martin and my beloved wife Mary Moore."

Witnesses: James Lindsey, John Martin.

- - -

D-28 Will in Archives. Dated 10 Sept 1800, proved Feb 1801.

JOHN KELL Wife: Rebeckah

"My children" mentioned, but number not stated.

"My boys Thomas and John" are to be bound to a trade .

Executors: Robert Hall and William Kell.
Witnesses: Jno. Riggs, Rachel (x) Millan.

- - -

D-29 Power of Attorney dated 16 Feb 1801, proved Feb 1801. from JOSEPH HART of Caswell County, N.C. "to my trusty friend JAMES MOORE, Cap't" of Orange County, N.C., to collect debts and accounts in Orange and Rockingham Counties, N.C. Witnesses: H. Brown, John Murray.

- - -

D-30 Will in Archives. Dated 10 July 1800, proved Feb / 1801.

KATY (x) BREWER

"My four children, to wit: Candice, Charlotte, William and Polly."

Exec's: "Trusty friends Samuel Carothers and Wm. Forsythe."
Witnesses: Wm. Strowd, James (x) Lloyd, Eliza. (x) Lloyd.

- - -

D-30 Will in Archives. Dated 25 Dec 1800, proved May 1801.

JOHN GANT Wife: Ann ,"all the land on the S. Side of Haw River", etc.

Sons: William Gant, John Gant,
James Gant, Isam Gant, Zacharia

Daus: Keziah Rippey, Sarah Gant, Mary Riggins,
Hannah Boish ?

Executors: wife Ann, and son Isom Gant.
Witnesses: W. Mebane, W.B.? Mebane.

- - -

D 33 Will dated 20 Feb 1801, proved May Court 1801.

WILLIAM EVANS wife: Margaret Evans

"my two sons Samuel and William Evans all my land"

daus: Catey, Betsey, Susanna Evans.
"All my furniture to be equally divided among my three girls"

Samuel Davis (no relationship stated)

Executors: "My son Samuel Evans and Margaret Evans."
Witnesses: Almon Mullan,Nathaniel Carrington.

- - -

D 34 Will dated 23 Feb 1801, proved May Court 1801.

BAXTER KING wife: Elenner King

daus: Mary, Hannah King, Nancy King, Dolley King, Elizabeth King. "until my young daughter comes of age"

sons: John, Nathaniel (he is to have "proper schooling")

"Mosby tract of land to be rented out"

Executors: wife Elinor and son John King.
Witnesses: John Adams, William Hogan, Charles King.

- - -

D 36 Will dated 1 March 1801, proved May Court 1801.

EDWARD HARRIS wife: Mary to have "plantation on Mountain Creek", etc.

sons: Sterling & Edward

daus: Mary & Elizabeth Harris, Delila

sons: Nathaniel and Willie all "my land and plantation lying upon Eno River" .. when they arrive at age 21. Willie (also spelled Wylley) is the youngest.

Executors: wife Mary Harris and friend James Walker.
Witnesses: Jesse Trice, James Moore, James Carrington, Jr.

- - -

D 38 Will dated 14 Jan 1800, proved May Court 1801.

SAMUEL (x) TURRENTINE wife: Mary

"Two youngest sons Absolom and Daniel" (they are under 21)

son: John "100 acres joining the lands of George Wilson"

son: Samuel "land lying on the east side of Buffalo Creek joining the lands of James Watson Senior."

- continued -

son: James "100 acres ... turning from Roark's corner west to
Jane Jamison's line .... to James Roark's."

daus: Lydia & Susanna (they are unmarried)
Sarah ...."and her son is to have 1 year's schooling"

"my Jane $10 " (no word omitted)

daus: Mary, Deborah and Martha $4 each

Executors: Wife, and son Samuel
Witnesses: John McMullen, Jno. Alston.

Codicil about burying ground dated 6 May 1801. Same witnesses.

- - -

D 40 Will dated 1 Nov 1800, proved May Court 1801.

JAMES GUTHRIE wife: Elizabeth

sons: James Guthrie, Robert Guthrie

"My four oldest daughters Ann, Mary, Margaret & Martha"

daus: Jean Guthrie, youngest Elizabeth Guthrie

grandsons: James & Robert Guthrie, sons of James Guthrie

grandsons: James Shanon, James Barnett, James Forrest,
James Mimenemy ? (McManamy ?)

Executors: "trusty friend David Mitchell and Isaac Raney".
Witnesses: Wm. McManamy, Jno. Sanders.

- - -

D 42 Will dated 25 March 1801, proved May Court 1801.

JOHN JOHNS wife: Elizabeth Johns

sons: Henry Johns, Thomas Johns

son-in-law: Thomas William Grice

"To my Kitty ? Johns" (no word omitted)

daus: Susannah, Elizabeth Johns, Patsey Johns

Executors: "Trusty friend John McCollock Sr and
James Allison."
Witnesses: Wm. Keeling, Wm. (x) Whitfield, George (x) Welsh.

- - -

D 43 Will dated 4 Dec 1800, proved May Court 1801.

WILLIAM FREEMAN

wife: Sarah Freeman "to raise and maintain my children"

son: George Freemen 100 acres "joining the land of David ...... and Thomas Dixon"

dau: Polly Trotman

sons: John Freeman and William Freeman

After wife's death her share of the estate to be divided equally among "my chilren Christian Freeman, Nancy Freeman, John Freeman, Betsey Freeman, Sally Freeman & Wm. Freeman."

Executors: wife Sarah Freeman, and George Freeman.
Witnesses: Hardy Hurdle, Joseph Terrill.

- - -

D 34 Will dated 19 Feb 1801, proved May Court 1801.

GEORGE NEWTON wife: Mary

"My two youngest children Sarah and John, and my daughter Lette's child Elizabeth to be schooled".

He speaks of "my children under age".

After wife's death property to be divided "between all my children and grandchild Elizabeth viz: Lette Newton, William Newton, James Newton, Henry Newton, Isaac Newton, George Newton, Robert Newton, Sarah Newton, John Newton, Elizabeth Newton daughter of Lette."

Executors: wife Mary and two sons Henry and George Newton.
Witnesses: James Latta,Jr., Henry Newton.

- - -

D 46 Will dated 6 June 1800, proved May Court 1801.

JOHN ROBERTSON wife a legatee, name not stated

sons: Hugh Robertson, Andrew Robertson

grandsons: John, Zachrias & Andrew Robertson

daus: Margaret Wilson, Elenor Johnson, Rebekka Guin

granddaus: Molly Robertson, Marget Robertson, Elenor Robertson, daughters of Andrew

Executors: wife, and Hugh Robertson
Witnesses: John Douglass, Robert Hatrick.

- - -

D 47A Will dated 20 April 1801, proved August Court 1801.

LEWIS (x) BREWER "weak in body" wife: Patience (one third)

daughter Nancy other 2/3 at her arrival at lawful age.

Executors: Nathan Dicks and Eli Harvey
Witnesses: John Stout, Adam Rinehart.

- - -

D 48 Power of Attorney from MARY (x) WILSON to "trusty friend William Cocke (Cooke ?) ". Dated 17 June 1801, proved August Court 1801.
Witnesses: John McCanless, Abraham Moore.

- - -

D 49 Will dated 2 July 1801, proved August Court 1801.

JAMES WATSON, SR. wife: Rosanna

sons: John, James, David, Jonathan

grandson: James, son of James

dau: Peggy "plantation I purchased of Henry Moore at the death of my wife ..."
dau: Elizabeth

Sole executor: son James Watson
Witnesses: James Moore, John Moore.

- - -

D 50 Will dated 3 July 1801, proved August Court 1801.

HENRY MORRAS "dear and loving wife"

At wife's death property to be divided "amongst my children and my son Henry's children."

sons: Thomas Morrass, Richard

grandson: John Morris (notice three spellings of name)

Executors: "trusty friends William Hogan and Thomas Brewer".
Witnesses: Wm. McCauley, David Hogan, Robert (x) Blackwood.

- - -

D 52 Will dated 14 July 1801, proved August Court 1801.

PHEBE (x) GRIMES eldest daughter Elizabeth Grimes

daus: Phebe Grimes, Lydia Grimes, Ann Grimes

sons: eldest James Grimes, Charles Grimes

"to Rebekah 5 shillings" (no relationship stated)

"My four children that is at home with me, viz: Elizabeth, Phebe, Lydia and Ann Grimes".

Executors: daughter Elizabeth Grimes and Thomas Wilson.
Witnesses: John Latta, Caleb Wilson

- - -

D 53 Will dated 12 Feb 1800, proved November Court 1801.

ELIZABETH (x) TINNING "being weak of body"

"To Elizabeth Grahams, daughter of John Grahams ..."

D 53 continued "to Mary Gresham"

"to my sister's daughter Sarah Thompson"
daughter
"to Fanny Walker/to John Walker" £ 10 when she comes of age.

"to Fanny Hall daughter to John Hall ten pounds when she is of such age to receive it."

"unto my cousin Richard Ball £ hard money."
"unto my cousin Wilson Ball £ hard money."

The remainder of her estate "unto John Grahams Sr. and his two sons James Grahams and George Grahams."

Executor: John Grahams
Witnesses: Caleb Simmons, James Tate.

\- - -

D 55 Will dated 17 March 1801, proved November Court 1801.

JOHN HOLDER wife: Mary Holder

youngest son: Aron Holder

10 shillings each to Abram Holder, Rhoda Vallentine, John Holder, Jr., Anny Morgan, Elijah Holder, Dannel Holder, David Holder. (No relationship stated to these 7 persons.)Children ?

Executors: "my loving Mary Holder and my two sons William and John Holder."
Witnesses: John Scoggins, Wm. Holder, Aron Holder.

\- - -

D 56 Will dated 2 April 1796, proved November Court 1801.

JOHN EDWARDS "very aged and infirm"

wife: Mary Edwards all estate during her life.

son: John Edwards 10 shillings

daus: Susannah Odean & Mary Campbell, 10 shillings each

sons: David Edwards, William Edwards, Sell Edwards and their children, 1 negro each.

He sets free a negro woman.

"To my son Henry Edwards" 5 negroes, etc.

Executors: son Henry Edwards and Zackfield Brewer.
Witnesses: Thomas Brewer, Elizabeth (x) Brewer).

\- - -

D 57 Will dated 27 July 1801, proved February Court 1802.

RICHARD WILLIAMS "in decline of life" Wife: Rachel

son: James 302 acres of land "and the money that is coming to me in Pennsylvania." (£113 money due him mentioned in a letter from my brother dated November 27, 1799."

daus: Hester, Martha, Rachel, Ann.
Rebeckah wife of John Wilkerson.

son: John Williams

Executors: wife Rachel, and son James Williams
Witnesses: Isaac Jackson, Owbert ? Faucett.

- - -

D 59 Will dated 2 April 1798, proved February Court 1802.

ADAM SMITH wife: Elizabeth

"My two sons and three daughters by my first wife".

Two plantations .. "one on which I now live containing about 197 acres, and another in Rowan County containing about 200 acres shall be divided into equal shares among all the children of my second wife Elizabeth ... 4 parts "

Executors: David Thornbury and George Brown, both living in Guilford County.
Witnesses: Adam Smith, Martin Strother, David Coble.

- - -

D 61 Will dated 11 October 1796, proved February Court 1802.

MARGARET CARSON "widow and relict of Alex'r Carson"

sons: Robert Carson, Samuel

"My three daughters Alice Mary and Elizabeth"

granddau: Margaret Clenny

Executor: son-in-law William Clenny
Witnesses: J. G. Rencher, Anne Rencher.

- - -

D 62 Will dated 5 February 1801, proved Feb Court 1802.

JOHN (x) GANDLEY to wife Mary 2/3 of estate

"to her (wife's) daughter Jean, other 1/3"

Witnesses: John Wilkinson, Francis Wilkinson, Robert Fossett.

- - -

D 62 Will dated 4th day 7th month 1800, proved May 1802.

ISAAC HARVEY (malster) wife: Martha Harvey

"Isaac Hannah Rachel Martha and Ruth one English shilling each".

"Five shillings to be divided among my deceased son William Harvey's children."

"Five shillings to be divided among my deceased daughter Edith Madden's children."

Son Nathan Harvey gets plantation.

Sole exceutor: son Nathan
Witnesses: James Newlin, ...

- - -

D 64 Will dated 24 February 1802, proved February Court 1802.

SAMUEL (x) McMULLEN "weak of body" wife a legatee

son: John $20

daughters Sarah, Margaret, Mary, Jane, and Rachel $1 each

sons: Samuel and Thomas $1 each

daughters Ann and Rebecca $1 each

son: James gets remainder of estate after mother's death

Executors: wife, and son James
Witnesses: Jesse Towel, John Towel.

- - -

D 66 Will dated 24 December 1794, proved August Court 1802.

JEREMIAH McCRACKEN wife: Sarah

brother: John

Executors: "Brother John McCracken and Sary McCracken."
Witnesses: William Clendennin, James Clendennin.

- - -

D 67 Will dated 20 April 1802, proved August Court 1802.

CHARLES (x) WILSON "in decline of life"

daughter Sally Wilson half of lands and plantation
" Rachel Dunn " " " " "

granddaughter: Elinor Dunn

Executors: "trusty friend Isaac Rainey and Robert McKee"
Witnesses: Sale Hatch, John Raney, Polle (x) McKee.

- - -

D 68 Will dated 7 June 1800, proved August Court 1802.

DAVID RANEY wife: Siney or Liney

"daughters Susannah Rainey, Jenny R., Margaret R., and Mary Rainey" each get a cow, etc, "when they see cause to leave their present home"

sons John Rainey and David Rainey and daughter Cathrin get five shillings each

son James Rainey gets all lands, etc

daughter Jinny

Executors: son James, and William Horne
Witnesses: Zaccheus Boroughs, Mark Barbee, Wm. Horn.

- - -

D 70 Will dated 24 May 1802, proved August Court 1802.

SARAH HERNDON, Widow (see note below)

daughter: Delilah Rhodes granddau: Sarah Jordan

sons: Lewis, James, George and Zachariah Herndon

daus: Mary Roberts, Sarah McCoy son: Reuben

Zachariah Herndon, Edmond Herndon, Ruth Roberts senior, Maryan Trice, Elizabeth Cole, Esther Barbee and Delilah Rhodes

Executors: Zachariah Herndon and Edmond Herndon
Witnesses: Thomas Steele, Joseph Bilbo.

Note by Ruth Herndon Shields: SARAH was the widow of George Herndon, whose will dated 8 May 1796 was proved at August Court 1796 and is recorded on page 85 in Will Book C. All the heirs named are identical except that George names his grandson George Roberts and does not name a granddaughter.

The descendants of George and Sarah Herndon are given in PART FOUR, HERNDONS OF THE AMERICAN REVOLUTION. See ad on last page of this book. I am a descendant through Delilah Rhodes.

- - -

D 71 Will dated 12 April 1802, proved August Court 1802.

THOMAS SHELTON wife: Catherine gets all estate

son James Shelton & daughter Mary Collar 5 shillings each

sons: Buckner, Frederick, Jeremiah and Thomas Shelton 5 sh.

- continued -

D 71 continued
dau: Rhoda Shelton feather bed, etc
son: John Shelton horse worth $40
dau: Elizabeth Shelton feather bed, etc
son: Edmund Shelton $40

Sole executrix: wife Catherine
Witness: Isaac Gattis.

- - -

D 73 Will dated 30 August 1801, proved August Court 1802.

SAMUEL PYLE son: Joseph Pyle

brother-in-law John Hall, his son Samuel Hall

brother Joseph Pyle and his son Samuel Pyle

Deborah Newlin, Daniel ...?....

Executor: John Newlin
Witnesses: ...?... ...?..., Dan'l Foust.

- - -

D 75 Will dated 27 March 1802, proved August Court 1802.

FRANCIS MORELAND wife: Nancy, all during her life

nephew: Joseph Moreland

Thomas Cooke, Francis Asbury and Richard Walcot.

"To John Major son of William Major deceased,
to Francis Moreland son of William Moreland,
to Francis Ashly son of William Ashly deceased " land, etc,
after the death of wife, Nancy Moreland.

Executors: Wm. Rhodes Jun'r, Page Patterson, John Major.
Witnesses: Thos. Steele, J. Dixon, John Hampton.
This will is signed by both Francis and Nancy Moreland.

- - -

D 76 Will dated 12 July 1802, proved November Court 1802.

ROBERT HUNTER wife: Nancy Hunter

daughter Frances Hunter to be made "equal with other daughters in household furniture"

sons: Samuel Hunter, James Hunter, Robert Hunter

daughters Marget and Jean and son Robert have had their full shares.

Executors: wife Nancy Hunter, and John Thompson, Esquire.
Witnesses: Robert Whitaker, Robert Hodge.

- - -

D 79 Will dated 2 March 1801, proved November Court 1802.

DANIEL BOOTH wife: Prissley

son: Gray Booth 20 shillings
" John Booth "plantation where he now lives known by the name of Hutson's plantation"
" Mark Booth 150 acres on "west of my mountain tract"
" Tapley Booth 125 acres joining Mark's
" Joseph Booth 175 acres joining Tapley
" Daniel Booth 245 acres known by name of Caselweary place
" Solomon Booth "one half of home plantation including dwelling house"
" Alphred Booth "other half of my Home Tract"

"My lot at the University to be sold".

daughter: Sarah Dixon 20 shillings

"To my six daughters namely Ruthey, Polly, Betty, Silvey, Ritty and Patty" ....

Executors: wife Prissley, son John Booth, and John Moore.
Witnesses: John Moore, Samson Moore, James (x) Daews ?.

- - -

D 80 Will dated 7 August 1802, proved November Court 1802.

JOHN (x) POWEL "weak in body" son: Oliver

wife? "loving Margaret Powel"

"Daughter Mary shall have just as much as the rest of her sisters

"To all my sons"

Executors: "loving son Josiah Powel and Thomas Powel"
Witnesses: Arthur Lovin ?, Lewis (x) Rhodes.

- - -

D 82 Will dated 18 July 1802, proved November Court 1802.

SAMUEL FREELAND wife Seely gets all estate for life

After wife's death "all my children to have an equal part".

No executor named.
Witnesses: Benjamin Shoarman, Joseph Rumbley, John (x) Whitten ?

- - -

D 83 Will dated 20 June 1802, proved November Court 1802.

JOSEPH BARBER wife: Marjary Barber

"My two children David and Elizabeth Barber " who are under age "to be schooled".

- continued -

"My stepdaughter Sarah Moore who is in the Western Territory".

Executors: "wife Marjary Barber and my brother Matthew Barber".
Witnesses: Jas. Boyle, Jean Barber, W.F.Thompson.

- - -

D 84 "State of North Carolina, Newberry District" Deed of Gift

from THOMAS CATES to his son Thomas Cates of Orange County, N.C. for a negro boy. Dated 29 November 1802, proved Feb Court 1803.
Witnesses: James S. Gilliam, Thos. Wadlington, Archibell Durham
Proved by the oath of Archibell Durham.

- - -

D 84 "State of North Carolina, Newberry District" Deed of Gift

from THOMAS CATES to his "loving daughter Ann Durham the wife of William Durham" of Orange County, N.C., for a negro girl.
Dated 29 November 1802, proved February Court 1803.
Witnesses: Thos. Wadlington, James S. Gilliam,
William Bedire ?, Archibell Durham.
Proved by the oaths of James S. Gilliam and Wm. Beaire ?.

- - -

D 85 Will dated 4 October 1800, proved February Court 1803.

HUGH CRAWFORD "old and infirm"

He leaves his wife Jenny "to the care of my only son Samuel".

daughter: Elizabeth Walker

Witnesses: William Freshwater, John Galbraith.

- - -

D 86 Power of Attorney from THOMAS H. PERKINS to "trusty

friend Francis Bullock" to collect debts due to the firm of Vestal and Perkins. (Vestal is deceased.) Witness: ..?.. Holt.
Dated 10 October 1801, proved February Court 1803.

- - -

D 87 Will dated 15 January 1783, proved February Court 1803.

GILBERT STRAYHORN

sons: David, John, William, James

"Grandsons Gilbert and John, sons of David" .... "house wherein I now dwell with 170 acres". They are both under 21 years.

son-in-law James Hart
grandchildren: Sarah and John Hart sons of James Hart

- continued -

D 87 continued

William Ansley (?) Ь 20,no relationship stated.

son-in-law John Strain

Executors: "My two sons-in-law John Strain and James Hart."
Witnesses: John Allison, John Ward ?, Thomas Scarlett.

- - -

D 89 Will dated 4 September 1802, proved February Court 1803.

LAZARUS (x) CATE "very weak of body" wife: Margaret

sons: William, John, Isaiah, Thomas and Benjamin Cate
"my five sons"

Executors: Culbird ? Burton, Henry Bunch.
Witnesses: Culbird (x) Burton, Henry Bunch,
Christian (his mark x) Burton.

- - -

D 90 Power of Attorney from JACOB SHORB of Frederick Co., Md.

to Archibald D. Murphey of Orange County, N.C.
Dated 16 Dec 1802, proved Feb Court 1803. Witness:
George Wilkins.

- - -

D 91 Will dated 22 December 1802, proved February Court 1803.

BARTHOLEMEW (x) STOVALL

wife Ann to have all his estate to use at her discretion "in raising my younger children."

This will is so confusing that I quote the following as written:

"My will and desire is that my executors shall pay unto my five children the wife of David Chandler five shillings specie - Thos. Stovall Bathew Stovall Mathew Griffin, George Stovall the same have already give them & they to have no other part of my estate unless my wife shall think to give it to them."

"My remaining children to witt / Susanna William Jane Frederick Henery & Anna Phebe & Nancy Wily & their ares (heirs) forever " ..

Executors: "wife Ann and real (?) friend & William Stovall
and Frederick Stovall."
Witnesses: Daniel Green, Elisha Manum (?)
Benjamin (x) Barber.

- - -

D 93 Will dated 12 December 1802, proved Feb Court 1803.

PETER (x) HELTON "very sick"   wife: Susannah

son: Abraham Helton 100 acres "he now lives on"
"   Peter Helton   100 "   " he formerly lived on"
"   James Helton   170 "   "including the old plantation"

"My eight daughters", names not stated.

Executors: Samuel Fogleman, and "John Cobble son of Adam".
Witnesses: Abraham (x) Helton, John Cobble,
Samuel Macq....?, Adam Starr.

- - -

D 94-99 Will dated 17 December 1802, proved Feb Court 1803.

ABSOLOM TATOM "of the Town of Hillsborough but now in the city of Raleigh."

"To my friends John Hogg, Catlett Campbell, David Ray, William Kirkland and Duncan Cameron "

"To Mary Willott wife of William Willott in the County of - (blank)- in the State of Tennessee" ... land on Harpeth River in the County and State aforesaid."

"To nephew Samuel Goodwin of the town of Fayetteville" ... "my house and lot in the town of Hillsborough".

"To my eldest brother Barnet Tatom" ...
"To my sister Elizabeth Hicks of Granville County" ...
"My brothers Abner Tatom, John Tatom, and William Tatom"
"To the children and heirs of my deceased brother Abel Tatom"
"To the children of my deceased sister Haritta Tulbylove"
"To the children of deceased sister Meriah Goodwin alias Newby, Samuel Goodwin excepted who is otherwise provided for".

Testator and William Moore have "interests in certain lands lying in Randolph County".

Executors: Samuel Goodwin, John Hogg, Catlett Campbell,
Duncan Cameron.
Witnesses: William Norwood, Ed. Jones, Gavin Alves,
W. L. Strudwick.

Codicil dated 17 December 1802 leaves to "Thomas Hogg the son of James Hogg" $200 to be placed at interest until he reaches 21 years of age. Same witnesses as above.

Friends to handle Tennessee lands: Major Abraham Maury (?), Gen'l Daniel Smith.

- - -

D 100 Will dated 24 January 1803, proved May Court 1803.

JAMES SHAW wife a legatee, name not stated

"To Betsy Shaw daughter of William Shaw (son of Sam'l)" ...

"My eight children"

sons: Joseph and William Shaw daughter: Fanny

"To my grandson James Shaw son of Levi"

Executors: "trusty friend James Dixon and my nephew Wm. Shaw."
Witnesses: Daniel Turrentine, Samuel White.

- - -

D 101 Will dated 24 March 1803, proved August Court 1803.

WILLIAM MEBANE wife: Rebecca 1/3 of estate

Robert Murdock large Bible, etc, and plantation after wife's death.

brother James 1/3 of estate
" David 1/3 of estate

"To my supposed son William Brown Mebane" he gives a slave.

Executors: "My brother James Mebane and my father-in-law Benjamin Rainey"
Witnesses: James Hutcheson, Ross Hutcheson.

- - -

D 103 Will dated 22 May 1803, proved August Court 1803.

THOMAS DURHAM wife: Lucey ? Durham

daus: Elizabeth Durham, Rebecca Durham, Susey ? Durham

sons: Aron, John, Thomas, Iley I., and Ezra Durham.

Executors: "friends William Durham and Thomas Cate".
Witnesses: Lysias Durham, William Hopson.

- - -

D 104 Will dated 26 February 1803, proved August Court 1803.

STWPHWN WILLSON wife: Sarah 1/3 of estate

to son John and daughter Sarah "land joining Mr. Tilley's "

"To William Dollar one English Crown besides what I have given him".
"To William Guess " " " " " I " " him"

Executors: William Cain and "my loving wife Sarah".
Witnesses: Thomas Latta, John Latta, Jr.

- - -

D 105 Will dated 25 August 1794, proved August Court 1803.

WILLIAM (x) DELEY "weak in body"

wife: Isble Deley, gets plantation during her lifetime,"then it falls to William Deley son of John Deley"

"Sister's children", names not given.

son-in-law James Gibens - his wife Catherine Gibens.
" " " George Reed - " " Mary Reed.

Wm. Deley Reed son of George Reed

Resey and Isbel Deley daughters of John Deley

William son of Samuel Ector

Executors: wife Isbel, and James Ector.
Witnesses: Samuel Ector, Joseph (x) Ector, Jr.

\- - -

D 107 Will dated 4 November 1802, proved August Court 1803.

JAMES BALDRIDGE wife: Martha

"Female children", names and number not stated. See below.
"Youngest daughter Martha White Baldridge"

sons: Malcolm and Josiah Walker Baldridge

"All my children to live with my wife until they marry".

Executors are to sell McDade plantation and lots in Hillsborough.

son: Stephen White Baldridge

"To Ann Baldridge"

daus: Elizabeth, Mary, Susanna, Charity, Jean, Margaret (all named Baldridge)

step-daughter: Elizabeth Moore

"940 acres of land upon Gasper River in the Western Country to be divided among my three sons Malcolm, Stephen W., and Josiah Walker."

Executors: trusty friends Samuel Turrentine, David White, James H. Bowman and Malcolm Baldridge.
Witnesses: David Allison, Joseph Hughes.

\- - -

D 109 Agreement between the heirs of the Estate of JAMES

ROBINSON, dec'd. William Robinson gets land on Little Creek. Others mentioned are Elisha Robinson, James Robinson. The paper is signed by Jesse (x) Beckum, James Robertson, Jane (x) Robertson, Elisha (x) Robertson.

Witnesses: J. Cook; Augustine Willis, Jacob Mosier ?. Dated 15 July 1803, proved August Court 1803.

- - -

D 110 Will dated 15 February 1803, proved Nov Court 1803.

JOHN (x) CARRINGTON "weak in body"

wife: Mary gets all estate during her life

son: Thomas Carington (1 bed and furniture)

Executors: "my two sons Nath'l Carington and Ephriam."
Witnesses: Jesse Rice ?, Benjamin (x) Carington.

- - -

D 111 Will dated 1 January 1798, proved Nov Court 1803.

JESSE RICE of Wake County, N.C. wife: Elizabeth

Executors: "my wife Elizabeth and my friend James Walker"
No witnesses.

- - -

D 112 Power of Attorney from JAMES MEBANE SENIOR to his son Alexander Mebane, both of Orange County, N.C., to sell land in Tennesse (county left blank) on Bartow's (Barton'n ?) Creek, "1000 acres granted by State of North Carolina to me for my military services." Dated 30 November 1803.
Witness: Archibald Murphey.

- - -

D 113 Power of Attorney from PATSEY ATKINSON of Caswell Co. N.C. to Archibald Murphey of Caswell Co., N.C., to collect the estate of her late brother RANSOM ATKINSON, late of Wayne Co. An advertisemant about his estate was published in the Raleigh Register.... money is in the hands of Simpson Smith. Dated 17 November 1803. Witness: Solomon Parks.

- - -

D 113 Power of Attorney from SAMUEL THOMPSON, weaver, of Orange County N.C. to John Boyle Junior of Orange County to sell land in Beautetort Co., Va. A tract containing 400 acres "entered in my name and at the instance of a certain Samuel Findley of the County of Beautetort".
Dated 26 November 1803; proved November Court 1803.
Witnesses: James Davis, James Palson ?.

- - -

D 114-118 Will dated 24 August 1801, proved Nov Court 1803.

THOMAS TRICE

"To my wife Sarey Trice one half of my property in Brunswick County, Virginia", etc.

Thomas Trice Carlton 400 acres "bounded by my home plantation Christopher Daniels and Robert Cambel's".

Polly Barby "200 acres bounded by my brother Edward Trice, Wm Cain and Page Patterson, running up Second (Creek) to the Cow Lick".

Ritty Barby 200 acres
Polly House 300 "
Nancy Carlton gets a negro girl

dau: Sally Barby wife of Joseph Barby gets two negroes
" Nancy House gets two negroes

Betsey Carlton wife of Leonard Carlton gets two negroes

"These six grandchildren Thomas Trice Carlton, William Carlton, Polly Barby, Ritty Barbee, Polly House, Betsey House" get 11 negroes.

Executors: brother Edward Trice, Lennard Carlton, John Moore.
Witnesses: Wm. Trice, Edward Trice, John Moore.

- - -

D 119 Will dated 27 November 1803, proved Feb Court 1804.

AQILIIA JONES wife: Hephsebeth

"My three sons John, Aquilla and James"

"Her (wife's) son William Hargis".

daughter Mary Jones

Testator's wish is that all the family stay together.

Executors: wife, and Reubin Smith.
Witnesses: David Ray, John Butner.

- - -

D 120-122 Will dated 13 April 1800, proved Feb Court 1804.

WILLIAM (x) PARTIN "weak in body" wife: Jane or Jean

To heirs of "my son John Partin deceased" 1 shilling.
To son-in-law Jesse Rigsby 1 shilling.

Sons: William Partin, Lennard 1 shilling each.

- continued -

sons-in-law: Henson Colther and Thomas Connaly 1 shilling
son: Charles Partin 1 shilling
son-in-law: Waller Herndon 1 shilling
son: Bennet Partin land joining Wm. Brewer, Alex. Strain, and John McCauley.
son: Lewis Partin land after wife's death

Executors: "trusty friend William Brewer and my son Charles Partin".
Witnesses: Isham Brewer, Waller Herndon, Holley her x mark Rigsby, Bennett Partin.

- - -

D 122 Will dated 8 January 1804, proved Feb Court 1804.

SAMUEL DICKIE wife: Cathren

(The name is signed DICKIE, but spelled two other ways.)

son: James Dicky
" Samuel Dickey, land in Caswell County

daus: Rachel Burd, Hannah Linch, Hester ? Cantrill

son: William Dickey, land in Caswell County.

dau: Susannah Linch

Executors: sons Samuel and William Dicky.
Witnesses: Sam'l Ector, Savana (x) Garison, her mark.

- - -

D 124 Power of Attorney from BENJAMIN PEELER to John Grant Rencher of the City of Wake. Dated 2 April 1804.
Witnesses: Thos. (x) Browning, John (x) May.

- - -

D 125 Will dated 10 July 1800, proved May Court 1804.

JOHN (x) STALCOP "sick and weak" wife: Elizabeth

sons: Solomon Stalcop, Thomas Stalcop (he is under 20 years)

daus: Elizabeth Stalcop Jr, Nancy Stalcop, Rachel Stalcop, Lydda Stalcop, Susannah Stalcop.

Executors: wife Elizabeth and son Solomon.
Witnesses: James Pyle, William Pyle.

- - -

D 127 This will is so confusingly worded that I copied it verbatim from the original in the Archives in Raleigh, N.C.

"July the 21st 1800

I, Samuel Thompson of the County of Orange and State

- continued -

of North Carolina   Just Account & legs (legacies ?)

Henry O'Daniel to Thirty Pounds Dr (debtor ?)
Joshua Thompson to Eighteen Pounds Dr
Samuel Thompson to Six Pounds Dr

I leave to my son Joshua Thompson
son Joshua son of Mary Paynes
Twenty Pounds

Samuel Bartly to have a child's part

Witness: Thomas Bradshaw ? "   Signed: his
Proved May Court 1804   Samuel x Thompson
mark

- - -

D 127 Will dated 3 January 1804, proved May Court 1804.

JOSEPH (x) CANTERIEL

sons: Isaac Canteriel, Benjamin Canteriel

daus: Rachel Hensley, Sally Davis

Sole executor: son Isaac Canteriel.
Witnesses: Andrew McClary, Conoley Walker.

- - -

D 129 Will dated 2 April 1804, proved May Court 1804.

SIMPSON (x) TAIT   wife: Catherine Tait

son: Zacheus Tait

Executors: "well beloved friend Anthony Tait, and wife Catherine."
Witnesses: Edmond Gilam, Wm. Street, Joseph Street, Senior.

- - -

D 130 Will dated 17 November 1803, proved May Court 1804.

JAMES (x) LINCH "very sick"   wife: Jean Linch

William Hughes and his wife.

"My three children (to wit) Elizabeth Linch, James Linch, and Aron Linch". All three are under age.

Executors: "my wife and her brother James Hutcheson."
Witnesses: Anth. Lovins, John (x) McCrory ?.

- - -

D 136 Will dated 13 March 1804, proved May Court 1804.

JEHU WHITTED   daughter: Anna

wife: Susanna "tract of land adjoining William Pickett, Eli

- continued -

 D 136 continued
Hill and others on Hill's Creek being part of the land that Wm. Courtney died possessed of."
"One house and part of lot #6 in the town of Hillsbouough now occupied by James Child."

daughter Anna brother Levi
"Should my wife have a child before my death ..."

He leaves £ 100 in trust with his father Wm. Whitted and brother Wm. Whitted Jr. for the benefit of a mulatto child Fanny. She is to have 6 months schooling, and be emancipated.

Samuel Bigeloe a legatee.
Testator has lands "in the Western Country."

sisters: Mary Bird (testator is guardian for her children)
Hannah Harris, Elizabeth Thompson, Susannah Thompson

Executors: father Wm. Whitted, brothers Levi and Wm. Whitted Jr, and William Harwood.
Witnesses: Will I ? Cain, Gavin Alves.

- - -

D 137 Will dated 20 December 1800, proved August Court 1804.

JAMES (x) CURREY "weak in body" wife a legatee, name not stated

sons: James
John "land joining Chisenhall's line"
"The three girls that is single", names not stated.

Executors: wife, and son James.
Witnesses: Silus Forest, Isaac Jones, James Currey.

- - -

D 138 Will dated 14 September 1804, proved Nov Court 1804.

SARAH McCRACKEN widow

"To Mary Paton wife of Robert Paton at whose House I now reside, and Polly Patton daughter of said Robert Patton"... (a long list of articles is given, and a list of notes due her.)

Executors: "trusty friends Robert Patton Senior and David Turrentine."
Witnesses: Robert Hodge, Robert Patton, Senior.

- - -

D 140 Will dated 20 February 1804, proved Nov Court 1804.

JOSEPH WELLS, Senior

son: William Wells "land on both sides of Cane Creek"
sons: John, Joseph, Nathan, Isaac Wells, $7 each

daughters: Margrate Gifford, Charity McDaniel $7 each
Mary A. Jamison ?, Rachel Underwood $7 each

- continued -

D 140 continued
granddaughter: "daughter of Jesse Wells deceased"

Elizabeth Wells (no relationship stated)

Executors: sons Isaac and William Wells.
Witnesses: Wm. Pike, John Pike Jr., John Marshill.

- - -

D 141 Division of the negroes in the Estate of RICHARD COCHRAN to Mrs. Turner, the widow of Richard Cochran, and his daughter Polly Dilhu Cockran.
Signed by: Joshua Holt, J. Scott, J'se ? Hall.

- - -

D 142 Will dated 19 March 1804, proved November 1804.

FREDERICK LOYD wife: Mary Loyd

sons: Lacey Loyd, Frederick and John Loyd.

Executors: "well beloved friend Thomas Brewer and Lacey Loyd"
Witnesses: Sackfield Brewer, Elizabeth (x) Brewer.

- - -

D 143 Will dated 2 January 1805, proved February Court 1805.

WILLIAM MURRAY

wife: Margaret to have all estate "for her and her children's support as it is this day for twelve years." James Barnhill & Isaac Hall are to help settle any disputes that arise during the twelve years.

sons: William, Robert Murray
"3 youngest" Andrew, Eli and John Murray

daughter: Margaret Bird

Testator has a saw mill and a grist mill.
He has land claims in Cumberland.

Executors: sons Robert and William.
Witnesses: Christ'r Swindell, Walter Murray, Rob't Tate.

- - -

D 146-148 Will dated 19 March 1804, proved Feb Court 1805.

JAMES HOGG sisters: Mary Elizabeth and Jean

neice: Jean Burgess
brother: Robert Hogg, deceased

"To my son Gavin Alves"
daughter: Robina Norwood

"My children Walter Alves, Gavin Alves, Helen Hooper and Robina Norwood, and to my grandchildren John Huske and Ann

- continued -

Alves Huske."

Executors: son Walter Alves and Gavin Alves.
Witness: James Wells.

- - -

D 148 Will dated 13 September 1803, proved May Court 1805.

THOMAS ROUNTREE wife a legatee, name not given

son: Joseph Rountree gets land on condition that he care for his mother.
sons: John and Thomas Rountree 5 shillings each

Lydia Cate and Rachel Jacobs 5 shillings each (daughters ?)

Money left in estate after wife's death to be divided into 8 shares and divided as follows: (no relationships stated) Andrew & Thomas 2 shares each, John, Charles, Lydia and Joseph, 1 share each.

Rachel, one cow
granddaughter: Elizabeth Hannah

No executor named.
Witnesses: Thompson McKissick, Wm. McKissick.

- - -

D 150 Will dated 4 May 1805, proved May Court 1805.

JONATHAN (x) JENKINS "sick and very weak" wife: Ann

Executors: wife, and "trusty friend John Wilbourn."
Witnesses: Ownley ?(x) Owen, Samuel (x) Owen.

- - -

D 151 Will dated 25 February 1805, proved May Court 1805.

THOMAS LEWIS wife: Jane

son: William "land on east side of Henry Lewis where he now/ lives"
" Fielding "land where I now live"

daughters: Frances, Elizabeth, Mary

sons: Robert, Henry, John

son-in-law: Nicholas Durning

Executors: "My two sons Fielding and Henry Lewis, and John Rhodes of Benjamin, and my loving wife Jane."
Witnesses: John Rhodes, Ben. Rhodes.

- - -

D 152 Will dated 25 June 1805, proved August 1805.

JOHN (x) KING "weak of body"

"Wife and two children Calvin and John five shillings each".

"My two sons Thomas King and Jeremiah King " under age.

Sole executor: father, Thomas King.
Witnesses: Julius King, John King.

- - -

D 154 Will dated 6 August 1803, proved August Court 1805.

MARTHA STRUDWICK

"to grandson Samuel Strudwick when he arrives at twenty..."
"in case of Samuel's death I give property to Edmund ..."

Sole executor: son Wm. F. Strudwick.
Elizabeth Kirby to have $50 "if she is with me at my death"
Witness: Elizabeth Sheppard.

- - -

D 155 Will dated 24 October 1793, proved August Court 1805.

JAMES BIRD (no wife mentioned)

"Youngest son Thomas Bird all my land I now possess."

"... the whole of my children saying Richard Empson Thomas Sarah Mary Susanna and Catherine each to have share and share alike" in moveable estate. (No punctuation.)

Executors: sons Richard and Empson Bird.
Witnesses: Alex. Mebane, Jas. Mebane, Jun'r.

- - -

D 156 Will dated 28 October 1804, proved August Court 1805.

HENRY McCLUER wife: Mary

son: James 150 acres and ½ of grist mill and all of saw mill
" John 180 "
" Henry (he is under age) 150 acres and "plantation I now live on" and ½ of grist mill

daughters: Elizabeth and Susannah 50 acres each
Sarah 5 shillings
Mary, Ann, and E.D. 50 acres each

granddaughter: Elizabeth (dau. of Sarah) 50 acres

Executors: sons James and John.
Witnesses: Wm. Hatchett, John McCullock, Eliz. McCullock.
"N.B. I will to my beloved son William 5 shillings."

- - -

D 158 Will dated 10 November 1800, proved August Court 1805.

GEORGE (x) FRIDDLE wife: Mary

sons: Casper, John and Henry Friddle, 1 shilling each
dau: Caty Garrot wife of Averot Gattot 1 shilling
" Peggy Lue wife of Michael Lue 1 shilling

"I say that it may be fully understood all my children by my first wife shall have one shilling each."

"My three youngest children (to wit) Caty Friddle Purley Friddle and Martin J. Friddle."

Executors: friends Ludwick Allbright Junr. and Jacob Graves.
Witnesses: Michael Holt, John ...land ?

- - -

D 160 Power of Attorney from JAMES TRICE to his brother William Trice, both of Orange County.
Dated 30 October 1805, proved November Court 1805.
Witnesses: Francis Barbee, Isaiah Marcum.

- - -

D 160 Will dated 20 August 1805, proved November Court 1805.

JOHN McKEE wife: Catherine "and family"

son: John McKee 500 acres
daus: Alizabeth McKee 250 acres, Mary McKee 250 acres
He speaks of "my three children"

Executors: Wife Catherine, James Clark and Robert McKee.
Witnesses: Thomas Clark, Agness Anderson.

- - -

D 162 Will dated 8 June 1805, proved August Court 1805.

JOHN NEWLIN

son: Nathaniel Newlin "the plantation I now live on"

"My other children namely Jas Newlin John Newlin Hannah Holladay and Mary Hadley."

"Five grandchildren of my son Eli Newlin deceased five pounds (to wit) Joshua and John Newlin Ruth Vestal Edith & Mary Newlin ..." (no punctuation)

No executor named.
Witnesses: John Carter, Anne Carter, Hannah Carter.

- - -

D 163A Will dated 17 December 1805, proved Feb Court 1806.

JAMES (x) COZART wife: Sarah

son: Hiram Brinkley Cozart "all my lands lying in Person Co. viz 1303 acres with the grist mill." He is under age.

sons: Hiram, David and William, all under age.

daus: Lively Brinklry Cozart, Edy Brinkley Cozart, Jemimah Cozart, Sarah Cozart, all under age. The three last are the youngest.

"I have left in the possession of James Tomison who married Charlotte four negroes ..."

Executors: wife Sarah,"and Court of Orange to appoint an Executor to act with my widow."
Witnesses: Alex. (x) McMullan, Rachel (x) Hopkins.

- - -

D 166 Will dated 2 February 1806, proved Feb Court 1806.

MARTHA WILLIAMS

sisters: Hester Williams and Nancy Williams
brother: James Williams

No executor named.
Witnesses: Isaac Jackson, John McMullin.

- - -

D 167 Will dated 9 September 1805, proved Feb Court 1806.

JAMES (x) MILIKEN wife: Rachel

sons: James (eldest), Elias, and George (youngest)

Executors: wife Rachel, and Jesse Miliken.
Witnesses: William Moore, William Robertson.

- - -

D 169 Will dated 15 February 1806, proved May Court 1806.

JOHN (x) ANDERSON wife: Lettice

daughters: Mary, Pheby and Ann

sons: Robert, John

Executors: sons Robert and John.
Witnesses: Thos. Armstrong, Robert Anderson, Wm. Anderson.

- - -

D 170 Will dated 9 May 1804, proved May Court 1806.

ROBERT (x) BURNSIDE He says "my seven children"

sons: Benjamin Burnside (eldest), John and James Burnside

daughters: Ruth, Hannah, Ann

Executors: Joseph Thompson, Owin Lindley.
Witnesses: Wm. Morris, James Lindley, Gracy ? Lindley.

- - -

D 172 Indenture bewteen ROBERT (x) BURNSIDE and Thomas Faucett, both of Orange Co., N.C. BURNSIDE sells land on Eno and Haw Rivers to Faucett. Dated 9 Nov 1798, proved 1806.
Witnesses: Owin Lindley, Chas ? Stubbins.

- - -

D 174 Will dated 26 September 1803, proved August Court 1806.

FRANCIS WILKINSON sons: John and William

He speaks of "my six children" but names only the two above, and David below.
Executors: sons John and David.
Witnesses: Joseph Thompson, ..?.. Hart, Thos. McCracken.

- - -

D 175 Will dated 29 August 1805, proved August Court 1806.

JAMES MURRAY wife: Sarah

son Jonathan, daughter Ann, and son James, 1 shilling each.

daughter Elizabeth everything after wife's death
" Ruth

Executrix: daughter Elizabeth.
Witnesses: Wm. Rainey, Jonathan (x) Murray.

- - -

D 176 Will dated 2 March 1803, proved August Court 1806.

GEORGE ALLEN

sons-in-law: James Mebane, David Mebane, David White, James Armstrong

son: Samuel Allen plantation joining lands of Robert Hodge and Robert Patton.

sons: William Allen George Allen, Alexander Allen

Executors: son-in-law David White, and Robert Hodge.
Witnesses: James Patton, Alexander Patton.

- - -

D 178 Will dated 13 January 1806, proved Nov Court 1806.

JACOB SENIOR ALLEN

son: Jacob Allen land on South side of Eno River
" William Allen land on North side of Eno

daus: Sally Allen, Betsey Allen, Hannah Allen
Nancy Latta, Syntha Scarlett

Executors: son-in-law James Latta, son Jacob Allen.
Witnesses: Wm. Cain Sr., John Kelly Sr., Cuthburt (x) Burton.

- - -

D 179 Will dated 13 October 1806, proved Nov Court 1806.

JOHN FAUCETT wife: Mary

"I leave my land to be divided equally to my children that shall live to come of age." Number and names not stated.

Executors: "friends John Ray and William Bradford."
Witnesses: Samuel Faucett, Thos. Bradford.

- - -

D 180 Will dated 23 September 1806, proved Nov Court 1806.

her
LESEY x ROGERS
mark

son: Laban Rogers (under age) all estate, including "my proportionate part of my deceased father's estate after my mother's death."

Executors: Richard Goat, Nathan Rogers.
Witnesses: James Sykes, Wm. A. Freshwater.

- - -

D 181 Will dated 19 November 1806, proved Nov Court L806.

EPHRIAM MITCHELL wife a legatee, name not stated

"Six of my sons Henry, David, Randall ?, James, Efram, and William."

daughter Patsey

children: Noah and Happey ? $15 each.

(This will has been checked with the original in the Archives. The writing is very bad.)

No executor named.
Witnesses: Stephen Robart, Nancy (x) Robart.

- - -

D 183 Will dated 15 Nov 1806, proved Nov 1806 or Feb 1807.

ISHAM GANT wife: Sally

"My children", all under age, names and number not stated.

Executors: brothers William Gant and James Gant.
Witnesses: J. Webb, A. Murray.

- - -

D 184 Will dated 8 July 1806 ?, proved February 1807.

MICHAEL ROBINSON

son: William 20 shillings
" David Robinson 20 shillings, a negro, 500 acres of land on Duck River
"James Robinson son of Alexander Robinson deceased" 20 sh.

daughter: Catherine Moore 5 shillings
son: Michael Robinson
grandson: John Robinson son of Michael "by his first wife Jane/Ray"
son: James Robinson "my large Bible"
daughter: Mary Moore 5 shillings
daus: Jinnett Ray wife of James Ray
Martha Ray, Nancy Rountree
son: Joseph Robinson 300 acres of land "lying on the waters of Duck River in the State of Tennessee, it being the third part of a tract of 1500 acres."
son: John Robinson 500 acres on Duck River
" Charles Robinson

"To heirs of my daughter Margaret McCallister" 5 shillings.
"To Jane Anderson daughter of Samuel Anderson" one negro child.
grandson: Michael Robinson Moore $20 "to help with his education."
Executors: friends Wm. Cooke, Thomas Roundtree, David Ray.
Witnesses: James Whitfield, Nancy (x) Wilson.

- - -

D 186 Will dated 18 November 1807, proved Nov Court 1807.

JOHN KING

"To friend George Wagoner 10 gallons of the whiskey James Walker promised to pay me."
To friend Charles Roberts, all his estate.

Executors: George Wagoner, Ephriam Roberts, James Walker.
Witnesses: Abner (x) Roberts, William Harris,
Milly (x) Arnold, Winnifred (x) Roberts.

- - -

D 187 Will dated 30 April 1806, proved February Court 1807.

JAMES McCADDAMS   wife: Rebeckah

sons: James McCaddams, James Hopkins

grandson: Absalom McCaddams

Executors; sons Jos'h McCaddams, James.
Witnesses: James McCaddams Jr., William Crutchfield.

- - -

D 189 Will dated 3 February 1807, proved Feb Court 1807 ?

WILLIAM MORROW of the Hawfields, "old and infirm"

son: William Morrow "plantation whereon I now live"
"   James Morrow   ""   "   he now lives"

daughters: Elizabeth Andrews ?, Margat Bryen ?, Jane Pickhard

"My son John Morrow doter Janey Banks (Parker ?) Morrow"
Janey is under age, her mother is Sarah Morrow.

Executors: son William Morrow and James Morrow and Jno.
Thompson.
Witnesses: Robert Grahams, William (x) Grahams, Jno. Thompson.

I have examined the original will in the Archives in Raleigh.
The writing is poor, name is spelled MURROW in the body of
the will but the signature is MORROW.

- - -

D 190 Will dated 11 August 1807, proved November Court 1807.

JONATHAN NICHOLS

grandchildren: Hannah and Nancy Riggs, Irven and John Riggs
John Nichols
"Heirs of my beloved daughter Hannah Riggs".

"To sons Jonathan Baldwin John and Amos Nichols"

Executors: sons Jonathan and Amos.
Witnesses: Jno. McMullen, James Daugherty.

- - -

D 192-4 Will dated 9 May 1807, proved May Court 1807.

WILLIAM (x) PICKET   wife: Elizabeth

"To India Pickett daughter of my son Jesse Picket.

granddaus: "Tempy and Edy Rigsby daughters of Jesse Rigsby"

daughter Elizabeth Rigsby   - continued -

sons: Mark Picket, Thomas Picket

"Thomas Picket and Jesse Picket .. the land and plantation where they live during their lives."

daughter Peggy Perry
grandson: Arche ? Rigsby "land where he now lives, formerly the property of David Grisham"

Executors: "worthy friends Mann Patterson, Wm. Rhodes Trice."
Witnesses: C. P. Patterson, William Rhodes.

- - -

D 194 Will dated 18 December 1806, proved May Court 1807.

JAMES RODGERS wife and "children as they grow up"

son: John "140 acres joining the line of Ceason ? Capps"
sons: James and William each get half of lands "joining George Fost and others", 150 acres

"My daughters, viz, Jean Ann Nelson and Polly"
Polly is the youngest.

Executors: "brother William Rodgers and my loving wife."
Witnesses: J. Scott, James Partin.

- - -

D 197 Will dated 5 February 1806, proved August Court 1807.

JEAN (or JANE) (x) McCANLESS No relationship stated to any of the legatees.

John McCanless
John Commins Senior, James McCanless, Elizabeth Hammetton
David McCanless "the mansion house", William McCanless

Executors: James H. Bowman, James Murdock.
Witnesses: John Trimble, Marget (x) Trimble, Sarah (x) Trimble.

- - -

D 199 Will dated 27 July 1805, proved August Court 1807.

JAMES FREELAND

grandchildren: Thomas Freeland "son of my son Thomas deceased"
Susan Freeland, daughter of Thomas deceased.

sons: James $1, John $50, have already received plantations

daus: Mary, "Jean Gibson wife of Andrew Gibson"

son: Joseph "all land I now possess"

Executors: Andrew Murdock, "and my son John Freeland."
Witnesses: Thomas Dickson, Stewart Dickson, Wm. Rainey.

- - -

D 201-203 Will dated 18 May 1807, proved August Court 1807.

JAMES MEBANE wife gets plantation, etc

daus: Elizabeth, Jenny, Nancy, Polley, Peggy

son: Alexander "200 acres in the State of Tennessee on the waters of Harpeth where he now lives."
" George "200 acres in Tennessee on waters of Harper"
" Robert "2000 acres in Tennessee in Jackson County"
" William "200 " " " on waters of Harper"
" Allen 200 " " " " " " "
" Nathaniel 200 acres in Tenn. " " " "
" James home plantation after wife's death
Other lands in Orange Co., N.C. and Tennessee are to be sold.

Executors: brother David Mebane, James Mebane, John Thompson.
Witnesses: Samuel Nelson, John Nelson, Edward Willson.

- - -

D 203 Will dated 14 September 1806, proved Nov Court 1807.
JOHN LINER

"My six children Mary James Sarah John Nancy Margaret".
Mary, Sarah and Margaret are living with their father.

Executors: "loving friends John Scott and Isaac Holt."
Witnesses: A. (x) Thompson, John Cook.

- - -

D 205 Will dated 27 March 1806, proved May Court 1806.

JOSEPH LOFTIN of Chapel Hill, N.C. Wife: Elizabeth

"My three children who are unmarried"
"To two sons Leonard and William ... lands I bought of John Morgan".
dau: Catherine "lands I bought of Bonds where Underhill lives".
daus: Vineter ?, Betsey
"Lands I bought of Thos Heath to be sold ".. in Craven County.

Executors: son Leanord Loftin and friend Daniel West.
Witnesses: Wm. Croom, Geo. Lane (Love ?), Thomas Collier ?.

- - -

D 206 Will dated 19 November 1806, proved Nov Court 1807.

JAMES CRUTCHFIELD

wife: Mary all estate, household furniture, etc, including "wheat at John Crawford's mill." This property to be divided among her children after her death. "All the property willed to her by John Steel."

James Crutchfield (under 21 years) "my road tract" 128 acres.

brother: Benjamin Crutchfield gets a slave, provided he completes a wagon on hand at Mathew Wilson's and Benjamin Crutchfield's shop. - continued -

brothers: John, William, Stephen ?, Anderson
"Property coming to me at the death of my mother I leave to Thomas and Stapleton."

John Pitts

Executors: wife Mary, and friend Jacob Geer (Greer ?).
Witnesses: Thomas Bradshaw, Wm. Shaw.

- - -

D 208 Will dated 16 September 1807, proved Nov Court 1807.

ELIHU WOOD "a farmer" wife: Elinor

"My four daughters Margaret Mary Rebecka and Lucy".

sons: William (under age), Hugh, Elihu (youngest)

Executors: "faithful friends David Ray and Robert Fausett, Sr."
Witnesses: Jno. Kelly Sen'r, John Trimble, Joseph Wood.

- - -

D 211 Will dated 16 June 1806, proved November Court 1807.

GEORGE McRAY wife: Sarah

son: James "land bought of Monhollen adjoining James Duke's"
daus: Susanna, Margret, Ann (she is under 18 years of age)
son: George (under 20) land joining John Hall & John Graham
dau: Sarah
son: John

Executors: wife Sarah, son James
Witnesses: Jonathan Harvey, James King.

- - -

D 213 Will dated 5 March 1805, proved Nov Court 1807.

HENRY (x) HORTON grandson: Henry McFarlan gets all lands

granddau: Mary Copley
son: Hugh Horton
dau: Elizabeth McFarlaine Thomas McFarlaine
"To my grandchildren of Sarah each and each to share alike (viz) Winnfred McMullen Susana Adams Mary Copley James McFarlain and William McFarlain." (No punctuation.)

Sole executor: grandson John McFarlain.
Witnesses: Jas. Walker, Moses Jones, Larcan his (x) mark McFarlain.

- - -

D 215 Will dated 18 October 1806, proved Feb Court 1807 ?

ALEXANDER (x) ROBBS "sick and weak"

All his estate goes to Benjamin Cantril, who is to set free his negro slave Peter, after ten years.

Witnesses: Hardy Hurdle, John Layne.

- - -

D 216 Power of Attorney from JAMES ALLAN MORGAN "being about to leave the State of North Carolina" to Chesley P. Patterson, "to lease, rent or sell ... lands bounded by Lemuel Morgan, Solomon Morgan, Christopher Barbee and Jarratt Yeargin."
Dated 19 November 1807, proved February Court 1808.
Witnesses: C. Barbee, John Morgan.

- - -

D 218 Power of Attorney from CASAN SWINDLE to Christopher Swindle, both of Orange County, N.C. Witness: James Mebane, Jr.
Dated 28 October 1805, proved Feb Court 1808.

- - -

D 219 Will dated 5 September 1807, proved Feb Court 1808 ?

JAMES CARSON son: Robert Carson

wife: Mary all estate during her life, including plantation and land that "now belongs to John McDade."

Executors: wife Mary, and William Clark.
Witness: Jesse Clark.

- - -

D 220 Will dated 11 November 1807, proved Feb Court 1808.

SABUT WOOD

grandchildren: Sabet Wood, Mary Wood, Hardy Wood, children of "my son Levin Wood."
dau-in-law: Elizabeth Wood, wife of Levin Wood
dau: Kezzia Wood
son: Isaac

Sole executor: son Levin Wood.
Witnesses: Joseph Clendennin, Jos. Harlow, George Coble.

- - -

D 221 Deed of Gift from MARGARET RIGGS to Sarah Hall· Shelton Hall and Jenny Hall (under age), all of Otange County, N.C.
Dated 19 September 1807, proved February Court 1808.
Witnesses: Jno. Riggs, James Woods, John Jimmason ?.

- - -

D 222 Will dated 23 November 1802, proved Feb Court 1808.

DAVID DENNING or DINNING

Dau: Margery Barber all estate, land on Laughlen's Creek, etc.

grandchildren: David Barber, Betty Barber
son: David Denning
dau: Isabella Moore

Executrix: Margery Barber.
Witnesses: John & James Boyles (Boylen ?), James Davis.

- - -

D 224 Will dated 20 November 1807, proved Feb Court 1808.

JOHN DUGLASS wife: Mary

"My five children John Duglass, George Duglass, Adam Duglass, Rosanna Duglass and Hannah Duglass."

"Peggy Walls and her son William Walls."

Executors: wife Mary, and son John.
Witnesses: James Cain, Thomas Holden, Henry Bunch.

- - -

D 226 No date on will, proved May Court 1808.

JONATHAN NICHOLS

mother: Sarah Dickson father: Jonathan Nichols

Witnesses: Jas. H. Bowman, Thomas Ray.

- - -

D 228 Will dated 10 June 1807, proved May Court 1808.

WILLIAM (x) BUSICK, SR "old and weak in body"

son: Caleb Busick
dau: Elizabeth Wood 5 shillings
son-in-law: Samuel Green 5 shillings
daus: Mary Willcox, Polly Conner ? 5 shillings each

"Son William Busick and Elizabeth Busick and Nancy Busick and Phebe Busick to be equally divided among them."

Executors: son William Busick and Henry Brannon.
Witnesses: William Brannock, Leah Branock.

- - -

D 229-231 Will dated 12 February 1808, proved May Court 1808.

ROBERT SR MORRISON

son: James all lands in Randolph County
" William "land where I now live and a piece of land I purchased from Wm. Carter adjoining the said place."

D 229-231 continued
son: Robert "land whereon my son William now lives"
daus: Hannah and Deborah $80 each 207 acres bought from Isaac Reynolds to be sold to pay them
"My daughters (viz) Jean, Catherine, Mary, Ruth, Hannah and Deborah."

Executors: son Robert, and James Newlin.
Witnesses: Wm. Carter, Danell Towell, Duncan Darroch.

- - -

D 231 Will dated 14 November 1807, proved May Court 1808.

DAVID (x) RAY "very sick" wife a legatee

sons: William (eldest), John, David, Hugh, James, Henry get 5 shillings each

daus: Rachel Gibson, Mary Becom 5 shillings each
Jenny Jones, Nelly Ricketts, 5 shillings each.

"son and youngest child Alexander", horse, etc.

Executors: wife, and John Pickard, elder.
Witnesses: John H. Pickard, John Grimes.

- - -

D 233 Will dated 18 Jan 1808, proved May or August Court 1808.

DAVID HALL wife: Elizabeth all lands

son: Hardy Almond lands after wife's death
" Thomas 5 shillings
dau: Delila 5 "
"daughters Sally Rebecca Betsey and Estey (Elsey ?)" get personal estate.

Executors: Abner Massey, wife Elizabeth.
Witnesses: Leonard Carlton, Wm. Shepard, J. Dixon.

- - -

D 235 Will dated 24 October 1807, recorded August Court 1808.

JOHN HARDIN wife: Sarah

son: John
"Four youngest daughters Polley, Sally, Betsy and Peggy."

No executor named. Witnesses: Jean Holt, Wm. Holt.

- - -

D 236 Mortgage from JAMES RIGGS to Andrew McBroom on a mare and a colt, etc, dated October 5, 1805, proved Nov Court 1808.
Witness: Ashahel Moore.

- - -

D 237 Will dated 19 June 1808, proved Nov Court 1808.

WILLIAM WOLF

Ann (relationship not stated, wife ?) gets plantation

sons: Peter, John, William (he is youngest)
daus: Barbara and Mary

His negro man to be hired out until he earns enough to repay his purchase price, when he is to be freed.

Witnesses: Benjamin Jackson, Joseph Clendennin.

- - -

D 239 Will dated 28 September 1808, proved Nov Court 1808.

PETER (x) FOUST "weak in body" wife: Mary, is pregnant

son: John Foust "plantation I bought of Joseph Stout", etc.
daus: Elizabeth Clap, Sarah Amick
son: Peter Foust under age
brother: Daniel

Exceutors: wife, and son John
Witnesses: Thomas Lindley, Jacob Marshall.

- - -

D 241 Will dated 8 October 1808, proved Feb Court 1809.

ELI McDANIEL wife: Elizabeth

sons: John and James, both married
daus: Peggy, Salley, Susy all under age

Executors: John McDaniel, James McDaniel.
Witnesses: Joshua O'Daniel, Jesse Miliken.

- - -

D 243 Will dated 10 October 1804, proved Feb Court 1809 ?

THOMAS ROBERTSON wife: Susannah

son: Abijah Ray

Executor: wife Susannah
Witnesses: John Clendennin, James (x) Daniels.

- - -

D 244 Will dated 25 November 1808, proved Feb Court 1809.

PETER (x) JEFFREYS wife: Lucy

Two slaves are to be emancipated.

Executor: John Young of the town of Hillsborough.
Witnesses: Robert Tinnen, James Lapslie.

- - -

D 244 Bill of Sale from WILLIAM BUSSICK, SR. to William Bussuck Jr. for $60, a sorrel mare and cow and calf.
Dated 24 February 1808, proved May Court 1809.
Witnesses: Elizabeth Bussick, Catherine (x) Bussick.

- - -

D 246 Power of Attorney from WILLIAM FORSYTHE to "trusty friend and son James Forsythe", both of Orange County.
Dated 17 July 1809, proved August Court 1809.
Witness: Barnett Forsythe.

- - -

D 247 Power of Attorney from WILLIAM BOND of Hillsborough, N.C., to friend James Webb of Hillsborough.
Dated 10 March 1809, proved August Court 1809.
Witnesses: William Whitted, James Whitted.

- - -

D 248 Will dated 13 April 1809, proved August Court 1809.

HUGH (x) McCADDAMS wife: Caty

sons: James, John, William and Isaac McCaddams $1 each
daus: Nancy McCaddams, Elizabeth Bason, Mary McCaddams $1 each
son: Hugh McCaddams land
" David McCaddams $1
" Tinnen McCaddams land
dau: Franky McCaddams one negro
son: Joseph, land, slaves

Executors: friends Joseph Moore and Robert Fossett.
Witnesses: Edward Fossett, Robert Tinnin, George Fausett.

- - -

D 250 Will dated 3 October 1808, proved August Court 1809.

REBECCA (x) McAdams

son: James and his daughter Rebecca
daus: Egness, Elizabeth Blair.

Witness: Samuel Crawford.

- - -

D 251 Will dated 9 May 1809, proved August Court 1809.

SAMUEL CHAMBERS wife: Sarah

son: James Chambers $1
sons: Samuel and William "land I purchased of John Railey"

daus: Mary Chambers, Elizabeth Railey, Hannah Lindley,
Grace Lindley

Executors: wife Sarah, and Owen Lindley.
Witnesses: John Thompson, Bennett Watson ?.

- - -

D 253 Bill of Sale from ANTHONY (x) COZART to Josiah Davis, both of Orange Co., N.C., for a slave girl Tamar for £ 500. Dated 20 May 1809, proved November Court 1809.
Witnesses: John Carrington, William Brinkley, Jr.

- - -

D 254 Will dated 25 May 1809, proved November Court 1809.

HENRY (x) PICKET "sick of body" wife: Indy or Judy

son-in-law: Ellick Grayham
granddau: Elizabeth Grayham

Executors: Ryly Vickers, ..?.. Guess.
Witnesses: Jesse (x) Picket, Lucy (x) Dolar, Mo. Guess.

- - -

D 256 Will dated 31 August 1809, proved Nov Court 1809.

DAVID (x) DUNN

sister: Nancy Love one half of property
brother: Drury Dunn other half of property

Witnesses: Isaac Hudson, Nathaniel Dunn.

- - -

D 257-258 Will dated 21 November 1809, proved Feb Court 1810.

ONLY (x) OWENS "sick and weak" wife: Sarah

daus: Nancy Jenkins and Elizabeth Lingo 5 shillings each
son: Belitha Owens 5 shillings
daus: Lear Pettigrew and Lavinia Pettigrew, 5 shillings each
sons: Samuel and John Owens 5 shillings each
son: Thomas Owens balance of estate

Executors: "trusty friends John Wilbon and John Jenkins."
Witnesses: Wm. Meadows , Charles Jenkins.

- - -

D 259 Will dated 10 October 1809, proved Feb Court 1810.

JOHN GRAHAM wife: Mary gets plantation etc, "to raise the children"
"Three sons James, George and Thomas Graham" all under age, to "be schooled".

daus: Jenny Walker $5, Ann Hall $5 and 1 negro man
sons: John Graham $25, etc, Robert Graham $25
dau: Fanny Walker $5
daus: Elizabeth Graham, Mary Graham, Charity Graham get a horse, cows, saddle, etc, each

Executors: wife Mary, and son John Graham.
Witnesses: David Bradford, James (x) Tate.

- - -

D 261 Will dated 12 March 1808, proved February Court 1810.

DARKIS (x) HAYS

Friends: Milly Beasley, Nancy Martin, Rachel Blanchard,
Ruthy Stark, the widow Stark, Phebe Stark,
Elizabeth Stark, Christin Hurdle

Executrix: Ruthy Stark
Witnesses: Hardy Hurdle, James Hurdle.

- - -

D 262 Will dated 14 August 1809, proved February Court 1810.

WORHAM GLEN wife: Nanny Glen

"My children (viz) Firy ? Glen, James Glen, David Glen, Nancy Wood, John Glen, Robert Glen and Sally Garrard."

Executors: Fery ? Glen and David Glen.
Witnesses: Thos. Reavis, Sally (x) Scoggins.

- - -

D 263 Will dated 11 September 1809, proved May Court 1810.

JESSE NEVILL wife: Elizabeth

"First children that have married off and gone from me, that is to say, Goodwick Kirk, Elizabeth Barby, Solomon Nevill, Benjamin Nevill, Jesse Nevill Jr", these have had their shares.

son: Samuel Parke Nevill
dau: Selah Nevill
son: Goodman Nevill (spelled Goodwin below)
" Wiley Whitwell Nevill
dau: Cynthia Aris ? Robertson

Executors: sons Goodwin Nevill and Samuel Parke Nevill.
Witnesses: Wm. Brewer, James Miles, Joshua Brewer.

- - -

D 265 Will dated 18 March ----, proved May Court 1810.

CHARLES COLLIER wife: Patty all estate

"My dear children", names and number not stated.

Executors: wife Patty, and friend Samuel Hopkins.
Witnesses: Edward Rigins, Rob't Campbell.

- - -

D 267 Bill of Sale from JOSHUA WEEDON of Orange County, N.C. to Quinton Anderson, horses and cow. Witness: James Anderson. Dated 9 February 1810, proved August Court 1810.

- - -

D 267 Will dated 8 September 1806, proved August Court 1810.

JNO. ARMSTRONG wife: Anne Armstrong

sons: Joseph, Thomas and James Armstrong 20 shillings each
dau: Margaret wife of James Willson 20 "
" Jinnet wife of John Hanks 20 "
" Mary wife of John Jesse 20 "
" Elizabeth wife of Isaac Jackson 20 "
" Catrenah wife of Absolom Cooper 20 "

Executors: wife Anne, "and my son John Hanks."
Witnesses: And'w McBroom, John Ray.

– – –

D 269 Will dated C July 1809, proved August Court 1810.

JOHN GATTIS

sons: Thomas & Alexander Gattis, land joining Joseph Kirkland
"To my daughter Martha or John Caldwell" 5 shillings
son: Samuel Gattis 5 shillings
"To my daughter Jinnet Morrow or William Morrow" 5 shillings
"" " " Sarah King or Nathaniel King" 5 "
sons: William Gattis and Isaac Gattis 5 shillings each

Executors: sons Thomas and Alexander Gattis.
Witnesses: Geo. Johnston, Mary Johnston, Joseph Kirkland.

– – –

D 271 Will dated 17 May 1810, proved November Court 1810.

WILLIAM (x) SCOTT wife: Mary Scott

sons:"John and William Mitchell Scott", Alexander and Thomas
daus: Jennet, Faney, Elizabeth, Mary

Executors: James Hutcheson, James Mc adam.
Witness: Samuel Crawford.

– – –

D 272 Will dated 20 August 1810, proved November Court 1810.

ABNER TAPP wife: Frances

He says "my fore children ... to raise my children.."

son: Richard Tapp
four daughters: Elizabeth, Susannah, Elethe

No executor named, no witnesses.

– – –

D 276 Will dated 28 August 1810, proved November Court 1810.

SAMUEL BENTON All estate goes to "John Taylor the younger my son-in-law of Hillsboro."
Executors: son-in-law John Taylor, friend Duncan Cameron.
Witnesses: Richard Henderson, Ed. Jones.

– – –

D 277 Will dated 4 December 1810, proved Feb Court 1811.

WILSON CHILD mother: Frances Child
of the town of Hillsborough

brother: Francis Child

"John Bruce, Charles Bruce & William Bruce sons of my brother-in-law Abner Bruce."

Executors: friends Archibald D. Murphey and John Taylor, Jr.
Witnesses: Henry Shutt, And. Brooks.

- - -

D 278 Will dated 9 March 1798, proved February Court 1811.

JOHN (x) COOK wife: Sarah Cook

son: Archibald Cook "plantation whereon he now lives"
" David Cook "" " " " " "
" Robert Cook
"All my children", number not stated.

Executors: son David Cook, and friend Hardy Hurdle.
Witnesses: Hardy Hurdle, H'm (?) Corgin.

- - -

D 280 Will dated 3 March 1810, proved February Court 1811.

LUDWICK ALBRIGHT

dau: Caty Holt wife of Jeremiah Holt
" Barbara Powel wife of Elias Powel

sons: John, Philip, Jacob, Ludwick, George & Daniel $10 each

"All my children tp wit: John, Barbara, Philip, Jacob, Ludwick, Caty, George and Daniel."

Executors: sons Ludwick and Daniel Albright.
Witnesses: Michael Holt, Rachel Holt.

- - -

D 282 Will dated 7 November 1810, proved Feb Court 1811.

CHARLES KING wife: Elizabeth

oldest son: Shurley gets land which was surveyed by Nathaniel and William King.
youngest son: Charles under age.

dau: Biddy
"son-in-law Charles Shaw and his wife Betsey" 10 shillings
grandchildren: William Franklin Shaw and Louisa Shaw

"To my bound servant John Cole ..." - continued -

Executors: Richard Blackwood, son Shurley King and wife Eliz.
Witnesses: Edwd. Robson, Wm. King.

- - -

D 286 Will dated 17 April 1811, proved May Court 1811. This will is not in the State Archives.

BENJAMIN RAINEY wife: Nancy

Michael Holt and Neil Bhon ? have bought land from testator.

daus: Nancy, Sally, Milly
son: John land in Tennessee on Turnbull Creek, 500 acres

"Sons and sons-in-law (to wit) John King, Isaac Rainey, Benjamin Abel Rainey and William Holt" land in Orange County, N.C. joining Guilford County line, Anthony Coble, etc.

grandson: Austin
He leaves his surveying instruments to his son Isaac.

Executors: son Benjamin Able Rainey and son-in-law Wm. Holt.
Witnesses: John Gant, Mason Tapley.
This will is also recorded on pages 295-299 in Book D.

- - -

D 289 Will dated 24 February 1807, proved Nov Court 1808.

LEWIS KIRK wife: Sarah

son: John Kirk

"My four eldest children viz William James Rebecca and Josiah."

Executors: friends Richard Stanford and Thomas Snipes.
Witnesses: Jon. Umstead, H. Forest, David Roach.

- - -

D 291 Deed from JAMES A. MORGAN to William Kirkland.
Witnesses: William Barbee, Edward ...?...
Dated 22 May 1809, proved November 1809.

- - -

D 292 Will dated 4 October 1799, proved May Court 1803.

JAMES ELLIOTT (no relationships stated except to wife)

wife: her name not stated, William Elliott is to care for her.

"To William Elliott all my lands on franchbord(French Broad ?) on James River on Haw River on Canocogiy ? Creek in Pennsylvania". (Seem to be four tracts in N.C. and another in Pa.)

- continued -

D 292 continued

Two shillings each to: John Murray, William Carter, James ..ad, Thomas Blak, William Pasmore.

Executor: William Elliott
Witnesses: John Murray, David Pasmore.

- - -

D 293 Will dated 16 September 1802, proved Feb Court 1804.

WILLIAM RHODES wife: Mary Rhodes

son: Benjamin Baker Rhodes
" John Rhodes (he has already received his part)
" William Rhodes

These eight daughters have already received their parts: Hannah Wotle (Whatley ?), Nanny Grism, Elizabeth Grisum, Molly Pattishall, Michel Horn, Amelia Herndon, Rebecca Herndon, Franky Barbee.

Executors: Chesley Page Patterson, John Rhodes, Benjamin Rhodes' son John, Benj. Baker Rhodes.
Witnesses: James Wilson, William Herndon, Henry (x) Trice, James Hutchins.

- - -

D 295-299 BENJAMIN RAINEY will. See D 286.

- - -

D 300 Power of Attorney from THOMAS HOUSE or HORNE "formerly of Orange County, N.C. but now of Chester District in the State of South Carolina" to William Holt. He revokes letters of Administration granted to John Strowd on the estate of his deceased son LILLTLEBURY HORNE ? who died in North Carolina. Dated 21 June 1811. Witness: B.A.Rainey.

- - -

D 301 Will dated 31 May 1808, proved November Court 1808.

W. A. FRESHWATER wife: Sally "to raise my children"

"My children to wit: Thadeus Freshwater, Chloe, Polley, Betsey, Luraney David Sally and Susanna Freshwater."

Executors: wife, and Hardy Hurdle.
Witnesses: Hardy Hurdle, Benj. Simpson.

- - -

D 303 Agreement between WILLIAM MINOR (now of age) and his former guardian JOHN STROWD (who was his guardian by the Chatham County, N.C. Court ... Witnesses: Bryant Strowd, Henry Strowd. Dated 14 January 1807, proved November Court 1807.

- - -

D 304 Will dated 26 March 1806, proved May Court 1806.

RICHARD CATE wife: Elizabeth

son: Abner Cate "land where he is settled"
sons: John Cate, Ephriam Cate
daus: Mary Hunt, Nancy Dossett

"My five children - Mary Hunt, Nancy Dossett, John, Ephriam and Abner Cate."

Executors: sons Ephriam and Abner.
Witnesses: James Latta, Shardick (x) Channeller.

- - -

D 306 Will dated 19 July 1810, proved August Court 1810.

JOHN (x) CRESWELL son: John Creswell

daus: Margaret Morrow, Easter Creswell
sons: William Creswell, Alexander Creswell

Executors: "trusty friends John Ray and Robert Faucett."
Witnesses: Thomas Vincent, Thomas Barnwell.

Codicil dated 30 July 1830 gives daughter Easter loom, etc.
Witnesses: John (x) Noble, John Creswell.

- - -

D 308 Power of Attorney from GEORGE RAY of Tennessee to JAMES MILLER of Orange County, N.C. Dated 11 May 1808, proved May 1808. Witnesses: Sampson Moore, John Hart.

- - -

D 309-311 Will dated 18 July 1801, proved May Court 1811.

JAMES FAUCETTE wife: Susannah

dau: Rachel Faucett
" Margaret Woods wife of Nathan Woods
" Mary Watham wife of Charles Wortham (spelled both ways)
" Lucy Smith wife of William Smith

He has unmarried daughters, names and number not stated.

Executors and friends to care for property: "well beloved friends Robert Faucett, Mathew Woods, Charles Watham and James Latta."
Witnesses: A. Tatom, George Anderson, Dun. Cameron.

- - -

D 312 Will dated 22 April 1811, proved May Court 1811.

HENRY SHUTT of the town of Hillsborough wife: Elizabeth

"My children" all under age, names and number not stated.

Executors: wife Elizabeth, and Thomas Ruffin.
Witnesses: J. Webb, J. Taylor.

- - -

D 314 Will dated --- 1811, proved May Court 1811.

SAMUEL ECTOR wife: name not stated

sons: Joseph, James, William
son: Hugh "land where John Dunnivan now lives"
daus: Margaret, Keziah son: Thomas

Executors: wife, and son Joseph
Witnesses: David Bradford,Sr., John Hughes.

- - -

D 316 Will dated 18 December 1810, proved May Court 1811.

SOLOMON BOOTH mother: Priscilla Booth

brother: Alfred Booth "my brothers"

Executor: brother Tapley Booth
Witnesses: John Moore, Sampson Moore, Betsey (x) Booth.

- - -

D 317 Power of Attornet from JONATHAN LINDLEY to "trusty friend JOHN NEWLIN. Witnesses: Thos. Whitted, Jon. Thomson. Dated 1 May 1811, proved May Court 1811.

- - -

D 317A Power of Attorney from JAMES RAY to friend JAMES WILLIAMS, both of Orange County, to sell land on a branch of Little River in Orange County conveyed from Rebecca McClennin to James Ray, and a tract conveyed by William Lindley to James Ray on the waters of Eno. Money is due James Ray from the estate of Michael Robinson, dec'd, who "removed before his decease to the State of Tennessee." Dated 17 November 1810, proved Aug 1811.
Witnesses: John Street, Justice Peace
David Ray, W. Cain.
signed:"James Ray of John."

- - -

D 318 Power of Attorney from WILLIAM KIRKLAND to GEORGE McNEILL and THOMAS RUFFIN, all of Orange County, N.C., to sell any of his property not devised by will to his wife Margaret Kirkland and his sons John Umstead and Alexander McKinzie. Dated 1 August 1811, proved August Court 1811.
Witness: Wm. Norwood.

- - -

D 320 Will dated 3 November 1792, proved August Court 1811.

JOHN (x) HODGE wife: Agness Hodge
"in low state of health"

son: Robert

"Two grandsons William & Joseph's sons John" each £ 10, when they come of age.

- continued -

sons: George, Samuel

Executors: wife Agness, and son Robert
Witnesses: Wm. Hodge, Jno. Herman.

- - -

D 322 Will dated 1 September 1811, proved Feb Court 1812.

CHARLES CHRISTMAS

All his estate is left in trust for the children named below, no relationship stated. He mentions a note he holds from his brother Nath. Christmas of the Mississippi Territory.

Estate left for the "raising of six children of Sarah Smith's (viz) John, Charles, Nancy, Patheny, William & Susannah & the raising and schooling of a child of Nancy Willocks (viz) Rebeckah."

Executors: Richard Christmas, Thomas Brewer, William Moore.
Witnesses: Wm. Moore, Joel Parish.

- - -

D 324 Will dated 20 December 1811, proved Feb Court 1812.

MATHAIS WILSON sister: Rachel Wilson plantation, etc.

friend: George Brown

"To William Wilson son of my brother Edward Wilson $20 to help with his schooling".

Executors: sister Rachel and brother William Wilson.
Witnesses: Thomas Gill, David Mebane.

- - -

D 326 Will dated 31 December 1811, proved Feb Court 1812.

JAMES CRAWFORD wife: Margaret

sons: William, Samuel he says"all my sons"
"Girls that is at home" names and number not stated.
dau: Hannah

Executors: son John Crawford and James Crawford.
Witnesses: Thos. Whitted, Jno. Thompson, James Morrow.

- - -

D 327 Will dated ---, proved February Court 1812.

DANIEL CLOUD wife: Nancy

sons: Joel, "to Daniel and David the tract of land on New Hope and mill I bought of John Mitchel"

daus: Martha, Margaret - continued -

D 327 continued
son: John No executor named.

Witnesses: Wm. Palmer, John Comb, Jesse ..?..

\- - -

D 328 Will dated 16 December 1811, proved Feb Court 1812.

ANDREW BROOKS mother a legatee, name not stated

sisters: Hannah, Sally Terrill

To Nelly Bryant all household furniture and bedding.
"Children of my brother William Brook and Joseph Terrill".
"Nephew James Brooks son of my sister Hannah."

No executor named. Will is not signed or witnessed.

\- - -

D 331 Will dated 24 February 1809, proved Feb Court 1812.

JOHN (x) SHADDY wife: Elizabeth
He owns a mill.

"All my children"
Molly wife of John Coble
Caty " " George A. Fogleman
John Shaddy
Rachel wife of George Fogleman
Jacob Shaddy
"youngest daughter and wife of Henry Steel"

Executors: "friend Michael Holt and my son Jacob Shaddy".
Witness: Frederic Kinney

\- - -

D 333 Will dated 11 March 1812, proved May Court 1812.

JAMES TAYLOR sister: Ann Taylor

father: John Taylor Executor: Thomas Taylor
Witnesses: John Anderson, Daniel Wilkerson, John Wilkerson.

\- - -

D 334 Will dated 25 May 1801, proved May Court 1812.

WILLIAM (x) CRABTREE granddaughter: Amelia

sons: Samuel, Abraham, James

Executor: son Samuel.
Witnesses: Samuel Thompson, Thos. Barton Jun'r,
Chas. Hughes.

\- - -

D 335 Will dated 30 March 1812, proved May Court 1812.
JAMES THOMPSON wife: Elizabeth

"All my children", number not stated.
sons: Levi (gets family Bible), John Thompson
dau: Sarah Woody

Executors: "beloved friends John Woody and Samuel Woody sons of James Woody."
Witnesses: John Whitted, Joshua Woody.

- - -

D 336 Will dated 17 March 1810, proved May Court 1812.

JOHN WALKER (no wife mentioned)

son: Peter Walker 100 acres on Duck River in Tennessee
dau: Mary Picket
Walter Picket
grandsons: John and James Walker, sons of William.
son: Andrew "remainder of my land on Duck River in Tennessee" and "plantation on which he lives".
grandsons: Peter and John, sons of Andrew Walker.
dau: Matty McCauley

Executors: sons Peter and William Walker.
Witnesses: James Mebane, John Wilson, James Murray.

- - -

D 338 Will dated 18 May 1811, proved May Court 1812.

BENJAMIN YEARGIN

wife: Sarah Yeargin "500 acres in Wilkes County on Cub Creek, on S.Side of Yadkin River, and near the Cour[t] House, Wilkesborough."
"Three of my children, Mark M. Yeargin, Harriett Forsythe, Bartlett Yeargin."
dau: Charlotte H. Young
son: Mark M. Yeargin 700 acres in Wilkes on Mulberry Creek.

Executors: wife Sarah, James Forsythe and Bartlett Yeargin.
Witness: David Strain.

- - -

D 339 Will dated 10 May 1812, proved May Court 1812.

HENRY (x) HASTINGS (heirs given in the order they are given in the will.)

dau: Mary Hastings
grandson: John Young
dau: Margaret Adams
grandson: Thomas Crabtree
daus: Isbell Collins, Elizabeth Watson, Ester Thompson
sons: James, Joseph, John, William and Henry Hastings.

Executor: son James Hastings
Witnesses: Andrew Watson, Arch. Crabtree.

- - -

D 342 Will dated 27 September 1810, proved --

MICHAEL SHOFNER

youngest son: Peter Shofner, "his four brothers"
son: Michael Shofner
dau: Magdalane

Executors: "sons-in-law Jacob Antony, Mathea (?) Fogleman."
Witness: Henry Cook, Jr.

- - -

D 344 Will dated 23 June 1812, proved --

ISHAM (x) THRIFT

wife: Mary gets land in Orange County "deeded from Wm. Strowd, deceased", and land in Chatham Co., N.C. "deeded from Jesse Buckner on the N.Side of Haw River on Wilkerson Creek."

"All my children, namely, Elizabeth Snipes, Susannah Booker, Perry Thrift, Sally Thrift, Delila Petty, Peggy Thrift, William Thrift, David Thrift, Drury Thrift, Isham Thrift, Polly Thrift, Frances Thrift, Nancy Thrift and Levicy Thrift." (14)

Executors: wife Mary Thrift and son David Thrift.
Witnesses: Bryant Strowd, P. Willis, Henry (x) Andrus.

- - -

D 346 Will dated 9 July 1812, proved --

PHILIP (x) EULICE wife: Elizabeth

sons: Henry Eulice, John Eulice, Actum (?) Eulice.

daus: Margaret Kimbro, Mary Linn, Molly Huffman, Eve Ross ?, Susanna Kimbro, Elizabeth Jones, Barbara Tracy.

"Children of my daughter Catherine Lineberry ... her daughter Eleanor Jones, ... Sophia Coble, George Lineberry and William Lineberry."

Executors: sons Henry and John Eulice.
Witnesses: Jonathan Hadley, John Arwick, Andrew (x) Shatterly.

- - -

D 347 Will dated 13 May 1812, proved --

EDWARD WILSON wife: Rachel

daus: Polly (unmarried), Nancy, Rachel
sons: William, Edward, Hugh
grandson: "my son Edward's son William"

Executors: daughter Polly and son William.
Witnesses: David Mebane, B. Burnsides.

- - -

D 351 Will dated 15 February 1812, proved --

JOHN PICKARD   wife: Peggy

dau: Sally (unmarried), her brother Alex is named as guardian.

"My three youngest sons, viz, Daniel, Jesse and Thomas."

.."rest of my sons and daughters, to wit, my sons Henry James John Alex'r Isaac Richard Elisha Michael and my daughters Rebecca Steel Fanny Crutchfield and Catherine Efland." (No punctuation.)

Executors: son Alex'r Pickard and grandson John H. Pickard.
Witnesses: Thomas Lasley, John Grimes.

- - -

D 352-358 Will dated 3 January 1812, proved --

GAVIN ALVES   cousin: Jane Burgess

aunts: Elizabeth Hogg, Jean Hogg

He sets free his slaves John and Esther. A negro boy, son of Esther, is to be bound out to learn a trade until he reaches 21 years of age, when he is to be emancipated. Legacies to each of these slaves.

brother: Walter Alves
sisters: Mrs. Hellen Caldwell, Mrs. Robina Norwood
sister-in-law: Mrs. Amelia Alves
neices: Ann Alves Webb, Mrs. Anne Henderson, Elizabeth Alves, Elizabeth Norwood.
nephews: John Huske, William, James and Thomas Hooper, James Alves, William Alves.
friends: the Rev. Joseph Caldwell, Dr. James Webb, Richard Henderson, Esq., Wm. Norwood, Esq. Catlett Campbell, Esq.

Executors: brother Walter Alves and friend Dr. James Webb.
Witnesses: James Child, A.B.Bruce.

- - - -

D 359-362 Will dated 29 January 1812, proved --

JOHN ALLEN   wife: Jennett

daus: Peggy, Sally, Jane ("Jenny"), all unmarried
sons: Abraham, George, Samuel
daus: Elizabeth, Nancy
grandson: John Allen

Executors: son Samuel, and Alexander Russell.
Witnesses: Ezekiel B. Currie, Alexander Russell, John C. Russell.

- - -

D 362 Will dated 4 November 1812, proved --

JOHN WILSON wife: Nancy

"My children",names and number not stated

Executors: "trusty friends James Walker and Herbert Sims."
Witnesses: James Webb, Thos. Latta.

\- - -

D 364 Will dated 23 October 1812, proved --

PETER (x) SMITH

mother: Hannah Smith to have all his estate during her life

"my four sisters namely Nancy, Susanna, Barbary and Polly Smith" to divide estate after mother's death.

Executors: "trusty friends John Hilton and John Cook."
Witness: Henry Cook,Jr.

\- - -

D 365 Will dated 13 August 1812, proved --

JACOB RILEY, SR.

son: Jacob Riley plantation, money, furniture, etc,
dau: Susanna Riley divided between these two children.

sons: Peter Riley, John Riley, 1 shilling each
dau: Caty Findly wife of Jacob Findly 1 shilling
" Mary Gray " " James Gray 1 "

Executors: sons Peter and Jacob Riley.
Witness: James Webb.

\- - -

D 366 Will dated 10 February 1813, proved --

WILLIAM RAY wife: Nancy Ray

son: James Ray
dau: Elizabeth Ray. No executor named

Witnesses: Elizabeth (x) Allison, Moses Gwinn.

\- - -

D 367 Will dated 9 January 1813, proved --

JOHN (x) McCRARY or McCRORY

sons: Robert and John land on Boyd's Creek
" Andrew McCrory, David McCrory
daus: Agness Fossett, Jane Scarborough

Witnesses: Samuel Crawford, James Murray. No executor named.

\- - -

D 368 Will dated ? proved --

WILLIAM HORN Wife: Agnes, all estate during her life.

"Unmarried children viz- John Tapley William Wesley Thomas Anderson & Nancy Ann Horn." (No punctuation, see below.)

Married children: Abel Horn, Sarah Griffin, Edith Younger.

three sons John Tapley William Wesley & Thomas Anderson Horn to receive plantation after wife's death.

Executors: wife, and John Tapley Horn.
Witnesses: G. Campbell, Peter Walker.

- - -

D 369 Will dated 17 December 1811, proved --

THOMAS CATE wife: Martha Cate

sons: Thomas Cate and John S. Cate, both under age
dau: Doratha Cate, under age
daus: Polly Cate, Martha Cate
sons: Isaih Cate, Thomas Cate

Executors: wife Martha, and "well beloved friend John Sykes."
Witness: Susannah (x) Durham.

- - -

D 371 Power of Attorney from JOHN C. McLEMORE of town of Nashville, County of Davidson, State of Tennessee, to HUGH MULHOLLAN of Orange Co., N.C., to make a deed to John Crutchfield for land on waters of Cane Creek joining Thomas Kirk and others, being the same land conveyed by William Kirkland ..." Dated 28 December 1812, recorded in Davidson Co., Tenn., 4 January 1813, in Orange County, N.C. --

- - -

D 373 Will dated 9 March 1812, proved --

DAVID HERNDON

dau: Frances
son: Larkin
daus: Clary, Martha
sons: Edmond, George
daus: Nancy, Rachel, Elizabeth, Rebecca
son: Martin Pearce

Executors: sons Edmond and George Herndon.
Witnesses: Jno. Landers, Elisha Rowark.
Note by Ruth Herndon Shields: Descendants of David Herndon are given in PART FOUR, HERNDONS OF THE AMERICAN REVOLUTION, by John Goodwin Herndon. See last pages of this book.)

- - -

D 374 Power of Attorney from JOHN (x) GEE planter of Rollins Fork of Salt River in Casey County, Kentucky, to HANSON COULTER of Orange Co., N.C., to collect a legacy from the estate of Thomas Odian (?) of Chatham Co., N.C.
Dated 9 April 1812, proved August Court 1812.
Witness: John Pendergrass.

- - -

D 375 Power of Attorney from JACOB ALBRIGHT of Madison County Georgia, to THOMAS POWELL of Orange Co., N.C., to collect from the executors of "my father LUDOWICK ALBRIGHT'S estate" ....
Dated 27 April 1812, proved August Court 1812.
Witnesses: Jas. Patterson, Thomas Kirk.

- - -

D 375 Power of Attorney from MARK M. YEARGIN of Orange County, N.C. to his brother BARTLETT YEARGIN, to sell land in Wilkes County, N.C. Dated 13 September 1812, proved Nov Court 1812.
Witness: James Forsythe.

- - -

D 376 SARAH YOUNGER administratrix of HENRY YOUNGER dec'd, "died on 2nd day of December 1812", gives her account of the slaves belonging to the estate, among Robert A. Younger the oldest son, John Younger the second child, and Richard Younger "the third and last child". Sarah is guardian to John and Richard. Dated 27 May 1813, proved May Court 1813.

- - -

D 377 Will dated 16 May 1813, proved May Court 1813.

HENRY O'DANIEL

Three brothers, Samuel, John and Joshua O'Daniel.
Four sisters, Susannah Pickard, Jane McDaniel,
Sally Hastings and Peggy Pickard.

Executors: James O'Daniel and Thomas Hastings.
Witnesses: Arch'd Holmes, John Grimes.

- - -

D 379 Will dated 24 July 1797, proved August Court 1813.

WILLIAM (x) RANY wife: Mary

son: David Rany
grandsons: William Baker (under age),
Wm. Rany Gwin (under age), William Rany

John Baker (no relationship stated)
brother: David Rany

Executors: wife Mary, and son David Rany.
Witnesses: Wm. Thrailkill, John Gil, Robert Duncan.

- - -

D 380 Deed of Gift from THOMAS HOLLOWAY of Orange County, N.C. to his son WILLIAM HOLLOWAY for a mare.
Dated 26 August 1813, proved August Court 1813.
Witnesses: Reuben Farthing, Thomas Holloway, Sr.

- - -

D 380 Will dated 15 June 1812, proved August Court 1813.

JOHN TAYLOR

son: Joseph Taylor daughter: Ann Taylor
"All my sons and daughters", names and number not stated.

Sole executor: Thomas Taylor.
Witnesses: Thomas Clarke, James McCord.

- - -

D 381 Will dated 14 July 1813, proved August Court 1813.

JAMES (x) WATSON, SR. wife: Margaret

sister-in-law: Elleanor Witted (?)

"My eight children-to wit- Helen Riley, James Watson, Rebecca Watson, Elizabeth Comb, Andrew Watson, Nancy Watson, John Watson and Robert Watson."

grandchildren: "Three children of Helen Riley -viz- Washington Riley, Elizabeth Riley and Rachel Riley."

Executors: wife Margaret, and son-in-law John Combs.
Witnesses: Abner Bailiff, John Dockery.

- - -

D 383 Will dated 16 January 1813, proved August Court 1813.

JOSEPH MOORE brother: John Moore

sister: Mary Ferguson plantation, slaves, etc, and after her death it goes to his brother John Moore.

Executors: John Moore, Sampson Moore, and sister Mary Ferguson.
Witnesses: John Allison, James Allison.

- - -

D 384 Will dated 2 June 1810, proved August Court 1813.

SACKFIELD or ZACKFIELD BREWER son: Thomas Brewer

granddaughter: Patsey Lindsey

great-grandchildren: "Two oldest children of my granddaughter Sarah Edwards" names not stated.
son: Ezekiel Brewer

- continued -

D 384 continued
grandsons: Sackfield and Henry Brewer, sons of Ezekiel
granddaus: Patsey and Polly Brewer, daughters of Ezekiel

dau: Elizabeth land on West side of Cane Creek joining Wm./ Hopson

granddaus: Mary Meachum, Sarah Edwards, Patsey Lindsey

"Great-grandson Peter Brewer son of my grandson Peter Brewer".

"My four surviving children Ezekiel and Thomas Brewer, Elizabeth Brewer and Rebecca Thompson."

Executors: sons Ezekiel and Sackfield Brewer.
Witnesses: A. Stanford, William Moore.

- - -

D 387 Will dated 14 September 1818, proved August Court 1813.

STERLING HARRIS

wife: Hannah "tract whereon I now live", slaves, lot in Hillsborough, etc.

dau: Charlotte Street wife of John Street of Hillsborough

Executors: wife Hannah, and "trusty friends Levi Whitted, James Phillips and William Kirkland."
Witnesses: John Young, J. Taylor, Theopilus Thompson.

- - -

D 389 Power of Attorney from PATSEY (x) RHODES to her father ACQUILLA RHODES to collect money due her from William Barbee. Dated 15 May 1813, proved November Court 1813.
Witnesses: Mann Patterson, David (x) Hinchey.

- - -

D 390 Will dated 29 September 1813, proved Nov Court 1813.

ROBERT (x) MILLIKEN wife: Jane gets land and mill

sons: John, Charles, Jesse; Robert and William get plantation after wife's death ; Haberson.

Executors: wife Jane, and sons Robert and William.
Witnesses: Joel Strong, Wm. Moore.

- - -

D 392 Will dated 19 July 1809, proved November Court 1813.

JOHN LINCH, SR.

sons: Jackson Linch and Cleaton Linch get plantation

daus: Rachel Linch, Gillee Linch

- continued -

D 392 continued
sons: Darling Linch, John Linch
daus: Sarah Jenkins, Olive Horner

Executors: James Latta and son Jackson Linch.
Witnesses: Henry Bunch, Rachel (x) Linch, Gillee (x) Linch.

- - -

D 393 Will dated 29 June 1808, proved November Court 1813.

JOHN WOODS wife: Ann Woods

son: David Woods

"All my children- viz- William woods, John Woods, Samuel Woods and Thomas Woods except Joseph Woods alias Joseph Baldridge."

Executors: sons Samuel and David Woods.
Witnesses: Jas. H. Bowman, John Hanks.

- - -

D 395 Will dated 7 October 1809, proved Nov Court 1813.

JACOB HUGGINS wife: Mary one-half of estate

son: Jacob Huggins other half of estate

Executors: "worthy friends John Campbell and Aaron Walker."
Witnesses: Jno. Campbell, Jas. Campbell, Joseph Hodge.

- - -

D 396 Will dated 4 August 1813, proved November Court 1813.

GEORGE CLANCY, SR. of the Town of Hillsborough, N.C.

wife: Rebecca
daus: Jenny Clancy, Polly Clancy & Sally Clancy, all under age.
son-in-law: William Palmer
sons: Jack Clancy and William Clancy to be sent to school, and then to be bound to trades.

Executors: wife Rebecca, and son Thomas Clancy.
Witness: A. B. Bruce.

- - -

D 398 Will dated 10 December 1813, proved Feb Court 1814.

JOHN WILKERSON wife: Rebecca

daughter Rebecca, under age, to be educated

Executors: "trusty friends James Lapslie and Daniel Wilkerson."
Witnesses: Moses Guin, Thomas Wilson, Jas. D. Hughes.

- - -

D 399 Will dated 8 February 1814, proved Feb Court 1814.

ELIZABETH (x) MURDOCK widow of James Murdock.

dau: Ann Murdock grandson: David Murdock, son of Ann

oldest daughter: Caty Murdock 5 shillings
dau: Mary Buchannon 5 shillings
sons: James and William Murdock 5 shillings each
grandchildren: John Murdock and Mary Murdock, ch. of James.
grandson: Robert, son of John Murdock deceased
granddau: Elizabeth Riggs, dau. of John Murdock deceased
" Elizabeth Murdock, dau. of James Murdock

Executrix: daughter Ann Murdock.
Witnesses: Thos. B. Patterson, Wm. Bowls.

- - -

D 401-404 Will dated 9th day 9th month 1813, proved Feb. 1814

JAMES NEWLIN "farmer" wife: Deborah

son: John
" Thomas "land on which I now live on the N. Side of Cane Creek" .. approximately 350 acres
" Nathaniel "my place over the creek ... 200 acres ... known by the name of Wait's place."
" William "plantation known by name of Waugh's place.."
" Jonathan "tract of land I lately purchased of Robert Green .. also my lot in Haywood."
daus: Deborah, Sarah, Mary, Ruth, Hannah

Executors: sons John and Thomas, and brother Nathaniel.
Witnesses: Jeremiah Hubbard, Margaret Hubbard.

- - -

D 4-4 Power of Attorney from SAMUEL TURRENTINE of the town of Hillsborough to JOHN TAYLOR and THOMAS CLANCY, ESQ.
Dated 27 Jan 1814, proved Feb 1814. Witness: Wm. Norwood.

- - -

D 406 Deed from JOSEPH COLLINS to ENOCH COLLINS for a mare.
Dated 1 April 1814, proved May Court 1814.
Witnesses: Edward McDade, Thomas Ray, Ashby Dunnagan.

- - -

D 407 Will dated 21 March 1814, proved May Court 1814.

DAVID H. NUNN mother: Elizabeth Nunn

brothers: Ilai Nunn, Hugh Nunn
sisters: Sally Nunn, Edith (Nunn) Thompson

Executors: brother-in-law Richard Thompson, and Thomas Clancy of Hillsborough.
Witnesses: I or J Witherspoon, F. Burnett.

- - -

D 408 Will dated 16 April 1812, proved August Court 1814.

ROBERT BERRY wife: Elizabeth

dau: Elizabeth Berry and her daughter Mary

sons: Robert Berry, Joshua Berry, Thomas Berry
Isaac Berry (not of sound mind, Henry care for him)
Henry Berry, David Berry, William Berry
"daughter Mary Kemp deceased's heirs one pound"
"son John Berry deceased's heirs one negro girl."

Executors: wife, and son Henry Berry.
Witnesses: J. Rountree, Wm. R. Robinson.

- - -

D 410 Will dated 23 March 1807, proved August Court 1814.

JAMES WILKINSON wife: Caty Wilkinson

son: William Wilkinson plantation, etc
dau: Mary Wilkinson "bed & furniture, mare & colt, etc"
daus: An Wilkinson and Susannah Ray 5 shillings each
sons: John Wilkinson, James Wilkinson 5 shillings each

Executors: "my wife Caty Wilkinson and my son Joseph Ray."
Witnesses: John Ray, James Clarke.

- - -

D 411 Will dated 14 July 1814, proved November Court 1814.

PAUL (x) MORGAN "very sick"

All estate to Isaac Jackson Senior. He is named executor.

Witnesses: Benoni Jackson, Hezekia s (x) Revel.

- - -

D 412 Will dated 21 October 1814, proved Nov Court 1814.

JOHN SAUNDERS All estate to mother, Lydia Saunders.

If anything is left after his mother's death it is to be divided between Patsy Proctor and Nancy Saunders.

Trustee and executor: William Henry Merritt.
Witnesses: Wm. Merritt, Thomas Merritt,

- - -

D 412 Will dated 17 September 1814, proved Nov Court 1814.

ISAAC JACKSON, JUNIOR farmer

No relationship stated to any of the legatees.
"To James Jackson, to Benoni Jackson " ... - continued-

D 412 continued

"to Elizabeth Randles and Mary Thompson" ...
"to Elizabeth McCain" ..
"to Isaac Jackson, .. to James Jackson"
"and Hetty Williams owes 3 dollard in which I allow to be buried."

Executor: J. Jackson.
Witnesses: Benoni Jackson, Mary (x) Jackson.

- - -

D 413 Deed from WILLIAM FAUCETTE to RALPH FAUCETTE for a negro girl and child. Witness: Philip Walker. Dated 28 November 1814, proved November Court 1814.

- - -

D 414 Will dated 6 September 1814, proved Nov Court 1814.

GEORGE RAY wife, name not stated , is pregnant ?

son: Michael Ray
daus: Jenny, Polly, Sally, Delilah, Matheran (Martha Ann ?)
"If my wife should have a male child ..."

Executors: "friend John Ray and Rankin McKee."
Witnesses: James Miller, R.R.Reade, Martin Murphey.

- - -

D 416 Will dated 26 August 1808, proved November 1814.

WILLIAM ARMSTRONG wife: Nancy

"My five children"
eldest son: Joseph Armstrong
daus: Isabella Armstrong, Marget Armstrong
sons: William Armstrong, James Armstrong

grandsons: Jesse Armstrong, James Watson Armstrong

Executors: sons Joseph and William Armstrong.
Witnesses: J. Rountree, Charles Rountree Jun'r.

- - -

D 418-420 Will dated 20 September 1814, proved Nov 1814.

SARAH HARDEN

son: John Harden "he having been provided for in the will of his father"
dau: Mary Prather tract of 150 acres called Powell's Place
"my three youngest daughters Sarah, Betsey and Peggy"
Peggy gets "tract whereon I now live, .. also the Rainey tract", etc.

Executors: "my good worthy friends Archibald D. Murphey, John L. Prather, and John Harden."
Witnesses: Thos. Scott, Rebekah Harden.

- - -

D 421-423 Will dated 24 November 1814, proved Feb Court 1815.

WILLIAM HOBBS, SENIOR wife: Easther

son: James Hobbs $1, he has had his share
daus: Mary Cheek, Elizabeth Chambers $1 each
sons: Thomas Hobbs, William Hobbs $1 each
son-in-law: Thomas Durham $1
sons: Jonathan, David, John, Harbard Hobbs
dau: Susannah Hobbs

Executors: wife Easther Hobbs, and trusty friend Thomas Latta.
Witnesses: Andrew Watson, Joseph (x) Weeks.

- - -

D 423 Deed of Gift from JOHN L. KIRK to his son JOHN L.F. KIRK for a negro girl. Dated 20 Nov 1812, proved Feb 1815. Witness: Sarah Kirk.

- - -

D 423 Receipt from SARAH KIRK. "Received of THOMAS GRIFFIN Ь 200 for a negro woman. Dated 4 Jan 1810, proved Feb 1815. Witnesses: John L. Kirk, James Minnis. "

- - -

D 424 Power of Attorney from GEORGE CHARLES of Russell Co., Va. to JOSEPH GIBSON of Guilford Co., N.C. to collect his part of the estate of "my father Michael Charles lately deceased of Orange County." Dated 22 July 1813, proved Feb 1815. Witnesses: Andrew Gibson, Zachariah Phillips.

- - -

D 424 Bill of Sale from JAMES MINNIS to JAMES CHAMBERS both of Orange County, N.C. Dated 2 March 1815, proved Feb Ct 1815. Witnesses: Andrew Watson, Joseph Stubbins.
Secutity: Thomas (x) Griffin.

- - -

D 425 Will dated 14 July 1814, proved February Court 1815.

JOSEPH WOODY wife: Sarah Woody

sons: Joshua Woody, Joseph Woody, Robert Woody
"All my children", number not stated.
"Patsy Jones which was bound to me"..

Executors: sons Joshua and Joseph Woody.
Witnesses: John Whitted, Thomas Whitted, Jun'r.

- - -

D 427 Will dated 20 September 1814, proved Feb Court 1815.

HENRY EVANS wife: Elizabeth (she is pregnant)

son: Asa land in Wake County, N.C.(he is under 9 years old)

"Archelus M. Thompson be sent to school 18 months" .. he is "to continue with my wife if they can agree".

Executors: "trusty friends Chesley P. Patterson, William Rhodes and Benjamin Rhodes."
Witnesses: John Rhodes, Thomas (x) Hutchings.

- - -

D 429 Will dated 18 April 1815, proved May Court 1815.

MARY (x) BIRD "in a low state of health"

son: John daughters, names not stated

Sole executor: son John
Witnesses: I or J Mebane, Alfred Compton, Jno. Umstead.

- - -

D 430 Will dated 27 February 1806, proved May Court 1815.

JAMES FULTON, "planter"

son: James gets estate
dau: Mary Rhodes wife of Thomas Rhodes 10 shillings
" Esther Warren wife of James Warren 10 shillings
" Jane " " " William Warren 10 shillings
" Margaret Garrard wife of James Garrard 10 shillings
" Sarah Edwards " " Thomas Edwards 10"

Executor: son James.
Witnesses: Thomas Latta, Jun'r, J. Watson.

- - -

D 431 Will dated 24 July 1814, proved May Court 1815.

HENRY (x) MARTIN wife: Sarah

sons: Robert Martin, George Martin
dau: Jane Browning wife of Edmund Browning
children: Elizabeth, Sally Wamick (Warnick ?) Rebecca Polly Nancy & Peggy Martin (only one comma)

Executrix: wife, "in whom I much confide."
Witnesses: Caleb Wilson, J. Watson.

- - -

D 432-434 Will dated 30 March 1815, proved May Court 1815.

GEORGE COBLE wife: Catherine

sons: John, David, Peter, William
daus: Elizabeth, Mary

Executors: Wife Catherine, and friend Isaac Patterson.
Witnesses: Levin Wood, M.G.Clay.

- - -

D 434 Will dated 8 March 1815, proved May Court 1815.

WILLIAM (x) MONTGOMERY wife: Eady
"weak in body"

sons: Hugh, John, Jonathan, James, David, Alexander
dau: Nancy
grandsons: "son Hugh's two sons James and Alexander"

Executors: John Latta Jun'r, and William Baldwin.
Witnesses: Hugh Montgomery, William (x) Woods.

- - -

D 436-438 Will dated 23 September 1814, proved May Court 1815.

WILLIS (x) ROBERTS wife: Sarah Roberts

stepchildren: Rebecca Harris, Ephriam Harris, Elzy Harris

"My own six children" to "be schooled".
daus: Menday Roberts, Loviney Roberts
sons: James Roberts, Jesse Roberts
daus: Sarah Roberts, Polly Roberts

Executors: Thomas Latta Sr., and Samuel Turrentine.
Witnesses: Joseph Armstrong, Peggy Armstrong, Eliz. (x) Trimble.

- - -

D 438 Will dated 18 April 1815, proved August Court 1815.

THOMAS LYNCH (This will is not in the Archives.)

brother: Jesse Lynch 300 acres joining William Paisley, James Forrest and others.
brother: Moses Lynch balance of 640 acre grant, etc.

Executor: brother Moses Lynch. Witness: Thomas Reeves.

- - -

D 439 Will dated 24 September 1814, proved August Court 1814.

ASEY his x mark BROWN Leonard Sears a legatee

"My mother Susannah Castlebury"
"My brothers and sisters", not named.

Executors: friends David George and Sampson Moore.
Witnesses: John Riggins, Gilly (x) Henderson.

- - -

D 440 Will dated 12 September 1814, proved August Court 1815.

JOHN ALSTON SR.

son: John 5 shillings "and all property I gave him when he left me"

- continued -

sons: George, James, Phillip, Lemuel, Alfred
daus: Polly, Patsy, Sally Pickett
son: Absolom 5 shillings & property "I gave him when he left/ me"
"grandson (son of Absolom) Calvin Alston"

Executors: son Absolom Alston and William Cain Jun'r.
Witnesses: William Cain Sen'r, William Smith.

- - -

D 441 Will dated 20 July 1813,proved August Court 1815.

WILLIAM (x) BOYLE "weak in body" wife: Ann

youngest son: John Boyle
son: James Boyle is to look after his brother John
daus: Mary Boyle, Jean Denning
grandson: Henry Boyle

Executors: son James Boyle, wife Ann.
Witnesses: John Boyle, James Boyle, Jas. Boyle.

- - -

D 443 Will dated 3 April 1815, proved August Court 1815.

JOHN BOYLE wife: Elizabeth

son: Hugh Boyle
"My three married daughters Rachel, Lavinia and Elizabeth."
"Two married daughters Ann and Martha."

Testator has land on Obine River in West Tennessee.

Sole executrix: wife Elizabeth.
Witnesses: George Garrison, Jas. Boyle, Mary (x) Moor.

- - -

D 445 Will dated 4 July 1815, proved August Court 1815.

NATHAN (x) ROGERS "sick of body"

wife: Nancy land on Boyd's Creek dau: Celia Ann
son: Idelet

Executors: wife Nancy, and "respected friend Lodwick Fear."
Witnesses: Thos. Scott, Alex Allen.

- - -

D 446 Will dated 17 February 1815, proved May Court 1815.

MARY (x) PRATT "very sick and weak" son: George Pratt

daus: Margaret Paul, Alsa Flintum, Caty Taylor

No executor named. Witnesses: Jas. Kerr, Jno. Piper.

- - -

D 447 Will dated 28 June 1815, proved August Court 1815.

JOHN COBLE wife: Catherine

sons: Peter, Samuel
"My four children that has had some property ", George, Catherine, Peggy, Mary.
"My three youngest children Henry & David & Milly" (Milly is youngest of all.)
sons: David (deceased ?),
Henry and Daniel get land on Stinking Creek

Executors: Jonathan Hadley and Adam Ingold.
Witnesses: Richard Proctor, Daniel Shofner, Eli (x) Rose.

- - -

D 449 Will dated 24 June 1811, proved August Court 1815.

HANNAH SHUGART

sons: William, Isaac and Nathan 1 shilling each
daughter: Rachel Shugart

Sole executrix: daughter Rachel.
Witnesses: Thomas Newlin, Nathaniel Newlin.

- - -

D 450 Agreement between the heirs of JOHN ALSTON. George Alston gives up claim. Signed by: A. Alston, Patsey (x) Alston, Solomon Jones, Christian Jones, Phillip Alston, L. Alston, Alfred Alston, Mary K. Alston, Mathew Pickett.
Witnesses: Susannah (x) Beaver, Henry Avrett.
(This original paper is in the State Archives.)

- - -

D 451 Will dated --, proved May Court 1813.

LEVI PENNINGTON wife: Margaret

Executors: wife Margaret, and worthy friend Archibald Murphey. No witnesses.
Proved by the oaths of John Umstead, John Stockard, and James W. Russell.

- - -

D 451 Will dated 1 October 1815, proved Nov Court 1815.

WILLIAM WILKINSON wife: Ann , whole estate

Executors: wife Ann, and David Wilkinson.
Witnesses: Samuel McCracken, John Plummet.

- - -

D 452 Will dated 19 April 1811, proved Nov Court 1815.

FISHER CLENDENNIN wife: Ann, is pregnant

oldest son: Thomas (under 21 years)
"My five sons, Thomas, Joseph, William, James & Fisher".
dau: Sarah (under 18 years)

"My apprentice William Izzel"

Executors: wife, and William Bradshaw Jun'r.

- - -

D 454 Will dated 24 June 1815, proved Nov Court 1815.

GEORGE LAWS wife: Sarah Laws

"To heirs of my deceased son William Laws, deceased son George Laws, deceased son Thomas Laws" 10 shillings each.

"My sons now living" names and number not stated.

Executors: sons Ezekiel and Leonard Laws, Thomas Latta, James Walker and Sterling Harris.
Witnesses: William Dollar, Thomas Latta.

- - -

D 455-457 Will dated 13 October, proved Nov Court 1815.

JOHN (x) NEALY or NEELEY wife: Mary

dau: Sally Cates 5 shillings , her son Nealy Cates
son: Isaac Nealy 5 shillings and Ł 50 to be divided among his lawful children
dau: Nelly Turrentine 5 shillings and Ł100 to her lawful ch.
" Elizabeth Bryant 5 " " Ł100 " " " "
" Rachel Pickle 5 " " Ł100 " " " "
" Polly Green 5 " " Ł100 " " " "
sons: John Nealy, Thomas Nealy
dau: Nancy Harris 5 shillings and Ł50 to her children
" Hannah Nealy Ł30 and to her son Green Nealy, etc.

Executors: friends Samuel Turrentine Sr and Benjamin Bullock "and my son John Nealy Jr."
Witnesses: Chas. Holman, Thos. Wilson, Joseph Woods.

- - -

D 457 Will dated 30 July 1815, proved November Court 1815.

DUNCAN D. BRIGGS

half-sisters: Mary I or J Alston, Kitty Alston
brothers: Samuel Briggs, John J or I Briggs.
half-brother: Calvin J. Alston
Duncan Briggs son of Samuel Briggs
Absolom Alston "all my books"

Executor: Absolom Alston Witnesses: James Webb, A.M.Dickson.

- - -

D 458 Will dated 9 February 1816, proved Feb Court 1816.

HIRAM (x) LOVE Hugh Finley "all my hogs"

sister: Margaret Harvey
brother: William Love
Mary Megomery ?
"brother Robert Love's child Dilly Ann Love"
brother-in-law: James Finley
brothers: John Love, James Love sister-in-law: Mary Love

No executor named. Witnesses: D.H.Harvey, William (x) Redum.

- - -

D 458 Will dated 21 February 1816, proved Feb Court 1816.

ROBERT (x) ANDERSON

"to Augusta Anderson and William Anderson the plantation where William Anderson did live, and 48 acres bequeathed to me Robert Anderson by my father John Anderson."

sisters: Mary, Phebe and Ann Anderson, and Letty Clark
brothers: John Anderson, Stewart Anderson
John Clark, John N. Clark

Executors: "trusty friend Wiley Shaw, Esq., and Major James Lapslie."
Witnesses: James McCluskey, Joseph Anderson, Alex. Anderson.

- - -

D 459 Will dated 9 February 1816, proved Feb Court 1816.

JAMES (x) TATE "very sick & weak" wife: Margaret

sons: Abner, Jesse, Joel, Robert
"Margaret Tate widow of James Tate deceased"
daus: Susannah, Elizabeth, Alse, Margaret

Executors: sons Abner and Jesse.
Witnesses: D. Bradford, Sr., James McCrory.

- - -

D 461 Will dated 19 February 1816, proved Feb Court 1816.

ZEPHANIAH TATE wife: Hannah

daughter: Polly Tate (under age)

Executor: "worthy friend Anthony Tate."
Witnesses: Jno. McMullan, John Hevy ?.

- - -

D 462 Will dated 10 January 1816, proved Feb Court 1816

VINSON (x) ROBERTS wife: Beersheba is pregnant ?

- continued -

sons: James, Morgan, George, Zephaniah.
      Calvin Henderson Roberts
daus: Lidda, Clary, Jemima, Peggy, Mary, Rebeckah
"My wife's daughter Nancy" 5 shillings

Executors: Thomas Compton and James Boling.
Witnesses: John Creswell, Jno. Landers, Erasmus (x) Compton.

- - -

D 464 Will dated 21 April 1815, proved Feb Court 1816.

ELIZABETH (x) WYATT "old and weak"

"My three children Joshua Wyatt, Frederick Wyatt, and Elizabeth Benson" get all her slaves.
"My son-in-law Benjamin Simpson" $1.

Executors: sons Joshua and Frederick Wyatt.
Witnesses: Anderson King, David King.

- - -

D 465 Will dated 4 January 1815, proved Feb Court 1816.

WILLIAM FAUSSETT, SEN'R

wife: Lydia land on Cane Creek
son: Ralph Faucett £5 "in addition to what I have given him"
" George " £5 " " " " I " " "
son-in-law: Abner Walker-£5 "in addition to what I have already given him with my daughter Polly"
son-in-law James Watkins and daughter Margaret
" " " Robert McCauley
daus: Eleanor Faussett, Lucia Faussett
sons: Robert, Eli, James Faussett

Executors: sons Ralph Faussett and George Faussett.
Witnesses: Rob't L. Mitchell, Caleb Wilson, James McCrory.

- - -

D 467 Will dated 29 December 1815, proved Feb Court 1816.

CHARLES ROUNTREE wife: Nancy

"My children, as they come of age", names and number not stated.

Executors: brothers Thomas Rountree and Joseph Rountree.
Witness: Jno. Rountree.

- - -

D 468 Will dated 24 March 1814, proved February Court 1816.

WILLIAM WHITTED, SR.

daus: Mary Bird, Hannah Harris ("she has but one child"),
      Elizabeth Holden, Susannah Thompson

- continued -

grandsons: Samuel Bigelow, William Whitted son of Levi
son: William Whitted
" Levi Whitted "land joining Isaac Holden's Mill Tract"

Testator emancipates his mulatto slave Dick.

Executors: sons William and Levi.
Witnesses: Thomas Flint, Henry Neal.

Codicil dated 4 August 1815. Daughter Mary Bird has died. Her legacy goes to "William Bird, James Bird, Sarah Walker, Nancy Thompson, Susannah Anderson, John Bird and Fanny Hamilton (children of the deceased Mary Bird) ..."

Witnesses: David Yarborough, J or I McKerall.

- - -

D 471-474 Will dated 10 March 1809, proved Feb Court 1816.

JOHN MOORE wife: Nancy

children under age: Mary, Nancy, Susannah, Lewis, Betsey, Sarah.
dau: Frances wife of John Hart
son: Thomas Moore ½ of tract of land in Tennessee on Blooming Grove Creek in Montgomery County. Thomas is living there.
son: Sampson Moore ½ of land in Tennessee, and tract in Orange joining Colonel Greene
son: Lewis other half of land in Orange County

Executors: wife Nancy, son Sampson, friend Mann Patterson.
Witnesses: P. Henderson, James (x) Davis, Richard (x) Davis, Christopher (x) Daniel.

- - -

D 475 Will dated 28 January 1814, proved August Court 1814.

JEREMIAH (x) GLENN wife: Patsey Glenn

sons: James, Thomas Anderson Glenn, George Washington Glenn
"To my daughter Nancy Woods's heirs"-£3
"To my daughter Feriby Watson's heirs"-£5
dau: Permelia Glenn
"To my daughter Polly Etheridge's heirs"-£5
daus ?: Kitty Horton Glenn, Lucy Glenn

Executors: brother William Glenn and James Latta, Esq.
Witnesses: Jno. Marshall, Demsey Wood.

- - -

D 476 Agreement about a road between LUDWICK ALBRIGHT and MICHAEL HOLT. Dated April 1816, proved May Court 1816.

- - -

D 477 Will dated 10 February 1816, proved May Court 1816.

MILDRED (x) GARRARD "very weak"

William Carrington and William Garrard 5 shillings each
"My son-in-law Joshua Childres" 5 shillings
"Heirs of my son-in-law George Bryant" 5 shillings
son: Daniel Garrard 5 shillings
dau-in-law: Elizabeth Garrard 5 shillings
sons: John Garrard, Jacob Garrard 5 shillings each
son: Carter N. Garrard bed, chairs
" Samuel Garrard " , " , and land
dau: Susy Garrard furniture, stock, etc.

Executors: friend James Walker, and Carter Garrard.
Witnesses: Lot G. Watson, Chuza Hopkins.

- - -

D 478 Will dated 1816, proved May Court 1816.

JAMES HANCOCK wife: Clarissa

sons: William and James Hancock $1 each
To deceased son Stephen Hancock's children $1 each.
dau: Betsey Franklin
sons: Robert Hancock, Nathan Hancock, Roger Hancock
dau: Polly
"two youngest children": sons Stanley and John Hancock.

Executors: wife Clarissa, and son Nathan
Witnesses: Tyree Glenn, Martin (x) Crutcher.

- - -

D 480 Will dated 11 April 1816, proved May Court 1816.

NATHAN HANCOCK

"brothers Robert Hancock & Roger Hancock & my sister Polly Hancock"
"My sister Polly's little daughter Henrietta" $100.

Executor: James Kimbrough.
Witnesses: Thomas Cottrell, Ira E. Arnold.

- - -

D 481 Will dated 19 February 1816, proved May Court 1816.

JOHN DOUGLASS

wife: Margaret all estate. Land bounded by William Cannon, James Graham, David Bradford and Jacob Garrison.

brothers: William, David and Henderson Douglass $2 each

- continued -

"Heirs of my brother James Douglass" $2

Executors: friends James Graham and George Garrison son of Jacob Garrison.
Witnesses: David Bradford Jr, Thomas (x) Bradford, George Graham.

- - -

D 482 Will dated 1st day 4th month 1816, proved May 1816.

ANNA ELIZABETH (x) CULBERSON

dau: Anna Elizabeth Culberson
" Rhoda McCracken

Executors:"Isaac Shugarts and my brother John"
Witnesses: Thomas Newlin, Henry Quakenbush.

- - -

D 483 Will dated 21 April 1816, proved May Court 1816.

ELI LINDSEY wife: Jane

sons: Josiah Bowman Lindsey, Martin Luther Lindsey.
daus: Ann Hodge, Polly Clark, and Sally Hodge "money now in hands of Willie Shaw, Esq."
dau: Eunice Lindsey bed & furniture, etc.
sons: John, Robert and James Lindsey, $3 each

Executors: wife Jane, and William McCluskey.
Witnesses: William Woods, J. Allison, John McDade.

- - -

D 484 Will dated 24 February 1816, proved May Court 1816.

ANN (x) BOYLE "weak in body"

dau: Jane Denning $5; etc
granddaus: Ann Boyle, Martha Boyle
son: John Boyle
dau: Mary Boyle gets most of estate

Executrix: daughter Mary Boyle.
Witnesses: Caleb Wilson, James Boyle.

- - -

D 485 Will dated 13 May 1816, proved May Court 1816.

JAMES (x) CARRINGTON "weak in body" wife: Ankey

sons: John & William $1 each with what they have already had
dau: Elizabeth $1 with what she has already received.
"The above the children of my first wife Jemima."

- continued -

son: James $1 besides what I have already given him
dau: Mary $1
"The children of my second wife Ankey"

Sole executor: James Latta. Witness: Thomas Latta, Sen'r.

\- - -

D 486 Will dated 25 December 1812, proved May Court 1816.

RICHARD STANFORD wife a legatee

"Two oldest daughters Ariana and Mary Mebane"
"Two youngest children Lawrence and Adeline"

Executors: friends Thomas Snipes Esq. and John Newlin.
Witness: Mark Durham.
Codicil dated 22 January 1814. No witness. Same heirs.

\- - -

D 489 Will dated 11 August 1810, proved August Court 1816.

EDMUND (x) GILLIAM wife: Sarah

sons: Edmund Gilliam
Charles and Burwell land on South-west side of Haw Riv.
David land on North-east side of Haw River
daus: Sarah Hurbin (?), Susannah Smothers,
Mary Bracken, Elizabeth Stalcop

Executor: son Edmund Gilliam.
Witnesses: Thomas Bradford Jun'r, David Bradford Sr.

\- - -

D 490 Will dated 2 April 1812, proved August Court 1816.

THOMAS CATE wife: Sarah Cate

son: Moses "150 acres where he now lives"
" John "150 acres " " " " "
" Ephriam "100 acres whereon he did dwell"
" Thomas 100 " "whereon I now dwell"

"My eleven children - Moses Cate, John Cate, Fanny Sykes, Martha Moore, Winney Sykes, Milly Roach, Huldah Cate, Tabitha Smith, Elizabeth Cate, Thomas Cate, Ephriam Cate."

Witnesses: Barnard Cate, Jean her x mark Cate .

\- - -

D 491-493 Will dated 19 April 1816, proved August 1816.

LUDWICK ALBRIGHT wife: Elizabeth

son: John Albright "tract of land he now lives on" etc.
" George " " " " " " " " "

-continued-

married daughters: "Mary Fogleman, deceased wife of John"
"Elizabeth Albright, wife of John"

son: Daniel "land whereon he now lives"
"Daughters not married-namely-Barbara, Martha and Sarah".
son: Isaac (unmarried, under 25) "land on S.Side of the Allemance"
son: Ludwick (unmarried, under 25) land on the S. Side of the Allemance.

Executors: "my brother Daniel Albright and my son John"
Witnesses: Mich'l Holt, Elias Albright, S. Harris.

- - -

D 494 Will dated 8 June 1816, proved Nov Court 1816.

HEZEKIAH (x) RHODES wife: Alementor Rhodes
"weak of body"

sons: Wesley and William
granddau: Mary Linnington Rhodes daughter of Wesley Rhodes
granddaus: Lucy Hall and Alsy C. Hall get cow and heifer "now in the possession of Henry Hall"

Executors: Wesley Rhodes and Absolom Alston.
Witnesses: L. Alston, Elizabeth (x) Cabe ?.

- - -

D 494 Will dated 22 March 1816, proved Nov Court 1816.

AARON BOLES

Henderson Haney "now about two years old", Nancy Haney
brother: John Boles $1
"$1 to each of my sisters"

Executor: friend Walter Murray.
Witnesses: Walter Murray, William (x) Criswell, Robert Fulton.

- - -

D 495 Will dated 2 March 1816, proved Nov Court 1816.

JACOB UMSTEAD mother, and "her daughter Jane"

"my brothers and sisters"
"my brother David's sons"
"" " John's " "

Executor: Elisha Umstead. Witness: Thornton McFarling.

- - -

D 496 Will dated 5 August 1816, proved Feb Court 1817.

JOHN CRAIG

He is to be buried near his wife Mary "who is gone before me"

son: Samuel (unmarried), son: Abraham
dau: Peggy (") " James -continued-

D 496 continued

"Elizabeth Russell and her children"
dau: Polly
grandson: John Long
granddau: "Elizabeth Craig of David"
"To each of my grandsons named for me $6."
son: Alexander
"My three granddaughters by David viz- Nancy Murdock, Polly and Sally Craig 5 shillings each"

Executors: nephew Isaac Craig and son-in-law Alex'r Russell.
Witnesses: Alex'r Russell, Isaac Craig.

- - -

D 498 Will dated 26 December 1815, proved Feb Court 1817.

ANDREW MURDOCK wife: Margaret

sons: Robert Nurdock, James Murdock
grandchildren: Andrew (under 21) and Betsey Murdock, children of James
" Andrew and Peggy Ann Craig, children of Abraham Craig
" Andrew Steel son of Joseph Steel, Peggy Steel
"To Andrew Murdock son of Thomas Murdock.."

Executors: son-in-law Abraham Craig and nephew James Mebane.
Proved by the oaths of James Mebane, William Sheppard, Reuben Smith and Thomas Whitted.

- - -

D 500 Will dated 24 November 1816, proved Feb Court 1817.

NANCY (x) MOORE

daughters Nelly, Margaret and Betsey get all estate, "cutting out all other heirs with five cents apiece."

Executors: Edward Couch, Alexander Gattis.
Witnesses: Thomas Gattis, Elizabeth Mason.

- - -

D 501 Will dated 31 July 1815, proved February Court 1817.

THOMAS (x) HATWOOD "low in body" wife: Nancy all estate

sons: Thomas Hatwood, John Hatwood 50¢ each
son-in-law: Robert Gee 50¢
dau: Jean Hatwood $1

Executors: friends Laban Andrews and George Smith.
Witnesses: James Reeves, Lacey Loyd.

- - -

D 502 Power of Attorney from SOLOMON NEVILL to his brother GOODMAN NEVILL. Dated 28 February 1816, proved Feb 1817.
Witness: John Craig.

- - -

D503 Will dated 21 April 1814, proved February Court 1817.

JOSEPH (x) McCULLOCH Testator owns a mill-stone quarry.
"weak in body"
son: John McCulloch "tract whereon he now lives on the S. Side of Toms Creek."
sons: George, William
son: Joseph "tract whereon he now lives which I purchased of John Tate, lying on both sides of Watson's Creek"

daus: Mary Johnston, Deborah Walker, Elizabeth

Executors: son George McCulloch and son-in-law Wm Walker.
Witnesses: Robt L. Mitchell, Thos. McCullock, Sam'l Edmiston, Andrew McCullock.

- - -

D 505 Will dated 22 February 1817, proved May Court 1817.

JAMES WHITTED wife: Attelia is pregnant

son: Nash Whitted

Executor: friend James Webb.
Witnesses: James Phillips, William I. Nash.

- - -

D 506 Will dated 8 June 1816, proved May Court 1817.

SUSANNAH (x) FULTON "low in health"

sons: Jesse Fulton, David Fulton, Samuel Fulton $2 each
granddaughter: Elsy Tate "my walnut chest"
son: Robert Fulton
great-granddau: Celia, daughter of Susannah Tate

Executor: "trusty friend William Bradford.
Witnesses: James Mebane. John Hughes.

- - -

D 507 Will dated 26 March 1814, proved May Court 1817.

BARNEY (x) TROXLER wife: Elizabeth $50, etc.

"Unto the heirs of Philipena Coble wife of David Coble" 5 sh.
"Daughter Mary's son John Albright" 5 shillings
son: Jacob Troxler 5 shillings
"Daughter Elizabeth Huffman wife of Peter Huffman" $20
"" Catherine McCamey " " James McCamey" $1
son: David Troxler "my chest and clothes and $50"
" Powell $30
" Barney 5 shillings
" George balance of estate

Executors: George Troxler and Isaac Holt.
Witnesses: Is'c Holt, Christopher Coble, Daniel Albright.

- - -

D 508 Will dated 7 January 1817, proved May Court 1817.

MATTHEW (x) RIPPY "old and weak in body"

He devises several slaves, land, etc. Mentions land he has already given away. Balance of estate to be sold and the money divided among "all my sons & daughters and the children of my daughter Jinney Garrett that is now dead." Daughters names are not stated.

Sons: John, Edward, Joseph, Thomas, James and Jesse Rippy.

Executors: friend Samuel Scott and son John Rippy.
Witnesses: Samuel Scott, John McCrackin.

D 509 Will dated 8 April 1817, proved August Court 1817.

HANNAH (x) RAY This will is so puzzling I give most of it as written. Checked with original.

.."to my eldest son James Massey James Lindley, to my youngest son Matthew Ray & my two grandsons the youngest sons of my daughter Lydia West, & Ann Wolf, at the decease of my two daughters a certain note of hand now in my possession on my son Matthew Ray for the sum of $95. Also all the money which I may die seized and possed of".

eldest daughter: Lydia West
youngest daughter: Ann Wolf

Executors: son Matthew Ray and John Stockard.
Witness: John Stockard.

D 510 Will dated 6 July 1817, proved August Court 1817.

STEPHEN SCARLETT wife: Sally

daus: Rachel and Cynthia Scarlett are unmarried
sons: James Scarlett (youngest), John Scarlett (eldest)

"7 daughters - Elizabeth Cain, Mary Latta , Sally Latta, Jane Latta, Susannah Cole, Rachel Scarlett and Cynthia Scarlett."

Executors: wife Sally and son James.
Witnesses: William Lewis, Henry Bunch, Abraham (x) Crabtree.

D 512 Will dated 16 August 1816, proved August Court 1817.

WILLIAM LAWS wife: Frances plantation on Flat River

son: Jonathan Laws land lying in Orange and Granville
" James Laws
sister: Elizabeth Laws - continued -

daughters: Jinney Waller, Polly Ferguson, Nancy Laws,
Rebecca Laws, Sally Laws, Margaret Laws,
Alsey Laws, Frances Laws

"My grandson David Laws son of my deceased son George Laws the tract of land on which my daughter-in-law Margaret Laws now lives." In case of his death it goes "to my grandson Charles Laws."

son-in-law: Elisha Umstead $5
granddaughter: Jemima Umstead

Executors: "Worthy friends Thomas D. Bennehan, William Roberts, Sr., and my son Jonathan Laws."
Witnesses: Mark Veazey, William Veazey.

- - -

D 514 Will dated 25 February 1817, proved Nov Court 1817.

MARY WOODS

niece: Emeline Dortch (under age) one-half of estate
nieces: Sally Dortch, Polly Dortch and Lucy Dortch, other half

Executor: Duncan Cameron.
Witnesses: James ? Kelly, Senior, Hugh Cain, Junior.

- - -

D 515 Will dated 13 November 1817, proved Nov Court 1817.

POMPHRETT HERNDON brother: James Herndon Jr half of estate

father: James Herndon $5
sisters: Polly Gorman, Nancy Barbee, Elizabeth Dickson $5 ea.
brother-in-law (half-brother) Macharine C. Herndon $5
Teresa N. Herndon (his half-sister) $5

sister: Sally Herndon other half of estate

Executor: brother James Herndon, Jr.
Witnesses: Ja mes Lynn, Charles H. Collier.

- - -

D 517 Will dated 29 March 1813, proved February Court 1818.

WILLIAM McPHERSON Checked with original will, writing bad.

wife: Phebe

"I give to my children as follows:
to Thomas and Mary Braxton,
to Othail (Othneil ?) & C ristain McPherson,
to Ruth Jonson (Tomson ?),
to Wm. & Betty McPherson,
to Daniel and Mary McPherson,
to Margaret & Jesse Pierce,"

- continued -

"to John and Hannah McPherson,
to Aaron and Phebe Lindley,
to Mary and Edward Stuart (Stewart ?),
to Ann and John Crutchfield,
to Edith and Mark Morgan, each two of them a Crown besides what they have already had".

"to my grandson Wm. McPherson(ye son of Enoch)" ..
"son Enoch and his wife Paray (Panay ?) .."

Executors: Daniel McPherson and John McPherson.
Witnesses: Jacob Nugent, Daniel McPherson, James Neal, Enoch McPherson.

- - -

D 518 Will dated 18 July 1817, proved February Court 1818.

LEWIS HERNDON (See back of this book for HERNDON genealogy)

wife: Polly "to keep our children together" and educate them
His lands in Wake County, N.C. to be divided among his 4 sons.

sons: Joseph (oldest), George, Lewis, Willis
dau: Polly

Executors: friends Joseph Boothe Jr. and Sampson Moore, and wife Polly.
Witnesses: Mark Beasley, Polly (x) Beasley, David (x) Castleberry.

- - -

D 520 Will dated 1 December 1817, proved Feb Court 1818.

JOHN EDWARDS,SR. wife: Lucy

son: Young Edwards 60 acres in Ash County -mill-on Dead Creek
" Allen Edwards
"To Stokes Edwards' children by his first wife to wit: Richard, Isaac & Allen, John, Nancy, Lucy & Cathery."

"great-grandchildren Rhoda, William & Mary, children of Richard Ricketts & Rebecca his wife."

sons: Stokes Edwards, John Edwards
daus: Elizabeth, Roda Ball

Executors: wife Lucy, son Allen, Brother Barry Cate, and Reuben Smith.
Witnesses: Elijah Graves, Ariana Graves.

- - -

D 521 Will dated 5 April 1817, proved Feb Court 1818.

ANNE WOOD widow of John Wood

daus: Nancy Robinson, Jane Wilson, Rebecca Thompson
nieces: Sally Wood, Ann Wilson
sons-in-law: Thomas Wilson, Samuel Thompson

- continued -

 D 521 continued
Executors: Thomas Wilson and Samuel Thompson "both of Orange".
Witnesses: Richard Holeman, Charles Holeman.

\- - -

D 522 Will dated 14 August 1817, proved May Court 1818.
EVE (x) SMITH
cousin-in-law: Peter Smith all estate

Witnesses: Frederick (x) Kimbro, Richard Proctor,
Isaac (x) Sharp.

\- - -

D 523 Will dated 17 February 1818, proved May Court 1818.

JOHN (x) WALKER wife: Judy

daus: Nelly Walker, Polly Ryals, Rebeckah Walker,
Betsy Walker, Letty Walker.
son: Benjamin Walker (under age)
daus: Emily Walker, Lucy Walker (both under age)

Executors: "Friends Herbert Collier & William Oldham & Judy Walker".
Witnesses: George Oldham, John (x) Oldham.

\- - -

D 525 Will dated 8 February 1817, proved May Court 1818.

JOHN LATTA wife a legatee, name not stated

children "to be schooled"
son: John "Little River plantation"
dau: Moriah

Executors: John Latta, Sr., and John Cabe, Esq.
Witness: Hugh Montgomery.

\- - -

D 526 Will dated 24 July 1817, proved May Court 1818.

JAMES WILKINSON wife: Susannah "to raise and school all our children"
sons: James and William, both under age
daus: Cata, Patsa and Sysannah Wilkinson

Executors: wife Susannah, and William Wilkinson.
Witnesses: Samuel Madden, Joseph Ray.

\- - -

D 527 Will dated 11 January 1813, proved May Court 1818.

JAMES TURNER, SR. wife: Mary

daus: Hannah, Sarah and Jane, all unmarried
sons: David Turner plantation, etc, James Turner 10 shillings
daus: Nelly Craig, Mary Holland, Ann, Christian Milligan 10 sh.

son: John Turner 10 shillings

Executors: wife Mary, and son David.
Witnesses: J. S. Smith, William (x) Smith.

- - -

D 529 Will dated 8th day 8th month 1813, proved May 1818.

BENJAMIN PIGGOTT

sons: Joshua (eldest), John Piggott
daus: Patience Cox(oldest), Elizabeth Wheeler $1 each
son-in-law: Jeremiah Cox $1
dau: Mary Keggs $1
son-in-law: Charles Davis $1
dau: Ruth Horniday $1
youngest son: Benjamin Piggott
grandchildren: Benjamin Piggott son of Joshua
" " " " John
Hannah Piggott dau of Benjamin
Mary Piggott " " "

Witnesses: Jeremiah Piggott, Thomas Marshall, Benj. Wheeler.

- - -

D 530 Will dated 25 March 1818, proved May Court 1818.

MORDECAI SOUTHERLAND

sons: Samuel (plantation); Ransom, William 10 shillings
daus: Frances Turner, Susannah Glen 10 shillings each
Polly Glen, Elizabeth Burton 10 shillings each

Executor: son Samuel.
Witnesses: Kennedy Haughton, Jas. Kimbrough.

- - -

D 531 Will dated 10 Febriary 1817, proved May Court 1818.

ROGER HANCOCK wife: Nancy

daus: Susannah Hancock, Polly W. Hancock, Betsy Hancock.
sons: Wesley Hancock "my big Bible"
Fletcher Hancock "my small Bible"

Sole executrix: wife Nancy Hancock.
Witnesses: Reubin Cardin, Jesse Branch.

- - -

D 533 Will dated 6th month 26th day 1816, proved May 1818.

JACOB MARSHILL wife: Margaret

son: Francis Marshill
dau: Ruth Hadley
dau-in-law: Ruth Marshill

- continued -

sons: William and John Marshill land on E side of Mary's Creek.
"heir of my son Jacob Marshill 5 shillings if demanded"
"" " " daughter Mary Hinshaw 5 shillings if demanded"
dau: Anna Thompson "2/6 if she comes to demand it"
"heir of my daughter Margaret Jones 2/6"
"" " " " Elizabeth Freeman 2/6"
"Ann Dunn feather bed ana furniture"

Executrix: wife.
Witnesses: Richard Thompson, Samuel Freeman, James Murray, Joseph Murray, J or I Hinshaw.

– – –

D 535 Deed of Gift from MORDECAI SCUTHERLAND to friend FEBE DOSSETT, bed and furniture, cow and yaerling, pine chest, etc. Dated 17 March 1818, proved August Court 1818.
Witnesses: Jas. Kimbrough, Tyree Glenn.

– – –

D 535 Will dated 10 July 1818, proved August Court 1818.

JOHN BARBEE wife: Esther

son: King Barbee dau: Sally
" Reuben Barbee $1 "with what he has already received"
" Zachariah
dau: Elizabeth (under age)
son: John "160 acres where I now live, etc."
" Gray "100 acres .. joining Bilbo and others.."

Executors: "worthy friend (actually his wife's brother) Zachariah Herndon" and King Barbee.
Witnesses: Zach. Herndon, William Hall, John Herndon.

– – –

D 537 Will dated 24 January 1813, proved August Court 1818.

JAMES WILSON

sisters: Maryann and Elizabeth get plantation, etc., they are to support his father and mother.

Executors: Ja mes Lapslie and Thomas Armstrong.
Witnesses: William Shepperd, Egbert Shepperd.

– – –

D 538 Will dated 28 January 1813, proved August Court 1818.

EDWARD WILSON wife: Mary

dau: Elizabeth $1, she has had her share.
son: Charles Wortham "all that I gave him when he left me"
dau: Sarah Hall gets a mare
son: William Wortham "all that he had when he left me", etc.
dau: Nancy Wilson $10 and what she had "when she left me"
son: John Wortham "all that I gave him when he left me", etc.
" James " " " " he got from me when he left me,"

- continued -

son: Alfred Wortham "plantation I now live on .. known as
Walker Tract .. he to have full possession after
the death of Mrs. Sarah Dunnagan."
" Samuel Wortham "tract where Mrs. Sarah Dunnagan lives"

Executors: wife, and son Samuel.
Witnesses: Joseph Armstrong, Peggy Armstrong.

- - -

D 539 Will dated 18 March 1818, proved August Court 1818.

WILLIAM LEWIS wife: Agnes

sons: Charles Lewis and Parsons Lewis
"only daughter Franky Lewis"

Executrix: wife Agnes Lewis.
Witnesses: James Nutt, Pomphrett Gooch.

- - -

D 540 Will dated 30 May 1818, proved August Court 1818.

JOSEPH HAMILTON wife: Martha

sons: James, John and William Hamilton

Executors: friends William Pickett and Archibald Hamilton.
Witnesses: Robert Gragson, Samuel McCaddams.

- - -

D 542 Will dated 18 June 1818, proved August Court 1818.

LEMUEL ALSTON

sisters: Christian Jones wife of Solomon Jones; Patsy
brothers: Absalom Alston, Philip Alston & Alfred Alston
sister: Mary Scott wife of Robert Scott
brother: George L. Alston
sister: Sally Pickett wife of Matthew Pickett
nephew: Lemuel Alston son of James Alston

Executors: "worthy friends and brothers Solomon Jones and
George L. Alston."
Witnesses: W. E. Roberts, Freeman Broadwell.

- - -

D 543 Will dated 14 July 1818, proved August Court 1818.

JACOB JEFFRIES

wife: Jane all estate, including "the Bounty Ticket of $3000
due by Major Thomas Donahoo".
"To each of my first wife's children, viz: Reuben Jeffries,
Mourning Jeffries, John Jeffries, Katie Ammons, Betsy Gray,
to each a dollar."

Sole executrix: wife Jane.
Witnesses: Rob't L. Mitchell, David (x) Hathcock.

- - -

D 544 Will dated 6 January 1812, proved August Court 1818.

STEPHEN WHITE

wife: Ann land on waters of Back Creek and Haw River
"To heirs of James Baldridge deceased " $2
sons-in-law: Samuel Mebane, William Hodge $2 each
sons: Stephen White, John White $2 each
sons: David land; James a mare
sons: Samuel $2; Joseph "land I now live on"

Executors: sons David and Joseph White.
Witnesses: James Palmer, Wm. Shaw, David Bryan.

- - -

D 454 Power of Attorney from JOHN ATKINSON to WESTWARD A. JONES, to collect from the "Sec'y of State of N.C. all the pay, bounty lands that is due ... from the state aforesaid for my services as a soldier of the Continental Line and on that Establishment ..." Witnesses: Wm. Leathers, John Darby. Dated 28 July 1808, proved February 1816.

- - -

D 546 Mortgage from GEORGE (x) PICKET to SAMUEL WILSON on a horse. Dated 23 February 1819, proved Feb. L819. Witness: Joseph A. Woods.

- - -

D 547 Bond - ROBERT HARRIS and WM. MONTGOMERY to RICHARD UMSTEAD. Robert Harris has purchased from Richard Umstead his interest in the estate of his brother Jacob deceased. Dated 20 January 1818, proved February Court 1818. Witnesses: Ezekiel Umstead, Jonathan Montgomery.

- - -

D 547 Deed from RICHARD CATE to SALLY CATE for a mare. Dated 9 June 1818, proved February 1819. Witness: Huldah Cate.

- - -

D 548 Deed from ALFRED or ALFORD CATE to NANCY CATE for two cows and calves. Dated 28 May 1822, proved August 1822. Witness: Huldah (x) Cate.

- - -

D 549 Will dated 21 March 1813, proved November Court 1818.

JOHN JOHNSTON wife: Isabel

sons: eldest David, second John, both under age
"each of my daughters as they arrive at age", not named

Executors: wife Isabel, and John Craig.
Witnesses: John Blackwoof, Margaret Johnston.

- - -

D 550 Will dated 10 April 1818, proved November Court 1818.

JOHN THOMAS wife: Elizabeth

Executor: worthy friend
Witnesses: Alexander Morphis, Micajah Thomas.

- - -

D 550 Will dated 5 September 1818, proved Nov Court 1818.

ALEXANDER RUSSELL wife: Elizabeth

sons: John Craig Russell, David, Robert Paistly Russell (under age)
son: Wright "land he now lives on"
dau: Jane Rodgers
son: Alexander "land I hold in Guilford bought of Jessup"
nephew: Joseph, surname not stated
unmarried sister, name not stated

Executors: sons John and Wright Russell, and Mathew Ray.
Witnesses: James Webb, James Turner.

- - -

D 552 Will dated 26 December 1818, proved Feb Court 1819.

ABRAM CRAIG wife: Jane

"Two oldest children are to receive a considerable legacy from the estate of Andrew Murdock dec'd. ..."
"My other children" , names not stated

Executors: friends James Mebane, George Johnston and John Freeland.
Witnesses: James Webb, James Craig.

- - -

D 553 Will dated 19 January 1819, proved February Court 1819.

JOHN WELBORN or WILBOURNE wife: Mary

"unto Duran Hampton wife of Nolan Hampton"
Alves and Nolan Hampton sons of Nolan Hampton
brother: Richard Wilborn
Robert Wilborn son of Richard
Lewis Wilborn
brothers: Edward and Zachariah Welborne 50¢ each
brother Thomas Welborne's children 50¢ each
sisters: Temperance Marshall, Susannah Ludlo Jones, Lida Slaughter
friends: Roland Cook, and John Hampton son of my wife,
He leaves 100 acres to his slave Jeremiah, who is to be freed.

Executors: friends Thomas Bennehan, Benjamin Bullock, and Nathaniel Carrington.
Witnesses: Samuel (x) Rush, John Suit, Jr., Robert Ashley.

- - -

D 555 Will dated 7 October 1815, proved February Court 1819.

ISAAC DALE wife: Margaret Dale whole estate

daughter Margaret Haddock $10

Executors: friends Thomas Holaday Sr."and my step-son Robert Andrew".
Witnesses: Lewis Hornaday, Dinah (x) Bittick.

- - -

D 556 Will dated 5 Jume 1818, proved February Court 1819.

WILLIAM (x) WOODS "sick and weak" mother: Elinor Woods

sister: Margaret Hopkins $1
brothers: Hugh Woods, Eli Woods
"brother-in-law Eli Woods husband of my late sister Lucy Woods deceased "my part of her part of the money coming from our grandfather Hugh Woods' estate."

Witnesses: Wm. Baldwin, Hugh Montgomery, Joseph Woods.
Executors: (named in Codicil) "My uncle Robert Faucett and my trusty friend James Jackson son of James Jackson Sr."

- - -

D 558 Will dated 14 March 1819, proved May Court 1819.

BENJAMIN WHIDBEE wife: Sally

son: Joseph (under age)
"All my children" (they all seem to be minors).

Executors: wife Sally, and brother-in-law William Holt.
Witnesses: John Harden, Lewis Holt.

- - -

D 559 Will dated 15 February 1816, proved May Court 1819.

THOMAS CARMICHAEL wife: Mary

sons: John Henry Carmichael, Archibald Carmichael
daus: Margaret Street, Nancy Smith, Jane Isley

Executor: son John Henry Carmichael.
Witnesses: John McMullan, Vance Laffatee.

- - -

D 560 Will dated 14 January 1819, proved May Court 1819.

WILLIAM FORSYTHE wife: Ma

"My children James Barnet John Margaret & Gilla & one sixth part to Anna Bailey's children" (no punctuation)
sons: John and Barnet get "landed estate" - continued -

daughter: Anna $10
"Friends Thomas Snipes and Elijah Graves trustees and guardian for my son John and his property for life".

Executors: son Barnet Forsythe and friend William McCauley.
Witnesses: Jno. Caruthers, Archibald Durham.

- - -

D 560 Will dated 30 March 1819, proved May Court 1819.

EDWARD PICKETT

son: John Pickett
" William Pickett
" James Pickett
dau: Mary Murry
" Margaret Roney
daus: Sarah McDaniel, Martha Murray
son: Walter Pickett

Executors: sons John and James.
Witnesses: James Mebane, J. A. Mebane.

- - -

D 562 Will dated 13 March 1819, proved May Court 1819.

JAMES (x) PYLE "sick in body" wife: Elizabeth

daughter Sally, "all my children" names not stated

Executors: wife Elizabeth, son William.
Witnesses: Wm. Hatchett, James Hicks, John Hicks.

- - -

D 563 Will dated 15 March 1819, proved August Court 1819.

THOMAS MOORE wife: Diana

"Four daughters- Elinor Moore (eldest), Diana Moore, Mary Moore, Sarah Moore."
"Daughters Jeney Moore, Marthy Moore and Elizabeth Moore"
sons: James Moore 10 shillings besides what he has received
Andrew Moore 10 " " " " " "
Thomas, Mathew, Robert

Executors: sons Andrew and Thomas Moore.
Witnesses: James Moore, Daniel Atkins.

- - -

D 564 Will dated 25 August 1819, proved November Court 1819.

JAMES WOOD

dau: Betsy Latta wife of John J. Latta
son: Willie Wood
dau: Nancy Lewis wife of Fielding Lewis
" Sally Wallace wife of Owen Wallace

- continued -

dau: Polly Chisenhall wife of Delancy Chisenhall

Executors: son Willie Wood, and John J. Latta.
Witnesses: Frederick Moize, Marstain (x) Crotckett ?

– – –

D 565 Will dated 22 November 1819, proved Nov Court 1819.

SAMUEL CARUTHERS wife: Sary

sons: John Caruthers, William Caruthers
"All my daughters", none named, some are married.

Executors: sons John and William.
Witnesses: William Brown, Levi Andrews.

– – –

D566 Will dated 10 January 1820, proved Feb Court 1820.

WILLIAM SMITH

"To William Smith son of John Smith (the grandson of my brother John) $50."
"To Ferze daughter of Robert Smith (son of John Smith) $50
"To Allen Compton the son of Erasmus Compton " $50
"To William O'Kelly the son of William O'Kelly" $50
"To Elender Smith the daughter of Polly Smith a note of $16 on John Ward."
"Unto Polly's children Jane, Ellender, Entricans (?) and Nancy" .. a tract of land. They are under age.

"My sister Mary McMund, Robert Smith (son of John Smith my brother), Joseph Smith and John Smith sons of Robert my brother" .. another tract of land.

Executors: Robert Smith (son of John Smith), and Robert Campbell.
Witnesses: John Landers, John Ward, Jacob (x) Huggins.

– – –

D 567 Will dated 11 June 1818, proved February Court 1820.

JOHN ECCLES wife: Jennet

daus: Elizabeth Eccles, Mary Eccles, Sarah Eccles, Martha Eccles (the last three under age ?)
son-in-law: Thomas Murray $1 besides what he has received
son: William Eccles

Sole executrix: wife Jennet.
Witnesses: Robert G. Mitchell, Junia Hall, James Barnard.

– – –

D 568 Will dated 30 September 1817, proved Feb Court 1820.

JOHN THOMPSON wife: Jennet

son: Thomas
dau: Rachel wife of John Russell
sons: James, William and John Thompson
dau: Jennet wife of George Johnston
daus: Ann Thompson, Elizabeth Grahams, Elender Thomas

Executors: brother Robert Thompson, son William Thompson.
Witnesses: W. Thompson, William (x) Gorly ?.

- - -

D 571 Will dated 20 November 1819, proved Feb Court 1820.

WILLIAM KING wife: Sarah

dau: Senea gets 1 filly
son: John $1
daus: Fanny, Elizabeth, Peggy $1 each
sons: William D. King, Marshal King, Pleasant King
dau: Sarrah gets bed and furniture

Executors: wife, and sons John and Wm. D. King.
Witness: Jonathan Tapp.

- - -

D 572 Will dated 8 December 1818, proved Feb Court 1820.

ROBERT (x) ANDERSON wife: Nancy

daus: Charity (she is married), Mary
sons: Robert, William (he is married), Alexander

Executors: friend William Maris, and son Alexander.
Witnesses: John Anderson, Wiatt Hickman.

- - -

D 573 Will dated 15 July 1811, proved February Court 1820.

MARY (x) McMUNN granddaughter: Ann

Executrix: daughter Sarah.
Witnesses: Alexander Findley, James Smith.

- - -

D 574 Will dated 25 November 1814, proved May Court 1820.

ROBERT McCULLEY He says "my seven children" ..

sons: Moore ? McCulley, William McCulley
dau: Sally McCulley

Executors: son Moore, and daughter Sally McCulley.
Witnesses: Daniel Johnston, John Boon.

- - -

D 575 Will dated 9 April 1820, proved May Court 1820.

JACOB GRAVES wife: Furby

dau: Betsy , unmarried
No relationship to : Mary Glass, Catherine Glass,
is stated. Daus ? Nelly (or Milly) Nease,
Barbara Graves, Betsy & Sarah Graves
son: Daniel Graves "tract whereon he lives"
sons: Elias, David, Bostian and John Graves

Testator owns a mill. His land joins that of Malachi Isley, Doctor Brehon, Frederic Shofner.

Executors: George Isley, Boston Graves, David Graves.
Witnesses: Is. Holt, Martin Nease, Jacob Anthony.

\- - -

D 577 Will dated 25 July 1815, proved May Court 1820.

THOMAS HOWARD, SR. wife: Elizabeth

son: James Howard
" John Howard
dau: Henrietta (unmarried)
" Betsy Watson
sons: Thomas Howard, Richard Howard

Executors: wife Elizabeth, and son Richard.
Witnesses: Thomas Scott, Stephen Glass.

\- - -

D 579 Will dated 10 December 1819, proved August Court 1820.

HENRY KECK wife: Elizabeth

son: Daniel
unmarried daughters: Sally and Caty
married daughters: Mary, Elizabeth and Barbara
"All my children, namely, Mary John Henry Elizabeth George Daniel , Barbara, David, William, Sally and Caty."

Executors: sons George Keck and David Keck.
Witness: Mich'l Holt.

\- - -

D 580 Will dated 28 July 1820, proved August Court 1820.

THOMAS ROUNTREE wife: Victory

He gives a rifle to Neil (?) Cate

Executrix: wife Victory. Witness: Wm. Armstrong.

\- - -

D 581 Will dated 30 June 1820, proved August Court 1820.

JOHN (x) COPLEY, SR. "sick and weak" wife: Sarah

son: Iley Copley dau: Jiney Copley

Executors: wife Sarah, and Moses McCown.
Witnesses: John Redman, Jr, Aquilla Roades.

- - -

D 581 Will dated 6 March 1820, proved August Court 1820.

ISAAC (x) JACKSON "very sick" father: James Jackson

sisters: Elizabeth and Ruth Jackson
sister: Sarah Cloud $1

Executor: trusty friend Levi Jackson.
Witnesses: A. G. Jackson, Jacob Jackson, Benoni Jackson.

- - -

D 583 Will dated 30 January 1819, proved August Court 1820.

JOHN BREEZE wife: Jenney Breeze

daughters: Patsy Breeze, Rachel Breeze, Polly Breeze, Jinney Breeze, Susa Breeze

Executors: friends Richard Breeze and Abner Bruce.
Witnesses: John McDade, A. B. Bruce, Patsy Breeze.

- - -

D 584 Will dated 24th day 2nd month 1820, proved Nov 1820.

NATHAN ALAN

wife: Martha her own land, which joins Robert Rains and Jacob Cox, inherited from her father.

Children: Ruth, Job, Miles, all under age.

Sole executor: trusty friend Ephriam Doan.
Witnesses: Soloman Alan, William Alan.

- - -

D 585 Will dated 12 October 1820, proved Nov Court 1820.

ISAAC HOLDEN wife: Elizabeth

son: Thomas Holden "my mills on Eno River", etc.
son: Isaac (under 21 years)
"My children Thomas W. Holden, Sally Holden, Elizabeth Holden, William Holden, Mary Holden, Harriett Holden and Isaac Holden".

- continued -

Executors: wife Elizabeth, son Thomas W. Holden, and friend John Taylor, Jr.
Witnesses: Tho. J. Faddis, Thomas Holden.

- - -

D 586 Will dated 27 August 1820, proved Nov Court 1820.

ANN (x) WILSON "low in health" son: John Wilson

granddaughter Polly "that lives with me"
" Betsy "" " " " "
grandson: Robert Wilkinson
son: Thomas Wilson $1
son-in-law: John Wilkinson 5 shillings
son: James Wilson $10
dau: Elizabeth Wilson balance of estate

Executors: Thomas Wilson and Elizabeth Wilson.
Witnesses: Joseph Latta, Caleb Wilson.

- - -

D 588-589 Will dated 11 January 1818, proved Jan Court 1821.

JAMES LAPSLIE

sister: Elizabeth Lapslie half of estate during her life
"I loan to Sally Bryant mother of my two supposed daughters .. Lavinia Isabelle Bryant and Jane Bryant".. both under age, half (of estate) now, rest after death of sister Elizabeth.

"Anderson Armstrong and Thomas Lapslie Armstrong sons of my nephew Thomas Armstrong"
"Seney Armstrong and Mitchell Armstrong children of the said Thomas Armstrong"

Executors: trusty friends Thomas Armstrong and Willie Shaw,Esq.
Witnesses: A. B. Bruce, Chs. Bruce.

- - -

D 590 Will dated 20 January 1821, proved Feb Court 1821.

MARY (x) RAINEY "in low state of health"

grandson: William W. Rainey
"grandchildren Mary A. Rainey & Pemelia E. Rainey"
dau-in-law: Ann P. Rainey

Executrix: daughter-in-law Ann P. Rainey.
Witnesses: Sam'l Craford, George Allison.

- - -

D 591 Will dated 8 July 1820, proved February Court 1821.

THOMAS READING wife: Mary

- continued -

"Children, namely: John Reading, Stephen Reading, Martha Beever, Mary Whitaker, Elizabeth Horn, Thomas Reading."

Sole executor: son John Reading.
Witnesses: John Redmon, Jones Cardin.

- - -

D 592 Will dated 15 July 1820, proved February Court 1821.

JAMES (x) ROBERTS wife gets all estate

"Two youngest sons James & Ellis" land after wife's death.
"All my other children" 10¢

Executors: William Roberts and Lewis Roberts.
Witnesses: Nathaniel Harris, Matthew (x) Ellis.

- - -

D 592 Will dated 23 September 1820, proved Feb Court 1821.

ELIZABETH F. (x) SAWYER "very weak and feeble"

All estate to sister Mary C. Sawyer.

Sole executor: friend and Uncle John Campbell.
Witnesses: E. Turner, John Landers.

- - -

D 593 Will dated 19 October 1819, proved Feb Court 1821.
JOHN LEIGH dau: Jane 5 shillings

son: Richerson 5 shillings
daus: Aleus (?), Caty, Lear, 5 shillings each
Susannah $20; Patsy & Dianna bed & furniture each

"Rest of estate to be sold and money divided between my under named children to wit: Jack B. Leigh, Sullivan Leigh, Washington Leigh, Richard Leigh, Samuel Leigh, Thomas Leigh, Ewel Leigh, Patsy Ellice, Nancy Garrard, Betsy Leigh and Dianna Leigh, eleven in all."

Executors: sons Jack B. Leigh and Sullivan Leigh.
Witnesses: Anderson Clements, Philip Alston, Isaiah Marcom.

- - -

D 594 Will dated 8 December 1820, proved Feb Court 1821.

JAMES (x) MILLER "low in health"

wife: "plantation I now live on"
daus: Susan, Jane, Lydia, Polly, Rebeckah
son: William "the plantation I bought of the Widow Trice"
" Jesse "200 acres joining Robert Walker and others"

- continued -

sons: John and George land after mother's death

Executors: son William Miller and Rachel Miller.
Witnesses: James Williams, John Riley, Joseph Latta.

- - -

D 595 Will dated 28th day 7th month 1816, proved May 1821.

JOSEPH ALBRIGHT wife: Barbara

dau: Sarah Nicholson
son: John Albright "the plantation on the Alamance"
" Andrew Albright "the plantation where I now live"

Executors: son Andrew Albright and son-in-law James Nicholson.
Witnesses: John Marshill, John Marshill Jr., Jacob Marshill.

- - -

D 596 Will dated 14 January 1820, proved May Court 1821.

JOHN BROWNING wife: Elizabeth

dau: Mary Browning son: Soloman Browning

grandchildren: "My four granddaughters children of Rachel Browning Elizabeth Sarah Frances & Milly" "The two sons of Edward Browning Isaac & Edward Elim."
son: Richard Browning 10 shillings (he owes his father $200)

Executors: worthy friend Robert Browning, and Soloman Browning.
Witnesses: James Hurdle, James Douglass.

- - -

D 597-598 Will dated 1 March 1820, proved May Court 1821.

JAMES MURRAY "old - infirm" wife: Jennit plantation, etc.

sons: John Murray, William Murray
daus: Rachel Walker, Elizabeth Craig, Margaret MCadams, Mary
son: James Murray
"my four sons" mentioned twice, only 3 are named.
He mentions "unmarried children"
nephew: James Madison Murray son of Walter Murray

Executors: William Murray, Elder, and son John Murray.
Witnesses: John McCawley, William Murray.

- - -

D 599 Will dated 12 March 1821, proved May Court 1821.

SAMUEL THOMPSON wife: Rebeckah plantation

"sons John B., Robert & Richard T. & my daughter Sally" get land in Tennessee.
sons: Ralph and Samuel get plantation after wife's death
"Three youngest daughters Betsy, Rebeckah & Patsy" all minors

- continued -

Executors: wife Rebeckah, Thomas Thompson and Joel Cloud.
Witnesses: Joseph Anderson, David W. Anderson.

- - -

D 600 Will dated 19 July 1821, proved August Court 1821.

SAMUEL STRAYHORN (no wife mentioned)

Son James and daughter Sally are both under age. They are to be educated.

Executors: friend Sampson Moore and Gilbert Hart.
Witnesses: J. Webb, James Hart.

- - -

D 601 Will dated 30 May 1821, proved August Court 1821.

RICHARD (x) GOTT in "low state of health"

wife: Catherine Gott 2/3 of estate
"Sarah Squires daughter of Thomas Squires" 1/3 of estate.

No executor named.
Witnesses: Jno. Umstead, Thomas Gill, Thomas Squires.

- - -

D 601 Will dated 28 May 1821, proved August Court 1821.

CULBIRTH BURTON wife: Christian Burton

sons: John, Samuel (youngest), Williamson, William

Executors: wife Christian, and sons Williamson and John.
Witnesses: John Link, Elizabeth Horner, John Burton, Henry Bunch.

- - -

D 602 Will dated 21 January 1818, proved August Court 1821.

ALEXANDER BORLAND wife: Susannah

sons: Andrew, Archibald, Abraham
"To William and John Borland living in the State of Ga." £25 ea
"Three daughters Susannah Jenney and Nancy" unmarried
"My daughters Elizabeth Moulder, Mary Stout, Sally Strayhorn"

Executors: wife Susannah, John Cabe, Andrew Borland, and Archibald Borland.
Witnesses: John Scarlett, Aron (x) Hunter, Robert Taylor.

- - -

D 603 Will dated 8 January 1817, proved August Court 1821.

JAMES CRAIG, SR. wife: Rebecca

son: William 10 shillings - continued -

daus: Nancy Mellett, Margaret Nichols 10 shillings each
son: Isaac 10 shillings
dau: Rebecca (unmarried)
son: David plantation

Executors: wife Rebecca, and friend John Blackwood.
Witnesses: John Blackwood, Samuel Strayhorn, Thomas Faucett.

- - -

D 605 Will dated 30 May 1821, proved August Court 1821.

GEORGE REEVES (no wife mentioned)

sons: John, George, James and Frederick Reeves
daus: Sarah Durham, Nancy Baldwin.

Executors: John Reeves and George Reeves.
Witnesses: William Brown, James Bishop, John Brown.

- - -

D 606 Will dated 20 September 1820, proved Nov Court 1821.

STEPHEN BECKHAM or BERKHAM wife: Catherine

daus: Nancy and Tabitha
sons: Joshua Joseph Thomas Leonard Caswell (no punctuation)
"John my grandson that lives with me" (surname not stated)
dau: Elizabeth has had her share

Executor: son Joshua.
Witnesses: D. Patterson, Isaac Patterson.

- - -

D 606 Will dated 20 October 1821, proved Nov Court 1821.

FREDERICK REED wife: Penny Reed

William Anderson a legatee, no relationship stated.

Executor: William Anderson.

Witnesses: Redding George, Sampson Moore.

- - -

D 607-609 Will dated 31 July 1821, proved November Court 1821.

DAVID RAY wife: Jane

brother: Robert Ray
son: Peter has already had land deeded to him
sons: Griffin, George and Tyree
Remaining estate to be divided into eight parts "to each of my children Peter, Ellen, Griffin, George, Petronilla, Peggy Jane and Tyree"

- continued -

D 607-609 continued
"William B. Jamison the husband of my daughter Ellen"
"To my friends Duncan Cameron and James Webb .. 1/8 part in trust for my son William."

"Duncan Cameron, James Webb, and Thomas Ruffin the guardians of all my infant children". These three also named executors.

Witnesses: Wil. Kirkland, Favid Woods.

- - -

D 610 Will dated 19 June 1821, proved November Court 1821.

DAVID GREESON wife: Mary

"My children William Elias Peter and Polly Greeson", no punctuation.

Executor: friend Ludwick Lowe.
Witnesses: W. R. Holt, Jas. Gibson.

- - -

D 611 Will dated 7 February 1811, proved Nov Court 1821.

MATHEW McCAULEY wife: Martha

sons: John, Charles, William, George and Mathew McCauley
daus: Jenny (Jane), Martha, Elizabeth and Elender
"Three youngest children George and Elender and Mathew" are under age.

Executors: friends George Johnston and John McCauley.
Witnesses: Wm. Brewer, Isham Brewer,
Cressy (Cassy ?) (x) Pickett (her mark).

- - -

D 612 Will dated 8 August 1821, proved Nov Court 1821.

ARCHIBALD NICHOLSON (Checked with original will, very bad writing.)
dau: Diley or Dilcey ? Davis Nicholson
daus: Caty Davis Nicholson, Nancy Nicholson
dau: Sukey Maras 10 shillings
grandson: Young Antony 10 shillings

Executors: George Fogleman and David Fogleman. No witnesses. Proved by the oaths of Delilah Nicholson, George Fogleman, William Clendennin, Joseph Murray and John Marshall.

- - -

D 614 Receipt from AMELIA (x) MORGAN to SARAH MORGAN, Executrix of Hardy Morgan deceased.
Dated 11 January 1803, proved May Court 1810.
Witnesses: John Daniel, J.G.Rencher, Ch. Barbee.

- - -

D 614 Bill of Sale from THOMAS R. CATE to JOHN S. CATE.
Dated 7 November 1818, proved Feb Court 1819.
Witness: Solomon Cate.

- - -

D 615 Bill of Sale from JAMES BARTON (or BOSTON) HORNE to ARCHIBALD HORNE for a gray mare colt, $150.
Dated 4 May 1817, proved February Court 1819.
Witnesses: Reuben Carden, Jacob Lemmons.
This original paper is preserved in the State Archives.

Last entry in Book D

ORANGE COUNTY WILL BOOK E

E 1 Will dated 18 November 1821, proved Feb Court 1822.

ADAM (x) WHITSEL wife a legatee, name not stated

daus: Elizabeth, Polly, Nancy

Executors: John Boon, Esq., John Troxler.
Witnesses: John Boon, David Troxler.

- - -

E 2 Will dated 7 January 1821, proved Feb Court 1822.

WILLIAM WHITTED, Sr. of Hillsboro, N.C. Wife: Mary

brother: Levi deceased brother: John
neice: Anne, daughter of Jehu
son: William Henry Whitted
dau: Eliza I.
grandchildren: "William Nash Whitted and Mary T. Whitted, children of my son James Whitted, deceased."
Attelia Whitted, widow of James.
"Anne Whitted deceased, daughter of Jehu".

Executors: James Webb, James Phillips.
Witnesses: Wm. Horton, John Scott.

- - -

E 7 Will dated 19 July 1821, proved Fenruary Court 1822.

JAMES LINN wife: Mary

"Wife Mary to make children with her equal with those that have left her." All children to have equal shares in estate.

Executors: Henry Barnhart and Eli Euliss.
Witnesses: John (x) Euliss, WM. Causey, Peter Linn.

- - -

E 7 Will dated 3 January 1818, proved Feb Court 1822.

ADAM (x) WHITSEL - continued -

sons: Ludowick (deceased), Jacob, Daniel, John, Henry,
and Christian Whitsel have all had land deeded to them
dau: Barbara is to have an amount equal to "my other daughters who are now married and left me."
daus: Caty, Mary. and Elizabeth Turley

Witnesses: Wm. Montgomery, John Boon.

- - -

E 9 Will dated 10 January 1822, proved Feb Court 1822.

TINNIN (x) McADAMS "in low state of health"

wife: Ann "My four children" to be "schooled"

son: Joseph Armstrong
daus: Mary, Peggy, Catey

Executor: John A. Mebane.
Witnesses: James Mebane, J. A. Mebane.

- - -

E 10 Will dated 10 August 1813 ?, proved Feb Court 1822.

DAVID ANDERSON son: Joseph

daus: Hannah Hill, Martha Anderson, Elizabeth Anderson

Executors: daughters Martha and Elizabeth, James Lapslie.
Witnesses: Thomas Armstrong, Robert Mitchell.

- - -

E 10 Will dated 30 January 1822, proved Feb Court 1822.

JOHN BRACKEN wife: Nancy

daughter: Julia Ann
brother: Joseph

Executors: brother Joseph, and Caleb Wilson.
Witnesses: James Blackwell, Wm. Ector.

- - -

E 11 Will dated 14 January 1819, proved Feb Court 1822.

GEORGE GARRISON wife: Margaret

daus: Lidia Brown, Susanna Phillips
son: Wm. H. Garrison
dau: Margaret Simpson
son: Zimree

Executor: Hall Garrison.
Witnesses: James Nicholson, Wm. Boswell.

- - -

E 13 Will dated 8 March 1813, proved February Court 1822.

MOSES HUTCHINS son: Thomas Hutchins

daus: Nelly Herndon, Hannah Herndon,
Elizabeth Evans, Peggy Turner

Executors: son Thomas, and C. P. Patterson.
Witnesses: C. P. Patterson, Sarah Patterson.

- - -

E 13 Will dated 7 February 1822, proved May Court 1822.

NATHANIEL CARTER

sons: Enoch, William, Henry, Brice
dau: Rebecca
sons: Nathaniel, Joshua

Executors: son Enoch, and John Newlin.
Witness: Elizabeth Rinstaff.

- - -

E 14 Will dated 28 December 1821, proved May Court 1822.

WILLIAM BRADFORD sons: Thomas and Joseph

dau: Sarah McCauley
grandsons: Hamilton and Grandison, sons of daughter Sarah
daus: Elizabeth Douglas, Margaret Ray, Jane Ray wife of Wm.

Executors: son David, and Robert Ray.
Witnesses: James Bradford, Thomas Reeves.

- - -

E 15 Will dated 15 May 1822, proved May Court 1822.

DANIEL (x) HUFFHINES "low in body" wife: Lucretia

daus: "heirs of Mary Farmer", Betsy Tickle, Caty Lowe,
Mary May, Susa (Lucy ?) Cornodle, Sally Lowe,
Christiner Cotner

sons: John, Jacob, George
He mentions George Cornable (Cornodle ?) as having a note.
George's father is also named George.

Executors: sons-in-law David Lowe and George Cornodle.
Witnesses: Joseph Gibson, Jeremiah Holt.

- - -

E 17 Will dated 8 December 1818, proved May Court 1822.

EPHRIAM CARRINGTON wife: Priscilla

sons: Morgan, John, Linton (?)
daus: Charlotte, Dicey, Polly - continued -

Executors: Herbert Lines, John I. Carrington "friends".
Witnesses: James S. Harris, Thomas Cottrell.

- - -

E 18 Will dated 7 March 1817, proved May Court 1822.

SUSANNA WARD son: William

son: James 20 shillings,
sons: Stephen, Thomas
daus: Sarah Clark, Asther Wells
son: Antony Ward
dau: Priscilla Free (?)
"To my daughter Susanna Pike heirs 20 shillings"

Execytors: son Stephen Ward, and David Patterson.
Witnesses: Isaac Patterson, John Coble.

- - -

E 19 Will dated 4 April 1822, proved August Court 1822.

JOHN (x) TICKLE wife: Mary

dau: Margaret Millar "tract on which she now lives"
daus: Catheriner Trollinger, Mary Huffhines, Barbary Tate.

"Grandson David Tickle's daughter Sally"
son: John

Executor: son John.
Witnesses: John H. Carmichael, Daniel Ockelreas.

- - -

E 20 Will dated 20 June 1822, proved August Court 1822.

JACOB (x) JOHNSON (Checked with original in Archives)

wife: Amy (?) "land I now live on which I purchased of Clement Massey."

Executrix: wife.
Witnesses: Sanders Riley, Warden Riley, Austin (x) Wesson.

- - -

E 20 Will dated 6 August 1822, proved August Court 1822.

GEORGE GRESHAM (or GRISHAM), SR. wife: Sarah

grandsons: George Washington Clinton, John Linnington Clinton, Samuel Harrison Clinton (youngest is under age, but can't tell which is youngest)
granddaughters: Sarah Clinton, Elizabeth Clinton, Nancy Clinton, Mary Ann Clinton.

Executors: "worthy friends Aquilla Rhodes and James Dollar son of Jonathan."
Witnesses: Moses McCown, James Dollar.

- - -

E 21 Will dated 9 June 1822, proved August Court 1822.

JOHN NELSON   wife: Janet.

sons: William, David, John, Samuel, Alfred, Paisley
dau: Isabella
son: James
daus: Marey (or Nancy), Margaret

no executor named
Witnesses: Samuel Nelson, James Tate.

- - -

E 22 Will dated 6 August 1821, proved November Court 1822.

JAMES JACKSON, SR.

sons: William, Jacob and James Jackson $5 each
daus: Susannah Latta, Mary Cloud, Sarah Cloud $10 each
daus: Elizabeth Jackson and Tuth Jackson "plantation where Abner Jackson now lives"

Executrix: daughter Elizabeth Jackson.
Witnesses: Wm. Nichols, Sr., Abner Jackson, Bradley Collins.

- - -

E 23 Will dated 23 October 1822, proved Nov Court 1822.

JOHN YOUNG of the Town of Hillsboro

wife: Nancy "my plantation bought of James Hastings", etc.

"Tiny children" mentioned, names and number not stated.

Executors: friends Levi Whitted and Thomas D. Watts.
Witnesses: James Webb, James L. Smith.

- - -

E 24 Will dated 6 April 1821, proved November Court 1822.

WILLIAM SHEPPARD

children: Wm. Sheppard, Betsy Ashe, Mary Ashe, & Susan Jane Hay.
dau: Sally Grove
sons: Egbert Sheppard, Henry James Sheppard
dau: Margaret L. Sheppard "640 acres in Tennessee in the Chickasaw Purchase", etc.

Executors: Dr. James Webb, David Yarborough.
Witness: John Haywood.

- - -

E 25 Will dated 29 July 1818, proved November Court 1822.

JOSEPH (x) COURTNEY "weak and indisposed"

Friend, relation, Thomas D. Watts all estate.   - continued -

Elizabeth Christmas is to be allowed to live where she is now for her lifetime.

"Loving friend and sister Frances Courtney"

Executor: friend Thomas Clancy.
Witnesses: Robert Glenn, Jane Glenn.

\- - -

E 26 Will dated 2 October 1820, proved Nov Court 1822.

MARY WOODS, widow (See will of Hugh Woods Jan 1794, D 1)

dau: Susanna Faucett
granddau: Rebecca P, Ray, daughter of Thomas Ray and his Mary.
dau: Sarah Ray
granddaus: "son John Woods two daughters Susanna and Peggy"
great-grand-dau:"Mary Mecia (?) Wood, daughter of my grandson Timothy Wood."
daus: Elizabeth Woods,Mary Ann Ray

Executors: son Joseph Woods, friend Robert Walker,
Witnesses: William Dunagan, Eli Woods, Wm. Baldwin.

\- - -

E 27 Will dated 22 May 1822, proved November Court 1822.

MARTHA (PATSEY) BREWER

sisters: Polly Miner, Fanny King, Elizabeth O'Daniel
Biddy Brewer (under age), Aris Brewer
brothers: William Brewer, Ransom Brewer, Morris Brewer, John Brewer

Her mother is living.

Executors: "beloved friends Thomas Brewer Sr, and Sackfield Brewer."
Witnesses: Thomas Brewer, Ezekiel Brewer.

\- - -

E 28 Will dated 27 February 1821, proved Nov Court 1822.

JAMES WOODY wife: Mary

sons: Hugh, Samuel, John
daus: Sarah, Mary, Rebecca, Charity, Hannah, Susannah, Jane, Ruth, Ellenor

Executors: sons Hugh and Samuel.
Witnesses: Enoch Morrison, Robert Graham.

\- - -

E 29 Will dated 25 October 1822, proved Nov Court 1822.

JAMES HASTINGS daughter: Easter Cate

sons: Thomas, Henry
daus: Nance Smith, Sarah Hastings, Hannah Smith, Margaret Lashley
youngest sons: James, John, Joseph

Executors: sons Thomas and Henry.
Witnesses: A. Watson, Joseph H. Latta.

- - -

E 30 Will dated 14 November 1822, proved Feb Court 1823.

JOSEPH PICKETT wife: Nancy

"Supposed son, John Copley, son of Dolly Copley.".. "Lives with me, raised by me, and bound by me - 17 February 1816."

Witnesses: Jacob Whitaker, Isley Copley.

- - -

E 31 Will dated 12 February 1819, proved Feb Court 1823.

ANNA ARMSTRONG son-in-law: Isaac Jackson

"To all my sons and daughters 10 shillings each," none named.

Executor: son-in-law Isaac Jackson.
Witnesses: Robert Whitted, Levi Whitted.

- - -

E 32 Will dated 5 October 1822, proved Feb Court 1823.

WILLIAM McKEE wife: Dolly or Polly

daus: Polly or Dolly McKee, Anne Wood
son: Rankin
dau: Victory Boring
sons: James, William
dau: Betsy Hargis
son: David

Executors: wife, and son Rankin.
Witnesses: William B. Roberson, James Murdock.

- - -

E 33 Will dated 25 July 1822, proved May Court 1823.

PETER (x) TICKLE "low and weak"

children: Mary Whait, John Tickle, Peter Tickle, Elizabeth Huffhines, Conrad Tickle, Henry Tickle.
son-in-law: Daniel Whait

Executor: Joseph Gibson. Witness: Anthony Coble.

- - -

E 34 Will dated 25 February 1823, proved May Court 1823.

MARY WHITTED

daughter: Eliza J. Whitted
son: Henry Whitted
grandchildren: Nash Whitted and Mary Jemima (or Terminia ?) Whitted get 1/3 of estate

Executor: James Webb
Witnesses: William Whitted, James Webb.

- - -

E 35 Will dated 25 July 1822, proved May Court 1823.

SAMUEL PEELOR wife: Elizabeth

son: Benjamin "when he comes of age".."old place whereon Iley Browning now lives"
grown sons: Cader Peelor, Michael Sherman Peelor, Pleasant Peelor, Anthony Redwine Peelor, Thornberry Peelor
daus: Sarah Peelor, Catherine Peelor

Executors: Moses Guess and Moses McCown.
Witnesses: Anthony Cole, Thomas James.

- - -

E 36 Will dated 5 February 1823, proved May Court 1823.

WILLIAM ANDERSON wife a legatee, name not stated

"Money put to interest till my youngest child comes of age then equally divided between my children."

Executors: worthy friends Joseph Allison and William Maris.
Witnesses: J.D.Hughes, Thomas Armstrong, Joseph Allison.

- - -

E 36 Will dated -- , proved August Court 1823.

DANIEL MAY wife: Barbary May

sons: David, William, Daniel, Jacob
daus: Mary Allbright, Barbary May, Catherine May

Executors: sons Jacob and William.
Witnesses: James Nelson, Samuel Curtis.

- - -

E 37 Will dated 7 February 1816, proved August Court 1823.

WILLIAM KEELING wife: Polley

"son William's three sons: John youngest, oldest son Benjamin, William"

- continued -

"son James Keeling and his two sons James and William"
son: Gregory Perry Keeling
"My other five children: Thomas, Rachel, Betsey, Polly and Ceney."

Executors: William and James Keeling and John Dunn.
Witnesses: Richard Breeze, Ast. Moore.

- - -

E 39 Will dated 6 February 1822, proved August Court 1823.

LUCY HILLYARD

She leaves all her estate to her daughters, because it is so small, though she loves her sons dearly.
Eldest daughter Nancy is to be guardian of the three other daughters, Lucy, Martha and Mary.

sons: William and John
Unimproved lot in Chapel Hill, N.C. is to be sold.

Executor: "Elisha Mitchell of Orange County."
Witnesses: William Pannill, Samuel Pannill.

- - -

E 40 Will dated 15 April 1820, proved August Court 1823.

JAMES PYLE wife: Sarah

sons: Isaac and Caleb $5 each
grandson: Henry Pyle son of Caleb
sons: William gets property, John $5, Joseph $50 "if living"
daus: Mary Whittenton, Rachel Cooke $5 each
grandson: Moses Pyle son of Isaac
" Garrett Pyle son of John
great-granddaughter: Rebecca Pyle (under 21)

Executors: William Matkins, William Brinkley.
Witnesses: Thomas Brown, James Danieley.
(Note: Mary Pyle married 15 Sept 1802 John Whittington.)

- - -

E 41 Bill of Sale from WILLIAM HINCHEY of Orange County to THOMAS M. JOHNSTON for bay horse, saddle and bridle, all household furniture, etc. Dated 13 July 1823, proved August Court 1823. Witnesses: C.W.Johnston, Matthew McCauley.

- - -

E 42 Will dated 15 December 1820, proved Nov Court 1823.

ISAAC HOLT wife: Mary

youngest sons: Archibald M. Holt and Isaac, not of age
son: Thomas S. Holt

- continued -

Maria D. Foust wife of George Foust
Emily Ray wife of William Ray
Thomas Rowan and wife Emily and to her children
"I leave on the Guliford Plantation of my wife .." etc.

Executors: Thomas Scott and George Foust, Jr.
Witnesses: Daniel Coble, Austin Coble, Frederick Kemruce ?, Thomas Scott, Wm. D. Murphey, A. D. Murphey.
Codicil dated 23 June 1821 names no new legatees.

- - -

E 47 Will dated 18 August 1823, proved Nov Court 1823.

JONATHAN DAVIS wife a legatee, name not stated

All children to have equal shares in estate. They are all under age now.

Executors: wife, and Colonel Joseph Allison.
Witnesses: E. Graves, Abram Parish.

- - -

E 48 Will dated 9 September 1823, proved Nov Court 1823.

PERRY MITCHELL

wife: Polly "land left me by will of my father at the death of my mother."

Executors: wife Polly, and Eli Murray.
Witnesses: Benjamin Burnside, John Compton.

E 48 Will dated 4 December 1807, proved Nov Court 1823.

LUDWICK WAYNICK

wife: Margaret "all to my wife unless she marry again , then to be returned to my children"

sole executrix: wife Margaret.
Witnesses: Thomas C. Scott, John Southard.

- - -

E 49 Will dated 15 February 1820, proved Feb Court 1824.

WILLIAM ANDREW, SR. (Indexed in Archives as ANDRUS)
"very aged"
sons: Starling land lying west of the Haw Branch
Archibel, Laborn 5 shillings
grandchildren: "lawful heirs of Elizabeth Edwards" 5 sh.
sons: Mark, John 5 shillings each
dau: Patsy Cheek 5 shillings
son: Henry 5 shillings dau: Ginney Cheek 5 shillings

- continued -

 E 49 Will of WILLIAM ANDREW, SR continued

sons: William 5 shillings, Archibald

Executors: sons Laborn and Mark.
Witnesses: Thomas Brewer, John ...?..

- - -

E 50 Will dated 19 April 1823, proved February Court 1824.

THOMAS LASHLEY (LESLEY in Archives) wife: Hannah

daus: Fanny, Hannah, Nicy, Henry Ray's wife, Jean, Rachel
sons: Thomas, Elijah, Alexander
Betsy, David Ray's wife

Executor: friend James Thompson.
Witnesses: Thomas Bradshaw, James Bradshaw.

- - -

E 51 Will dated 1821, proved February Court 1824.

WILLIS (x) MONK wife: Mary

sons: Andrew, John
"I have given all my children their portion I alloted for them."

Executors: wife Mary Monk, and Ezekiel Hailey.

- - -

E 52 Will dated 5 February 1824, proved Feb Court 1824.

RACHEL (x) MILLER "in low state of health"

sons: William, Jessey
daus: Lydia Miller, Polly Miller, Rebecca Miller
sons: Jarge (under age), John
sister: Sally Hall "my loom"
sons-in-law: Samuel Bird, James S. Cate 5 shillings each

No executor named.
Witnesses: John I. Freeland, Daniel Cloud.

- - -

E 53 Will dated 1 January 1823, proved Feb Court 1824.

JOHN McCAULEY

wife: Mary R. "land I may inherit from my father by Will at his death ... to be divided between my children, if any, if none then in that case whole shall be divided equally between Maria and Martha Lea, daughters of Gabriel B. Lea, Esq."
sister: Mary Ann Lea
brother: Robert W. McCauley
brother-in-law: William M. Lea

Executor: Joel B. Lea. Witness: Robert Morrow.

- - -

E 54 Will dated 26 November 1823, proved May Court 1824

WILLIAM PICKETT wife: Elizabeth

sons: Edward, Joseph and William (youngest)

"The whole of my children, Edward, Patsy, Polly, Eliza, Emily, Joseph, Lucretia, William."

Executor: Gabriel B. Lea.
Witnesses: I. S. Smith, Elizah Pickard.

- - -

E 55 Will dated 11 May 1824, proved May Court 1824.

JOHN HOLT wife: Melly

"My three children: Elizabeth, Hezekiah, Milly."

Executor: cousin William Holt.
Witnesses: Peter L. Ray, Mason Tarpley.

- - -

E 56 Will dated 9 January 1823, proved May Court 1824.

JOHN HUTCHINS dau: Polly wife of William Lewis

Executors: daughter Polly lewis, and son-in-law Wm. Lewis.
Witnesses: Philip Alston, William Lynn, J. Dickson.

- - -

E 57 Will dated 8 January 1824, proved May Court 1824.

DAVID HARDEE wife: Winney

sons: John, William, Thomas
daus: Polly Wells, Elizabeth Crisp, Sally Hardee, Martha Carlton Thompson
granddaughter: Martha Winnefred Thompson

Executors: wife,and Sally Hardee , Mr. Willie Shaw, Miles / Wells.
Witnesses: Alston Moore, John Moore.

- - -

E 58 Will dated 31 October 1816, proved May Court 1824.

THOMAS KELL son: William

"Three children Robert, Thomas, Elizabeth

Executors: William Kell and Thomas Riggs.
Witness: John Latta.

- - -

E 59 Will dated 18 February 1824, proved May Court 1824.

SAMUEL PYLE wife: Susannah

sons: Joel, Alfred, William
He speaks of property to be kept in hands of executors for "all my children", but only the three above are named.

Executors: Isaac Patterson, Alexander Albright
Witnesses: Stephen Ward, Leven Woods, John Pike,Jr.

- - -

E 60 Will dated 20 May 1824, proved August Court 1824.

WILLIAM MARSHILL wife: Mary

daus: Elizabeth (unmarried), Rachel, Ann
son: William "plantation he now lives on"
sons-in-law: Benjamin Dixon, Winlock (?) Reynolds, Solomon Stout
dau-in-law: Elizabeth Marshill

Executors: son William, and son-in-law Benjamin Dixon.
Witnesses: Solomon Allen, John (x) Sheirdan (?).

- - -

E 61 Will dated 2 March 1824, proved August Court 1824.

NATHANIEL KING, SR. wife: Sally

son: Thomas
daus: Polly, Sally, Fanny

..."property equally divided between all my children now living."

Executors: wife Sally; and sons Nathaniel and William.
Witnesses: John Adams, John McCauley, N. I. King.

- - -

E 62 Will dated 16 November 1823, proved August Court 1824.

JOHN McDANIEL wife: Margaret

sons: Eli, John, Alexander
daus: Elenor, Elizabeth, Margaret, Jean, Susannah
son: James

Executors: sons Eli and James.
Witnesses: John Stockard, Richard Thompson.

- - -

E 64 Will dated 3 July 1824, proved November Court 1824.

PETER WALKER wife: Elizabeth

nephew: William Walker son of William Walker deceased

- continued -

nephew: Peter Walker, son of "my brother Andrew"
"Lemuel Pickett son of John"
neice: Sarah Walker "daughter of my brother Andrew"

Executors: brother Andrew Walker, and nephew John Pickett.
Witnesses: Wm. I. Bingham, Vicy King, Nancy Hamilton.

- - -

E 65 Will dated 18 August 1824, proved Nov Court 1824.

JOHN LONG aunt: Polly Freeland

uncle and aunt: Samuel Craig and Peggy Craig
cousin: Elizabeth Craig
half-brothers: George Long, Thomas Long, James Long,
Charles Long, Anderson Long, 5 shillings each
half-sisters: Nancy Long, Catherine Long, 5 " "
"To my brother William Long's children he had of his wife Peggy" 5 shillings each.
"To the man who succeeds me as Captain of my Company, my Military equipage .."etc.

Executors: friends Isaac Craig, John Freeland.
Witnesses: Isaac Craig, James Freeland.

- - -

E 66 Will dated 1 April 1824, proved November Court 1824.

JOSEPH LATTA wife: Sarah

"All my children: Mary P. Latta, John Cabe Latta, Nancy A. Latta, Elizabeth L. Latta, Caroline L. Latta." (John a minor.)

Executors: trusty friends Thomas Latta and James Latta.
Witnesses: John Riley, John Ray, Sr.

- - -

E 68 Will dated 28 July 1824, proved November Court 1824.

JOHN RHODES wife: Patsy

sons: Pleasant, John, Benjamin
daus: Polly, Sally, Betsy, Patsy

Executors: Christopher Barbee Jr, Pleasant Rhodes, and Benjamin Rhodes.
Witnesses: Sampson Moore, F ? H. Ta ylor.

- - -

E 67 Will dated 5 June 1823, proved November Court 1824,

JOHN LATTA son: Thomas

"son John's two children John and Maria" - continued -

sons: James, Joseph
sons-in-law: Robert Walker, Robert Davis
William Faucett, Thomas Holloway Jr.
grandsons: William and John Holloway

Executors: sons Thomas and John Latta.
Witnesses: James Allison, Robert Davis.

- - -

E 70 Will dated 10 January 1823, proved August Court 1824.

State of Tennessee, Roane County 4th Monday in April 1823 Court. "An instrument in writing was produced in Open Court and proved by oath of Samuel Eskridge and Abigail Johnston who made oath that the said FRANCIS CHILDS signed, sealed and published the said instrument as his last will and testament in their presence.

I, FRANCES CHILDS of Orange County, N.C. now in Roane County Tennessee, and I give and deliver to my son, Samuel, one-halfof my estate. To my wife, Martha, rest of estate. Hereby appoint executors: Simon Turner of Murray County. "

- - -

E 71 Will dated 12 August 1822, proved February Court 1825.

HENRY THOMPSON wife: Priscilla

dau: Mrs. Nelly Baldridge
dau: Sally - her estate is to be held in trust for her during her life by Catlett Campbell, James Child, William Huntington.
granddaughter: Susan Thompson "daughter of said Sally"

Executors: Thomas Clancy, John Scott.
Witnesses: James Phillips, J. H. Hand.

- - -

E 73 Will dated 4 July 1822, proved February Court 1825.

JACOB ALBRIGHT "beloved wife"

sons: John, Solomon, William
"After just debts paid money to be equally divided between my daughters" names and number not stated.

Executors: son Solomon and son-in-law John Albright.
Witnesses: Andrew Albright, Henry Garrott.

- - -

E 74 Will dated 5 May 1817, proved February Court 1825.

WILLIAM (x) HOLDER wife: Mourning

Children: Chesley, William, Daniel, Polly, John, Hosea, Lydia, Nancy, Elijah, Elisha.
Executor: son Chesley. Witnesses: Thos. Flint, Harrison Christian.

- - -

E 75 Will dated 6 December 1824, proved Feb Court 1825.

LESLIE O'KELLY wife: Nancy

"My children", names and number not stated.

Executor: brother Franklin O'Kelly and brother-in-law John McCuiston.
Witnesses: Henry Moring, William Hudson.

- - -

E 76 Will dated 24 August 1823, proved Feb Court 1825.

SARAH YEARGAN daus: Charlotte Nunn, Harriet Forsythe

son: Mann Patterson
Milly , daughter of Mann Patterson
"Four oldest daughters of Mann Patterson", not named.
son: Bartlett Yeargan

Executor: Mann Patterson
Witnesses: B. Cheek, W. I. Dillard.

- - -

E 76 Will dated 29 July 1824, proved Feb Court 1825.

WILLIAM HENRY WHITTED wife: Frances

sister: Eliza Jane Murphey
brother James
brother's children: William Nash Whitted
Tarmesia Mary Whitted

Executor: Dr. James Webb.
Witnesses: Thomas Ruffin, James Child, James Webb, John Street

- - -

E 78 Will dated 20 April 1821, proved February Court 1825.

JOHN O'DANIEL

sons: John, Henry, James, Jesse, Green
daus: Jane Cates, Peggy Thompson
"Peggy Thompson's three daughters Nance, Jane and Anne Thompson are to have her part" (is Peggy deceased ?)
"Nancy Basket, John Basket, and William Basket sons and daughter of Susannah Basket"

Executors: son James, and Thomas Thompson.
Witnesses: Ezra Durham, John Durham, Henry O'Daniel Sr.

- - -

E 80 Will dated 29 November 1824, proved May Court 1825.

ELIZABETH HOWARD daughter: Henrietta

granddau: Elizabeth Christmas Howard, daughter of Richard

Executor: Stephen Glass
Witnesses: W. Thompson, Reuben Smith.

- - -

E 81 Will dated 12 July 1812, proved May Court 1825.

JAMES WILSON wife: Henrietta

son: Samuel gets a colt son: William "small colt"
daus: Dicey, Sally, Henrietta, Jean
"Granddaughter Mariah daughter of my deceased daughter Dradeyann (?)."
sons: John D. Wilson and George Wilson, both under age.
" Hiram "my plantation"; James to "live where he is for 3 yrs"
son-in-law: James Turrentine $1. After wife's death her share t
"All my children, namely: James, Archelaus, William, Samuel, John D, George Wilson, also Nancy, Polly, Dicey, Sally, Henrietta and Jeane, "except Hiram, who has land left to him."
Executors: wife Henrietta and Samuel Turrentine.
Witnesses: S. Turrentine, Alex. Turrentine, Arch. Turrentine.

Proved by oaths of Thomas Clancy and William Hall who swore that they were acquainted with the handwriting both of Samuel and Alex Turrentine and that they believe their names subscribed as witnesses to the foregoing will are in the proper handwriting of the said Samuel and Alex Turrentine."

\- - -

E 82 Will dated 12 March 1825, proved May Court 1825.

JAMES BARNWELL wife: Susan

"Three youngest daughters Susan, Nancy and Elenor".

Children: Robert, Catherine, John, William, Susan, Nancy, Elenor, James

Executors: wife Susan, and son John.
Witnesses: Ellis Malone, William Murray, Andrew Murray.

\- - -

E 84 Will dated 28 January 1825, proved May Court 1825.

THOMAS VINCENT

sons: John, William, James, Thomas
daus: Sarah Morrow, Polly Byrd, Elizabeth Vincent

Executors: sons John and William.
Witnesses: Thomas Reeves, Wm. Creswell, Gab. B. Lea.

\- - -

E 86 Noncupative will of WILLIAM W. HALL dated 4 June 1825,

proved by the oaths of William Hall Sr., Joseph Allison and Joel Reynolds at August Court 1825.
All estate left to Alex G. Hall, no relationship stated.

\- - -

E 86 Will dated 7 September 1824, proved August Court 1825.

JOSEPH BOOTHE, SENIOR wife: Sarah

son: Joseph

"Grandchildren Joseph B. Herndon, George Herndon, Lewis, Willis and Mary Herndon are to receive the share of their deceased mother, Mary Herndon."

daughter: Rosy Reach (Beach ?)
granddaughter: Mary Yates daughter of Rosy Reach
daus: Elizabeth Stone, Tabitha Hudson, Delilah Yates, Sally George

Executors: Wm. Yates, Sampson Moore, and wife Sarah Boothe.
Witnesses: David George, David Castleberry.

Note by Ruth Herndon Shields: This BOOTHE family and their descendants are given in HERNDON-HUNT and ALLIED FAMILIES by Lillie Boothe Nesbitt and Edna Hilliard White Wood, published 1930. The HERNDON grandchildren's ancestry will be found in HERNDONS OF THE AMERICAN REVOLUTION, PART FOUR, by John Goodwin Herndon. (See last page in this book.)

- - -

E 87 Will dated 10 March 1825, proved August Court 1825.

WILLIAM LEATHERS

" ... property to be divided equally between my wife and children .... to be kept together until one of them marries or comes of age ..." Number and names of children not given.

Executors: brother Fielding Leathers, and Tignal Jones.
Witnesses: James Webb, Westward A. Jones.

- - -

E 88 Will dated 20 August 1822, proved August Court 1825.

JOHN FLINTHOM (FLENTHOM ?) wife: Alsey

son: Clement
daus: Elizabeth Campbell, Sally Flinthum
Legacy to Nancy Carr (relationship not stated) .."if she will come into this county and visit her relations, nothing if she will not come."
son: James No executor named.

Witnesses: Archibald Borland, Thomas W. Holden.

- - -

E 89 Will dated 28 August 1818, proved Nov Court 1825.

PETER INGOLD wife a legatee, name not stated

son: Adam

- continued -

He says he leaves "nothing to other heirs".
William Ingold is mentioned in description of land boundaries, no relationship mentioned.

Executor: son Adam.
Witnesses: Jacob Sherer, John Garrett, Peter Ingold.

- - -

E 90 Will dated 6 April 1825, proved Nov Court 1825.

CHARLES HOBSON wife: Zernah

daus: Peninah and Lydia, both under age.

Executor: William Thompson.
Witnesses: John Thompson (two of them), Libri ? Moffitt.

- - -

E 90 ADAM SPRINGER sisters: Mary Springer, Eve Partin

brothers: David Springer, George Springer

Executor: "Trusty and beloved friend Sebastian Graves."
Witnesses: Benj. Burnside, John Coble.

- - -

E 91 Will dated --, proved November Court 1825.

DAVID NELSON brother-in-law: David Craig

brothers: William, John, Samuel and Alfred Nelson.
sisters: Mary Nelson, Margaret Nelson
brother: Paisley Nelson
mother: Jennett Nelson

Executors: James Tate and David Mebane.
Witnesses: David Mebane, James Tate.

- - -

E 92 Will dated 16 April 1824, proved November Court 1825.

JOHN DAVIS wife: Elizabeth

sons: Anderson, James, John, William
daus: Sally Beville, Nancy Raney, Frances Beville
son: Robert
daus: Mary Davis, Elizabeth Gattis
son: Wyatt

Executors: son James, and Sampson Moore.
Witnesses: Jack B. Leigh, Anne Leigh.

- - -

E 94 Will dated 20 November 1822, proved Nov Court 1825.

JONATHAN JORDAN wife: Mary

son: George daughter: Nancy

grandson: Jacob granddaughter: Polly Jordan

"To each and all my other children the property they have already received of me." Names and number not stated.

Executors: James Hutcheson, George Hurdle.
Witnesses: David Perkins, James Paul.

- - -

E 95 Will dated 13 September 1825, proved Nov Court 1825 ?

JOHN B. VINCENT

brothers William and James, and sister Betsey

niece: "Elizabeth Bird, daughter of my sister Polly Bird."

Executors: Brothers William and James.
Witnesses: Gabriel B. Leigh, Ashford Walker, Wm. C. Patrick, James Weldon.

- - -

E 96 Will dated 24 April 1820, proved February Court 1826.

RICHARD BENNEHAN daughter: Rebecca Cameron

son: Thomas D. Bennehan

"1,000 for the propagation of the gospel of Jesus Christ."

Witnesses: Samuel Yarborough, Wm. M. Shaw
Executors: son Thomas D. Bennehan, and Duncan Cameron.

- - -

E 97 Will dated 3 April 1818, proved February Court 1926.

WILLIAM McCAULEY James Allison's lot in Hillsboro is mentioned.

son: John
dau: Jane McCollum
sons: Matthew, Charles
grandson: William, son of John
grandsons: Benjamin and James, sons of Matthew
" James Reeves; William, son of Charles
dau-in-law: Catred ? McCauley, widow of son James
son-in-law: William Trousdale and Catred his wife

Executors: George Johnston, Alex. Gattis, Wm. Kirkland.
Witnesses: Matthew McCauley, James McCauley.

- - -

E 99 Will dated 22 March 1823, proved February Court 1826.

JUDY CLAPP

"Children of my daughter Barbara formerly wife of John Powell."
son: John

daughter: Caty, wife of John Hobbs
"   Sophia, wife of Jacob Foust

Executor: son John Clapp.
Witnesses: Joel C. Yancey , Wm. Smith.

- - -

E 99 Will dated 28 January 1826, proved Feb Court 1826.

JOHN STRAIN   wife: Marian ? Miriam ?

sons: David, Alexander, James, Samuel
dau: Mary Strayhorn
daus: Elizabeth Strain, Sarah Strain
grandchildren: Jane Strayhorn and Samuel Strayhorn

Executors: son David Strain, and son-in-law Bryant Strayhorn.
Witnesses: Charles W. Johnston, Wm. Kirkland, Chas. R. Yancey.

- - -

E 101 Will dated 29 October 1825, proved Feb Court 1826.

GEORGE TROXLER   son: John, under age

eldest daughter: Adeline Warren, wife of Briscoe Warren
daughter: Franky Rich, wife of Henry Rich
unmarried daughters, names not stated: "my two other daughters that may remain after one other is married."

Executors: son-in-law Briscoe Warren, and Wm. Montgomery.
Witnesses: D. Albright, B. Troxler.

- - -

E 103 Will dated 29 October 1825, proved Feb Court 1826.

MARY CRAIG

She is to be buried at New Hope (Presbyterian) Meeting House where "my husband and many of my relatives are buried."

grandchildren: "William, Peggy and Polly, children of my deceased son Samuel."

Executors: Wm. Kirkland and Charles D. Johnson.
Witnesses: George J. Johnston, Joseph Kirkland.

- - -

E 105 Will dated 11 November 1825, proved Feb Court 1826.

JOSEPH TATE   wife: Mary   - continued -

daughters: Polly and Alice
son: Griffith Tate. Legacy to him "if said Griffith Tate ever return to the county."
sons: James, Joseph, William, Robert
dau: Elizabeth Taylor
"All property divided between five sons and three daughters, Polly and Alice."

Executors: sons William and Robert
Witnesses: John Hughes, William Gattis.

- - -

E 106 Will dated 6 September 1824, proved Feb Court 1826.

ROBERT DOCKERY wife: Caty

nephew: "Sister's son John Withey (?)

Executors: Richard Breese and Caty Dockery.
Witnesses: S.M.McCracken, John (x) Dockery, R. Breese, Paton ? Dockery.

- - -

E 107 Will dated 22 December 1825, proved Feb Court 1826.

ROSANNAH COTNER grandson: Aaron Cotner

relationship not stated to : Barbary Hunt, Eve Stonor, Mary Alexander, Peter Cotner, Susannah Kinney

"To Louis Cotner, Grace Cotner and Rosannah Gifford all rest of my property."

Executors: Isaih Hornaday and Samuel Hymer.
Witnesses: Micajah Thompson, Job Evans.

- - -

E 107 Will dated 6 February 1826, proved May Court 1826.

ROBERT WALKER wife: Elenor

daughter: Elizabeth Patterson "to be excluded"
sons: John, William, Robert, Philip, and George W. Walker (George is under age)
daus: Sally, Polley, Peggy, Jane
granddaughter: Elizabeth Walker

"To Rev. WM. M. Green in trust for Protestant Episcopal Church in this state, $25."

Executors: sons John and William.
Witnesses: Wm. B. Jamison, Ezekiel Laws.

- - -

E 109 Will dated 5 March 1826, proved May Court 1826.

PHILIP WALKER, SR. sons: James, Alexander

dau: Jinney
sons: Conley, John, Philip
dau-in-law: Peggy Walker
dau: Mary Crawford

Executor: son Connerly Walker.
Witnesses: Thomas Reeves, Ralph Faucett.

- - -

E 111 Will dated 1 December 1825, proved May Court 1826.

WILLIAM SHEPPERD son: James

"Heirs of Henry Shepperd"
daus: Mary, Caty, and heirs of Elizabeth
"Rest of property divided between my six daughters" names not stated.

Executors: "Sampson Moore as an executor for Susanna Thrower", Christopher Barbee and Sullivan Leigh.
Witnesses: Richard Leigh, Berry Holden.

- - -

E 112 Deed from HENRY EDWARDS, SR. to JOHN EDWARDS of Chatham Co., N.C., for a negro boy. Dated 10 April 1826, proved May Court 1826. Witnesses: Henry Edwards, Jr., Isaac Durham.

- - -

E 113 Will dated 20 April 1824, proved .... 1826.

HENRY NEAL wife: Lydia

Part of property to be "divided between my children and my Wife's sister Nancy Furguson."
dau: Martha Turner wife of James Turner
grandson: Henry Turner son of James

Executor: James Webb.
Witnesses: F.B.Phillips, W. Whitted.

- - -

E 115 Will dated 19 May 1817, proved August Court 1826.

JOHN KELLY, SR. wife: Mary

granddaughters: Peggy and Sally Lockhart, $50 each
grandsons: Isaac, John K., Billy and David Lockhart, $1 each
Remainder of estate to "wife Mary Kelly and her six children, to wit: Kesiah Bane, Nancy Kelly, Dolly, Betsy, my son John, and Charity Kelly."

Executors: James Cain, Archibald Cain, Thomas Bain.

- - -

E 117 Will dated 1 July 1824, proved August Court 1826.

ISAAC JACKSON, SR. wife: Mary

daus: Elizabeth Reynolds, Ruth Pickett
"daughter Mary Thompson's children" their mother's portion
To Benoni Jackson (relationship not stated) 50 acres
son: James Jackson "my plantation"
To "rest of lawful children 50¢ ... which have all been portioned off before."

Executors: James Jackson, Benoni Jackson.
Witnesses: Brice Jackson, Jno. Jackson.

- - -

E 118 Will dated 3 April 1826, proved August Court 1826.
This will is not indexed in the State Archives.

MASON TARPLEY

wife: Elizabeth, plantation and ten slaves, etc.
sons: James, Abraim, William, Henry

unmarried daughters Sarah, Elizabeth, Dolly, Milly, Nancy, "if they should marry they be furnished by my executors such things as can be spared & value it that the other married daughters may be equal."

Witnesses: Peter L. Ray, John Isley.

- - -

E 120 Will dated 26 May 1826, proved August Court 1826.

WILLIAM ANDREW wife: Hannah, west end of land joining Joseph Thompson's.

son: Isaac
granddaughter: Olive Newlin
grandson: William Andrew son of John Andrew
"Sons and daughters, namely, Henry, Sarah, John, Robert, Samuel, William, James, Aaron and Hannah."

Executors: son Isaac, and son-in-law Nathaniel Newlin.
Witnesses: Joseph Marshill, Thomas Thompson.

- - -

E 121 Will dated 17 June 1826, proved Nov Court 1826.

LEONARD (x) SMITH wife: Mary

son: Daniel Smith "all lands" after wife's death

Executors: Andrew Shearen, Daniel Smith, John Furguson.
Witnesses: Peter Spoone, Robert Marshill.

- - -

E 122 Will dated 13 September 1825, proved Nov Court 1826.

BENJAMIN (x) JACKSON   wife: Letty

sons: John, Alfred, Malehu
daus: Nancy, Charity, Bien ?, Polly, Ruth, Love, Edy

Executor: John Long, Jr.
Witnesses: D. Patterson, Jones Rivers.

- - -

E 122 Will dated 23 December 1825, proved Nov Court 1826.

BENJAMIN (x) BARBEE   wife: Phoebe

son: Gabriel
daus: Jemima Rainey, Polly, Betsey
grandson: Francis, son of Gabriel
son: Gray

Executors: Gabriel Barbee, William Cooke.
Witnesses: Isaiah Marcum, William Cooke.

- - -

E 124 Will dated 16 August 1826, proved November Court 1826.

DANIEL (x) FOUST   wife: Sarah

Friend Robert Graham plantation known as Lindley place, 226 acres.
Nephew, Daniel Foust, son of Peter "plantation known as Marshill place". Also "new entry".

Executor: Robert Grahams.
Witnesses: John Newlin, Solomon Allen, William Allen.

- - -

E 125 Will dated 18 September 1826, proved Nov Court 1826.

HENRY (x) COBLE

wife (name not stated) "to live on and be suppotred by sons on plantation."

sons: George, Henry (plantation), David, Peter
daus: Elizabeth, Eve, Peggy, Mary, Barbara, Sally, Catherine

Executor: son Peter.
Witnesses: John Long, Sr., William Patterson.

- - -

E 125 Will dated 8 August 1826, proved November Court 1826.

WILLIAM FLINTOFF   wife: Mary Flintoff

daughter: Jane Flintoff "clock of Library"   - continued -

son: William R. Flintoff "at lawful age my watch", etc.
" John T. Flintoff "at lawful age my desk and six volumes of books"

Executors: wife Mary, and William Robson.
Witnesses: John Blackwood, William Hinchey.

- - -

E 127-129 Will dated 26 October 1826, proved Nov Court 1826.

THOMAS BAIN wife: Keziah

daus: Rachel, Keziah, Sarah
"three youngest children, Ellenor, Mary and Charity"
son-in-law Thomas Heartt and his four children Harrul Walton Heartt, Henry Jackson Heartt, Harrison Bain Heartt, and Julian Heartt.

sons: Nathaniel (oldest), John

Executors: sons Nathaniel and John.
Witnesses: E. Graves, Thos. Armstrong, Wm. Clark.

- - -

E 130-133 Will dated 17 November 1826, proved Nov 1826.

JOHN ALAN name is spelled Allen in will, but signed Alan.

sons: John Allen (Chatham Co.), Peter (Chatham Co.),
Joseph, Herman (land in Randolph Co. on Mill Creek),
Nathan Allen (Orange Co.) deceased
grandchildren: Ruth Allen, Job Allen, Miles Allen, children of Nathan
sons: Solomon Allen (Orange Co.), William Allen

wife: Rachel
dau-in-law: Martha Allen, widow of Nathan $1
son: Joel
daus: Phoebe, Hannah

Executors: sons Joseph, Herman, Solomon and William.
Witnesses: Peter Stout, Jesse Dixon, Joseph Dixon.

- - -

E 134-136 Will dated 3 March 1824, proved November 1826.

BARNARD CATE wife: Jane

grandsons: Joel, Joshua, sons of Joseph
son Bernard's heir David
son David's two sons: James and Sanders
son Thomas' " " : Joseph and Vinson

- continued -

daus: Rebecca Cate, Ann Cate, Mary Cate, Sarah Cate,
Jean Cate, Rosannah Cate

Executors: John Sykes, Robert Hastings, Wm. Thompson.
Witnesses: John Workman, Wm. Workman, W. Thompson.

- - -

E 137-138 Will dated 3 August 1822, proved February Court 1827

ROBERT FAUCETT

"To Mrs. Martha Strudwick- my faithful old slave Luce- if Mrs. Strudwick dies before I do, I leave Luce to Mrs. Grove, widow of late Wm. B. Grove of Fayetteville."

Legay to son Robert Faucett if he returns to North Carolina to claim it. He does not know where he is.
sons: James Faucett, William Faucett
"To Wm. Tudor, whom I have raised ..."

Executors: Rev. John Hanks, cousin James Faucett, John Faucett, son of Henry.
Witnesses: Thomas Ruffin, Patrick H. Winston.

- - -

E 139 Will dated 17 August 1826, proved May Court 1827.

JESSE THOMAS son: Nehemiah Thomas

To Elenor Ripper "case of drawers"
daus: Jane Donnerly, Caty Thomas, Mary Hubbert
grandson: Thomas Thomas
grandchildren: Nancy, Caty (surnames not stated)

Executor: Nehemiah Thomas
Witnesses: Robert Lackey, John (x) Underwood.

- - -

E 140 Will dated 7 December 1826, proved May Court 1827.

JAMES (x) DAVIS wife: Elizabeth

sons: Sampson Moore, James Roberson

Executors: Dr. Hudson N. Cave, nephew James Davis.
Witnesses: R. Henderson, Isaac Molett, Abner (x) Parry.

- - -

E 141 Will dated 21 January 1827, proved May Court 1827.

GEORGE FAUCETT wife: Martha

son: Ray daughters: Nancy, and another not named

Executors: brother Edward, Samuel Tate Sr, Wm. Murray.
Witnesses: Willis Sellars, Sam'l Crawford.

- - -

E 143 Will dated 13 February 1823, proved August Court 1827.

RACHEL ARMSTRONG

niece Anne Glass, daughter of Stephen and Betsy Glass

Executors: Thomas Ruffin, Archibald D. Murphy.
Witnesses: A. D. Murphy, Victor M. Murphy.

- - -

E 143-145 Will dated 25 March 1825, proved August Court 1827.

BENJAMIN (x) RONEY wife: Catherine

daus: Margaret Eason, Nancy Bryan, Catherine Pickett
Mary Clendennin, Sally McCadams, Elizabeth Trowlinger
Catherine and Benjamin Clendennin children of Mary
sons: James Roney, Andrew Roney, John Roney
grandchildren: Benjamin and Catherine (under 21) McAdams, children of daughter Sally McAdams

Executors: son Andrew Roney, son-in-law John Trolinger.
Witnesses: Robert A. Younger, Joseph Barker.

- - -

E 145 Will dated 2 June 1827, proved August Court 1827.

SAMUEL (x) STEWART wife: Elizabeth

daughter: Anna (unmarried)
sons: Samuel, James, Charles, John
grandson: Samuel Stewart

Executors: friend Joseph Thompson, and son James Stewart.
Witnesses: Wm. J. Clendennin, Robert Thompson, Wm. Bradshaw.

- - -

E 146 Will dated 10 June 1827, proved August Court 1827.

JAMES CRAIG, SR. wife: Ellen

daughter: Ann Craig
son: John M. Craig gets plantation after mother's death
" James A. Craig "plantation where he now lives"
" William I. Craig

Executor: John McCauley.
Witnesses: John Lewis, John M. Craig, John McCauley.

- - -

E 147 Will dated 7 March 1827, proved November Court 1827.

SALLY LEWIS REEVES sister: Martha E. Reeves

brother George Washington Reeves gets three negroes "provided
- continued -

my brother John Claiborn Reeves shall succeed in obtaining property left him by his brother William B. Hill, deceased, to amount of the three last named negroes."

Executor: father Willis Reeves. Witness: W. Reeves.

- - -

E 148-149 Will dated 19 February 1820, proved Nov Court 1827.

JESSE (x) RIGSBY "weak in body" wife: Elizabeth all estate

Executors: wife Elizabeth, and friend and relation Mark Pickett.
Witnesses: C. P. Patterson, John Anderson.

- - -

E 149 Will dated --, proved November Court 1827.

WILLIAM HALL, SR. son: Alexander G. Hall

daughters: Polly, Jinney

Witnesses: Sam Woods, Thomas Bowls.

- - -

E 150 Will dated 30 October 1827, proved Nov Court 1827.

LETTY (x) SANDERS

grandson: Henry Neal, son of John Neal
" James Monroe Neal, son of John Neal
granddau: Eliza Neal, daughter " " "
"To John Rhodes, son of Benjamin Rhodes, deceased."
sons: Jordan and Henry, 5 shillings each "if demanded"
dau: Franky "5 shilling if demanded"

Executor: friend James Rainey.
Witnesses: Alfred Horne, Riley Neal.

- - -

E 151 Will dated 23 December 1826, proved Nov Court 1827.

DAVID COBLE

son: George "plantation whereon his widow now lives"
" John "part of plantation known as Horniday Place"
" Eli "plantation whereon I now live"
" David other part of Horniday place

Daughters Barbary, Mary, Margaret, Catty, Elizabeth, Sally, and Nancy have already received their parts.

Executors: son John Coble, and Michael Writsel.
Witnesses: D. Patterson, ...? .....? (illegible).

- - -

E 152 Will dated 9 July 1827, proved November Court 1827.

SARAH MORGAN

All estate after debts are paid to grandchildren Thomas Morgan, Hardy Morgan, Sally Morgan, Lemuel Morgan, James Ruffin Morgan and Mary Emeline Morgan.

Son James A. Morgan is to be testamentary guardian and executor until youngest grandchild reaches 21 years of age.

- - -

E 153 Will dated 16 February 1828, proved Feb Court 1828.

THOMAS (x) NICHOLS

His wife Hannah is to have all his property and slaves. At her death property is to be divided between his brothers and sisters , names not stated.

Witnesses: John Bane, Tho. Jeff. Faddis.

- - -

E 153 Will dated 31 January 1828, proved Feb Court 1828.

WILLIAM (x) TATE wife: Rachel all property

children: Joseph, Alfred, Margaret, Mary

Executors: wife Rachel Tate, and friend Joseph Eaton.
Witnesses: Robert Tate, James Tate.

- - -

E 155 Will dated 7 July 1827, proved February Court 1828.

JOSIAH CLIFTON wife: Catron is pregnant

"My three daughters- Emily, Amy and Mahala Cliftons"
sons: James K. Clifton, John J. Clifton, James Clifton

Executors: son John J. Clifton, and friend Isaac Kirby.
Witnesses: John Moring, William H. Lewter.

- - -

E 156 Will dated 8 May 1827, proved February Court 1828.

JAMES (x) ADAMS wife: Nancy

dau: Isabella Allen 5 shillings
sons: James Adams, John Adams 5 shillings each
dau: Dianna Adams, property after wife's death

Executrix: daughter Diannah Adams.
Witnesses: Thomas Brown, Robert Lackey.

- - -

E 157 Will dated 10 April 1827, proved May Court 1828.

MARY (x) HALL mother a legatee

brothers: Anderson Hall, Junah Hall
friend: Sarah Pyle side saddle and one fly wheel

Witnesses: Jehu Hall, William Hall.

- - -

E 159 Will dated 27 March 1828, proved May Court 1828.

SAMUEL (x) GARRARD sister: Susan Garrard to have "rent of my old place with exception of store house"

James Garrard
Ann Leathers daughter of Fielding Leathers
Mary Webb Warren
Henry Warren "all other lands- watch- kitchen furniture
Willie Shaw Jr "books bonds property real and personal belonging to concern of Garrard and Shaw, and should he go into mercantile business I give him the storehouse - all with the understanding that he marry with the consent of his father and Uncle- otherwise to Anny Warren.

Executors: Henry Warren, Samuel Yarborough

- - -

E 160 Will dated 19 February 1816, proved -- 1828

STEPHEN MESSER (x) SMITH wife: Susannah

daus: Catherine Gates - 5 shillings, Mary Smith, Johannah Parker, Elizabeth Horner - 5 shillings
sons: Leonard Smith and William Smith under age, to receive plantation and grist-mill, etc, when of age
daus: Sarah Smith, Dice, Agnes
granddaughter of daughter Mary named Jinnet
"My grandson of my daughter Sarah named John" 2 years school

Executors: Jacob Waggoner, John .
Witness: Thomas Hall.

- - -

E 161 Will dated 13 January 1827, proved August Court 1828.

WILLIAM ANDERSON wife: Lucinda

dau: Margaret Anderson
sons: Henry Anderson and William Anderson, both under age
dau: Minerva Anderson

Executor: William Merritt.
Witnesses: Franklin O'Kelly, Pleasant Barbee.

- - -

E 162 Will dated 17 March 1828, proved August Court 1828.

ISAAC McCADAMS wife: Peggy

son: Wiley
daus: Jane (youngest, under age), Rebeckah,
Fanny Long (oldest) wife of William Long

Executor: son-in-law Moses Whitsett.
Witness: John Trolinger.

- - -

E 163 Will dated 10 April 1828, proved August Court 1828.

RICHARD FAUCETT wife: Rebecca

"My two single daughters Nancy and Elizabeth"
daughter Susannah Durham
son: Thomas Samuel Faucett, under age

Executors: wife Susannah, and Samuel Strayhorn.
Witnesses: Samuel Faucett, Thos. Latta, Jinney Faucett.

- - -

E 164 Will dated 19 July 1827, proved August Court 1828.

HARDY HURDLE

sons: James Hurdle, Henry Hurdle, George Hurdle
dau: Nancy Garrison and her children
" Sarah McCulley $5, Rachel Hurdle
sons: Thomas Hurdle, Benjamin Hurdle, Josiah Hurdle
son: Jacob Hurdle (under 21)
grandson: Hardy Beasley "land I purchased from Jonathan Jordan"
"my son-in-law Samuel Beasley and his wife Milly Beasley"
"to the children of my daughter Sarah McCulley wife of John McCulley viz: William McCulley, Hardy McCulley, Miles McCulley Milley McCulley and Sarah McCulley."
daughter Milly Beasley's children $25 each

Executors: "My seven sons"
Witnesses: Robert A. Younger, James M. Scott.

- - -

E 167-171 Will dated 22 September 1824, proved 1828.

"JONATHAN LINDLEY of Orange and State of Indiana"

Wife: Martha
son: Jonathan
dau: Catherine McVey
sons: Thomas Lindley, William Lindley
daus: Sarah Hadley, Deborah James, Hannah Braxton, Mary Dixon,
Quine Esther Clark, Ruth Farlow, Ellenor Chambers
to Rebecca Henley 8 acres of land
"To sister Deborah Newlin, $100"

daughter: Gubelma (under age)
"my big Bible"

- continued -

 E 167-171 will of JONATHAN LINDLEY continued

"To William and Jonathan Dicks ....
son: Zaccheus $5, "I deeded him his plantation some time ago"

He devises many tracts of land in Orange County, N.C. and in Orange County, Indiana.

Executors: sons Thomas and William "my sole and whole executors in the State of Indiana and all the Western Country", and John Newlin "my sole executor in the State of North Carolina."
Witnesses: Owen Lindley, Thomas Maris, Aaron Maris.
Probated in Paoli, Orange County, Indiana, 25 July 1828.

- - -

E 173 Will dated 3 July 1827, proved November Court 1828.

STEPHEN (x) CARROLL indexed in State Archives as CARRELL
"weak in body"

wife: Elenor son: Benjamin

Executors: wife Elenor, and William Lewis.
Witnesses: James Berry, James Dollar.

- - -

E 174 Will dated 19 September 1827, proved Nov Court 1828.

MARY WORTHAM All estate to daughter Elizabeth Wilson.

Sole executor: son-in-law Samuel Wilson.
Witnesses: Joseph Armstrong Jr, John Wilson, Peggy Armstrong.

- - -

E 174 Will dated 10 March 1823, proved February Court 1829.

BENJAMIN (x) WHEELEY wife: Dorothy
"weak in body"

son: Benjamin Wheeley
daus: Susannah Wheeley, Dorothy Wheeley and Betsey Wheeley
son: Philip Wheeley
He says "my seven children" only five named.

Executors: sons Benjamin and Philip.
Witnesses: Edward Eubanks, James (x) Blackwell.

- - -

E 175 Will dated 10 August 1827, proved February Court 1829.

JOHN RAY, SR. wife: Sally

dau: Margaret Robinson wife of James
daus: Sally Robinson, and Lydia McKee wife of Rankin McKee
"Susy Ray, widow of my son Joseph Ray, deceased."

- continued -

sons: John Ray and David Ray
dau: Susan Ray

Executors: son David Ray, and Richard Nichols.
Witnesses: Samuel Madden, Alex. Smith.

- - -

E 178 Will dated 9 September 1828, proved Feb Court 1829.

SAMUEL BYRD Father and mother are living.

"My desire is that my daughter Susannah Byrd be taken by my sister Caty Kimbrough to raise"

"My two sisters-in-law and two brothers-in-law namely: Rebeckah, Polly, George and John Miller."

"To my brother Thomas Bird's daughter Mary $50"

"Brothers and sister: James Bird, Empson Bird, Caty Kimbrough, and Elizabeth Flowrence"

Executors: Thomas Lynch and Gabriel B. Lea.
Witnesses: Gabriel B. Lea, Thomas Bird, Sr.

- - -

E 180 Will dated 1 February 1827, proved Feb Court 1829.

JOHN WILSON wife: Eunice

daus: Rhoda Wilson, Martha Wilson, Ann Atwater
"To my daughter Nancy Tripp's children, to wit, Martha Tripp, Elizabeth Tripp, Eunice Tripp, Polly Tripp, Millicent Tripp, John Wilson Tripp and William Blumer Tripp, $50 each."
grandson: Wilson Atwater
daus: Millicent Pritchett, Lois Cole, Elizabeth McCauley

Executors: friends Wilson Atwater and Charles McCauley.
Witnesses: Wm. McCauley , Goodman Neville, Richard Thompson.

- - -

E 182 Will dated 25 June 1829, proved May Court 1829.

JOHN UMSTEAD

"To Morgan Hart .. home plantation where I now reside."

His slave Dicey and her two children are to be freed.

To friend John Umstead Kirkland "land on Obion River in State of Tennessee."

Executors: Catlett Campbell and Thomas D. Bennehan.
Witnesses: James Webb, Wil Kirkland, Hugh Waddell.

- - -

E 183 Will dated 21 April 1829, proved May Court 1829.

CHARLES McCAWLEY wife: Mary

daus: Eliza McCawley, Sarah McCawley, Mary Jane McCawley
sons: William McCawley, James McCawley
" Johnston, Archibald and Henry Crawford McCawley, the last three are all under 21 yaers of age

Testator's father, now desceased, was William McCawley.

Executor: John McCawley, son of Matthew.
Witnesses: Joseph Kirkland, James Long.

- - -

E 185 Will dated 8 November 1826, proved May Court 1829.

JOHN LINK wife a legatee, name not stated

sons: Silas M. Link, William
"When all my children come of age", only two (above) named.

Executor: son Silas M. Link. Witness: Ed. Strudwick.

- - -

E 186 Will dated 5 May 1819, proved May Court 1829.

GARRETT GARRISON daughter: Mary $5

sons: Levi Garrison, John Garrison
daus: Rebecca 5 shillings, Eleanor Garrison
sons: George, Jehu

Executors: sons Levi and George
Witnesses: William Bribkley, Henry Hurdle.

- - -

E 188-190 Will dated 22 November 1828, proved August 1829.

THOMAS WILSON wife: Jane

daus: Nancy, Fanny
sons: Anderson, Caleb
dau: Elizabeth wife of Solomon Latta
grandsons: Jackson Latta, Asahel M. Latta, Caleb H. Latta
"My sons that have married and left me" not called by name.
"Children of sons Charles and Robert"

Executors: sons Anderson and Caleb.
Witnesses: James Holeman, Richard Holeman.

- - -

E 191 Will dated 7 January 1829, proved August Court 1829.

WILLIS (x) TREWIT or TRUET or TRUETT, spelled three ways
"weak of body"
Wife: Nancy - continued -

two oldest sons: John and Levi $1 each
two youngest sons: Spencer and Willis
daus: Gatsey Hall and Mary Danley $1 each
three youngest daughters: Eleanor, Elizabeth and Nancy

Executors: son Levi Truett, and Robert A. Younger and William Brinkley.
Witnesses: Josiah Hurdle, William Benson.

- - -

E 192 Will dated 23 June 1829, proved August Court 1829.

WILLIAM (x) CLARK (ROCK) signed with a mark CLARK.
(This will is not in the State Archives.)

Daughter: Nancy Clark

Executor: friend James Clancy.
Witnesses: James Webb, Henry Yarborough.

- - -

E 193-195 Will dated 5 June 1829, proved August Court 1829.

JAMES JACKSON, SR. wife: Nancy

He devises many tracts of land, among them land "willed by George Riggs Sr. to his daughter Nancy my wife and Rachel wife of Amos Nichols and Nancy Riggs". He has bought land from Levi Whitted, Jacob Jackson, Margaret Jackson, James Glenn, James & Ruth Jackson, John & Polly Collins, ... Carter & wife Catherine, Betsy & Ruth Jackson.

sons: James, George and Anderson Jackson.

Executors: wife Nancy, and son James.
Witnesses: Michael Ray, Thos. W. Holden.

- - -

E 195-200 Will dated 6 January 1813, proved August 1829.

SAMUEL THOMPSON wife: Isabell

son: Richard Thompson and his son Samuel
dau: Nelly Barton wife of John Barton "Kennedy's place adjoining lands of Wm. Strayhorn" 200 acres
grandson Stephen Barton son of Nelly Barton
unmarried daughters: Frances, Hannah, Phoebe

Executors: wife Isabell, and William Norwood.
Witnesses: David Yarborough, James Child.
Codicil dated 11 Nov 1815 says grandson Samuel Thompson has died. Witnesses: Wesley Debruler, Levi McCollum.
Another codicil dated 20 August 1823, same witnesses.
A third codicil dated 28 Sept 1824 says that daughter Phoebe is now married to James Clancy, names son James Thompson.

- - -

E 201 Will dated 12 May 1824, proved November Court 1829.

JOHN FADDIS, SR. of the Town of Hillsborough

wife: Nancy all estate during her life

"My two children, Nancy Womack and Thomas J. Faddis."
granddaughters: Eliza Womack, Mary Jane Womack
Jacob P. Womack, husband of daughter Nancy, also called Ann.

Executors: wife and son Thomas J. Faddis, and Jonathan P. Sneed.
Witnesses: James Webb, F. B. Phillips.

- - -

E 202 Will dated 3 August 1824, proved November Court 1829.

RICHARD BIRD wife: Rachel

daughters Catherine Kimbrough and Elizabeth Florence

"My granddaughter Nancy Bird, daughter of my son Thomas Bird deceased" under age.

sons: Samuel, James and Empson Bird

Executors: sons James and Samuel.
Witnesses: Thomas Reeves, John Reeves.

- - -

E 203 Will dated 16 October 1829, proved Noc Court 1829.

WILLIAM PIKE son: John Pike

daus: Abigail Pike, Mary Pike, Nancy

"Heirs of daughters Hannah and Priscilla deceased"

Executor: friend William Thompson.
Witnesses: Wm. Albright, John Thompson, John Thompson.

- - -

E 204 Will dated 19 October 1829, proved Nov Court 1829.

THOMAS or JOSEPH (x) LAYCOCK, SR. This will is in the Archives. It is endorsed on the back "Will of Thomas Laycock".

wife: Rosea $1

sons: William and Joseph get land on both sides of Eno River

daus: Nelly Cates, Elizabeth Scarlett, Sally Scarlett, Delilah Scarlett, Disey Laycock, Easter Laycock

Executors: son Joseph, and Frederick Moize.
Witness: John (x) Warren.

- - -

E 205 Will dated 20 August 1829, proved Nov Court 1829.

RICHARD (x) MARCUM wife: Anna

son: Wilie "tract he now lives on"
" William "tract he now lives on"
sons: John and Spencer "land where my father lived and died"
son: Aaron "plantation I now live on"
daus: Cynthia (unmarried), Polly Sorrell
son: Willis $40 (mentioned in codicil, made same day)

Executors: worthy friends Thomas Bilbo and John Bilbo.
Witnesses: William B. Williams, John D. Carlton.

- - -

E 207 Will dated 28 May 1829, proved November Court 1829.

JOSHUA (x) HORNE, SR. wife: Mikey
"very weak" (She was Michel Rhodes)

sons: John and Joshua "all my land"

daus: Milly Redding, Alsey Cates, Viney Hinchey ?, Betsy Brockwell, and Polly Neel 5 shillings each

Executor: friend James Rainey.
Witnesses: Pleasant Rhodes, Young E. Rainey.

- - -

E 208 Will dated 22 November 1820, proved Nov Court 1829.

HENRY O'DANIEL wife: Margery

sons: Samuel, John, Joshua
daus: Susana Pickhard, Jeane McDaniel, Sally Hastings, Margaret Pickhard
grandson: William O'Daniel son of John
grandsons: Henry and William sons of William

Executors: Thomas Hastings and Thomas Brewer.
Witnesses: John O'Daniel Jr., Jesse O'Daniel.

- - -

E 209 Will dated 27 August 1829, proved February Court 1830.

MELCHI McDANIEL

son: William McDaniel "plantation known as the Henry Hasten place"
dau: Martha Smith wife of William Smith "my plantation"
Elizabeth Britt daughter of Celia Britt "my plantation known as James Minnis plantation on E Side of Cane Creek"
Eli Britt son of Celia Britt "plantation where I now live" on E Side of Cane Creek.

Executors: David Roach and William Thompson.
Witnesses: Thomas G. Willis, Alfred Pickard, Henry O'Daniel.

- - -

E 211 Will dated 5 December 1829, proved Feb Court 1830.

ELIZABETH (x) WALKER

sisters: Margaret McCullay, Nancy Byrd
Andrew Walker
"To John Picket's children: Juliann and John Quincy"
"To William Picket's (deceased) Children: Joseph, Lucrecey, William, and Vicey Byrd."

Executor: worthy friend James Forest.
Witnesses: Thomas Lynch, James Forest, John Forest.

- - -

E 212 Will dated 2 December 1829, proved Feb Court 1830.

ANN (x) LONG
"weak in body"

daughter: Nancy Long
" Mary Long

sons: James Long, Thomas Long, Anderson Long, George Long, and Charles Long, 50¢ each
"My granddaughter Eliza Long daughter of Mary Long"

Executor: son George.
Witnesses: Wm. H. Woods, John Brown, William McCauley.

- - -

E 213 Will dated 23 January 1830, proved Feb Court 1830.

LETTICE (x) McCULLEY

Albert Hamilton, son of William Hamilton
Thomas McCulley "all my pewterware"
William Hamilton "all balance of estate"

Executor: "friend Henry Hurdle".
Witnesses: Chesley F. Faucette, Edward Fausett.

- - -

E 213 Will dated 6 August 1828, proved February Court 1830.

MARY KELLEY

sister: Keziah Bane

sisters: Nancy and Betsy to have her share of the undivided estate of their father
"To Sally Lockhart $15 for her services to me in my sickness"

Executor: Thomas W. Holden.
Witnesses: Hugh Cain, John Lockhart.

- - -

E 215 Will dated 10 May 1826, proved May Court 1830.

JOHN (x) IVEY

wife: Mornning

daus: Nancy Holder $1, Sally

- continued -

sons: Joseph Ivey, Andrew Patterson, John $2, William $2

Executor: friend John Carethers.
Witnesses: Archibald Durham, Thomas Lloyd.

- - -

E 216-218 Will dated 3 May 1830, proved May Court 1830.

NICHOLAS JONES

wife: Nancy "land which joins Samuel Evans and Ephriam Carrington deceased"
wife's father David Parker of Granville County, N.C.
son: William land in Granville County on "Nap of Reed Creek" joining land of George Roberts deceased, James Roberts, Edward Jones Sr, and others
son: Washington Jones (under age)
dau: Polly Jones (under age)
daus: Ma rtha Ann Jones and Rebecca Jones (both under age)
son: Willis Simpson Jones land on Flat River

Executors: brother Henry W. Jones of Granville County, and son Washington Jones.
Witnesses: Willis Bowling, John J. Carrington.

- - -

E 219 Will dated 30 April 1830, proved May Court 1830.

MIRIAM (x) STRAIN "low in health"

sons: James, Samuel, and David get land, Alexander 50¢
granddaughters: Mary Strayhorn, Jane Strayhorn
dau: Mary Strayhorn wife of Bryant Strayhorn
dau: Elizabeth Elkins

Executor: John McCauley.
Witnesses: Wm. D. Strain, John Strayhorn.

- - -

E 220 Will dated 25 September 1827, proved May Court 1830.

ELIZABETH (x) BREWER "old and infirm"

nieces: Betsy Oldham, Mary Ann Bracher ?
brothers: Ezekiel Brewer, Thomas Brewer
sister: Rebeckah Hopson

Executor: friend Thomas Snipes of Chatham County.
Witnesses: W. S. Snipes, George W. Morrow.

- - -

E 221 Will dated 25 February 1830, proved May Court 1830.

SARAH (x) STRAIN brothers: James and Samuel Strain

She holds a note on her mother Maryann Strain (actually Miriam, see E 219) - continued -

sister: Mary Strayhorn wife of Bryant Strayhorn
" Elizabeth Elkins

"My six nieces: Mary Strayhorn, Jane Strayhorn, Elizabeth Strayhorn, Mary Strain, Elizabeth Strain and Sarah Strain."

Executor: Bryant Strayhorn.
Witnesses: Samuel Strain, Alex, Gattis, Mary Strayhorn.

- - -

E 222 Will dated 7 May 1827, proved May Court 1830.

THOMAS (x) HART, SR. "weak of body"

daughters: Rebecca and Susannah get all his land
son: Fin Hart

Executor: son Fin Hart, and Thomas McCracken.
Witnesses: Jo. Hart, John W. McCracken.

- - -

E 223 Will dated 3 January 1826, proved August Court 1830.

EDWARD (x) BOSWELL "weak in body"

two eldest sons: Craven and John
"Mary Boswell widow of my son Thomas Boswell deceased"
"three other sons: Edward, Mathew and James Boswell"
grandson: Brown Boswell
"My three married daughters, namely, Susannah Leachman (?), Nancy Wilkerson, Catherine Graham."
daughter: Charlotte Boswell
son-in-law: Thomas Sulivan $1
" " " James Wilkerson $1
granddaughters: Julia Ann Bracken (under 18), Catherine Graham
grandchildren: William Sulivan, Craven Sulivan, "Nancy, Catherine and Elizabeth Sulivan"

Executors: son James Boswell, and George Graham.
Witnesses: Andrew Hughs, Thomas Fitch.

- - -

E 224 Will dated July 1827, proved August Court 1830.

ROBERT MOORE wife: Isabel

granddaus: Keziah Moore, Sally Tate, Isabel Tate
"To Anthony Tate, James Faucett Moore, David Moore, Robert Moore, William Moore, 10 shillings each"
His plantation to grandsons, sons of Thomas Moore: Robert Moore, William Moore, David Moore, Absalem Moore.

Executors: Absolem Harvey and Juneah Hall.
Witnesses: James Moore, Thomas Moore.

- - -

E 226 Will dated 8 December 1825, proved August 1830.

HUGH MONTGOMERY wife: Rebecca

sons: James and Alexander (legacy), William $1
dau: Lydia Woods wife of Alfred Woods $1
"To Hambleton James Alexander and Hugh one dollar as they arrive to age 21" (no punctuation)

Executors: wife Rebecca, and friend Thomas Holden.
Witnesses: Eli Woods, John Woods.

- - -

E 227 Will dated 11 August 1828, proved August Court 1830.

WILLIAM MILLER wife: Rebecca

"My children", names and number not stated.

Executors: friends Dr. Edmund Strudwick and William Bowls.
Witnesses: James Webb, Jesse Miller.
Codicil dated 2 Feb 1830 says that wife is to have life estate. Witness: James Webb.

- - -

E 228 Will dated 4 February 1823, proved August Court 1830.

MARY (x) THOMPSON "weak in body"

"To my sister Hannah Thompson all my money in the hands of my brother John Thompson." (Her father was Thomas Thompson.)

Executors: friends Thomas Thompson and Robert Thompson.
Witnesses: Jo Clendennin, John Thompson.
Codicil mentions Thomas, Nelly and Mary Thompson.

- - -

E 229 Will dated 31 July 1830, proved August Court 1830.

EDWARD McDADE

daughter: Peggy McDade
niece: Peggy McDade daughter of brother John McDade
"Mrs Elizabeth Wilfong saddles, etc. in my shop"

Executors: friends John McDade and Thomas Clancy.
Witnesses: J.W ? Smith, Wm. Nelson.

- - -

E 229 Will dated 23 November 1829, proved August 1830.

WILLIAM BLACKWOOD

daus: Hannah Selph, Elizabeth Allen, Mary Craig 50¢ each
son: John Blackwood 50¢
daus: Martha Craig, Jane McCauley, Ann Potts 50¢ each
daus: Margaret Long, Sarah Gattis 50¢ each - continued -

 E 229 Will of WILLIAM BLACKWOOD continued

sons: William Blackwood, James Blackwood 50¢ each
daus: Nancy, Catherine and Fanny "all my land, furniture" etc.
grandson: Anderson, son of daughter Ann Potts

Executors: sons John and William Blackwood.
Witnesses: Wm. C. Blackwood, Franklin L. Blackwood.

- - -

E 231 Will dated 4 August 1830, proved August Court 1830.

SOLOMON WOOD wife: Elizabeth all during her life

Henry Wood
brother James Wood brother-in-law Ezekiel Haley

Executor: wife Elizabeth, and brother-in-law Ezekiel Haley.
Witnesses: Arch'd Cain, J. B. Leathers.

- - -

E 231 Dated 15 October 1830, proved Nov Court 1830.

JOHN (x) ALBRIGHT SR. "weak of body"

daughter: Barbara Garrat "all the land I own with all appurtainances."
daus: Betsey Clap and Philipenia Swing
Sally Holt wife of Thomas Holt
Abraham Clap

Executors: Andrew Albright, John Garrat Sr.
Witnesses: Henry (x) Thomas, William (x) Holt.

- - -

E 232 Will dated 13 August 1830, proved November Court 1830.

PETER L. RAY wife: Elizabeth B. Ray

children: David L. Ray (under age), Mary E. Ray, Griffen L. Ray

Executors: William Holt, Sr, and Jeremiah Holt, Sr.
Witnesses: James Bleat, William Tarpley.

- - -

E 233 Will dated 28 August 1830, proved Nov Court 1830.

WILLIAM CRESWELL wife: Jane is pregnant ?

nephew: William Brown Creswell
" Wesley Morrow

Executor: George A. Mebane.
Witnesses: B. Breeze, William Mebane.

- - -

E 235 Will dated 21 March 1825, proved Feb Court 1831.

ELIZABETH (x) FAUCETT

son: Joseph Faucett , estate of late husband David Faucett
" James Faucett $50
granddaughter Elizabeth Ann Bain (under age)

Executors: James Faucett and Joseph Faucett.
Witnesses: A. Armstrong, WM. B. Ringstaff.

- - -

E 236 Will dated 25 September 1830, proved Nov Court 1830 ?

WILLIAM WOODS wife: Elenor all during her life

daus: Anne and Asenath
He mantions "all my children", seems to have married daughters.
David Dickey is to have board and lodging for 1 year.

Executors: son John S. Woods and son-in-law Robert Redden.
Witnesses: Samuel Paisley, James Clark.

- - -

E 237 Will dated 15 January 1831, proved Feb Court 1831.

EMPSON BIRD wife: Polly

"Two oldest daughters Eliza Bird and Citty Bird"
"Three youngest Martha Bird, John Bird, Richard Bird"
"Land I bought from Catherine Redding to be sold".
"Sister Betsy Florence should take and raise Eliza"
"Sister-in-law Nancy Kirkpatrick should take and raise Citty"
"Cousin Sarah Walker take and raise my daughter Martha"
"Uncle James Dickey should take and raise my son John"
"Friend George Jordan find a place for Richard if necessary"

Executor: George Jordan.
Witnesses: Jehu Bird, James Bird, Charles Jordan.

- - -

E 239 Will dated 17 February 1831, proved Feb Court 1831.

RICHARD DAVIS sons: Archibald and Miles Davis 50¢ each

daus: Dellila King, Sarah Montgomery, Mary Jenkins 50¢ each
son: John Richard Davis 50¢
" Thomas Capper Davis half of estate
daus: Winnifred Beville and Fanny Trice other half

Executors: friends John L. Moore and James N. Patterson.
Witnesses: J. L. Moore, Nancy Moore, James N. Patterson.

- - -

E 240 Will dated 8 March 1831, proved February Court 1831.

JOHN (x) CARRIGAN "sick and weak" "present wife "

"wife and daughter Tempe" (unmarried) - continued -

"son Hugh (he is under age) by my present wife to share equally with other children"

Executor: trusty friend Samuel Child.
Witnesses: Alves Cheek, James Cheek.
Codicil, dated same day, says son-in-law James Roach has "my permission to build himself a house near where Thomas Dodson now lives, and at end of Dodson's rent take over possession of 10 acres around house as long as wife and daughter Tempe live".

- - -

E 241 Will dated 14 January 1831, proved Feb Term 1831.

NATHANIEL CARRINGTON

son: Nathaniel M. Carrington all real estate
daus: Ruth Carrington, Dolly Cozart, Polly Cozart wife of Dovy
daus: Fanny wife of J.J.Carrington and Dessy Harris wife of Edward Harris, 10¢ each, they have had their portions
sons: William Carrington (10¢), Eaphriam and Alfred

Witnesses: James Webb, P.H.Ma ngum.

- - -

E 243 Will dated 28 March 1831, proved February Court 1831.

STEPHEN GARROTT wife: Betsey all property for life

Children to receive property after wife's death.

Executrix: wife Betsey.
Witnesses: F. Moize, Lewis Hutchins.

- - -

E 243 Will dated 16 May 1829, proved February Term 1831.

PRISCILLA DUNCAN dau: Elizabeth White $1

estate to daughter Lucy Duncan and son Charles N. Duncan

Executor: friend James Forest.
Witnesses: Wm. P. Forest, A. Forest.

- - -

E 245 Will dated 28 January 1831, proved Feb Court 1831.

BARNABAS O'FAIRHILL wife: Nancy one third

"No bequests to any of her (his wife's) children".
sister: Jane Woods
niece: Anne Kelly

Executor: Thomas Clincy of Hillsborough.
Witnesses: Thomas D. Watts, John Scott.

E 247 Will dated 22 May 18--, proved August Court 1831.

JOSEPH MOORE

sons: William Stanford Moore 100 acres, Carter Moore (married)
daus: Patsey Bird, Celia Reynolds, Susan (unmarried)
sons: Peyton P. Moore and Joseph Moore balance of land

Executors: Peyton P. Moore and Jehu Bird.
Witnesses: James Mebane, James Picket.

- - -

E 248 Will dated 4 June 1831, proved August Court 1831.

SUSANNAH (x) RAY "weak of body"

She leaves slaves and household furniture to her step-mother Sally Ray, and after her death to brother David Ray.

sister: Sally Robertson wife of Joseph Robertson
Lydia McKee wife of Rankin McKee
"To the heirs of George Ray dec'd, the heirs of Joseph Ray, John Robertson and Michael Robertson sons of James Robertson deceased, James Ray and John Ray, that is to say, six equal parts." Peggy Jane Ray, daughter of David Ray.

Witnesses: Robert Reding, J.H.Mangum.
Executor: Richardson Nichols.

- - -

E 250 Will dated 30 May 1830, proved August Court 1831.

LYDIA (x) DILLARD "weak of body"

"Four youngest daughters viz: Eliza, Caroline, Martha and Mary Jane"
She has thirteen children, but only four are named.

Executor: son Willis.
Witnesses: Wm. R. Herndon, Polly (x) Blake, David Roberts.

- - -

E 251 Will dated 20 July 1831, proved August Court 1831.

WILLIAM WHYTE "of the Village of Chapel Hill"

wife: Lucy
"My three children namely Thomas Whyte Rebecca Ann Whyte and Joseph Whyte."

Executor: friend John McCauley.
Witnesses: D. B. Alsobrook, Thomas E. Taylor.
Codicil dated 8 August 1831, signed with a mark, same witsesses, mentions "my plantation which I lately purchased of William Barbee Sr known as Creage (?) Mill Tract".

- - -

E 253 Will dated 16 February 1831, proved August Court 1831.

ANDREW HUNTER   wife: Susannah

son: Alexander Hunter
daus: Elizabeth Hunter, Jane Loyd, Frances Hunter,
Frances Hunter, Eliza Hunter, Christa Hunter,
Harriet Hunter
son: Thomas Hunter
"... that my first wife's children have nothing more than they have received .."
daus: Nancy Loyd and Sary Cate

Executors: Thos Hogan and John Careathers.
Witnesses: Hasten Poe, Reuben C. Poe.

- - -

E 255 Will dated 10 May 1825, proved August Court 1831.

ELIZABETH (x) HALL

daus: Phebe Dickey, Joannah McAdams $1 each
sons: Jeremiah Hall, Samuel C. Hall $1 "
dau: Mary Hall
daus: Nancy Plummer, Elizabeth Harvey, Sarah McAdams $1 each
son: Anderson Hall

Executor: son Anderson Hall.
Witnesses: John Hall, William Hall.

- - -

E 256 Will dated 24 October 1830, proved August Court 1831.

JOSEPH BAKER SR.

daus: Margaret Murray, Susey Clarke
"My granddaughter Eliza H. Baker daughter of my son Nathaniel Baker (now deceased). She is under 21.
son: Joseph Baker

Executors: friend John Trolinger, and son Joseph Baker.
Witnesses: Wm. H. White, James A. Craig.

- - -

E 257 Will dated October 1819, "republished" 13 September 1827, proved August Court 1831.

LUCY (x) JEFRES   granddaughters: Milly and Lucy

grandsons: Ja mes Samuel and Cato (surnames not stated)

Executor; Fielding Leathers.
Witnesses: Robert Faucet, James Webb.

- - -

E 258 Will dated 1 May 1831, proved August Court 1831.

HENRY (x) MOIZE   wife: Lucy

Daughter Frances Moize gets his land.
"My children Allen Moize Nancy Roberts Elizabeth Tilly Keziah Tilly and Frances Moize."

Executor: brother John Moize.
Witnesses: Frederic Moize, Willia P. Mangum.

- - -

E 259 Will dated 26 February 1831, proved 1831.

ROBERT HARRIS   wife: Casserna

"sons Marcus ? Harris William Harris & Harrison Harris"
daus: Bulia; Tempy and Edny (last two under age)
sons: Nathaniel, Archer

Executors: Silas M. Link, and son Marcus Harris.
Witnesses: Duncan Cameron, Thomas D. Bennehan.

- - -

E 261 Will dated 17 October 1831, proved Nov Court 1831.

ISAAC (x) JONES   wife: Catherine

sons: Samuel Stockard Jones, John Orange Jones
daus: Elizabeth Jones and Frances Jones, both under age

Executor: brother Samuel Jones.
Witnesses: Jeremiah Holt, V. M. Murphey.

- - -

E 262 Will dated 24 August 1831, proved November Court 1831.

SARAH (x) THOMPSON

oldest daughter: Ann Thompson
"next eldest daughter Jilsey ? Roundtree
daughter Rebecca Bird and her children
sons: John Thompson (eldest), James, Thomas Thompson
"   Lawrence, Joseph and Nicholas Thompson

Executors: son Nicholas, and friend James Forest, Esq.
Witnesses: Peter Walker, Mathew Brown.

- - -

E 263 Will dated 14 January 1829, proved Nov Court 1831.

MARGARET WATSON   dau: Helen Riley

son: James Watson
daus: Rebecca Watson, Elizabeth Comb
son: Andrew Watson   - continued -

 E 263 Will of MARGARET WATSON continued
dau: Nancy McCamal ?
son: John Watson and his daughter Margaret Watson
" Robert Watson

Executor: son Robert Watson.
Witnesses: Js. R. Watson, Farmer Smith.

- - -

E 265 Will dated 8 June 1831, proved November Court 1831.

SAMUEL WARE wife: Gilly

"My daughter and son", names not stated.

Executrix: wife.
Witnesses: Chesley M ? Patterson, Isreal (x) Turner.

- - -

E 265 Will dated 22 October 1831, proved Feb Court 1832.

DANIEL LYNCH wife: Polly "may be pregnant"

He purchased tracts of land from John Horner, Thomas W. Holden and Alves Nichols.

children: Sarah Ann Lynch, Logan Lynch

Executrix: wife Polly. Witnesses: John Allen, John Horner.

- - -

E 267 Will dated 11 September 1829, proved Feb Court 1832.

ELIZABETH (x) ROGERS "weak and infirm" son: Theopilus

Elizabeth Webb, daughter of John Webb

All her grandchildren to have equal shares "except Idlett Rogers who I consider has gotten a good share from his grandfather William Rogers's Estate".

Executor: James A. Craig.
Witnesses: John Cheek, Sarah (x) Freshwater.

- - -

E 268 Will dated 15 February 1832, proved Feb Court 1832.

THOMAS (x) JAMES wife: Elizabeth

He speaks of his children .."until my youngest child comes of age ... my three sons ..."

Executor: "worthy friend James Rhodes".
Witnesses: Silas M. Link, Wm'son Burton.

- - -

E 269 Will dated 20 May 1827, proved May Court 1832.

JOSEPH THOMPSON

".. children taht are herein named Elizabeth, Abel, Enoch, Thomas, Edith, Lydia and Sarah .."

Executors: "my two sons Abel and William Turner".
Witnesses: Samuel McCracken Sr., Samuel McCracken Jr.

- - -

E 270 Will dated 5 February 1832, proved May Court 1832.

WILLIAM WHITAKER wife: Nancy

daus: Polly Cardin, Nancy Whitaker, Ann Whitaker
son: John (schooling 1 year), Burton
" Thomas, Isaac, William and Divid Whitaker

Executor: son William Whitaker.
Witnesses: Robert Gresham, James Horn.

- - -

E 271 Will dated 7 January 1823, proved August Court 1832.

FRANCES CHILD "of the Town of Hillsborough"

son: Samuel Child "lot where I now live, lot # 117"
grandsons: Samuel Child and William McKerall

Executors: "worthy friends James Webb and F. Nash"
Witnesses: Thomas Clancy, James Child.

- - -

E 272 Will dated 13 January 1832, proved August Court 1832.

WILLIAM (x) BRANNOCK

sons-in-law: David Gilliam and William Taylor 10 shillings ea.
sons: William Brannock 10 shillings, Alexander N. Brannock
"My two daughters Delilah Brannock and Angel M. Brannock my lands".

Executor: "my son-in-law Henry Brannock in whom I much confide"
Witnesses: Wright Brannock, George Thomas, Henry Brannock, Sr.

- - -

E 273 Will dated 14 June 1832, proved August Court 1832.

PARRIS PEARSON wife: Mary

"My children- to wit- Stephen Thomas John M Joel Jane Marcom Sarah Trice Rachel Massey and Eliza Colliear" (no commas).
"To my son Green 50¢"
"To my grandson Silas Green Clark"
"daughter Ann Collier and Mary Moore $2 each"

Executors: "sons William and Edward Collier".
Witnesses: R. S. Leigh, W. D. Carlton.

- - -

E 275 Will dated 5 May 1829, proved August Court 1832.

JACOB GARRISON

"grandson Henry Garrison plantation on which I now live, joining the lands of Henry Hurdle and his mother Nancy Garrison"

son-in-law: Henry Hurdle
grandsons Jacob and John Jorden plantation on Tom's Creek
son-in-law Job Walker "plantation on Stoney Creek known by the name Bracken's old place" 200 acres
son-in-law Thomas Bradfprd $500
daughter Rachel Walker 100 acres on Stoney Creek known as "Burch's old place, and "each of her children $50"
"My grandchildren, children of my daughter Mary Dickey $100 each except George"
granddaughters: Mary Jordon and Levina Jordon
grandchildren: Elizabeth and George King
daughter: Margaret Hurdle
grandson: Granderson Garrison
"That John Walker pay to Rachel Walker" note due.

Executors: son-in-law Henry Hurdle, and friend William Brinkley.
Witnesses: Thomas Trewett Sr, Thos Trewett, Jonathan Harvey.

- - -

E 277-279 Will dated 27 February 1826, proved August 1832.

JOSEPH SHAW grandson: Benjamin J. Kinnion

daughter Maria Kinnion, and to her children
son: Joseph B. Shaw
"daughters of my son Joseph"
grandson: Joseph John Shaw
daughter Drusilla Ann Hargis .. "her daughters"
daughter Catherine H. Horton "and to the children of her daughter Maria B. Hargis"
daus: Elinor Ann Ray, Rebecca E. Shaw, Fantitina Joys Shaw
son: Neal H. Shaw
grandsons: Neal H. Horton, Anthony W. Horton
sons-in-law: John Warren, James M. Wheat (?) 10 shillings each
" " " Paul Kennion, Dennis Hargis 10 shillings each

Executrix: daughter Fantitina J. Shaw.
Witnesses: Murrell Breesse , Thos. V. Hargis, J. P. Sneed.

- - -

E 280 Will dated 7 June 1831, proved August Court 1832.

HENSON (x) COULTER, SR. wife: Lizzy

sons: Anderson Coulter, Charles Coulter , 50¢ each
"deceased son Thomas Coulter or his heirs" 50 ¢
daughter Jane Fan
sons: Allen Coulter, Asa Coulter, Ashley Coulter

- continued -

daus: Miloy Pendergrass and Fanny Pendergrass 50¢ each
dau: Milly Coulter $200
"My illegitimate daughter now bearing and known by the name of Eliza Coulter , $200."
"My three last sons viz Sherly ? Coulter, Bartlett Coulter and Fanning Coulter," lands, etc.

Executors: friends William Barbee Sr., and Thomas H. Taylor.
Witnesses: Henry Thomson, John Sparrow, Chas. R. Yancey, Ashley Coulter.

- - -

E 282 Will dated Jul7 1832, proved November Court 1832.

JAMES (x) CRABTREE

sons: Richard, John and Abram Crabtree, $1 each
dau: Charlotte wife of James Jackson $1
dau: Fanny " " James Crabtree, land
daus: Sally, Elizabeth and Polly Crabtree, land
son: Clement Crabtree

Executor: Son Clement Crabtree.
Witnesses: Allen Cain, James Myrick.

- - -

E 283-285 Will dated 16 September 1832, proved November 1832.

JOHN McCAULEY wife: Nancy F. McCauley is pregnant

sons: William, James, Mathew McCauley
son: Charles John Franklin McCauley
dau: Marthy E. Morrow and her husband John Morrow
daus: Nancy Flutcher McCauley, Mary McCauley, Ellen Jane McCauley, Orella Dow McCauley, Verlina Ann McCauley, Lucinda

Executor: brother Mathew McCauley. Witness: Thos. D. Watts.

- - -

E 285 Will dated 6 May 1831, proved November Court 1832.

JOHN HICKS son: John Hicks

daus: Frances Hicks, Jane Hicks
sons: John Hicks, Thomas M. Hicks

Executors: sons James and John.
Witnesses: James Trewett, Wm. Brannock.

- - -

E 287-288 Will dated 30 June 1830, proved February 1833.

JAMES (x) STRAYHORN, SR. "weak in body" wife: Rachel

daus: Elizabeth Strayhorn, Polly Strayhorn - continued -

sons: James, John, William

He devises "tract which I purchased of James Hart", "
"tract which I purchased of my nephew Gilbert Strayhorn and John Strayhorn sons of my brother David deceased, and which was willed to them by their grandfather Gilbert Strayhorn, Sr."

Executor: son John Strayhorn.
Witnesses: J. M. Kerall, Thomas Crabtree, Wilsom McKerall.

- - -

E 289 Will dated 1 February 1833, proved Feb Court 1833.

AARON WALKER wife: Sarah

sons: Levi Walker, Empson Walker
"daughter Nancy Shaw wife of John W. Shaw"
"daughter Harriett Crawford wife of Philip Crawford"
son: Freeman Walker

Executor: son Dr. Levi Walker.
Witnesses: J. S. Smith, John Walker, James Walker.

- - -

E 290 Will dated 11 November 1832, proved Feb Court 1833.

JOHN FARRAR Wife a legatee, name not stated.

Children, names not stated, to "be schooled".

No executor named. Witnesses: Hunter McCauley, Joseph Barbee.

- - -

E 291 Will dated 10 September 1827, proved May Court 1833.

JOSEPH (x) WOOD wife: Polly

dau: Elizabeth Chisenhall son: James Wood

Children: Solomon Wood, Henry, Joseph, Sukey Glenn, Nancy King, Mary Chisenhall, $1 each.

Executor: son James Wood.
Witnesses: Frederick Moize, Dempsey Wood.

- - -

E 292 Will dated 3 March 1832, proved May Court 1833.

BETSY (x) LEIGH "sick in body"

sisters: Nancy Garrett; Anna Leigh
brothers: Thomas Leigh, Sullivan Leigh

Executor: brother Sullivan Leigh.
Witnesses: Joseph Dickson, William Leigh.

- - -

E 294 Will dated 21 April 1833, proved May Court 1833.

WILLIAM GUESS

"My seven children Margaret, Sarah, James, Nancy, Frances, Joseph and Wilson" $400.
son: Moses
"Balance to be equally divided among all my children, Mary intermarried with David Warren, Rebecca intermarried with James Dollar; John, Elizabeth, George, Thomas, Margaret, Moses, Sarah, James, Nancy, Frances, Joseph and Wilson."

Executor: son Moses.

- - -

E 294 Will dated 31 January 1833, proved May Court 1833.

WILLIAM BARBEE wife: Sarah

"infant daughter June (or Jane ?) Barbee"
son: James Barbee "tract where he now lives"

Executor: "worthy friend" John W. Wilson.
Witnesses: Caleb Wilson, An. Watson.

- - -

E 296 Will dated 18 January 1832, proved May Court 1833.

JOSEPH WARD wife: Charity

Son Robertson, daughters Sally Parham, Patsy Blailoc, Bethany, sons Ransom, William and Josiah, daughter Elizabeth Moor, sons Isham (or Isaac ?) and John, 50¢ each. These all seem to be children of his first wife.

Daughters Rebecca Moor, Mary Ward, Jennet, son Edwin, daughter Louisa, sons James and Marvil, daughter Nancy Ann (unmarried), "my last wife's children aforementioned".

Executors: wife Charity, and brother-in-law James Law.
Witness: Thomas Howard.

- - -

E 297 Will dated 20 March 1833, proved May Court 1833.

DAVID RAY Wife a legatee, name not stated.

step-mother: Sally Ray
sister: Susannah Ray deceased
daughter Peggy Jane Ray

He says "until my youngest child that may be living arrives at age of twenty-one."

Executor: Richerson Nichols.
Witnesses: John Hanks, John Smith, Charles Ray.

- - -

E 298 Will dated 10 May 1831, proved May Court 1833.

WINNEY her x mark HARDEE

daughter: Sally Shields

daughter: Polly Wells $1 "besides what I have given her
son: William Hardee
daus: Martha Carlton Thompson, Eliza Wells
grandchildren: Luiza Hardee, Caroline Gordan, Whitmell H. Hardee
"Three of my son John's children, namely Henrietta, Luvina Daniel and Frances W. Hardee."
"All my son William's children" (not named)
"All my daughter Martha C. Thompson's children"
"All my daughter Eliza Wells' children"

Executors: son William Hardee, son-in-law Benjamin Wells.
Witnesses: J. A. McDade, H. C. McDade.

– – –

E 300 Will dated 25 June 1830, proved May Court 1833.

RICHARD CHRISTMAS (He devises many slaves and other property.)

To Miss Betsy Cooper for her care of him in his infirmities, $100, slave, furniture, etc.

Legacies to Richard Glass, son of Stephen and Betsy Glass, and to his parents.
Dr. James A. Craig
Niece Mary G. Christmas
" Nancy Christmas daughter of my deceased brother James
" Henrietta Christmas dau. " " " " "
nephews: John and William sons " " " " "
"My niece Mary Edward Green daughter of my nephew John Green of Warrenton."
Niece, Mary Young widow.
Ann Christmas Lytle ? niece of my deceased wife.
Mary Smart " " " " "
Peggy Lankston " " " " "
"My niece Mary Powers wife of Richard Powers"

Executor: Dr. James A. Craig.
Witnesses: A. D. Murphey, Arch'd Murphey, V. M. Murphy.

– – –

E 302 Will dated 16 October 1828, proved August Court 1833.

ELIZABETH (x) LAWS

friend: Thos. D. Bennehan

Mary Furgerson wife of John Furgerson
"To William Laws son of my nephew Leonard Laws"

Executor: Thos. D. Bennehan.
Witnesses: Wm. Horner, Sam'l Yarborough.
Young Dorch, A. Williams.

– – –

E 303-305 Will dated 2 April 1826, proved August 1833.

WILLIAM (x) BREWER wife: Dorothy

"Four sons of my son Isham Brewer (viz): Joseph, Benjamin, Washington and Isham."

grandchildren: William Hatch, George B. Hatch,& Sally Hatch.
"My three grandchildren (viz) William B. Bredges, Elizabeth C. Bredges, and Mary I. Bredges."
"Jane Brewer and her six children Joseph and Benjamin & Washington & Isham & July & Polly."

Executors: trusty friends Thomas Weaver and Joseph Brewer.
Witnesses: Jessey Nevills, John Crabtree, William Thompson.

- - -

E 306 Will dated 9 July 1833, proved August Court 1833.

MOSES HARVEY or HERVEY ? wife: Hannah

"All my children", not named except daughter Grace.

Executors: Worthy friends Samuel Woods and John Newlin.
Witnesses: Robert Cheek, Isaac Andrews.

- - -

E 307 Will dated 21 June 1833, proved November Court 1833.

JOHN HOLMES wife: Catherine

son: Nicholas unmarried son: William
unmarried daughters: Ann and Jane
"their three married sisters who have left me"

"All my children namely, Mary, Hannah, Sarah, William, Henry, Ann, Joseph, Nicholas and Jane."

Executor: son William Holmes.
Witnesses: William Paine, John Stockard, John (x) Paine.

- - -

E 308 Will dated 2 November 1833, proved Nov. Court 1833.

CASON CAPPS wife: Mary

sons: Robert and James, "William now in the Western Country"
"Nelly McDaniel, Milly Carter & Mary Stout & their children"
None of the property shall fall into the hands of their husbands Joseph McDaniel, Joseph Carter and Samuel Stout.

Executors: sons Richard and James.
Witnesses: James Moore, Thomas Scott.

- - -

E 309 Will dated 10 May 1832, Proved November Court 1833.

BETSY (x) GRAVES son: Elijah

"My two granddaughters Selina F. Graves and Betsy C. Graves my four wheel carriage and harness."
"Grandson Ralph Lewis Graves son of Elijah"
"Grandsons Jessey Dixon Graves and Elijah Calvin Graves, sons of my dear Henry."

Executor: son Elijah.
Witnesses: Archibald Andrews, Isaac Durham.

E 311 Will dated 13 August 1822, proved February Court 1834.

JOHN (x) DANNELLEY "frail and old" wife: Nancy

dau: Rosanna Smothers $1 son: James Dannelley $1
" Priscilla Rumbley $1 " John Dannelley $1
daus: Sarah and Margaret Dannelley

Executors: daughters Sarah and Margaret Dannelley.
Witnesses: Robert Lackey, Thomas Woody.

E 311 Will dated 3 December 1833, proved Feb Court 1844.

ARCHIBALD (x) FINDLY "weak in body" Wife: Ann, all estate.

"My children Brice Andrew and Morau" (no punctuation) children are under 21 years of age.

Executors: trusty friends John A. Faucett & Levi McCollum.
Witnesses: Geo. W. Bruce, John Newman.

E 313 Will dated 23 October 1833, proved Feb Court 1844.

WILLIAM (x) PRICHARD wife: Milly

dau: Rodah Prichard
son: Nelson "land on south side of Price's Creek"
son: Wilson
dau: Nancy Prichard (under age)
son: Edmond Prichard

Executors: "trusty friends Wilson Prichard and Nelson Prichard."
Witness: Goodman Nevill.

E 315 Will dated 2 February 1832, proved May Court 1834.

JOHN (x) ROBERTS "son's daughter Mary Roberts"

"son William's son John Wesley Roberts"
Executor: son William. Witnesses: Nath. Newlin, Sarah Andrews.

E 315 Will dated 18 January 1832, proved May Court 1834.

THOMAS (x) KING "far advanced in years"

wife: Elizabeth land adjoining James Walker and others
youngest son: Thomas King
daus: Dicey King and Marsha ? Ann King

executors: friend James Leathers, and wife Elizabeth.
Witnesses: W. J. Duke, James Leathers.

- - -

E 316 Will dated 13 February 1833, proved May Court 1834.

WILLIAM RAY, SR.

son: James Ray
" William Ray
" John Ray

dau: Jane Hopkins
" Sally Rhew

"Grandsons James and John Ray sons of Thomas Ray deceased"
(other children of Thomas) William, Rebecca, Charles & Bogan.

Executor: Richison Nichols.
Witnesses: Adam Dikson, Wm. Dickson.

- - -

E 317 Will dated 5 September 1829, proved May Court 1834.

JOHN REDMOND, SR. (Names is spelled Redmon in will but is signed Redmond.)
Daughter Margaret Redmon gets all estate during her life.
Grandson John Riley,Jr gets land after Margaret's death if he stays to care for her.
John Redmon, Jr.
Sally Riley wife of John Riley
Nancy Redden wife of John Redden
Elizabeth Browning wife of James Browning

Executor: worthy friend Willoughby Hudgins.
Witnesses: William Chamblee, John Riley.

- - -

E 318 Will dated 18 March 1833, proved May Court 1834.

WILLIAM (x) M'CADDAMS "on the decline" wife: Fanny

daus: Nancy M'Caddams and Margaret M'Caddams
son: Hugh,"and his son William M'Caddams"
" Samuel
" James M'Caddams "my plantation in the North East corner of the county called the Robson place"
dau: Catherine Thomas
son: William M'Caddams

Residue of estate "equally divided between .... M'Caddams, Samuel M'Caddamd James M'Caddams Catherine Thomas Martha

- continued -

Redden William M'Caddams Nancy M'Caddams Margaret M'Caddams."

Executor: Edward Benson.
Witnesses: Stephen Benson, William Benson.

- - -

E 319 Will dated 12 March 1832, proved May Court 1834.

JOHN REEVES All estate to son Thomas Reeves.

Exceutor: Thomas Reeves. Witness: Thomas Lynch.

- - -

E 319 Will dated 12 May 1834, proved May Court 1834.

JOSEPH DICKSON "far advanced in years"

Daughter Mary M. Herndon, and her two sons Maturine C. Herndon and Coslett M. Herndon.
"My granddaughter Mary Ann now the wife of Anderson Ferrell."
son: Alexander C. Dickson
granddaughters: Mary Ann Dickson and Caroline Dickson
"Respected friends Hugh Waddell and Robert William Dickson and Presley H. Mangum Esquires attorneys-at-law" trustees to hold estate for "my daughter Julia Newell Dickson and my grandson Robert William Dickson" until he arrives at mature age.

Caroline Dickson now the wife of Joseph Marcom.

Executors: Hugh Waddell, Robert WM. Dickson, Presley H. Mangum.
Witnesses: Joseph Marcom, F. Bilbo, Elizabeth (x) Rigsby, Mary (x) Marcom.

- - -

E 321-323 Will dated 5 February 1823, proved May Court 1834.

CHRISTOPHER BARBEE He devises numerous slaves, etc.

son: Francis
son: William lands on Morgan Creek, and "lands on Bolind's Creek which I bought of Tapley Booth"
dau: Elizabeth who married Samuel Allen
" Nancy " " Edward Jones
" Susanna " " Wm. Henry Merritt
"Some years ago being visited by my granddaughter Polly Allen daughter of my daughter Elizabeth who then lived in the State of Tennessee, I loaned to her a certain negro ..."
grandsons: Christopher Allen, Willis Jones

Executors: son William, and friend Mann Patterson.
Witnesses: J. Henderson, N. I. King, Maurice Henderson.

Codicil dated 31 January 1826 annuls legacy to grandson Willis Jones. Witnesses: Wm. Chalmers, John Hutchins, Wm. McCauley.

- - -

E 324-328 Will dated 14 December 1827, proved November 1834.

WILLIAM CAIN the older.

daughter: Polly Southerland "tract called Fannings ... which formerly belonged to my brother Timothy Cain"
son-in-law (married to Charity Cain) Willie P. Mangum, lot in Hillsborough
son: William Cain
daughter Ann Davis and her husband Edward Davis and children
"grandsons William Cain, William R. Southerland and William Cain Davis"
"To Eliza Moore (daughter of Philip Moore) a bureau, one of those used by my deseased daughter Martha."
dau: Peggy Cain

Executors: friend Duncan Cameron, and son William Cain.
Witnesses: Thos. D. Bennehan, Sam'l Yarborough.

- - -

E 329 Will dated 28 October 1834, proved Nov Court 1834.

WILLIAM RHODES (He was a son of William and Delilah (Herndon) Rhodes. See Delilah's will, F 6.)
WIFE (name not stated, but she was Penelope Trice) gets estate to "raise" and "school" children.
"All my children" mentioned, names and number not stated.

Executor: "worthy friend Zachariah Trice".
Witnesses: Henry Trice, Sr., Chesley P. Trice, Henry D. Trice.

- - -

E 330 Will dated 6 December 1834, proved Feb Court 1835.

JONATHAN (x) DOLLAR "far advanced in years"

daus: Milly, Sally, Cynthia
Mary Rhodes (relationship not stated)
son: Jonathan Dollar

Executor: son Jonathan Dollar.
Witnesses: W. S ? Pratt, T(homas) Bilbo, William Lynn.

- - -

E 331 Will dated 13 February 1834, proved Feb Court 1835.

ALEXANDER WALKER

brothers: Conoley Walker, James Walker, Philip Walker
"Margaret Walker widow of William Walker"
Samuel Crawford $1 John Walker

Executor: brother Conoly Walker.
Witnesses: C. F. Faacette , Robert Fausett.

- - -

E 332 Will dated 8 December 1834, proved Feb Court 1835.

ROBERT H. FAUCETT "my mother Phebe Dickey"

"My two sisters and brother (viz) Aby Dickey Elizabeth Dickey and Isaac Newton Dickey all my land ..."

Executors: "Uncle Absolem Harvey and Junia Hall."
Witnesses: James Pickett, James Hart.

- - -

E 334 Will dated 22 November 1834, codicil dated 5 Dec 1834, proved February Court 1835.

MARY (x) THRIFT "weak of body"

daus: Nancy Rosser, Elizabeth Snipes, Polly Lloyd
"son Isham Thrift's children"
She says "all my children", but does not give number.

Executor: James Rosser.
Witnesses: B. Strowd, Wilson Atwater.

- - -

E 335-338 Will dated 18 August 1834, proved Feb Court 1835.

STEWART DIXON

wife: Sally home plantation and part of Hulgan Tract
eldest son: James Dixon "Turrentine Tract" of land
son: Joseph Dixon "Kirk Tract of land which runs to Haw River" joins Hufman.
son: Thomas Dixon "Patton Tract"
" John Dixon "McCracking Tract"
" William Dixon "balance of Hulgan Tract" & "Freeman Tract"
daughter Mary Wilkins wife of William Wilkins
daus: Martha Morrow, Hannah Dixon, Margaret Dixon, Nancy Dixon, Sally Dixon

Executor: son Thomas Dixon.
Witnesses: John Trolinger, Alex Mebane, Elijah Pickard.

- - -

E 338 Will dated 31 July 1828, proved May Court 1835.

JACOB (x) ANTHONY, SR daughter: Mary Moser

"My other twelve children" names not stated.
eldest son: Jacob

"I was born the first day of May 1745".

Executors: son Henry Anthony, Adam Wrightsel.
Witnesses: A. W. Albright, ...?.. ...?.... (a foreign name).

- - -

E 339 Will dated 16 June 1833, proved May Court 1835.

THOMAS (x) McCRACKEN, SR. "weak of body" wife: Priscilla

"All my children- viz- Joseph, Robert, Stephen, Alexander, Abigail, Martha, Thomas."

Executor: son Thomas McCracken.
Witnesses: John Hart, Samuel McCracken.

- - -

E 341 Will dated 21 April 1835, proved May Court 1835.

THOMAS FREELAND "all my brothers"

father: John Freeland "my land which he now lives on adjoining Charles Johnston, John Blackwood and others"
sister: Martha Cloud

Wxwcutor: worthy friend John Blackwood.
Witnesses: James J. Blackwood, David K. Blackwood.

- - -

E 342 Will dated 25 April 1835, proved May Court 1835.

WILLIAM (x) LOYD,SR. wife: Hannah

sons: Thomas, William, Pleasant, Green and John Loyd
daus: Sarah Loyd, Mary Poe, Nancy Jones, Elizabeth Loyd
daughter Rebecca William's children

Executor: John Careathers..
Witnesses: Levi Andrews, William Careathers.

- - -

E 343 Will dated 11 February 1835, proved May Court 1835.

MARY (x) DICKIE in "feeble state of health"

"son Zachariah Dickie - and his children"
grandsons: E. M. Dickie, Franklin Dickie
granddaus: Margaret Dickie and Mary Dickie
dau: Margaret Dickie

Executor: J. D. Hughes.
Witnesses: James Clark, John Reding, Jr.

- - -

E 344 Will dated 1 November 1830, proved May Court 1835.

DIANNA (x) MOORE

All to daughters Elennor Moore and Mary Bowls.

Executors: worthy friends Thomas Moore and Anderson Moore.
Witnesses: Isaac Jeffreys, James Moore.

- - -

E 345 Will dated 19 February 1831, proved May Court 1835.

ANDREW (x) McCULLOCK, SR. "weak of body"

friend: James Kerr of Caswell County
niece: Polly Smith land joining William Barbee
Land and slaves to "my nephew Andrew Forgason, now of Ireland", provided he comes to America.

Executors: worthy friends James Kerr and James Hurdle.
Witnesses: Solomon Browning, Wm. Cantrell, Connoly Walker.

- - -

E 247-249 Will dated 3 March 1835, proved May Court 1835.

THOMAS ARMSTRONG   wife: Elizabeth

son: Anderson Armstrong
"My children Anderson, Asenath, Thomas Lapslie and Frances E. Armstrong (Frances is under 21) "

"Daughter Asenath Curree and son-in-law John Currie" ... "her children Thomas Anderson, Ann Elizabeth and such other children as she may have..."
son: Thomas Lapslie Armstrong slaves, and "all my interest in a tract of land lying in Montgomery County, Ga."
son: James Armstrong has had his part

Executors: Anderson Armstrong and Thomas L. Armstrong.
Witnesses: William Clark, Jno Bane, Thos. P. Paul.

- - -

E 350 Will dated 27 October 183-, proved May Court 1835.

FREDERICK FONVILLE   Wife a legatee, name not stated.

sons: Asa and Brice, both under age
married daughter Hannah and her son Brice
" " Edna " " dau Palina
" " Sarah
daus: Mary, Fanna
sons: William ($1) and his son Washington, James ($3), John $1

Executor: son-in-law Thomas Grahams.
Witnesses: Jacob Somers, Chesley F. Faucette.

- - -

E 351-352 Will dated 21 September 1834, proved May Court 1835.

THOMAS RHODES, SR.   son: Noah Rhodes

"My granchildren Jane Medley (Medlin), Wesley Rhodes, Wiley Rhodes and Artemesia Rhodes children of my son Noah Rhodes."

son: Thomas Rhodes , his children, "his present wife SallY" get "tract where he now lives that I purchased from William Riley."

- continued -

son: James Rhodes "tract whereon he now lives"
dau: Hannah Rhodes Bunch.
" Belinda wife of Abel Cain "tract I purchased of Henry/
" Elizabeth Guess wife of Thomas Guess now of the State of Kentucky
"To the children of David Warren which he had by my daughter Polly Rhodes"

Sole executor: Silas M. Link.
Witnesses: Archibald Cain, Wmson Burton.
(Names of other grandchildren will be found in equity suit papers about the settlement of this estate. In State Archives)

- - -

E 353 Will dated 10 September 1834, proved May Court 1835.

MANN PATTERSON

Wife Mary Patterson and her seven children namely Jane, Martha, Caroline, Mann, William, David and Robert, 2200 acres on the waters of New Hope adjoining the lands of William Cain, Wm. Jenkins, Wm. Robertson and others...

son: John T(apley) Patterson
"Caroline and Ferdenon M. Patterson daughter and son of John T. Patterson."
son: James N. Patterson
daus: Sarah M. Rhodes, Nancy M. Strayhorn
" Amelia H. Boroughs, Mary A. Patterson

Executors: friends James Webb, James N. Patterson and John C. Rhodes.
Witnesses: Robert Davis, Elias Batchelor, Thomas (x) Henderson.

- - -

E 355-357 Will dated 18 November 1834, proved May 1835.

THOMAS HOLLOWAY, SR. wife: Lydia

"My children John, Williamson, Sarah, Lydia Caroline, and Milly Holloway". "Said three daughters" all under age ?
son: Bennehan Holloway
"children of my son Samuel Holloway"
Susannah Whitaker
"the heirs of my daughter Polly Woods"
daughter Lucy Whitaker
David Holloway, William Holloway
"heirs of Elizabeth Trice"
Hannah Latta, Ann Farthing, Agatha Harward (married)
Thomas Holloway, Sarah Holloway, Fanny Leathers,
James Holloway, John Holloway, Williamson Holloway,
Lydia Caroline and Milly Holloway.

Executors: friends James Latta, John Leathers, and Williamson Burton.
Witnesses: Archibald Cain, William Piper.

162 Codicil to will of THOMAS HOLLOWAY, SR.

Daughter Ann Farthing, her son Hargis Farthing, his deceased father Reuben Farthing. Witness: Silas M. Link.

- - -

E 358-361 Will dated 26 July 1831, proved August Court 1835.

MARTIN PALMER

William Huntingdon and Thomas Clancy trustees for property left to son William Palmer, and then to his children.

son James Palmer and his children
daughter Mary and her husband Roswell Huntingdon
" Sarah and her husband John Rasberry
son-in-law Thomas Clancy and his wife Nancy
daughter Elizabeth Peacock wife of Richard Peacock
" Temperance Faucett wife of John Faucett
" Agnes wife of Henry G. Parish

Executors and trustees: Thomas Clancy and Wm. Huntingdon.
Witnesses: J. W. Norwood, James Faucett.

- - -

E 362 Will dated 23 July 1834, proved May Court 1835.

THOMAS BIRD, SR.

wife: Nancy ... "I lay no claim to the property that my wife Nancy possessed when I married her".
son: Thomas
"All my children", names and number not stated.

Executors: son William, and friend Thomas Reeves.
Witnesses: Thomas Reeves, William Bird.

- - -

E 363 Will dated 17 March 1835, proved August Court 1835.

WILLIAM G. CLENDENNIN wife: Isabel

"All my children", names and number not stated.

Sole executor: James Johnston.
Witnesses: Alfred Thompson, Patterson Thompson, James Clendennin.

- - -

E 363 Will dated 26 September 1817, proved August Court 1835.

JOSEPH CALDWELL wife: Helen

step-son: William Hooper, Esq. niece: Margaret Caldwell

Executors: William Hooper, Esq., James Webb.
Witnesses: John L. Bailey, Pleasant H. May.

- - -

E 365 Will dated 15 December 1832, proved Nov Court 1835.

THOMAS FITCH

"Grandson Thomas Fitch son of my son James Fitch" tract on west side of Stony Creek joining Jacob Greeson, to Tom's Creek .... James Graham's line... "
son: Empson Fitch
dau: Mary Fitch
" Barbara Barker wife of George Barker
" Susanna Younger wife of Joseph
son: James Fitch $1
" William Fitch $2

Executors: friend George Martin, and son Empson Fitch.
Witnesses: Caleb Wilson, John Fitch.

- - -

E 366 Will dated 5 October 1833, proved Nov Court 1835.

BENJAMIN (x) TUTTERTON in "feeble state of health"

dau: Elizabeth Blalock $1 "besides what I have given her"
son: Barenton Tutterton $1 " " I " " him
daus: Lainey Tutterton and Polly Tutterton get all estate

Executor: William Paul.
Witnesses: J. D. Hughes, R. Thompson.

- - -

E 367 Will dated 25 January 1834, proved Nov Court 1835.

PETTER WAGGONER wife: Margaret

son: Daniel
Daughters Barbary Elizabeth Catherine Margaret Mary Rosanna Hannah (no punctuation).
"Granddaughter Nancy Waggoner daughter of Peter , deceased."

Executors: son Daniel Waggoner, and George Smith.
Witnesses: John Boon, Jonathan Harvey.

- - -

E 368 Will dated 19)ctober 1835, proved Feb Court 1836.

TEMPERANCE PRIMROSE

"Six of my children (viz) William Primrose, Rachel Wheeler, Frances Culberhouse, Ann Chisenhall, Thomas Primrose, and George Primrose."
"To heirs of James Primrose deceased"
"To Aga Primrose daughter of Pegga Primrose Dec'd."
Nine shares to "John Primrose Elizabeth Garrard Mary Stem William Primrose Rachel Wheeler Frances Culberhouse Ann Chisenhall Thomas Primrose and George Primrose."

- continued -

Executors: son and daughter John Primrose and Elizabeth Garrard.
Witnesses: Thomas Flint, Lewis Hutchins.
This will is recorded again in Book F page 114.

- - -

E 369 Will dated 5 June 1825, proved February Court 1836.

JOHN O'DANIEL

All his estate to his brothers Henry and Jesse O'Daniel.
If brothers die without issue property goes to Anne Waddleton and John Baskett of South Carolina.
No witnesses. Ececutors: brothers Henry and Jesse O'Daniel.

- - -

E Will dated 10 November 1832, proved Feb Court 1836.

PHEBE (x) GRIMES

sisters: Elizabeth Grimes $5, Anna Grimes $5,
Rebecca Montgomery widow of Hugh Montgomery $5
sister: Lydia Grimes land and all other property

Executors: "Loving friend Anderson Wilson", and sister Lydia.
Witnesses: Caleb Wilson, Samuel Turrentine,
Martha Wilson, Absolem Turrentine.

- - -

E 371 Will dated 5 February 1834, proved Feb Court 1836.

SARAH YOUNGER widow, "aged and infirm"

son: Robert Younger all money on hand
"Heirs of my son John E. Younger" $1
to son Richard Younger , plantantion, etc; and to his son John, "my plantation on Boyd's Creek where I lately resided"

Executor: son Richard Younger.
Witnesses: Jas. Grahams, Robert Fausett.

- - -

E 371 Will dated January 1835, proved Feb Court 1836.

ROBERT MOORE father: James Moore

"sister Margaret, James and sister Sally Crutchfield and John Moore"
"sister Margaret Jones"
He devises lands on waters of Cain Creek -to wit- Lashley Tract .. joining James Moore & Wm Morrow', the Griffin Tract joining Wm. Smith & John Crofford (Crawford) ...

Executors: John Jones and John Moore.
Witnesses: Henry O'Daniel, Elizabeth (x) Moore, Jesse O'Daniel.

- - -

E 372 Will dated 22 December 1835, proved Feb 1836.

PETER S. CLARK sister: Elizabeth Weaver.

wife: Susannah, land near Woody's Ferry, etc.

Executors: wife, & " friend Jediah Smith of Guilford County."
Witness: John Moore.

- - -

E 373-375 Will dated 10 September 1835, proved Feb 1836.

ALEXANDER ALLEN Wife a legatee, name not stated.

Infant son Alexander, son John, daughters Fanny, Mary, Jane and Nancy. (All the children seem to be minors.)

Executors: "friend and kinsman George Mebane and my brother-in-law John Scott."
Witnesses: James Patton, James White.

- - -

E 375 Will dated 22 April 1830, proved Feb 1836.

ROBERT TINNEN sons: Thomas and David

sons: Catlett C. Tinnen & Robert Tinnen "plantation which joins Joseph Allison".
"My four daughters Margaret, Jennet, Elenor and Mary" ...
Grandsons: "Robert Clark (of Jos) and Robert Tinnen (of Thos)"
"My bound girl Polly Deneal ..."

Executors: sons David Tinnen and Robert Tinnen.
Witnesses: J. Taylor, James Lindsey.

- - -

E 377 Will dated 12 January 1836, proved Feb 1836.

MARTHA (x) PRICE. All estate to grandson Thomas Johnson Crabtree.
Executor: "trusty friend John Crabtree".
Witnesses: Goodman Nevill, John Couch.

- - -

E 378 Will dated 18 November 1834, proved May 1836.

MARTHA (x) MULHOLLAN, widow of Thomas.

To friend Samuel N. Tate all her property in trust for sons John Mulhollan and Samuel Mulhollan. At their deaths to"the children of my son Hugh Mulhollan deceased."

Executor: Samuel N. Tate. Witnesses: C. C. Smith, James Tate.

- - -

E 379 Will dated 14 April 1827, proved May 1836.

JOHN HUGHS, SR. Wife a legatee, name not stated.

son: Thomas Hughs. daughter: Elizabeth

son: Samuel Hughs land on Reedy Fork
sons: John and Andrew Hughs have already received land

Sole executor: son Andrew Hughs.
Witnesses: Robert Bevell, Michael Strader.

- - -

E 380 Will dated 11 May 1836, proved May Court 1836.

WILLIAM H. PARKER "weak in body"

wife: Jane plantation in Person County "known by the name of the Aldrige Tract ... lying on waters of Flat River"
dau: Anzalette M. Parker
His plantation in Orange County known as Vincent Tapp tract to be sold.

Executor: George C. Ray.
Witnesses: Hugh Woods, H. Terry, Edward Riley.

- - -

E 381 Will dated 11 May 1836, proved May Court 1836.

PHILEMON HOLT wife: Sarah

"My children namely Mary S. Holt, Jane Holt and Wilkins Holt" all minors.
"My bound boy Granville Simpson now living with me to be schooled."

Exceutors: wife Sarah, and brother Jacob Holt.
Witnesses: Sarah Holt, Jonah Dobyna, Elizabeth W. Waggoner.

- - -

E 382 Will dated 18 April 1835, proved May Court 1836.

WILLIAM KELL wife: Anna

dau: Sally granddaughter: Charlotte Kell
grandson: William Gates
great-grandson: Allen Kell son of Charlotte Kell

No executor named. Witnesses: James Webb, James Webb, Jr.

- - -

E 382-384 Will dated 17 May 1828, proved May Court 1836.

GEORGE FOUST wife: Barbara

son: Daniel Foust 250 acres in Guilford County "which I bought from my brother John Foust and John Cook"
son: George Foust plantation where he now lives, with a piece joining it "which I bought from William Ray"

- continued -

son: Peter Foust "land which I bought from Old Woman Ray and her son Robert".."likewise a part of the tract I bought from James Ray from the Fayetteville Road to the Alamance".."land I bought from Old Aaron Sharp"
son: William Foust "plantation I bought from John Ray" "100 acres I bought from the heirs of the Widow Ray"
son: Henry Foust "plantation whereon I now live" and 50 acres bought from James Tinnen, & "plantation I bought from David Efland"

daughter: Catherine wife of John Clap
" Barbara " " Joseph Bason
" Sally " " Jeremiah Holt
granddau: Sally daughter "of my son John Foust Deceased", half of plantation John Foust lived on.
great-granddaughter: Barbara Catherine Albright
He owns other tracts of land which are to be sold.

Exceutors: sons George, Peter, William and Henry Foust.
Witnesses: Joseph Clendennin, John Holmes, A.D.Murphey.
All the above witnesses died, and the will was witnessed again 18 September 1833 by: Thomas Ruffin, Will K. Ruffin.

- - -

E 385 Will dated 18 January 1836, proved May Court 1836.

VINES GUYE wife: Elizabeth "to raise my children"

Children (names and number not stated) all seem to be minors.

Executors: wife Elizabeth, and James Womble.
Witnesses: Tho. Prendergast, William Miles.

- - -

E 385 Will dated 6 April 1836, proved August Court 1836.

ELIZABETH (x) KING widow of John "weak in body"

James Wyate $1 - "his son John Wyate my well-beloved grandson" (under age)
Empson Byrd $1-"his oldest sons Thomas & John Byrd $2"
Daughter Levina King and sons John and Hezekiah King "tract whereon I now live".

Executors: son John, and daughter Levina King.
Witnesses: Thomas A. Horn, Levi Truet. ...

- - -

E 386 Will dated 8 July 1836, proved August Court 1836.

DICY (x) HARRIS "weak in body" brother: William Harris

"Brother William Harris' four oldest children -- Narcissa Ann, Rufust, Mary, Lucy."

- continued -

 E 386 Will of DICY HARRIS continued

Amelia Ball, Temperance Harris, Eliz. Mangum, Nathaniel Harris

"Elenor Piper, Drady Parker, Temperance Harris, Edna Harris, Elizabeth Harris, Ducey Harris my neices."

Sole executor: nephew Williams Harris.
Witnesses: James C. Roberts.

- - -

E 387 Will dated 24 September 1824, proved August Court 1836.

EDWARD THOMAS wife: Elizabeth

sons: Neamia Thomas, Richard Thomas
"Six daughters Nelly Hollen, Hannah Cook, Nancy Hubbert *, Elizabeth Thomas, Jenney Thomas & Caty Thomas."
* (Nancy Thomas married in Orange Co. 24 March 1809 James Hub/bard.)

Executrix: wife Elizabeth.
Witnesses: D. Albright, Israel Holt.

- - -

E 388 Will dated --, proved August Court 1836.

JAMES MOORE

"The property that will fall to" daughter Patsey Smith not to be subject to any debts of Hosea Smith.

Sons Robert and John Moore to be guardians of property.
Witnesses: Jesse O'Daniel, Henry O'Daniel.

- - -

E 388-390 Will dated 16 October 1829, proved -- ?

WILLIAM KIRKLAND wife: Margaret

His estate is very involved. He is indebted to David Yarborough. He appoints his son John Kirkland and his-son-in-law Thomas Ruffin Trustees and Executors.

"My four children Alexander, Mary, Susan and Phebe"
Married daughter Martha.
He speaks of "my four younger children", it is not clear whether they are the four named above.

No witnesses.

Page 391 is blank.

E 392 Will dated 4 July 1836, proved November Court 1836.

MOSES ATWATER wife: Anney or Amey ?

sons: Gehiel, Jahaza, Wilson get lands which join James Norwood, Maderson Cook, Isham Smith. - continued -

E 392 Will of MOSES ATWATER continued
He speaks of his mill purchased from Fearington.

daughters: Lois Strowd and Celia Strowd.
"All my children (viz) Wilson, Edmund, Jahaza, Gehiel,
Lois Strowd and Celia Strowd."

Executors: sons Wilson and Jehaza.
Witnesses: J. H. Norwood, Martha Bilbow.

- - -

E 393 Will dated 4 August 1836, proved November Court 1836.

ISABEL JOHNSTON youngest daughter: Fanny

daughter: Jane Thompson
"All my children", number not stated.

Sole executor: James Johnston.
Witnesses: Ja mes Patton, Samuel Patton.

- - -

E 394 Will dated 15 November 1836, proved Nov Court 1836.

JOHN (x) MINNIS "weak of body"

son: James (he has had his part) $1
dau: Jane Taylor $1
son: William Minnis half his land joining Jos Thompson
dau: Lavinia Minnis " " " " " "
grandson: Ashburn Minnis
son: Allen Minnis $1
dau: Margaret Gant $1
"My pension if any be due" to be collected.

Executor: friend William F. Jones, and son William Minnis.
Witnesses: Samuel Jones, Alf. Nelson.

- - -

E 395 Will dated 19 October 1836, proved Nov Court 1836.

JAMES MELVIN wife: Catherine

sons: Louis, John (to be educated), James, Elias
"Four daughters Mary, Elizabeth, Nancy and Matilda."

Executors: son Elias, and Boston Iseley.
Witnesses: Julius S. Bracken, Christian Iseley,
James Melvin, Jr.

- - -

E 396-400 Will dated 5 August 1824, proved August 1836.

ANTHONY (x) THOMPSON wife: name not stated

son: Anderson Thompson
" William " land "whereon he now lives"

- continued -

son: Marmaduke Michael Thompson "land on Beaver Creek joining Barney Clap & others"
son: Anthony
Daughter Polly has had one of her hands injured. She is to have $150 more than other children.

"My children- to wit- Nancy Jane Anderson Letty William Dilly Marmaduke and Anthony and my daughter Polly."

Executrix: wife.
Witnesses: Michael Holt, Alfred A. Holt, Joel C. Yancey.

Codicil dated 7 June 1826 revokes bequest to daughter Jane, wife of John James.
Daughter Nancy has been advanced $50 "for the moving of her and her family from the State of Tennessee."
$50 to Archibald D. Murphey, who advanced this $50 to Nancy "without my consent."
Witnesses: Michael Holt, Alfred A. Holt.

— — —

E 400-401 Will dated 12 January 1836, proved Nov Court 1836.

JOHN LONG, SR. wife: Mary W. Long

son: Alphonso to continue at school until he is 18½ years old
"My store to be kept in operation", store goes to Alphonso.
"His sister Flora (Alphonso's) "
"Each of my first wife's children Nancy, John, Rebecca, Sally, Polly, Rachel" $200, with what they have already received.

Executors: "John Newlin and his son James Newlin."
Witnesses: D. Patterson, A. Shearer, Fred'k Brown.

— — —

E 402 Will dated --, proved November Court 1836.

JAMES MOORE "The property that will fall to my daughter Nancy Sykes and to the heirs of her body" not to be subject to the debts of William Sykes.
Guardians of property: sons Robert Morre and John Moore.
Witnesses: Jesse O'Daniel, Henry O'Daniel.

— — —

E 402-403 Will dated 9 February 1837, proved Feb Court 1837.

DAVID (x) STRAIN wife: Jane

son: John Strain
unmarried daughters: Sarah and Elizabeth Strain
son: William Strain

Executors: sons William and John.
Witnesses: N. I. King, J. Mullchey, David McLean.

— — —

E 404 Will dated 16 December 1836, proved Feb Court 1837.

CHARLES McCAULEY wife: Elizabeth ½ estate

son: Matthew other ½ of estate- he is to be educated
brother: Matthew McCauley 150 acres on Cub Creek and land on E side of Morgan Creek known as Brewer or Tilly land "including my saw mill"
brother: George McCauley "who now resides in the State of Tennessee"
He speaks of "wife and my family".

Executors: brother Matthew McCauley and friend Bryant Strowd.
Witnesses: Charles King, Henry McColum, John Cheek.

- - -

E 406-407 Will dated 18 December 1836, proved Feb Court 1827.

RACHEL (x) STRAYHORN widow of James

son: William Strayhorn
grandsons: Thompson and James Strayhorn
granddaughter: Rachel Strayhorn
son: John Strayhorn
dau: Polly Bowland
grandchildren: Willie Strayhorn Maleacy A. Strayhorn
sons: John Thompson, John Strayhorn

Executors: friends Andrew Bowland and Samuel Strayhorn.
Witnesses: Aaron Strayhorn, William (x) Strayhorn.

- - -

E 408 Will dated 11 January 1837, proved Feb Court 1837.

JAMES RAY, SR. legatee: Sally Daugherty

grandson: James Ray granddaughter: Elizabeth Ray
granddaughters: Polly Cole and Rosanna Jones

Executors: grandson James Ray and worthy friend Hezekiah Terry.
Witnesses: Charles Wilson, Jon R. McKee.

- - -

E 409 Will dated 12 March 1830, proved February Court 1837.

JOSEPH FREELAND wife a legatee, name not stated

sons: William and Thomas, both under age
daus: Sally and Mary, both under age

Witnesses: W.F.Hogan, James Gattis.
Executor: brother John Freeland, appointed in codicil dated December 1836.
Witnesses to codicil: W.F.Hogan, Thomas Hogan.

John J. Freeland qualified as executor.

- - -

E 410 Will dated 7 December 1836, proved Feb Court 1837.

ELIZABETH (x) Strayhorn niece: Rachel Strayhorn

nephews: Thompson and James Strayhorn
Emmely Malone
sister: Polly Bowland
"Three brothers William, John and James Strayhorn"
mother: Rachel Strayhorn

Executors: worthy friends Andrew Bowland and Bryant Strayhorn.
Witnesses: S. Strayhorn, J. S. Smith.

- - -

E 410 Will dated 12 December 1836, proved Feb Court 1837.

PHEBE (x) BARBEE

daus: Gemima Hopkins, Mary King
grandson: Francis Barbee
granddaughters- "all the daughters of Gabriel Barbee" ...
"Durcilla Nancy Noe Phebe Ann Barbee" (no punctuation)
"To Luvinia Matley 50¢ she is to have no more of my estate"
dau: Elizabeth Rencher

Executor: Gabriel Barbee.
Witnesses: Isaah Marcum, David Malone.

- - -

E 411 Will dated 13 July 1832, proved May Court 1837.

NANCY (x) CLOUD "weak of body"

daughter Martha Bailiff wife of Abner Bailiff
"My children Samuel Cloud, Martha Bailiff, Joel Cloud, Daniel Cloud, David Cloud, John Cloud, Mary Beavers and Sarah Nichols & my grandchildren Nancy Cloud daughter of Samuel, Nancy Cloud daughter of Joel, Daniel Cloud son of Joel, Daniel Bailiff son of Abner Bailiff, and Daniel Cloud son of David Cloud."
Nathaniel J. Palmer, Esq.

Executor: friend Catlett Campbell.
Witnesses: David Murdock, Matthew Futral.

- - -

E 412 Will dated 24 April 1837, proved May Court 1837.

JOHN SCARLETT wife: Scyntha

sons: Allen, Page and Henderson Scarlett
daus: Nancy, Mariah and Delilah Scarlett.
grandson: John Gaston Carrell
dau: Nancy Elizabeth Carrell

Executor: son Page Scarlett.
Witnesses: Silas M. Link, Susan McQuiston.

- - -

E 414 Will dated 6 May 1834, proved May Court 1837.

WILLIAM ROBERTS

"Five of my children- Winnefred, John, Jacob, David and Mahala" (Winnefred and Mahala are unmarried)
sons: Willis, William, Charles and Elisha
"My son Richard's two children Wesley and Eliza"

Executors: sons Jacob and John. Witness: Elisha Umstead.

– – –

E 415 Will dated 9 February 1837, proved May Court 1837.

DAVID (x) McCROREY "sick in body"

son: David "my plantation adjoining Wm. Faucett, ... Sellers, James Mebane .."
son: William
"brother John McCrorey's son Thomas McCrorey"

Executor: "Anderson Thompson, true and faithful friend."
Witnesses: Samuel Tate, Thomas McCrorey.

– – –

E 416 Will dated 30 July 1834, proved May Court 1837.

NATHAN (x) HARVEY "my advanced age" wife: Agness

son: Anthony
daus: Mary and Elizabeth
son: Isaac

Executor: "worthy friend Samuel Woody".
Witnesses: John Newlin, Z. Bingham, Elenor Guthrie.

– – –

E 417 Will dated 3 January 1833, proved May Court 1837.

STEPHEN WARD wife: all estate during her life

Stephen Ward son of William Ward
" Pike " " William Pike
" Elliott son of Abraham Elliott
" Wells " " Nathan Wells
} $50 each
" Moon " " James Moon $25
Leah Siler wife of Jeremiah Siler $100

Remainder of estate in 7 equal parts to: 1 part to Susannah Ward's children, 1 part to William Ward's children, 1 part to ..?.ster Wells' children, 1 part to Priscilla Free, 1 part to James Ward's children, 1 part to Thomas Ward's children, 1 part to Antony Ward.

Executors: John Long,Jr., and Benjamin Way.
Witnesses: A. Shearer, Geo. C. Mendenhall.

– – –

E 418 Will dated 29 July 1836, proved May Court 1837.

SALLY MITCHELL

"My graddaughter Frances E. Potter daughter of Thomas Potter late of the County of Granville deceased" (Frances is a minor). "My granddaughter Caroline Mildred Pratt daughter of Moses S. Pratt late of Orange County deceased" (Caroline is a minor). "My daughter-in-law Caroline Mitchell widow of my son James" "Granddaughters Lucy and Martha Mitchell daughters of Robert B. Mitchell deceased."

Executors: "James Mallory late of the County of Granville in this State but more recently of the State of Alabama", and friend John Hutchins of Orange County.
Witnesses: J. W. McGee, John Hutchins.

- - -

E 420 Will dated 30 April 1835, proved August Court 1837.

ROBERT KING "aged and infirm"

son: Benjamin King
"To heirs of my daughter Foster $1"
dau: Rebecca Walker wife of Philip Walker $1
" Nancy Wallis " " Peter Wallis $1
" Sally Barber
" Clarecy Faucett wife of Robert Faucett

Executors: son-in-law Robert Faucett and friend James Grahams.
Witnesses: William Barber, Nathan Findley.

- - -

E 421 Will dated 10 July 1837, proved May Court 1837.

ELIZABETH (x) SNIPES Willis Snipes $1

Mary Shelby wife of John Shelby $1
Sarah Masey " " Lonnie ? Masey $1
Dempsey Snipes $1, Oren Snipes $1

Thomas Snipes and Robert Snipes, Martha Snipes and Elizabeth Snipes get proceeds of sale of "my land in Chatham County".

Executors: friends Thomas M. Durham and James Rosser.
Witnesses: James Lloyd, Mary Lloyd.

- - -

E 422 Will dated 27 April 1837, proved August Court 1837.

JOHN (x) DANIEL "advanced in age" wife: Susannah

After wife's death property to: "David Carlton & Nancy his wife & their sons William & Henry & daughters Margaret Marcum and Nancy Leigh " ..
"Henry Trice Sr ... during his life and at his death to Henry Pearson". Henry's daughter Amelia Trice, his son Page Trice , his daughter Sarah Lynn, his daughter Frances, son Henry Trice,

daughter Susannah."
"To my grandson John Carlton" the Patterson tract of land.
"To John Couch's three children he had by Susannah Carlton" $100 each.
"To Wesley Carlton's three children , $100 a piece"
"grandson Page Trice" 150 acres .. "where he now lives"
" Henry Trice "balance of my land"
" William Carlton
granddaughter Elizabeth Marcum

"Daniel Carlton guardian for John Couch's and Wesley Carlton's children as to the money I left them."

Executors: Henry Trice Sr. and Daniel Carlton.
Witnesses: R. Henslee, Mark (x) Pickett, Joseph White.

- - -

E 424 Will dated 7 July 1837, proved August Court 1837.

WILLIAM (x) STRAYHORN

Mother-in-law is to take his "children to raise them."
Children are to be "schooled." Names and number not stated.

Executor: William Duskin or "Heart or my brother Aaron".
Witnesses: E. Strudwick, Walter A. Norwood.

- - -

E 425 Will dated 30 June 1837, proved August Court 1837.

JOSHUA (x) THOMPSON daughter: Polly Thompson

son: James Thompson
dau: Patsy Curry wife of William Curry
" Ruth Thompson wife of James Thompson

Executors: son James Thompson, and Richard Tapp.
Witnesses: Geo. W. Bruce, W. H. Thompson, Abel Thompson.

- - -

E 426 Will dated 9 October 1834, proved August Court 1837.

SAMUEL NELSON, planter. daughter: Ibby Allen

son: David Nelson (of Tennessee)
dau: Betsey Stephens (of Tenn.) "three slaves she received from me when sheremoved to Tennessee"
daus: Peggy Dunn, Ginney
sons: George, Samuel
"Samuel Allen son of my daughter Ibby"

Executor: son George. Witnesses: Alf Nelson, James A. Craig.

- - -

E 428-429 and here the number skips to 500.
Will dated 14 May 1837, proved August Court 1837.

ENOCH McPHERSON wife: Sarah - continued -

dau: Sarah
" Mary Dask ? "land I purchased of John Pyle"
son: Eli "the Nall place"
"Grandchildren the children of my son James, by name Enoch John Aren William & Wright".
dau: Phebe "the Dowdy place"
He frees his two slaves.

Sole executor: son William McPherson.
Witnesses: James McPherson, Isaac Andrew, John Davis.

- - -

E 501 Will dated 24 February 1837, proved August Court 1837.

LEWIS (x) HORNADAY wife: Dinah

son: William "plantation on which he is now living" and Cotner place.
son: John land "known as the Dale plantation"
Brother: Simon shall have the benefit of the Pike plantation for three years.
daus: Susannah Foust, Polly Stafford, Ruth Wells, Rebecca Hill, Hester Alexander
sons: Simon, Ezekiel
son: Lewis "the Dixon place"
Dinah Marshall

Executors: son William Hornaday and friend William Thompson.
Witnesses: John McPherson, R. Freeman.
Codicil made orally during his last illness 25 August 1837.
Witnesses: Henry Stout, Dinah (x) Hornaday.

- - -

E 508-509 Will dated 11 July 1833, proved November Court 1837.

DAVID WHITE wife: Betsy

grandchildren: David White Kerr, Margaret Graham Kerr
son-in-law: Samuel Kerr
Fanny White daughter of Samuel White
John Allen son of Alexander Allen

Executors: son-in-law Samuel Kerr, and brother-in-law Alexander Allen. Witness: James A. Craig.

- - -

E 509 Will dated 18 August 1837, proved Nov Court 1837.

REBECCA (x) BIRD Son, James J. Bird, to be educated.

Executor: James Bird. Witness: Thomas Reeves.

- - -

Book E has been re-bound, and the last few pages are badly scrambled, hence the confusion in page numbers here.

E 503-505 Will dated 6 January 1837, proved August 1837

ALFRED MOORE "of Moorefields"

"My son-in-law Francis Nash Waddell of the State of Louisiana" whole estate. Waddell has looked after the affairs of testator during his long illness.
Sister, Sarah Moore to have use of Moorefields plantation in Orange County, she is unmarried. His daughters, Augusta, Emma and Caroline (all unmarried) to live with their Aunt Sarah at Moorefields.

Sole executor: son-in-law Francis Nash Waddell.
No witnesses. The will was found among his valuable papers 1 August 1837, after his death.

- - -

E 505 Will dated 31 January 1837, proved Nov Court 1837.

SAMUEL THOMPSON wife: Elizabeth

daughter: Rebecca Cloud
sons: William, Solomon and David Thompson
Daughter Nancy Sytayhorn is not of sound mind.
granddaughter: Rachel Strayhorn
dau: Rachel Lindley

Executors: wife Elizabeth, and son Solomon.
Witnesses: J. Allison, John McDade.

- - -

E 507 Will dated 25 October 1837, proved Nov Court 1837.

ANDREW WILLIAMS, Blacksmith wife: Phebe

He speaks of his blacksmith shop at Staggsville.

"My children", number not stated.
Daughters, Sally, Matildy and Annis to have beds they have / made.

Executor: James Leathers.
Witnesses: P. C. Cameron, Fendal Southerland.

- - -

E 510 Will dated 17 July 1837, proved November Court 1837.

RALPH (x) FAUCETT, SR. wife: Martha

daus: Sarah Weedon, Emelia Wilson
son: William Faucett
daus: Martha Wilson, Charity Dickey, Rachel
sons: Ralph Faucett, Bracken Faucett
dau: Clarissa (unmarried)

Executor: friend Robert Gillam.
Witnesses: Robert Faucett, Snelson Love.

- - -

E 511 Will dated 1823, proved Nov Court 1837.

GEORGE (x) THOMAS

sons: William Thomas $1, Josiah Thomas $3
daughter Mary Thomas to have all his lands
" Elizabeth to live with Mary

Executors: Sam'l Crawford and John McCauley.
Witnesses: A. McCauly , Joseph Tate.

- - -

E 512 Will dated 15 May 1834, proved November Court 1837.

ANDREW BURNS "weak and infirm" wife: Martha

eldest son: William Burns gets "Blackwood tract" of land
son: Samuel Burns "land joining Alex. Craig ... David Strayhorn's line"
son: Andrew Johnson Burns land joining Wm Robson and Mary / Flintoff
dau: Margaret Mitchell Burns (unmarried)
" Mary Strain wife Alex Strain

Executors: sons William and Samuel Burns.
Witnesses: C. W. Johnston, William Duskin, John Boroughs.

END OF BOOK E

BOOK F, page 1 Will dated 9 Sept 1837, proved Feb Court 1938.

JOHN SHAW

Daughters Jane Walker, Elinor Street, Kitty Armstrong, Clarissa Crawford, Verlinda D. Vincent.
sons: John W. Shaw, William V. Shaw, Joseph W. Shaw
John W gets land he lives on, on Jordan Creek ... corner of William Cantrell's line and the land he bought from Anderson Watson .. another tract on West side of big branch running with James Walkers' line
Joseph W gets land on S side of Jordan Creek near Connaly Walker's .. to Gibson's corner ..., etc
William W ... land joining Samuel Couch.. and Rachel Walker

Executors: son John W. Shaw, and son-in-law James Walker of Caswell County.
Witnesses: Obediah Hurdle, John Squires, Edmisten ? Love.

- - -

F 3 Will dated 5 September 1837, proved Feb Court 1838.

LYSIAS DURHAM

daughters: Tabitha Gear, Mary Jane (a minor), Susannah L.
sons: David, Dudley, Tarleton

Executors: friends Wilson Atwater, Manly Snipes.
Witnesses: R. C. Poe, Antho. Durham.

- - -

F 4 Will dated 9 September 1837, proved Feb Court 1838.

ANN PHILLIPS   son: Benjamin

daus: Polly, Hannah, Rachel
daughter Lucretia is non compos mentis- she is to live with brother-in-law Boston Iseley and his wife. Her share to go to Boston Iseley and Rachel.

Executor: Boston Iseley.
Witnesses: Jesse Thompson, John Lewis, Abner (x) James.

- - -

F 6 Will dated 18 December 1837, proved Feb Court 1838.

DELILAH RHODES

"Son Zachariah Rhodes' three children (viz) Lowry Jane, Cozby Ann, Claudeus Jasper"

children: Sarah Hutchins, George W. Rhodes, Dicey Rhodes, Caroline Jane Rhodes, Penney Patteshall, Mary Hurley, Delilah Patteshall, Milley Smith.

Son William Rhodes' children"

Witnesses: Samuel Couch, Wm. Trice, Jr.
The above will does not state that these are her children, but papers in the equity suit for distribution of the estate give all the relationships. Delilah is the widow of William Rhodes, and the daughter of George Herndon and Sarah. See D70.

- - -

F 7 Will dated 3 July 1838, proved August Court 1838.

ANN WILKERSON   sons: James, Francis & John Wilkerson

daus: Frances Wilkerson, Polly Wilkerson, Nancy Pickett, Margaret McDaniel, Elizabeth Wilkerson

Executors: son Francis Wilkerson, and John Wilkerson.
Witnesses: William Wilkerson, Robert G. Tinnen.

- - -

F 8 Will dated 23 December 1836, proved August Court 1828.

SAMUEL McCRACKEN   sons: John and Thomas

Executors: son Thomas McCracken, and James Tate.
Witnesses: Sam'l N. Tate, Thomas Squires.

- - -

F 8 Will dated 15 December 1837, proved August Court 1838.

JAMES TATE

son: David "home plantation at present occupied by Chas Cox"
sons: George and Samuel N. Tate   - continued -

 F 8 Will of JAMES TATE continued
George Marlet (no relationship stated)
son-in-law: John Squires
Thomas Gill "$70 to be paid by my son Sam'l N. Tate"

Executor: son Samuel N. Tate.
Witnesses: C. C. Smith, Thomas McCracken.

- - -

F 9 Will dated 22 June 1838, proved August Court 1838.

WILLIAM SUTHERLAND Mother: Mary A. Sutherland

Executor: William Cain of Hillsboro.
Witnesses: George W. Jones, Menerva R. Cain.

- - -

F 10 Will dated 7 November 1837, proved May Court 1838.

JOSEPH (x) FENNELL (or FERRELL ?)

"To my five daughters namely Betsy Williams, Patsy Lester, Nancy Kelley, Catherine W. Castleberry, Sally S. Lewter, what they have received" and $1 each.
Daughter Patience F. Fennell, all estate.

Executrix: Patience F. Fennell.
Witnesses: Henry Moring, John S. Moring.

- - -

F 11 Will dated 11 March 1837, proved May Court 1838.

MARTHA RAY "wife of George Ray, deceased"

dau: Martha Ann wife of Anderson Jackson
daus: Delila Nickols, Polly Jackson, Jenny Collins
To friend James Jackson (of James) in trust "for my daughter Sally Hopkins, wife of Cuza Hopkins" ...
sons-in-law: Bradley Collins and Cuza Hopkins $1 each
sons: Michael Ray, James Collins
granddaughters: Martha A. Collins and Martha D. Hopkins

Executor: James Jackson (of James).
Witnesses: Levi Whitted, Thos. W. Holden.

- - -

F 13 Will dated 10 December 1837, proved May Court 1838.

ISAAC CANTRELL wife: Rutha

"Children", number and names not stated.

Executrix: wife Tutha Cantrell.
Witnesses: John Tapscott, Joseph Simpson, George W. Taylor.

- - -

F 14 Will dated 10 May 1834, proved May Court 1838.

EZEKIEL VEAZEY of Granville County wife: Frances

daughters: Mealey Jarrot and Thersday (?)
son: Leonard
Other children he does not name.

Executors: son Edward Veazey, and friend Elijah Hester.
Witnesses: William Veazey, John C. Veazey.

- - -

F 16 Will dated 12 July 1838, proved November Court 1838.

JOHN PATTON

Sisters Margaret and Elizabeth to live on home plantation. "Andrew Patton to have a support as long as he continues with them."

Executor: friend John Thompson.
Witnesses: Stephen Scarlett, John Hamilton.

- - -

F 17 Will dated 12 July 1838, proved February Court 1839.

THOMAS MARCOM

sons: Nathan, Isaiah, Thomas.
"Son Edmond's children, William and Henderson M. Marcom."
granddaughters: Mary Moring and Nancy Marcom.
dau: Elizabeth Carlton
daus: Amelia Dodd, Celia Cates, Polly Shepherd, Patsey Williams
Lewis Caudle (no relationship stated)

Executors: sons Isaiah and Nathan Marcum.
Witnesses: Cornelius (x) Cook, Benj. Marcom.
This family and descendants are given in HERNDONS OF THE AMERICAN REVOLUTION, PART FOUR, See last page in this book.

- - -

F 19 Will dated 7 December 1838, proved Feb Court 1839.

WILLIAM TRICE, SR. wife: Frances

sons: Zachariah, William, James
dau: Penny
granddaughter: Penny Dillard
Willis Dillard "land adjoining Widow Daniel... to repay him cost of Philpot and Barbee debts which he paid as security for my son James Trice."

Executors: sons Zachariah and William Trice.
Witnesses: Richard Henslee, F. Bilbo.

- - -

F 21 Will dated 12 December 1832, proved Feb Court 1839.

LETTY (x) NEECE

"My oldest daughter Milly" ... "balance of my girls"
son: Elias
Powel Anthony, Eli Sharp, Polly, Prisee (relationship not stated)
Executors: Powel Anthony, Eli Sharp.
Witnesses: Hiram Steel, Isaac Sharp.

- - -

F 22 Will dated 18 December 1838, proved May Court 1839.

REBECCA MONTGOMERY daughter: Lydia Woods

sons: Hamilton, Hugh, James, Alexander

Executor: son Hamilton Montgomery.
Witnesses: John Woods, James T. Roberts.

- - -

F 23 Will dated 9 June 1839, proved August Court 1839.

ANDREW McCAULY wife: Mary

daughter: Jane Long
niece: Martha Nobel tract including the place where John Fitch ? now lives"
John Nobel (note on George & James Graham); Robert Nobel
niece: Mary Nobel (note on Gabriel B. Lea)
son: Johnson McCauly tract adjoining Margaret Watson

ExecutorsL Johnson McCauly and John Nobel Jr.
Witnesses: Robert Fausett, C. F. Faucette.

- - -

F 25 Will dated 30 May 1839, proved August Court 1839.

JOANNA FARTHING "widow of Reuben Farthing"

sons: Hargis Farthing, Thomas Farthing, John Farthing
dau: Nancy Watkins Farthing
sons: William Farthing, Abner Farthing.

Executors: William Farthing and Abner Farthing.
Witnesses: Harris Wilkerson, I. Gooch.

- - -

F 26 Will dated 16 March 1832, proved August Court 1839.

WILLIAM BROWN wife: Ruth

dau: Ann Brown granddaughter: Polly Ann Cabe
sons: Mathew, John, William, Jehu, and Allen Brown

Executors: sons Mathew Brown and Allen Brown.
Witnesses: Daniel Wilkerson, John Wilkerson.

- - -

F 28 Will dated 27 May 1839, proved August Court 1839.

WILLIAM HORNADAY wife: Mary

son: Alfred plantation that formerly belonged to Christopher Hornaday
son: Balam home plantation, "including land devised to me by my brother Lewis Hornaday deceased."
minor daughters: Anna, Hester, Jemima, Mary Ann, Ruth Elinor
daus: Sally, Rebecca

Executors: son Alfred Hornaday, and friend Wm. Thompson.
Witnesses: Jer. Piggott, B. Adams.

\- - -

F 29 Will dated 25 May 1835, proved November Court 1839.

JAMES HART

son: Samuel land "where he now lives on E side of Raleigh Rd.
sons: David, William, James
daus: Betsy, Miriam, Jane
grandchildren: Sarah Strayhorn James Strayhorn
sons: John, Gilbert, Samuel

Executors: son David Hart, and friend Catlett Campbell.
Witnesses: A. Mivkle, John U. Kirkland.

\- - -

F 31 Will dated 19 February 1838, proved Nov Court 1839.

JAMES HERNDON wife: Mary M. Herndon

son: Maturine C. Herndon "part of tract bought ftom Robert Campbell and a lso the Hall tract"
son: Coslett M(axwell) Herndon
daus: Elizabeth Carlton, Terminia Herndon, Nancy Barbee
grandson: Lorenzo J. Vann
"Children of my son James" $1

Executors: Thomas Bilbo, Anderson Ferrell.
Witnesses: Aquilla Herndon, Sullivan Leigh.
James Herndon was a son of George and Sarah Herndon. See D70.

\- - -

F 33 Will dated 17 August 1839, proved November Court 1839.

WILLIAM TAYLOR

eldest son: Harrison Taylor "plantation called Faucett place"
" dau: Nancy Taylor
second son: Henderson Taylor
" dau: Juda Betsy Taylor

Executor: Harrison Taylor
Witnesses: William Bowls, Hugh Woods.

\- - -

F 34 Will dated 8 March 1837, proved November Court 1839.

WILLIAM L. DURHAM

son: Archibald Durham "children of my son Thomas"
"granddaughter Nancy Durham wife of Mark Durham"
"children of son Isaac Durham deceased"
" " " daughter Susannah Jolley deceased"
" " " daughter Frances Lacy deceased"
"My five sons: Archibald, Isaiah, William, John and Thomas"

Executors: "three sons Archibald Durham, William Durham, John Durham". Witnesses: R. C. Poe, B. Strowd.

- - -

F 35 Will dated 27 July 1835, proved November Court 1839.

HARDEMAN DUKE

Daughter Betsy and her husband John Duke - after Betsy's death her children to have her part.

Executors: trusty friends Willie P. Mangum, John Moize.
Witnesses: Benjamin Hester, Charity A. Mangum, William P. Mangum.

- - -

F 38 Will dated 17 January 1834, proved Nov Court 1839.

THOMAS LLOYD wife: Delilah

sons: Sidney S. Lloyd, Thomas M. Lloyd
"two youngest sons Lorren O. Lloyd, Atlas J. Lloyd"
daughters: "Sintha Hunter and her children"
Elizabeth Lloyd, "Frances Barbee and her children", Cornelia A. Lloyd, Sephonia C. Lloyd
Testator's land is on Phill's Creek.

Executors: wife Delilah, and sons Sidney S. and Thomas M. Lloyd.
Witnesses: B. Strowd, Henry McCollum, Hasten Poe.

- - -

F 41 Will dated --, proved -- JAMES MILES or MILER ?

Wife: Nancy Miles No witnesses or executor.

- - -

F 42 Will dated 7 January 1840, proved Feb Court 1840.

ELI WOODS wife: Margaret R. Woods

son: John Washington Woods
daus: Lucy Ann Woods, Ellen Woods, Margaret Ray Woods, Adaline Woods, Elizabeth Brown Woods

Executors: wife Margaret R. Woods, and Samuel Turrentine.
Witnesses: Hezekiah Terry, Charles Wilson.

- - -

F 43 Will dated 4 January 1840, proved Feb Court 1840.

JAMES BARBER wife: Ellen

daughters: Sarah Jane, Mary Ann
friend: Samuel Ellett

Executor: John W. Wilson.
Witnesses: Nathan Findley, A. N. Watson.

- - -

F 45 Will dated 28 November 1839, proved Feb Court 1840.

JAMES PATTEN wife: Elenor

"All my children, namely, Samuel, Margaret, James, Jane, Isabel, Johnston, Mary, George, Nancy, Elenor, William and Alexander." "Younger children shall get as much schooling as the older ones have had."

Executors: Wife Elenor, and James Johnston.
Witnesses: Alexander Patton, Sam'l King.

- - -

F 46 Will dated 11 July 18 , proved February Court 1840.

JESSE MILLER wife: Margaret

"Jesse Miller and other five children".... not named.

Executor: Henry Whitted.
Witnesses: A. C. Murdock, Alvis Nichols.

- - -

F 47 Will dated 7 October 1839, proved Feb Court 1840.

MARY A . PALMER

sons: James N. Palmer, Nathaniel Palmer, John C. Palmer.

No executor. Witnesses: Thomas Fawcett, R. W. Lassiter.

- - -

F 48 Will dated 11 April 1840, proved May Court 1840.

HENRY (x) TRICE sons: Chesley P. Trice, Henry D. Trice

daughters: Nanny Pearson, Frances Trice, Amelia Trice,
Elizabeth Marcum, Sarah Lynn

Executors: Chesley P. Trice and son-in-law William Pearson.
Witnesses: James N. Patterson, David Vickers.

- - -

F 50 Will dated 21 March 1839, proved May Court 1840.

EUPHENCE B. KERR son: Samuel Kerr

daughters: Eliza Jane Kerr, Susan Kerr (both under 18 ?)
She speaks of "the boys" but names only one son, Samuel.

Executors: "trusty friends Samuel Kerr and James Whitsett."
Witnesses: Austin Whitsett, John McJean ?.

- - -

F 51 Will dated 26 February 1840, proved May Court 1840.

ELEANOR HOPKINS son: Gilbert

daughters: Bashaba, Mary.

Executors: two daughters Bashaba and Mary.
Witnesses: Nathaniel Harris, Oxford Moize.

- - -

F 52 Will dated 19 January 1835, proved May Court 1840.

STEPHEN JUSTICE (The name is spelled Justus in the will, but is signed Justice. I have checked the original will in the Archives, writing very bad.)

wife: Anna

"Beloved friend Stephen Pleasants" gets a slave.
"Stephen Farthing son of William Farthing deceased" $100.
"To the children of Elder William Worel (?) deceased" $200.
Heirs of my two brothers Davy and Allen Justus $300.
" " " sister Kyer (?) or Lizy (?) Robertson $300.
" " " sister-in-law Mary Lloyd (?) Floyd (?) deceased
Matildy Perry $100
William Roberts, son of Paschal Roberts $100
Stephen Brown $300, Phelemon Lacy $300
$1000 to foreign missions

Executors: Anna Justus, and Stephen Pleasants, Sr.
Witnesses: Thomas Weaver, William Roberts.

- - -

F 53 Will dated 17 October 1839, proved May Court 1840.

HENRY FOUST wife: Caroline R. Foust

sons: Robert M. Foust, William M. Foust

Executor: brother-in-law William M. Mebane.
Witnesses: William Holt, Mich'l Wm. Holt.

- - -

F 54 Will dated 18 April 1840, proved August Court 1840.

JANE ALLEN sons: John Allen, Alexandrico

daughter: Mary Jane Executor: John Scott.
Witnesses: James White, Thomas Lashley.

- - -

F 56 Will dated 21 June 1840, proved August Couty 1840.

JOHN (x) CHRISTOPHER wife: Pollay

sons: James Christopher "my Finley tract"; John Christopher
grandsons: "Pollay Stuerts two sons John C. Stewart, Calvin B. Stewart"
other children: Elizabeth Compton, Jane Scott, Nancy Christopher, Sideny Smith, Frances Ward, Eliza Ward, Matty Christopher.

Executor: Thomas Lynch. Witnesses: James Ward, Empson Walker.

- - -

F 57 Will dated 18 October 1838, proved August Court 1840.

MARY (x) WILBOURN sons: Nolen Hampton, John Hampton

grandson: Noah, son of Nolen

Executors: John Hampton and Allen Waller.
Witnesses: Wm. J. Roberts, G. Hopkins.

- - -

F 58 Will dated 22 May 1838, proved August Court 1840.

JOHN (x) POOL, SR. daughter: Sarah

sons: Isaac Pool, John Samuel

Executor: Lewis Hutchins.
Witnesses: Harris Wilkerson, Thos. W. Gooch.

- - -

F 59 Will dated 28 August 1837, proved August Court 1840.

HENRY ALBRIGHT son: Joseph Albright

daughters: Catheron, Elizabeth, Polly

Executors: "my sons, Nickolas and Joseph."
Witnesses: Levin Wood, Daniel Coble.

- - -

F 60 Will dated 6 March 1838, proved August Court 1840.

GEORGE NEASE wife: Molly

sons: Jacob, Sampson, Anson, George
daughters: Sally and Polly

Exceutor: Jacob Nease.
Witnesses: Mich. Holt, Edwin N. Holt, W. A. Carrigan.

- - -

F 62 DAVID McCRORY No date, proved August Court 1840.

son: James daughter: Mary Jane
brother-in-law John Albert

Executor: James Johnston. Witnesses: Giles Mebane, Robt. S. White

- - -

F 63 Will dated 5 April 1840, proved August Court 1840.

SAMUEL WILSON wife: Elizabeth

sons: Charles and John, plantation after wife's death
son: Felix "plantation where he now lives"
His two other plantations known as the Turner place and the Ray place to be rented.
daughters: Sally Roundtree, Elizabeth Dickson,
Nancy Nichols, Harriet Walker.
"My three daughters now in the west: Lotty Cates, Jane Taylor and Polly Roland (or Robards ?)".

Executors: sons Charles and John Wilson.
Witnesses: Jas. Holeman, Alex. Robinson.

- - -

F 65 Will dated 14 December 1827, proved August Court 1840.

JOHN SOUTHWARD daughters: Sally, Polly, Tempey

sons: Macklen Southward, Gilliam, Charles, James, Carter, John
"My sons Macklen and James guardians for my son John".

Executors: sons Macklen and James.
Witnesses: James Moore, Daniel Barnet.

- - -

F 68 Will dated 23 June 1840, proved August Court 1840.

JOSHUA JOHNSON wife: Sarah

sons: Hiram, and Calvin (youngest, under 21)
dau: Anna Johnson
" Mary, wife of Joseph Haskins "land on Deep River in Guilford County whereon my sister now resides".
daus: Susanna, Lydia

Testator owns a tannery in Chatham County with Wm. Albright. He owns mills in Guilford County, and stock in Cain Creek Cotton Factory.

Executors: Joseph Huskins, Calvin Johnson, Anna Johnson.
Witnesses: Jno Long, Jesse Hargrave.

- - -

E 72 Will dated 26 May 1840, proved November Court 1840.

WILLIAM MORTON wife: Sarah

sons: Benjamin F. Morton, Jacob Morton, Henry H. (under 21)
daughter: Martha Morton
Joseph Gillam , husband of daughter Mary deceased $5.

Executor: son Benjamin F. Morton.
Witnesses: James Hicks, Lemuel W. Simpson.

- - -

F 72 Will dated 5 October 1840, proved Nov Court 1840.

GEORGE KEEK or KECK ? wife: Polly

son: George Alexander
"All my children", number not stated, they all seem to be minors.

Executors: wife Polly, and William A Carrigan.
Witnesses: Jonathan Job, John C. Troxler.

- - -

F 76 Will dated 23 May 1839, proved November Court 1840.

JOSEPH ARMSTRONG

wife: Peggy, is to receive numerous items, including "settee now in the possession of James B. Leathers" also "all my right in the sale of the Jonathan Watson lands". He speaks of "her own four children or her grandchildren."
daughters: Mary Ann Parker, Parthenia Leathers, Nancy Coggin
This is a long will, many pieces of land are devised, and many slaves.His father was William Armstrong.

Executors: Jesse P. Parker, George T. Coggin, John B.Leathers.
Witnesses: Andrew Gray, S.C.M. Gray, Wm. J. Gray, Enos Ross.

- - -

F 80 Will dated 23 August 1838, proved Nov Court 1840 ?

JOHN HENDERSON wife: Frances

sons: Pleasant, Thomas, James, and John Henderson
daughters: Elizabeth Pearson, Sarah Perry, Dicey Perry, Martha Henderson, Eliza C. Henderson.
"Heirs of daughter Polly Stowers"

Witnesses: A. W. Clemebts, John D. Carlton.
Executrix: wife Frances Henderson.

- - -

F 82 Will dated 20 May 1835, proved November Court 1840.

SARAH FREEMAN (This will is not in the State Archives.)

husband: Richard Freeman, land in Chatham County on Rocky River.

Executor: John Newlin. Witnesses: John Pope, M. H. Britt.

- - -

F 83 Will dated 26 May 1840, proved Feb Court 1841.

ABNER (x) MASSEY (this will is very confusingly worded.)

sons: William Massey $1, Armon
married daughters: Christilly Prosper ?, Corrinda Chancery $1
other children John Massey, Hardy Massey, Joel (under 21), Kellister Massey, Valinia or Lavinia Massey, Louisey Massey, Miriam Massey" $118 debt due me by John Massey to be paid to the seven children named above.

"I will that my seven children single stay together until Joel Massey becomes 21."

Executors: sons John Massey and Armon Massey.
Witnesses: S. W. Fowler, Thos. R. Shepherd.

- - -

F 84 Will dated 11 January 1839, proved Feb Coyrt 1841.

ZERNAH HOBSON widow

daughters: Lydia Hadley, Peninah Hobson, Emily Hobson.
"Peninah to have the motherly care of my young daughter Emily Hobson."

Executor: friend Frederick Stafford.
Witnesses: Wm. Thompson, Peninah Hobson, John Thompson.

- - -

F 86 Will dated 12 February 1834, codicil dated 14 Feb 1837, proved February Court 1841.

ISBELL (x) THOMPSON

daus: Fanny, Hannah, Ellen Barlow
son: Richard
"to Phebe Clancy"

Executor: friend James Webb.
Witnesses: Wm. Norwood, John Bylers ?.

- - -

F 87 Will dated 14 March 1841, proved May Court 1841.

DRURY (x) JEFFRAS wife: Sylvia

sons: Andrew, Eaton, Stephen, Henry, Addison - continued -

daughters: Betsy, Sylvia, Partha, Tempy Corn, Polly Burnett.

Willy Corn (grandson ?) granddaughter: Peggy Jeffrass

Executors: Andrew Jeffrass, Eaton Jeffrass.
Witnesses: Hugh Jeffrass, Charles Jeffrass.

- - -

F 89 Will dated 1 November 1833, proved May Court 1841.

JOSEPH KIRKLAND, SR. son: Joseph King

daughters: Ann King, Elizabeth, Jinney Strayhorn
"Children of deceased son William: Samuel Kirkland, Joseph Kirkland, Johnston Kirkland, William and John Kirkland, Peggy Kirkland, Betsy Kirkland, Isabel Kirkland."
granddaughters: Margaret King and Jinney King
grandchildren: Mary, Peggy and Patsy Craig

Executors: Charles W. Johnston and Joseph Kirkland.
Witnesses: Alex. Gattis, C. W. Johnston, Thomas Gattis.

- - -

F 92 Will dated 29 March 1826, proved May Court 1841.

LAZARUS TILLEY wife: Elizabeth

sons: John and Thomas $1 each

Executrix: wife Elizabeth.
Witnesses: Wm. Horner, Robert Edwards, Willie P: Mangum.

- - -

F 93 Will dated 25 January 1841, proved August Court 1841.

WILLIAM LEIGH brother: Richard Leigh

sister: Susan Trice
The will mentions that testator's wife was a daughter of David George.

Executor: father, name not stated. Witness: S. W. Fowler.

- - -

F 94 Will dated 15 January 1837, proved August Court 1841.

MARY (x) GRAHAM daughter: Mary Garretson

grandson: John Graham, son of James
"Mary Graham, daughter of my son George"

Executor: son James. Witnesses: Thomas Reeves, Wm. Hamilton.
At date of probate, the witnesses having removed from the State, the will was proved by Chesley F. Faucett, Esq., and Lemuel Lynch.

- - -

F 96 Will dated 12 June 1841, proved August Court 1841.

MARGARET J. McDADE Father: John McDade, Sr.

Mother: Lavinia relationship not stated: Lucinda McDade

Executor: John McDade. Witnesses: Ast. Moore.

- - -

F 97 Will dated 1 September 1828, proved August Court 1841.

HENRY BRANNOCK, SR. wife: Elizabeth

sons: William, Henry, Edmund, James, Wright, Thomas
daughter: Sarah

Executors: Henry Brannock and Edmund Brannock.
Witnesses: John Foster, Alex. N. Brannock, William Makins.
Codicil dated 6 May 1833, after the death of Henry.

- - -

F 100 Will dated 12 September 1834, proved August Court 1841.

THOMAS TATE daughters: Ann and Ginny

son: Samuel Tate granddaughter: Luiza

Executor: son Samuel. Witnesses: Joseph Tate, Samuel Tate.

- - -

F 101 Will dated 4 January 1841, proved August Court 1841.

ABNER TATE sister: Alsa Tate brother: Jesse Tate

Executor: brother Jesse. Witnesses: Andrew Ross, David Barber.

- - -

F 102 Will dated 18 November 1836, proved August Court 1841.

THOMAS THOMPSON wife: Elizabeth

son: John son-in-law: William Thompson
"All my children", number and names not stated.

Executor: son John Thompson.
Witnesses: W. Bradshaw, Jno. Thompson.

- - -

F 104 Will dated 9 January 1840, proved August Court 1841.

CHRISTOPHER (x) HORNADAY John Tague ? (Teague ?)

"The four daughters of John Tague (?): Polly, Patty, Kisiah, and Jemiah"
"The four sons of John Tague: Isiah, William, Christopher, Edward," $25 each.
sons: John, Solomon, Samuel, Isaiah Hornaday. - continued -

grandson: Christopher, son of John Hornaday $100
" Daniel, son of Isaiah Hornaday $25
granddaughter: Priscilah, daughter of Isaiah $25

Executor: friend David Patterson, Sr.
Witnesses: John Foust, Benj. Way, Weston (x) Low (or Law).

- - -

F 106 Will dated 22 October 1840, proved Nov Court 1841.

EDWIN G. (or T) THOMPSON wife: Eliza

son: George Sidney Thompson

Executrix: wife Eliza.
Witnesses: James N. Thompson, Wm. Pickard.

- - -

F 107 Will dated 4 April 1837, proved Nov Court 1841.

SAMUEL SCOTT wife: Nancy

sons: John Scott, Henderson Scott
daughters: Jane Allen, Fanny Scott and Hannah Murphy
granddaughter: Nancy Scott "daughter of my son John Scott"
"Fanny Allen, daughter of Alexander Allen deceased"
Executors: John Scott, Henderson Scott.
Witnesses: John Trolinger, Benjamin Trolinger.

- - -

F 110 Will dated 13 April 1841, proved November Court 1841.

JESSE (x) JAMES, SR. son: Thomas James

wife: Elizabeth "tract whereon I now live"

Other heirs: William James, Milly Redmon, Sarah Rhodes, George James, Elizabeth Dollar, Jesse James, Rebecca Rhodes, Russell James, Riley James, Polly Baldwin.
"To the children of my son Thomas James $1."

Executor: "trusty friend James Latta, Sr."
Witnesses: Silas M. Link, John Holloway, Jr.

- - -

F 112 Will dated 17 August 1841, proved Nov Court 1841.

HANNAH KIRKPATRICK sons: Joseph, Paisley

daughter-in-law: Nancy Kirkpatrick
granddaughters: Hannah Kirkpatrick, Elizabeth Kirkpatrick, Caroline Kirkpatrick, Sarah Jane Kirkpatrick, Frances Kirkpatrick
grandson: Samuel

Executor: Paisley Kirkpatrick.
Witnesses: Thomas Jones, Alex N. Wood.

- - -

F 114 Will dated 19 October 1835, recorded May Court 1836. TEMPERANCE (x) PROMROSE. This will is recorded in Book E on page 368. With the will is a statement of the property she has already given the legatees.

- - -

F 115 Will dated 23 March 1840, proved February Court 1841.

THOMAS S. COX Father: Charles Cox

sisters: Margaret, Nancy, Caroline, Elizabeth, Isabella
Trustee to hold property for his mother Elizabeth Cox, then it goes to his father, then to his sisters.

Trustee and executor: Osmond F. Long.
Witnesses: Steve Moore, Jas. Sneed.

- - -

F 116 Will dated 30 March, 18--, proved February Court 1841.

WILLIAM NORWOOD wife: Robina

sons: John W. Norwood, Joseph Norwood, James H. Norwood, William, Walter
daughters: Eliza, Jane, Helen
"Son James H. Norwood's wife and children", names not stated.

Executors: sons Joseph and John.
Witnesses: O. F. Long, H. Webb.

- - -

F 119 Will dated 18 December 1840, proved Feb Court 1842.

ABNER (x) ROBERTS "weak and low"

daughters: Elizabeth Casey, Sarah Roberts, Vinney Roberts
sons: Thomas Roberts, Moses Roberts, Abner Roberts
son: Ivey Roberts $1
"granddaughter Susan Rew, daughter of my son Jesse Roberts, deceased"
"granddaughters Elizey Ann, Caroline & Winny Roberts, daughters of my son Moses Roberts"

Executor: friend Elijah Hester.
Witnesses: Mark Roberts, Presly Roberts.

- - -

F 121 Will dated 6 March 1841, proved February Court 1842.

THOMAS LATTA wife: Elizabeth

sons: Joseph H. Latta, John W. Latta
daughters: Ann Durham, Mary Long
"My seven daughters Elizabeth, Elenor, Jane, Arena, Amelia, Rachel and Fanny" (unmarried).

Executors: sons Joseph H. Latta and John W. Latta.
Witness: James C. Latta.

- - -

F 124 Will dated 20 December 1842, proved Feb Court 1842.

DANIEL WILKINSON wife: Elizabeth

sons: Thomas (oldest), John, William and Samuel Wilkinson
Daughters mentioned, names and number not stated.

Executors: sons Thomas and John.
Witnesses: Samuel McCracken, Allen Brown.

- - -

F 126-129 Will dated 20 January 1842, proved May Court 1842.

MICHAEL HOLT "I was born 11 July 1778"

sons: William and Edwin M. Holt.
"My two grandchildren, children of my deceased daughter Jane- to Edwin M. Holt,Jr., to Eliza Ann ..."
"My grandchildren, children of my daughter Nancy M Carigan, namely Alfred William Robert John and James Carigan certain slaves now in the possession of their father Wm. A. Carigan."

Many tracts of land and many slaves are devised.
$200 to enclose with brick or stone burying plot "graves in the garden."

Executors: sons William R. and Edwin M. Holt, and Wm. A. Carigan.
Witnesses: Wm. Smith, A. T. Finley.

- - -

F 130 Will dated 5 October 1837, proved May Court 1842.

LABAN (x) ANDREWS "weak in body" wife: Rebecca

son-in-law: Aron Trip
son: Green daughter: Hannah
" John
"My children- David, William Henry Nancy Cates Berry Willie Elizabeth Trip Green & Delia Robards" (no commas).
He says "my four daughters".

Executors: sons David and Berry.
Witnesses: E. Graves, A. Graves, J. Caruthers, Ruffin Andrews.

- - -

F 132 Will dated 27 October 1817, proved May Court 1842.

GEORGE (x) SMITH wife a legatee, name not stated

"All my children, viz, David Smith Joseph Smith William Smith, George Smith & Wesley & Suckey Smith Nancy Smith & Sally Smith". "Two youngest sons George & Wesley".

Executors: friends Thomas Whitted and Thomas Brewer.
Witness: Thos. Brewer.(He was blind when the will was proved.)

F 134 Will dated 24 March 1842, proved May Court 1842.

JOSEPH THOMPSON wife: Elizabeth

sons: Samuel and Thomas to have his mill together

"Daughter-in-law Lavina Thompson tract whereon she now lives", after her death "to my son Robert Thompson's children, to wit: Jinnett Elizabeth Joseph Samuel Elender Lavina Thompson"
son: John Thompson
daughters: Elinor Foust and Rachel Morrow, land which is to be "divided by Daniel Foust and John Morrow"
son: Joseph Thompson

Executors: son Thomas Thompson, and son-in-law Daniel Foust.
Witnesses: John Thompson, James Paris, Jno. Thompson.
- - -

F 136 Will dated 8 March 1842, proved May Coyrt 1842.

JAMES (x) CARRELL wife: Polly

youngest daughter: Ellin (under age)
sons: Lemuel, John, Dixon get land; William gets $2
grandson: James McColum $2
"My nine children Lemuel & John & William & Dixon Candis & Cinthy & Martha & Elizabeth & Ellin."

Executor: son William Brewer.
Witnesses: James Reaves, Calvin Carrell.
- - -

F 137 Will dated 29 June 1842, proved August Court 1842.

ANDREW WATSON wife: Nancy

dau: Tempy T. Watson
" "Margaret Watson wife of Wilson Watson and her two children Alexander Watson and Juliana Watson"
sons: Julius Watson, James M. Watson
"Daughter Elizabeth Durkey dec'd wife of ..... Dorkey"
son-in-law: Samuel Riley $5

Executors: son Julius Watson and son-in-law Wilson Watson.
Witnesses: Levi McCollum, S? L. Turner.
- - -

F 139 Will dated 23 January 1839, proved August Court 1842.

WILLIAM DUKE, SR. sons: John Duke, William Duke

daughter: Polly Leathers wife of Moses Leathers
son: Green
"Heirs of daughter Dicey Bobbitt".
daughter: Reny Mangum wife of W.G.Mangum
" Bedy Oakley wife of Vincent Oakley

Executor: Ellison G. Mangum. Witnesses: Jeff Horner, Orford / Moize.

F 142 Will dated 7 June 1842, proved Nov Court 1842.

NANCY MOOR (She was the widow of John Moore. See D 471)

To William F. Strayhorn
son-in-law: Samuel Strayhorn
granddaughters: Mary E. M. Strayhorn, Nancy Craig
grandsons: Samuel Strayhorn, Thomas Strayhorn
daughters: Frances Hart, Nancy Hart, Susannah Yergan,
Sally Pratt, Elizabeth Allen

Executor: grandson William F. Strayhorn.
Witnesses: D. W. Craig, James N. Craig.

- - -

F 143 Will dated 17 October 1842, proved Nov Court 1842.

WILLIAM (x) McCULLOCK wife: Patience Jane

"All my children", names and number not stated.

Executor: uncle John McCullock.
Witnesses: Alex. Dickson, Joseph McCullock.

- - -

F 144-152 Will dated 7 April 1842, proved Feb Court 1843.

DAVID MEBANE wife: Elizabeth

sons: Alexander, George A., Wiley, Anderson and Sidney.
daus: Betsy Mitchell, Jane (Jenny) Thompson, Fanny Walker,
Martha Ann Holt
granddau: Julia Ann Curry
"Elizabeth Elbridge daughter of my deceased son Elbridge"
grandson: David son of George A. Mebane
son-in-law John Thompson

Executors: sons Alexander and George A. Mebane.
Witnesses: James A. Craig, Samuel Tate.
Codicil dated 26 April 1842.

- - -

F 152 Will dated 22 December 1834, proved Feb Court 1843.

JAMES (x) STANFORD son: Robert Stanford

daus: Peggy Stanford, Jinny Stanford, Elizabeth Dixon.
grandson: James Stanford son of Alexander

Executor: son Robert. Witnesses: Peyton P. Moor, Wm. McCrory.

- - -

F 153 Will dated 24 May 1836, proved February Court 1843.

ALEXANDER GATTIS wife: Rosanna

"My four sons John, William, Alexander & Thomas " all lands.
Son James has already received land.

- continued -

198 Will of ALEXANDER GATTIS concluded
daughters: Elizabeth, Jane and Margaret

Executors: wife Rosanna, son John M., and friend Charles W. Johnston.
Codicil: same date, "to son Samuel $1".
Witnesses: Thomas Gattis, C. W. Johnston.

- - -

F 155 Will dated 25 April 1842, proved May Court 1843.

PETER F. PERRY wife: Patty

"My three sons Samuel, William, Persullas (?)" $100 each.
"My five sons Manly Murphy Peter Henry John A. Mangum Edward Norris"(no punctuation) "all my land".

Executors: son William Perry and George Johnston.
Witnesses: Nathaniel Newlin, Samuel Perry.

- - -

F 157 Will dated 10 August 1842, proved May Court 1843.

ELENOR (x) WOODS

grandchildren: James Hopkins, Rebecca Hopkins, Harriet Hopkins.

Executor: "Trusty friend Henry Whitted."
Witnesses: James Montgomery, Lydia (x) Grimes.

- - -

F 158 Will dated 17 February 1843, proved May Court 1843.

NANCY (x) ROBINSON All to Alexander Robinson.

Executor: Alexander Robinson. Witness: Jas Holeman.

- - -

F 159 Will dated 3 September 1838, proved May Court 1843.

JAMES ALLISON wife: Elizabeth

son: John gets land adjoining Edward Riley
" Joseph

Executor: friend Caleb Wilson. No witnesses.
Proved by the testimony of Joseph Allison.

- - -

F 160 Will dated 7 January 1843, proved May Court 1843.

JAMES (x) HUTCHERSON wife: Sarah

"Daughter Patian and her husband George McCrary" land joining said McCrary, Thomas Tyrell and others ... adjoining Sally Allen

- continued -

and A. Mebane and others"

Balance of estate to be divided between "all my children."

Executors: George McCray, and friend George Hurdle.
Witnesses: Henry Bason, Stephen White.

- - -

F 162 Will dated 8 August 1841, proved August Court 1843.

PETER (x) MOSER wife: Barbara

Executors: Ephriam Mitchell, Levy Moser.
Witnesses: Martin Moser, Bostian Moser.

- - -

F 163 Will dated 13 1842, proved August Court 1843.

MIRIAM (x) STRAIN

sons: David Strain, Samuel D. Strain, John Strain
dau: Miriam Strain son: William D. Strain
D. Strain "interest in estate of son Alexander Strain,dec'd"
granddaughters: Miriam Crutchfield, Miriam Tate, Miriam Nelson.
Miriam Freeland, Miriam Davis

Executor: son Samuel D. Strain. Witness: Samuel S. Clayter.

- - -

F 164 Will dated 7 June 1843, proved August Court 1843.

POLLY (x) RONEY

"My two daughters Catherine Prater & Mary Ann McCray".
"My only and beloved grandson William R. Prater."

Executor: friend John Roney.
Witnesses: Henry Bason, John White.

- - -

F 165 Will dated 30 November 1842, proved August Court 1843.

JOHN STRAYHORN daus: Jane, Patsy Trice

sons: David Strayhorn, Bryant Strayhorn
dau: Polly Davis
"grandchildren whose father and mother is dead."

Executors: son Bryant Strayhorn and son-in-law Alex. Craig.
Witnesses: David Hart, David Craig.

- - -

F 167 Will dated 16 January 1843, proved August Court 1843.

HENRY (x) DOLLAR wife: Elizabeth

son: William Dollar
daus: Mildred and Cinthia Ann Dollar

Executrix: wife Elizabeth.
Witnesses: Silas M. Link, John C. Burton.

- - -

F 168 Will dated 20 September 1842, proved Nov Court 1843.

THOMAS WEAVER wife: Sarah

eldest daughter: Winnie C Lloyd
" son: William G. Weaver $10
second son: Isham S. Weaver
grandsons: Samuel and George Weaver, sons of Isham
son: John H. Weaver
daus: Mary C. Weaver, Elizabeth C. Weaver
youngest son: Thos S. Weaver

Executors: William G. Weaver and John H. Weaver.
Witnesses: W. H. Merrett, George W. Purify.

- - -

F 170 Will dated 13 March 1843, proved November Court 1843.

SARAH WALKER (See the will of Aaron Walker, E 289)

sons: Levi Walker, Empson Walker
daus: Harriet Crofford(Crawford), Nancy Shaw
son: Freeman Walker

Executor:son Levi Walker.
Witnesses: Thos Lynch, John Compton.

- - -

F 171 Will dated 17 September 1835, proved Nov Court 1843.

OSBOURNE SNIPES All estate to wife Martha Snipes.

He leaves "to any other legal representatives or heirs" 50¢.

Executor: Bennett T. Blake.
Witnesses: Ellis G. Blake, Jno P. Cook.

- - -

F 172 Will dated 8 March 1843, proved November Court 1843.

JOHN WALKER wife: Hannah

Two daughters Mary (Polly or Dolly) Walker and Hannah M. Walker.
son: Adam D. Walker pnantation called "the Tate place".

Executors: friends Sam M. Douglas, Absalom Hervey.
Witnesses: John C. Douglas, James Gilliam.

- - -

F 174 Will dated 9 November 1843, proved Nov 1843.

JOHN BLACKWOOD wife: Mary

He devises property "in Town of Hillsboro adjoining lot of Thomas Faucett ... now occupied by Charles Cooley." And a tract of land on Eno River joining John McCauley. A tract called "the Mountain Tract."

daus: Mary Strayhorn, Margaret McCauley
sons: David K. Blackwood, John J., and Johnston Blackwood

Executor: David K. Blackwood.
Witnesses: C. W. Johnston, James Gattis.

- - -

F 175 Will dated 26 November 1842, proved Nov Court 1843.

JESSE O'DANIEL All estate to his brother Henry O'Daniel.

Witnesses: Wm. (x) O'Daniel, William Perry.

- - -

F 176 Will dated 5 August 1826, proved May Court 1843.

DANIEL ALBRIGHT wife, name not stated

"Son-in-law William Montgomery and daughter Sarah."
"My grandchildren", number and names not stated.
His wife is to choose an executor.
Witnesses: Elias Albright, John Clapp.

- - -

F 178 Will dated 27 March 1841, proved February Court 1844.

THOMAS (x) GRIFFIN "weak in body"

"I lend to Peggy Griffin the use of my plantation which Alfred Pickard now lives on".
"Peggy Pickard wife of Alfred Pickard"
"Peggy Pickard's two sons James Pickard and Thomas Pickard"
"brother James Griffin and his wife"
"Lilla Wicks & Rebecca Wicks daughters of Jenny Wicks" both under age, $1000 each.
friend Hugh Waddell $500
friends Jesse O'Daniel and Henry O'Daniel balance
stepson Thomas Griffin $200

Executors: friends Hugh Waddell and Jesse O'Daniel.
Witnesses: B. Strowd, Thos. M. Durham, R. Stanford.

- - -

F 179 Will dated 21 November 1843, proved Feb Court 1844.

WILLIAM CLENDENNIN wife: Jean

"..daughters Hanor S ?, Nancy Ann, Sarah M., and Letitia ? or Lavinia ? Cornelia ? Bradshary ? so long as they live single "
In another place Sarah Margaret is mentioned. - continued -

son: William Clendennin (unmarried)
"daughter Caroline who is married"

Executor: "friend and neighbor John Stockard."
Witnesses: George Clendennin, Fisher Clendennin.

- - -

F 181-184 Will dated 20 July 1843, proved Feb Court 1844.

HENRY (x) TROLINGER, SR. wife: Polly

eldest son: John Trolinger
" dau: Betsy Gant son-in-law: Jonathan Gant
sons: Henry Trolinger Jr, Joseph
dau: Catherine Freshwater
"children of my deceased son Jacob Trolinger as they arrive at age"
dau: Mary Raney
"daughter Peggy Tarpley and her husband Henry Tarpley"
grandson: Moses Trolinger
granddaughter: Adaline Freshwater

Executors: sons John and Joseph Trolinger.
Witnesses: Daniel A. Montgomery, Thos. Dixon.

- - -

F 184 Will dated 23 July 1836, proved February Court 1844.

JOHN COOK, SR. daughter: Sarah Thomas

granddaughter: Elizabeth R. Wagner

Sole executor: William Brannock.
Witnesses: Daniel White, John Hicks.

- - -

F 186 Will dated 30 September 1841, proved Feb Court 1844.

ANDREW (x) McCAULEY grandson: John W. McCauley

"Sarah McCauley, widow of my son Robert dec'd" $2.
son-in-law: Gabreal B. Lea
grandsons: John and Andrew Lea (under 21)
granddaus: Hannah Moore, Martha Lea
Andrew J. McCauley

Executor: Gab. B. Lea. Witnesses: Wm.Ward Sr, John Barnwell.

- - -

F 187 Will dated 23 August 1840, proved February Court 1844.

MARY (x) JONES brother: Johnson Jones

sister Margaret Jones, and sister Levina Woods and her daughter Matilda Woods

Executor: Johnson Woods. Witnesses: Wm. Shaw, Alex'r M. Woods.

- - -

F 188-190 Will dated 18 March 1843, proved Feb 1844.

JOHN PICKETT wife: Catherine

dau: Julia Ann Pickett (unmarried)
sons: Samuel & John Quincy Pickett
dau: Elizabeth W. Wilkinson

Sole executor: friend Thomas Lynch, Esq.
Witnesses: J. Allison, C. E. Tinnen.

- - -

F 190 Will dated 23 April 1843, proved May Court 1844.

PRISCILLA (x) CARRINGTON "advanced in years"

son: Morgan
dau: Polly Parrish wife of James Parrish
" Dicey Cozart wife of Wm. Cozart of Person County

Executor: George W. Jones.
Witnesses: Willis Bowling ?, David Parrish, George W. Jones.

- - -

F 191 Will dated 12 December 1842, proved May Court 1844.

JAMES CLARK wife: Ann

dau: Grace (unmarried)
" Sarah Hughs
Hannah H. Dickey
granddau: I.B.Bethiah Lindsey
grandson: James C. Lindsey
son: Stephen Clark $1

son: James W. Clark

His land on Eno River joins John Compton, Wm. Allison, & others.

Executors: sons James W. and Stephen Clark.
Witnesses: Lemuel Wilkinson, Alexander Findley.

- - -

F 193 Will dated 8 April 1844, proved May Court 1844.

JOSEPH D. HUGHES daughters: Jane, Eliza

"My wife Sarah and her four children Rice (?) Ann John and Sidney are to have my lands lying near Person County" 500 acres. Children all seem to be minors.

"My eight children Anderson Thomas Samuel Jane Joseph Franklin Paisley and Eliza" (no punctuation).

"Whatever may be coming to me from the estate of James Clark deceased" ...

Executors: sons Anderson and Samuel.
Witnesses: Monroe Allen, I or J. C. McDaniel.

- - -

F 195 Will dated 27 March 1844, proved May Court 1844.

JOSEPH (x) WHITE wife: Nancy

mother: Mary Couch
daus: Susanna Craig, Nancy Cole
sons: Thomas White, Joseph White
Land he purchased of Moses H. Turner to be rented.

Sole executor: Thomas White.
Witnesses: Jas. N. Patterson, Sam Couch, Anderson (x) Rhodes.

- - -

F 197 Will dated 18 March 1839, proved May Court 1844.

JOHN (x) RUMBLEY wife: Elizabeth

"Two infant children John Severn (?) Rumbley and Rachel L. (?) Rumbley".
son: Thomas Rumbley 150 acres "Adam's Old Tract" which he now lives on
sons: James, Edward and William, $1 each with what they have had
"son Aron Rumbley's heirs $1"

Executrix: wife Elizabeth. Witnesses: Benj. Hurdle, John Pyle.

- - -

F 198 Will dated 8 February 1841, proved May Court 1844.

FRANCIS JONES "late of the county of Chatham, but now of the town of Hillsboro" .."in advanced age and feeble"
son-in-law James S. Smith of Hillsboro plantation on Pokeberry Creek joining John Hackney, Joseph Bynum, James Kirby & others 2000 to 2700 acres (in Chatham) in trust for "only child and daughter Delia Smith wife of the said Dr. James S. Smith"

grandson: Dr. Francis J. Smith another plantation in Chatham joining Isaiah Cole, Wm. Merritt, 1800 acres.
grandson: James Sidney Smith
granddau: Mary R. Smith plantation in Orange on Price's Creek

Sole executor: James S. Smith.
Witnesses: A. Parks, Thomas Faucett.

- - -

F 200 Will dated 24 February 1839, proved May Court 1844.

JOHN FREELAND, SR. wife: Nancy

"All my children", number and names not stated.
Deceased son Thomas Freeland.

Executors: son John J. Freeland, grand-son-in-law Ralph Faucett.
Witnesses: C. W. Johntson, John Blackwood, James J. Blackwood.

- - -

F 203-205 Will dated 15 June 1841, proved May Court 1844.

THOMAS HORNER, SR. wife: Sarah

daus: Mary Parker, Elizabeth Cabe, Lucretia Holeman $1 each
"Three sons William Horner, John Horner & Jefferson Horner
land on Flat River joining Nathaniel Harris & Elizabeth King."

Executors: sons William and Jefferson Horner.
Witnesses: Francis Epperson, L.C.Ellis ? (Ellus ?)

- - -

F 204-206 Will dated 8 May 1844, proved May Court 1844.

NICHOLAS ALBRIGHT wife: Ann

eldest son James P. Albright "tract on which he now lives"
son: John G. "tract on which he now lives" on Haw River
sons: Henry Albright, William P. Albright (under 21)

Executors: wife Ann, and William M. Rogers.
Witnesses: Calvin C. Graves, Mich'l M. Holt.

- - -

F 206 Will dated 2 June 1844, proved August Court 1844.

JOSEPH W. ALLISON wife: Susan

oldest daughter: Margaret Jane Allison
daus: Mary N. Allison, Susan G. Allison
son: Joseph Washington Allison (undera age)
He speaks of his wife's "raising the children".

Sole executrix: wife Susan.
Witnesses: Hezekiah Long, James Allison.

- - -

F 208 Will dated 25 July 1844, proved August Court 1844.

JOHN McDADE wife: Levina

sons: James B. & Patterson H. McDade plantation after wife's / death
son: Henderson C. McDade "100 acres where he now lives"
" John A. McDade "100 " " " " " "

Executor: friend Joseph Allison.
Witnesses: John Kelly, Joseph Smith.

- - -

F 210 Will dated 26 July 1844, proved August Court 1844.

ELIZABETH GASKELL "younger daughter Drusilla Gaskell"

"My three daughters Mary Gaskell Susan Gaskell & Drusilla."

Executor: friend James A. Craig.
Witnesses: Randolph C. Mabrey, George Crawford.

- - -

F 212 Will dated 18 April 1844, proved August Court 1844.

WILLIAM GATTIS wife: Rebecca

"All my children", names and number not stated.

Executrix: wife Rebecca. Witnesses: D.D.Pane, Nath'l ? Bain.

\- - -

F 213 Will dated 29 December 1842, proved August Court 1844.

ELIZABETH (x) CLINTON son: Jesse Clinton

"Milly Watson's daughter Elizabeth Ann Watson"
No relationship stated to: Milly Anderson, Susan Clark, John Clinton, Samuel Clinton, Mary Dollar $1 each.

Executor: son Jesse Clinton.
Witnesses: James Stag, Washington Duke.

\- - -

F 214 Will dated 27 March 1843, proved August Court 1844.

REEVES MANGUM wife: Martha

"All my children", names and number not stated.

Executor: son William.
Witnesses: Thos. W. Gooch, Harris Wilkerson.

\- - -

F 215 Will dated 13 June 1840, proved August Court 1844.

NATHAN MANN Nancy Lasley "pension money due me".

Sole executrix: friend Nancy Lasley.
Witnesses: Thos. Pendergrast, Andrew J..?...

\- - -

F 216 Will dated 8 April 1839, proved August Court 1844.

SOLOMON CATE wife: Mary

"son Thomas and Anna"
"little William must be bound to some trade"

Executor: son Thomas. Witnesses: Thomas Sykes, Anna (x) Cate.

\- - -

F 217 Will dated 30 March 1841, proved August Court 1844.

ELENOR (x) ROGERS youngest son: Will Rogers (unmarried)

son: James Rogers
"Four daughters Jane Holt (?), Ann Albright, Elenor Johnson, and Mary Foust."

- continued -

"only sister Jane Rogers wife of Wm. Robess (?) the elder"
grandsons: sons of daughter Elenor Johnston, John and James, both under 21 years of age
son: John Rogers

Executor: son William Rogers.
Witnesses: Thomas Ruffin, Milton S. Holt.
Codicil, no date . Daughter Elenor has died. Granddaughter Sally Rogers (unmarried" has waited on "me most kindly and faithfully". Witnesses: John Rogers, Milton S. Holt.

- - -

F 220 Will dated 17 September 1843, proved August Court 1844.

MARY (x) HERNDON, widow (She was the widow of Elias Herndon who died intestate in 1828.)
"My children, that is, Elizabeth Mason wife of John Mason, Reaney Jenkins wife of Joseph Jenkins, Matilda George wife of Ezekiel George, William Herndon and Martha Herndon my (two) grandsons the heirs of Gustin Herndon, and Madison Herndon my grandson son of Stanford Herndon, heirs of my daughter Mary wife of Berry Mason; Joseph Mason, Adison Mason, Leroy Mason, Elizabeth Mason, Nancy Mason."

Berry (Littleberry) Mason $1

Executor: friend John Mason.
Witnesses: John Marcom, Willis Marcom.

- - -

F 222 Will dated 8 July 1844, proved August Court 1844.

DANIEL HUFFMAN wife: Elizabeth

married daughters: Rachel, Polly or Patty, Catherine Lydia and Sally
youngest daughter: Susan
son: John "200 acres on which he now lives"

Executor: son John.
Witnesses: Joseph J. Trolinger, Daniel A. Montgomery.

- - -

F 224-226 Will dated 5 May 1838, proved November Court 1844.

THOMAS BREWER wife a legatee, name not stated

son: Thomas
daus: Elizabeth Oldham, Maryann Bradshaw, Margaret Snipes Martha Lindsey

granddaus: Polly Strowd, Rosanna Turner, Nancy Cate
grandsons: Wesley Edwards, William Edwards, Thomas Edwards

Executors: son Thomas Brewer, Thos. Oldham & Wm. Bradshaw.
Witnesses: David Roach, David Williams.

- - -

F 227 Will dated 25 September 1844, proved Nov Court 1844.

WILLIAM (x) O'DANIEL brother: John O'Daniel

sisters: Lavina and Margaret

Executor: brother John. Witnesses: John Jones, Henry Ray.

– – –

F 227 Will dated 21 September 1838, proved Nov Court 1843.

CATHERINE (x) HORN son: John Horn $1

"Daughter-in-law Elizabeth Horner (?) and her three children namely Nancy Catherine Horn, William Page Horn and Norflet Anderson Horn". (It is Horner in the book in Hillsboro. I have not checked the original will which is in Raleigh. R.H.S.)

Sole executor: James N. Patterson.
Witnesses: Jane Cole, Susannah (x) Rainey.

– – –

F 229-233 Will dated 10 October 1838, proved Nov Court 1844.

BARNEY (x) CLAP wife a legatee, name not stated

son: Emanuel land on Bever Creek
daughter Polly "of unsound mind"
"Daughter Penny John Lacy's (?) Lue's (?) wife".(The clerk's writing is very poor. There were Lacy and Lue families near.)

Daughters: "George Clap and wife Barbara, Frederick Sherer ? and wife Peggy, John Lue ? and wife Penny, Ceatty ? Clap wife of Isaac Clap, Sally Kime ?, John Lowe and wife Nelly".

Executors: sons David Clap and Emanuel Clap, and son-in-law John Low.
Witnesses: Wm. Smith, Wm. Artz, Mich'l Holt.
Codicil dated 5 February 1842, names no new heirs.

– – –

F 233 Will dated 20 August 1844, proved November Court 1844.

SARAH MONTGOMERY mother: Elizabeth Albright

"My four youngest children Harriett Cornelia Barbary & William .... until the youngest child shall reach the age of 15"
"All my children", names and number not stated.

Executor: son Daniel A. Montgomery.
Witnesses: James B. Montgomery, Hiram Whitsell.

– – –

F 235 Will dated 19 April 1834, proved Nov Court 1844.

ARMOUR KING, SR. wife: Rach

sons: Jennison or Jeremiah $2, Armer
daus: Elender, Margret, Sarah
sons: Samuel, Henry $2, Garrison $2
daus: Rachel, Nancy and Mary $2 each
"granddaughter Mary the daughter of Elender"

No executor named. Witnesses: Jas Lover ?, Jas MCray.

- - -

F 236 Will dated 3 February 1843, proved --

ELENOR (x) GARRISON legatee: Brise F. Garrison

brother: George Garrison brother: John 1 shilling
brother Levi Garrison's heirs 1 shilling
sister Mary Pyle's heirs 1 shilling each
sister Rebecca Pyle's heirs 1 shilling each

Executor: brother George Garrison.
Witnesses: Benj. Hurdle, Edward (x) Thompson.

- - -

F 238 Will dated 5 Debruary 1842, proved August 1844.

WILLIAM RILEY

sons: Samuel, Copeland and William Riley
sons: Warden and Judson Riley land on McGowan's Creek bought from Enoch Thompson.

dau: Polly

Sole executor: son William Riley.
Witnesses: Hugh Waddell, F. N. Waddell.

- - -

F 238 Will dated -- , proved November 1841.

JOHN HUFFIND wife: Rachel

Jackson Mury (or Munn) no relationship stated.

No executor named. No witnesses.

- - -

F 240 Will dated 20 July 1844, proved February Court 1845.

JOHN (x) COBLE (listed as CABLE in index in Archives)

wife: Catherine youngest son: Benjamin Coble
oldest son: John second son: Phillip
daus: Barbary Wirick ?, Elizabeth Tickle, Sarah Wirick ?
"..unto Warner Cardin if he stays and works with family until he is twenty-one..."

Executors: son Benjamin Coble, and George Tickle.
Witnesses: Adam (x) Strader, Lewis Lowe ?, Archibald Murphy.

- - -

F 242 Will dated 9 December 1844, proved Feb Court 1845.

HENRY (x) EULIS sons: George and John

daughter Peggy wife of Tobias Clapp
" Catherine wife of Daniel Spoon
son: Allen
daughter Reney $1, her daughter Lucritta (?) $200
" Nancy wife of N. Holt
"George son of Elizabeth Kimbrow " $50

Executors: Powel Kimbro, George Eulis, Peter Eulis.
Witnesses: William Moser, John Kimbro.

- - -

F 244 Will dated 3 January 1845, proved Feb Court 1845.

GEORGE (x) BAKER "low state of health" wife: Barbary
(Indexed in State Archives as BARKER)

"sons Thomas Isreal & John Baker having left me and married"..
C.B. Baker George Baker Mary Baker & Susan Baker (no punctuation, and no relationship stated)

Executor: son John Baker.
Witnesses: Snelson Love, Samuel P. Foster.

- - -

F 245-247 Will dated 11 January 1845, proved Feb Court 1845.

CATLETT CAMPBELL He speaks of "my kindred in Virginia."

"Children of my deceased sister Mary Ann Burke"
sister Nancy Marbury ? sister Sally Turner
nephew James Burke of Alleghany County, Va.
sisters: Permelia Waugh, Judy McGinnis

Executors: Nephew James Burke, friends John U. Kirkland, Osmond F. Long and John W. Norwood.
Witnesses: Jas C. Norwood, Thos N. Burke, Wm. Ward.

- - -

F 248 Will dated 5 March 1845, proved May Court 1845.

JEMIMA (x) CABE "weak and feeble"

"To my daughter Mary Burton the plantation I purchased of my son-in-law John Brown" grandson: John Burton
granddau: Mary A. Burton
son: William Cabe
dau: Rachel Claytor
"All my children"

Executors: son-in-law John Brown and Samuel S. Claytor.
Witnesses: Allen Brown, Thomas Piper.

- - -

F 249 Will dated 26 October 1841, proved May Court 1845.

ELIZABETH ESTES

"My neices Mary Jane & Caroline Evans" lands on Eno River, and "my residence in the Town of Hillsborough"
neice: Catherine Evans "house on Churton Street"
neices: Isabelle Bridges, Mariah Dodd
sister: Mrs. Peggy Nash
Mrs. Sarah Grove widow of Wm. B. Grove
"Mary Whitted daughter of my late neice Eliza Whitted" (the 3rd Codicil says "of Alabama")
"friends Mrs. Josiah Turner, Mrs. Attelia Whitted and Mrs. Eliza Bingham"
"To Mrs. Elizabeth Thompson my neice a daughter of Mrs. Mary Seawell & wife of Mr. Thomas"
Harriet Barton
"To Eliza Turner & Mary Turner daughters of Josiah Turner"
"Mrs. Susan Mebane wife of James Mebene Jr."

Executors: friends John W. Norwood and James Dodd of Fayette/ville.
Witnesses: O.F.Long, A. Mickle.

Codicil #1 dated 18 Nov 1843, Witnesses: J.Webb Jr., H.Y.Webb.
Catherine Evans is now the wife of John Turner,
Isabella Bridges wife of Young Bridges.

Codicil #2 dated 24 Feb 1844 revokes bequest to Harriet Barton
" #3 dated 10 March 1844, and #4 dated 2 August 1844 name no new heirs.

\- - -

F 253-255 Will dated 24 February 1844, proved Feb Court 1845.

JAMES LEATHERS wife: Elizabeth

son: John Leathers
" William Leathers "tract where he now lives joining Wm Lipscomb & others" (200 acres)
" Moses Leathers 500 acres
" Kintchin Leathers land joining Durham Hall (200 acres)
daughter: Elizabeth
Zachariah Rhodes "who married my daughter Sally", & children
"My children, viz, John Leathers William Leathers Moses Leathers Kintchin Leathers Patsey Holloway wife of James Holloway Edney Green wife of William Green & Elizabeth single"..

Executors: sons John and Moses Leathers.
Witnesses: Harris Wilkerson, Benton Ray.

\- - -

F 256 Will dated 22 April 1845, proved May Court 1845.

SAMUEL McDANIEL "my dear father"

"My three single sisters Sally Peggy & Jane" - continued -

 F 256 Will of SAMUEL McDANIEL continued

"My two single brothers William and Jesse"
brother Henry and sister Elizabeth

Executor: brother William McDaniel.

- - -

F 256 Will dated 24 March 1843, proved May Court 1845.

POLLY (x) HARRIS

son Arlos Harris land joining John Brewer & Josiah Turner.

Exceutor: son Arlos. Witnesses: J. Turner, Jas. R. Brewer.

- - -

F 257 Will dated25 September 1844, proved May Court 1845.

ALVIS NICHOLS wife: Polly

"My children" names and number not stated.
He mentions "plantation whereon William & Elenor Faucett now live" and "plantation whereon Jacob Jackson Sr now lives"

- - -

F 258-260 Will dated 7 April 1845, proved May Court 1845.

JAMES GARRARD

sons: William, James and Sherwood Garrard
son Wilson Garrard to make deeds (Clerk's writing very bad)

Executors: sons James and Sherwood Garrard.
Witnesses: Silas M. Link, James Latta.

- - -

F 260 Will dated 30 April 1845, proved May Court 1845.

ELZY HOPKINS all estate to wife Sarah

"My children ... as they grow up" no names given.

Executors: "my father-in-law John Ray and his son Benton Ray".
Witnesses: E. Strudwick, J. B. Leathers.

- - -

F 261 Will dated 22 June 1844, proved May Court 1845.

WILLIAM (x) HOPSON wife: Harriett

deceased son Wiley
son: Wm. Henry Harrison Hopson plantation on N.E.Creek of New/Hope
dau: Rebecca Tapp wife of Richard Tapp $10
" Rosannah Tapp wife of Vincent Tapp $10
" Sally Barbee $10

Executor: friend William Thompson.
Witnesses: W. Bradshaw, Elijah Pickard, R. Stanford.

- - -

F 262 Will dated 16 July 1830, proved May Court 1845.

GEORGE (x) PAISLEY "low and weak" wife (see note below)

sons: Joseph and John (All the children seem to daus: Luisa and Mary Ann be minors.)

Guardians and executors: Johnston Freeland and Moses Gibson.
Witnesses: Joseph Gibson, Josn Freeland, John Paisley.
George Paisley married in Orange Co,1 Feb 1810 Elizabeth Freeland, bondsman was Johnston Freeland.

- - -

F 264 Will dated 28 May 1845, proved August Court 1845.

THOMAS McCRACKEN wife: Susan all estate, except

$100 to "my nephew Thomas McCracken son of my brother John"

Executor: Thomas P. Paul. witness: Sam'l N. Tate.

- - -

F 265 Will dated 13 February 1845, proved Nov Court 1845.

THOMAS COUCH

All estate goes to his brother William Couch except one slave girl to Thomas White.

Witnesses: Abner Copeland, James N. Patterson.

- - -

F 266 Will dated 2 July 1844, proved November Court 1845.

SAMUEL TURRENTINE wife: Ann

"brother Absalom Turrentine's two oldest children Samuel W. Turrentine (under age) and Mary I. (or J) Turrentine"
neice: Seliny Ann Turrentine
Martha A. Wilson
brothers: Absalom and Daniel 100 acres called "Kell Tract"

Executors: Charles Wilson and Daniel Turrentine.
Witnesses: Joseph Brown, John L. Brown, C. Wilson.

- - -

F 267 Will dated 21 September 1840, proved November 1845.

CONNALLY WALKER "far advanced in age" wife: Elizabeth

All estate to daughters Jane Walker and Mary Walker.
His three sons William, Samuel and Phillip Walker have all received their portions.

Executors: son Samuel and daughter Jane Walker.
Witnesses: John W. Shaw, Obediah Hurdle.

- - -

F 268 Will dated 4 April 1845, proved November Court 1845.

REBECCA (x) DOLLAR

daughter Susan Dollar all money on hand, all notes due her, and "pension due me from the United States"
"My grandson William Glenn son of James Glenn"

Executrix: daughter Susan. Witnesses: J. Turner, James Turner.

- - -

F 269 Will dated 19 December 1839, proved Nov Court 1845.

ROBERT MORROW wife a legatee, name not stated

sons: Vincent, Josiah, Robert J, and George W. Morrow.
daus: Eliza A., Mary Jane, Elizabeth M., Julee Nancy
sons: Sidney Mebane, George Washington Morrow
"son Elbridge's heirs"

Executors: sons Vincent and Josiah.
Witnesses: Thomas Reeves, Robert Whitted.

- - -

F 271 Will dated 14 June 1839, proved February Court 1846.

JOSEPH ARMSTRONG wife: Frances

sons: John Armstrong, Thomas D. Armstrong
daus: Frances Clendennin, Jinney Walker, Elizabeth Tate, Henrietta Tate, Parthena Faucett
grandchildren: Joseph McAdams, Mary Rippy, Peggy McAdams, Catherine McAdams
"Little grandson Joseph Tate, Betsy Tate's son" .. "my shotgun"

Executors: sons-in-law John Tate and John Faucett.

- - -

F 273 Will dated 22 August 1845, proved February Court 1846.

NANCY (x) CRUTCHFIELD grandson: John Workman

daughter: Nancy Stubbins
sons: John, Enoch and James Crutchfield

Executor: son Enoch.
Witnesses: Richard Tapp, James H. Thompson.

- - -

F 274 Will dated 3 November 1845, proved Feb Court 1846.

BENJAMIN (x) CARROLL wife: Nancy

son: Alsey Carroll
"Ilai Copley and his wife Claricey"
Dicey James, Luvico ? Glenn - continued -

sons: Eli Carroll, Archibald Carroll, Charles Carroll, Benjamin Carroll, Clement Carroll and Stephen Carroll 50¢ ea.

Executor: son Alsey Carroll. Witnesses: W.N.Pratt, Thos. White.

- - -

F 276 Will dated 25 June 1845, proved February Court 1846.

TIRZA (x) SWEANEY

neices Nancy and Martha Oakley, daughters of Barton and Amelia Oakley (both neices are under age)

Executor: George W. Jones. Witnesses: John Duke, John Hill.

- - -

F 277 Will dated 23 May 1840, proved May Court 1846.

JOHN (x) NOE "under bodily affliction"

sons: George Noe, Daniel Noe
daughters Sally, Nelly Noe land on Stinking Quarter Creek
son: Solomon balance of land
married daughter Mary 5 shillings

Executor: Edwin Holt, Esq.
Witnesses: Mich. Holt, Jno.A.M.Fadyen, Christian --

- - -

From this point I give only the name of the testator, date of the will and date of probate, except for the two or three I had already abstracted earlier. All are in Book F.

Book F page #	testator	date of will	proved
279-281	FREDERICK (x) SHOFFNER	23 October 1845,	May 1846
283	SAMUEL PATTON, SR	25 July 1846	Aug 1846
285	HANDY WOOD	8 August 1846	" "
286	EDWARD J. WARD	31 July 1846	" "
288	JOHN WALKER	15 November 1844	" "
290	ANDERSON HALL	7 March 1846	" "
293	ROBERT McCADAMS	13 June 1846	" "
294	JAMES THOMPSON, SR. "old and feeble"	22 July 1833	" "
296	MARY (x) FINN or FENN	14 February 1846	" "
297-300	LOFTIN K. PRATT	4 August 1846	" "

Book F	name of testator	date of will	proved
301	MARGARET (x) WALL	16 August 1838	Aug 1846
304	ELI EULISS	8 September 1846	Nov 1846
303	JOHN MORROW	23 July 1846	" "
305	MARTHA (x) BENSON	10 August 1842	" "
306	WILLIAM HOLT	20 April 1842	" "
308	WILLIAM FOUST	18 August 1846	" "
309	AQUILLA (x) JONES, SR. "old and weak"	26 November 1843	" "
310	JOSIAH ATKINS, SR.	23 November 1839	" "
312	JOSEPH A. WHITE	3 October 1846	" "
314	JOSHUA SUMMERS	25 August 1846	" "
315	YOUNG (x) DORCH	1 October 1846	" "
317	DANIEL ALBRIGHT	30 October 1846	" "
319	MARTHA (x) McCAULEY	24 October 1846	" "
322-6	JOHN (x) EULISS	10 December 1845	" "
327-9	EMANUEL CLAPP	2 August 1846	" "
330	SUSANNAH ESTHER BAKER	23 October 1843	" "
331	MARTIN COBLE	8 August 1846	Feb 1847
331-3	MASTING CHEEK	26 March 1841	" "
334	JOHN WOODS	30 July 1845	" "
336	HENRY O'DANIEL	2 February 1846	" "
337-9	MOSES GUESS	19 March 1842	" "
240-2	JOHN JONES	17 October 1846	" "
343	MARGARET (x) McCULLOCK	24 January 1845	" "
344-5	THOMAS BOWLS	13 February 1839	" "
346	EDWIN ISELEY	16 September 1846	" "
348	JAMES (x) ECTOR	1 September 1846	May 1847
349	WILLIAM WILKINSON	29 May 1845	" "

Book F	name of testator	date of will	proved
350	CHARLES (x) PETTIGREW	31 October 1844	May 1847
351	ELIZABETH BURTON	16 July 1845	" "
354	JAMES LINDSEY	7 April 1847	Aug 1847
355	JAMES (x) CARTER	8 March 1831	" "
357-8	JOHN THOMPSON	17 February 1847	" "
359-61	JOSEPH ANDERSON	3 July 1847	" "
362-4	STEPHEN GLASS	31 July 1847	" "
365	MARGARET (x) PATTON	6 August 1846	" "
366	THOMAS (x) BARTON "weak in body"	14 June 1847	" "
368-9	DAVID (x) CASTLEBERRY	19 May 1847	" "
371	JAMES PHILLIPS	27 October 1847	Nov 1847
373	REBECCA (x) DAVIS	11 July 1844	" "
375-7	THOMAS D. BENNEHAN	28 April 1845	" "
378	JAMES (x) HAILEY	22 October 1847	" "
379	MARGARET (x) HERNDON	16 August 1847	" "
	All her estate to her sister Elizabeth. It consists partly of her share of the undivided estate of her father William Herndon. Wits: Wm. Trice, Noah Trice.		
380-3	GEORGE FOGLEMAN	28 February 1843	Nov 1847
	" " codicil	3 September 1846	" "
383	JAMES W. McCAULEY	21 July 1847	" "
	"late of the State of Tennessee, but now at the home of Wm. McCauley (his relative) of Orange County."		
386	DAVID PATTERSON	4 December 1839	Nov 1847
388	JOHN TAYLOR	13 November 1847	" "
389	JAMES RIGGS	24 July 1847	" "
390	ARLAS (x) HARRIS "weak in body"	September 1847	" "
392	JAMES ROSS	11 January 1836	Feb 1848
394	ISABELL (x) CLENDENNIN	22 October 1847	" "
395	SIMPSON RHEW	20 June 1847	" "

Book F	name of testator	date of will	proved
396	FRANCES (x) COOK "weak in body"	10 August 1846	Feb 1848
398	NATHAN HOOKER	24 December 1847	" "
400	ELIZABETH (x) BLACKNALL	5 January 1848	" "
401	FIELDING (x) LEWIS	27 February 1847	" "

wife: Nancy daughters: Mary and Nancy
"sons and daughters" ... "rest of my children that has married and left me"
Executor: son John C. Lewis.
Witnesses: Joseph Proctor, John Pool.

402	HARVEY I. ROUNDTREE	29 October 1847	Feb 1848
404	GEORGE (x) FOSTER	29 January 1846	May 1848
406-9	JOSEPH FREELAND	2 July 1846	" "
409-11	MARGARET (x) KERR "old"	4 July 1843	" "
412	ELIZABETH THOMPSON	13 August 1842	" "
413	RACHEL (x) JACKSON	13 April 1848	" "
414	WILLIAM ROGERS	27 January 1845	" "
416-8	WILLIAM ECTOR	26 June 1848	" "
419-21	GEORGE ISELEY	24 February 1845	Nov 1848
422-4	SARAH F. DURHAM	8 April 1847	" "
425	JANE (x) STEVENS	2 March 1845	" "
427	HETTY (x) WILLIAMS	24 September 1847	" "
428	WILLIAM (x) FOGLEMAN	8 December 1848	Feb 1849
430	NATHANIEL HARRIS	30 June 1846	" "
432	MARTIN MURPHY	26 September 1848	May 1849
433-7	RICHARD CRABTREE	21 May 1841	" "
	" " codicil	13 October 1843	" "
439-43	LEVI WHITTED	10 June 1845	Aug 1849
	" " codicil	17 April 1849	" "
443	DANIEL HOGAN	7 May 1844	" "
445	MARGARET (x) RIGGS	18 May 1828	" "
447	ANN (x) GRIMES	27 March 1846	" "

Book F	name of testator	date of will	proved
449	WILLIAM BOWLES	1 September 1827	Nov 1849
451	ROBERT (x) BLACKWOOD "low state of health"	28 September 1849	Feb 1850
452	JOHN (x) GATES "in affliction"	30 January 1849	" "
453	JANE (x) WILSON	5 September 1841	" "
455	DANIEL GREEN	22 April 1850	May 1850
456	ALEXANDER HATCH	21 November 1845	" "
458-62	WILLIAM H. MERRITT	18 July 1850	Aug 1850
462-5	DANIEL PARKER "in advanced age"	24 August 1844	" "
466	HENRY EDWARDS, SR.	20 July 1844	" "
467	DAVID ROBERSON	24 December 1849	" "
469	DAVID (x) WILLIAMS "in feeble health"	27 April 1849	" "
470	DICEY (x) SPARROW	14 June 1850	" "
472	DANIEL BOOTHE	18 August 1850	Nov 1850
474	ANNA DEBRULER	29 August 1850	" "

This concludes the wills probated during the year 1850.

I found six original wills among the second series of Orange County wills preserved in the State Archives in Raleigh, N.C. which are not now on record in the will books in Hillsboro. The date of probate on these wills is not known. I give them in order of their dates.

GENET (x) McCOWN, widow "very weak" dated 9 July 1785

grandsons: James Johnston and James Odonel $20 each
granddaus: Jean Johnston and Jean Odonel (O'Donnel)
daus: Jean Johnston and Agness Odonel
"My grandchildren Thomas John Jean & Charles Johnston and likewise Jean Susiana William John and Henry Odonal ... above named nine children...."

Executors: John Thompson Miller and Thomas Brad .... (torn).
Witnesses; Chas Clindennin, Wm. Clindennin, Thomas Bradshaw.

220 Codicil to the will of GENET McCOWN dated 10 Oct. 1792.

"my son-in-law John Johnston married to my eldest daughter Jean " 5 shillings
"my son-in-law John ODonal married to my youngest daughter Agness" 5 shillings

Witnesses: James Thompson, Thomas Thompson, Chas. Clindennin.

\- - -

JAMES McMUNN Will dated 31 December 1802, proved --

wife a legatee, name not stated son: William 5 sh.
daughter: Ginny Brease 5 shillings
Ann Hargis 20 shillings James Lindcey 5 shillings
daughter: Elizabeth 5 shillings

Witnesses: Alexander Finley, Wm. Smith.

\- - -

ABRAHAM I. (x) WHITAKER Will dated 10 December 1803, proved --

wife: Martha
sons: William and Abram Whitaker land bounded by John Redmond's Cardin's & Jacob Allen's lands
son: Jacob land "where John Poteet formerly lived now belonging to Thomas Holloway"
youngest son: James Whitaker
sons and daughters Isaac Whitaker
daus: Joana Holliway, Hannah Barbee, Elizabeth Riley, Mary Riley

Executors: John Cabe and Henry Bunch.
Witnesses: Henry Bunch, John (x) Morris.

\- - -

THOMAS (x) GUINN Will dated 18 June 1822, proved --

wife: Mildred all estate during her life
son: Joseph Guinn $1
dau: Elizabeth Vickers wife of David Vickers $1
" Mary Jane Quinn estate after wife's death

Executors: friends Reuben Cardin & Frederick Moize Esq.
Witnesses: Thomas (x) Christian, Benton Clark.

\- - -

THOMAS (x) CRABTREE Will dated 10 March 1826, note on back says "recorded February 1833"

wife: Caty

"Children Harriet Tempe Martha Anne Abram, George, Jacob Samuel" (punctuation as given)
"To my children John Thomas William, Peggy, Nancy Hunter (?) Hetty, Susanna Elizabeth one shilling each having heretofore advanced them".

- continued -

Executors: "brother William Crabtree and James Crabtree son to my brother Abram."
Witnesses: J. Taylor, Thos. Hargis.

- - -

THOMAS COUCH There are two drafts of this will, the first is dated 14 January 1828, the second is dated 27 January 1829.

son: Thomas Couch "one-half the land I bought of Wm White and part of the tract I bought of Joseph White ... lying on the W side of Piney Mountain Cr.
son: Hardin Couch "Peelor tracts adjoining Aquilla Rhodes and the heirs of Benjamin Rhodes."
sons: Isaac Couch, Jacob Couch, William Couch, Samuel Couch
daughter Rachel White $10, Thomas White $10, Joseph White Jr $10, Nancy White $10, Susannah White $10.

No executor named, no witnesses, but signed by Thomas Couch.

- - - - - -

Every will abstracted in this book is preserved in the State Archives with the exception of the nine listed below.

name of testator	date of will	recorded in Book
LYNCH, THOMAS	April 1815	D 438
MOORE, JAMES	proved 1836	E 402
MURDOCK, ANDREW	December 1815	D 498
RAINEY, BENJAMIN	April 1811	D 286
STRAYHORN, GILBERT	1783	D 87
TARPLEY, MASON	April 1826	E 118
TATE, JOSEPH	November 1825	E 105
WOOD, SABUT	November 1807	D 220
WORTHAM, MARY	September 1827	E 174

- - - - - -

CORRECTIONS

D203 The name is JOHN LINN instead of Liner. He is "advanced in age and infirm."
D263 Nancy McDaniel instead of Nancy McCamal. A check of Orange County marriages shows that Nancy Watson married 18 September 1817 John McDaniel.
E207 Vicey instead of Viney Horne.
E417 After "Susannah Ward's children, Wm Ward's children" it should read Esther, instead of Stephen, Well's children

During the period covered by this book Orange County Inferior Court met quarterly, in February, May, August and November. For part of this time it began on the fourth Monday of the month and lasted several days, sometimes going over until the first of the following month.

- - - - -

INDEX The name of the testator is in capitals.

Name of the testator is in capitals.

Name of testator is in capitals

Name of testator is in capitals

Name of testator is in capitals

MARRIAGES mentioned in these wills which do not appear in the collected marriage bonds of Orange County. Indexed by brides.

bride	groom	date of will	testator
Albright, Philipenia	.... Swing	Oct 1830	J. Albright
Alston, Christian	Solomon Jones	Jun 1818	Lemuel Alston
" , Mary	Robett Scott	" "	D542
Boswell, Susannah	.... Leachman	Jan 1826	Edward Boswell
Carmichael, Jane	.... Iseley	Feb 1816	Thos Carmichael
" , Nancy	.... Smith	" "	D559
Cozart, Charlotte	Jas Tomison	Feb 1805	James Cozart
Dale, Margaret	.... Haddock	Oct 1815	Isaac Dale
Deley, Catherine	James Gibens	Aug 1794	Wm. Deley
" , Mary	George Reed	" "	D105
Dickie, Hannah	.... Linch	Jan 1804	Samuel Dickie
" , Hester	.... Cantrill	" "	" "
" , Rachel	.... Burd	" "	D122

Their sister Susannah Dickie m in Orange Moses Linch.

Edwards, Rebecca	Richard Ricketts	Dec 1817	John Edwards

MARRIAGES not in the collected bonds.

bride	groom	date of will	testator
Edwards, Mary	.... Odean	Apr 1796	John Edwards
" , Susannah	.... Campbell	" "	D56
Eulice, Barbara	.... Tracy	Jul 1812	Philip Eulice
Foust, Elizabeth	.... Clap	Sep 1808	Peter Foust
Friddle, Caty	Averot Garrott	Nov 1800	Geo. Friddle
" , Peggy	Michael Lue	" "	D158
Forrester, Jemima	Harris Woods	Nov 1800	B. Forrester
Gant, Hannah	.... Boist	Dec 1800	John Gant
" , Keziah	.... Rippy	" "	" "
" , Mary	.... Riggins	" "	D30
Harvey, Edith	.... Madden	Jul 1800	Isaac Harvey
Hastings, Marg't	.... Adams	May 1812	H'y Hastings
Horn, Edith	.... Younger	pr. 1813	Wm. Horn
Lindley, Hannah	.... Braxton	Sep 1824	Jon Lindley
" , Quinton Esther	..... Clark	" "	E167
McAdams, Eliz	.... Blair	Oct 1808	Reb McAdams
McPherson, Ann	John Crutchfield	Mar 1813	William
" , Iddith	Mark Morgan	" "	McPherson
" , Margaret	Jesse Pierce	" "	D517
" , Mary	Thomas Braxton	" "	"
" , "	Edward Stewart	" "	"
" , Phebe	Aaron Lindley	" "	"
" , Ruth	..... Johnson	" "	"
Newlin, Hannah	..... Holloday	Aug 1805	John Newlin
" , Mary	..... Hadley	" "	D162
Owens, Elizabeth	..... Lingo	Nov 1809	Only Owens
Primrose, Eliz.	..... Garrard	Oct 1835	Temperance
" , Frances	..... Culberhouse	" "	Primrose
" , Rachel	America Wheeler	" "	E368

Their sister Ann Primrose m in Orange 1824 Sam Chisenhall.

bride	groom	date of will	testator
Rhodes, Mary	..... Pattishall	Sep 1802	Wm. Rhodes
" , Eliz.	..... Gresham	" "	D293
" , Frances	..... Barbee	" "	"
" , Hannah	..... Whatley	" "	"
" , Nancy	..... Gresham	" "	"

Marriages of 3 other Rhodes daughters are recorded in Orange.

bride	groom	date of will	testator
Robertson, Elenor	..... Johnson	Jun 1800	John
" , Margaret	..... Wilson	" "	Robertson
" , Rebekka	..... Guin	" "	D46
Rountree, Rachel	..... Jacobs	Sep 1803	T. Rountree
Shaddy, Caty	Geo A. Fogleman	Feb 1809	John Shaddy
" , Molly	John Coble	" "	D331
" , Rachel	George Fogleman	" "	"
" , ...	Henry Steel	" "	"
Sheldon, Mary	..... Collier ?	Apr 1802	Thos Shelton
Stovall, ...	David Chandler	Dec 1802	Bart. Stovall
Trice, Sally	Joseph Barbee	Aug 1801	Thomas Trice
Troxler, Philipena	/David Coble	Mar 1814	Barney Troxler
Ward, Asther	..... Wells	Mar 1817	Susanna Ward
" , Druscilla	.... Free ? Tree ?	" "	" "
" , Sarah	..... Clark	" "	E18
" , Susannah	..... Pike	" "	"
Wells, Margrate	..... Gifford	Feb 1804	Joseph Wells
" , Mary	..... Jamison	" "	" "
" , Rachel	..... Underwood	" "	D 140
Wilson, Rachel	..... Dunn	Apr 1802	Chas. Wilson
Woods, Susanna	James Faucett	Oct 1820	Mary Woods

****

OMISSIONS AND CORRECTIONS (2 pages) March 1966
by the compiler, Ruth Herndon Shields, to

ABSTRACTS OF ORANGE COUNTY, NORTH CAROLINA, WILLS 1800-1850

Page Testator (All additions are indexed, unless so stated.)

17 D105 WM DELEY - son: "John Deley the 200 acres whereon he lives (Samuel Ector to make the deed) Not indexed

27 D169 JOHN ANDERSON - add- daughter: Lettice

31 D192 WM PICKETT-add-"Daughter Nancy Bryant and her husband Williamson Bryant" not indexed

32 D192 3rd line should read "Joseph Pickett & Jesse Pickett ..."

33 D203 Testator is LINN, not Liner.

43 D277 WILSON CHILD - William Bruce should be Wilson Bruce.

49 D334 WM CRABTREE- add- daughter Nancy not indexed

50 D336 JOHN WALKER-add- "son William Walker 450 acres ..."etc..

D339 HENRY HASTINGS - "grandson Thomas Crabtree" is son-in-law.

61 D418 SARAH HARDEN - dau: Jean Whitsett, 200 acres in Caswell.

64 D434 WM MONTGOMERY - add- son: William

65 D JOHN BOYLE - strike married from "My three married daus ... The married daughters are in the line below this.

73 D491 LUDWICK ALBRIGHT - add- married daughters "Mary Fogleman, deceased wife of John, Elizabeth Albright wife of John"

75 D500 Testator is NANCY MASON , not Moore.

80 D522 The Testator is EVE (x) SMITH.

82 D538 Testator is EDWARD WORTHAM, not Wilson.

85 D550 ALEX. RUSSELL - add- daughter: Polly
son: William "my land warrant for 800 acres now in the hands of I.G.McLemore of Tennessee."

86 D555 ISAAC DALE - wife's name is Deborah.

103 E26 MARY WOODS - add- grandson: Joseph Woods

107 E42 ISAAC HOLT - Thomas Rowan's wife is Eliza M, not Emily.

108 E49 WM ANDREW, SR - add- "grandchildren Milly, William & Dolly Cate, 5 shillings each."

E51 WILLIS MONK - add - Witnesses: Andrew Hailey, James Nutt.

109 E55 JOHN HOLT - wife's name is Nelly, not Molly.

Page Testator. All corrections are indexed unless so stated.

110 E59 Testator is SAMUEL PIKE, not Pyle.

112 E67 JOHN LATTA - Executors are Thomas & James Latta, not John

E71 HENRY THOMPSON - Witness is J.H.Bland, not Hand.

118 E101 GEORGE TROXLER - add - wife: Peggy Troxler. Not indexed.

E103 MARY CRAIG - grandchildren are "William, Peggy, Polly & Patsy, children of ..." Patsy not indexed.

124 E137 ROBERT FAUCETT - add - "friend Duncan Cameron"

125 E143 BENJAMIN RONEY - add- son: Benjamin Roney

129 E162 ISAAC McCADAMS - Exec. is brother in law, not son in law

E167 JONATHAN LINDLEY-add- "To sister Deborah Newlin, $100."

135 E207 JOSHUA HORNE, SR-add- sons: Alford, William, 5 shillings daughter is Vicey

136 E213 LETTICE McCULLEY - Executor is "friend Hardy Hurdle".

148 E277 JOSEPH SHAW - add - grandson: Joseph B.S.Hargis.
E280 HENSON COULTER, SR - add - son: Henson Coulter.

153 E303 WM BREWER - add - daughter: Sally Weaver

165 E375 ROBERT TINNEN - add - "My four daughters , Margaret, Jennet, Elenor and Mary."

171 E407 RACHEL STRAYHORN - add - son: James Strayhorn

174 E420 ROBERT KING - "To heirs of my daughter Elizabeth Foster.

178 F1 JOHN SHAW - add - granddaughter: Eliza Walker

189 F76 JOSEPH ARMSTRONG - add - Witness: Enos Ross.

208 F229 BARNEY CLAPP - add - son Christian,"deceased son John".

214 F273 NANCY CRUTCHFIELD - add - son: Benjamin Crutchfield.

Also add to the INDEX, HILLYARD, John, Wm. E39